A TRAINING SCHOOL FOR ELEPHANTS

Also by Sophy Roberts

The Lost Pianos of Siberia

A TRAINING SCHOOL
FOR ELEPHANTS

Sophy Roberts

Atlantic Monthly Press
New York

First published in 2025 in Great Britain by Doubleday
an imprint of Transworld Publishers

First Grove Atlantic hardcover editon: April 2025

Typeset in 11/15.25pt Sabon Next LT Pro by Jouve (UK), Milton Keynes

ISBN 978-0-8021-6486-5
eISBN 978-0-8021-6491-9

Printed in the United States of America

Library of Congress Cataloging-in-Publication data is available for this title.

Atlantic Monthly Press
an imprint of Grove Atlantic
154 West 14th Street
New York, NY 10011

Distributed by Publishers Group West

groveatlantic.com

25 26 27 28   10 9 8 7 6 5 4 3 2 1

For Anne and Johnny

'All continents are dark continents, half the time.
But the darkness is not empty.'

—TEJU COLE,
Black Paper: Writing in a Dark Time

'Better to know. I always think it's better to
know than not to know . . . You hear people say,
"Why do people always talk about colonialism? It's over".
But no, it's not. Because until we are more open about
understanding its consequences, it's not over.'

—ABDULRAZAK GURNAH,
in conversation with Kunle Ajibade

'It was impossible to keep a real course, the path wound so.'

—VERNEY LOVETT CAMERON,
Journal, 13 February 1874

Contents

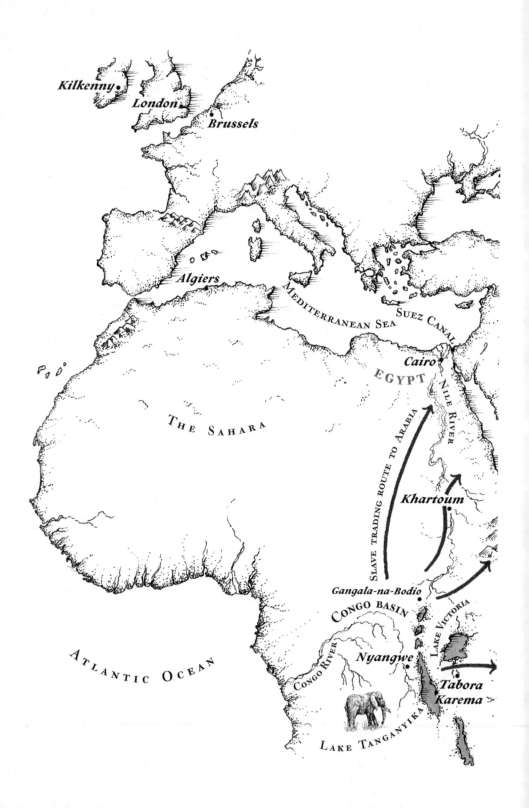

Kilkenny

London

Brussels

Algiers

MEDITERRANEAN SEA

SUEZ CANAL

Cairo

EGYPT

THE SAHARA

NILE RIVER

SLAVE TRADING ROUTE TO ARABIA

Khartoum

Gangala-na-Bodio

CONGO BASIN

LAKE VICTORIA

Nyangwe

Tabora

Karema

CONGO RIVER

ATLANTIC OCEAN

LAKE TANGANYIKA

Author's Note

THIS BOOK TRACES THE forgotten story of an 1879 European expedition in Africa – one of the first stabs at a colossal, brutalizing vision waiting to unspool in a scramble for its resources. Not long after, at the Conference of Berlin of 1884–5, Africa began to be crudely divvied up by Europe's colonizing powers, which changed the continent's political, economic, ecological and belief systems for ever. I followed in the expedition's footsteps to interrogate this pivot in the world order, my approach weaving together archive research and reportage with the arc of a journey. Those layers of past and present meant confronting numerous patterns of domination.

The map on pp. x–xi carries modern place names with nineteenth-century equivalents given in parentheses. In the pages that follow, you'll find a blend of both depending on the context. The map on p. 310 details the loose dominions of some of the main ethnic groups that occupied the region in 1879 when this expedition took place. These groupings still exist in and around the countries of Tanzania and the Democratic Republic of Congo, or DRC. Understanding that ethnic geography helps with the imaginative leaps needed to erase current national boundaries shaped largely by the colonizers.

The main thrust of the expedition's journey begins in Zanzibar. The route then winds from the shores of East Africa to Lake Tanganyika, the border territory where modern Tanzania rubs up against the DRC. Tanzania was called German East Africa from 1886 to 1916. After the First World War, the region came under British control, and was known as Tanganyika Territory. In 1961, the country gained its independence, and following union with Zanzibar in 1964, became the United Republic of Tanzania. The turbulent nomenclature of the DRC (which is a different country from the much smaller Republic of Congo) is another story. The region was called the Congo Free State from 1885 to 1908 when it was in the private ownership of King Leopold II of Belgium, and the Belgian Congo from 1908 to 1960. With independence came a new run of names in rapid succession, including Zaire. For simplicity, I've generally used 'Tanzania' and 'Congo' throughout.

The colonizers, it would seem, didn't let their ink run dry in the African sun. When they weren't sweating off a malarial fever, they were filing trunkfuls of official reports, field journals, letters and newspaper articles to their consuls, editors and benefactors. This abundance was a direct reflection of literate power at the time, composed in English, French, German and Arabic. I've relied on those written sources from the 1870s and 1880s, which are detailed in the Select Bibliography and Notes. Meanwhile, the African oral tradition, and the role of intermediaries, guides and interpreters, was largely unacknowledged by nineteenth-century European documentarians. With a few exceptions, Africans were rarely named, and often not in full. I've tried to find a better contemporary balance with oral history, although I know there are problems with representation (women, for instance, aren't given the same voice as men). I haven't changed the name of any living person. My reasons are not just journalistic, but to counter the deletions of the past.

In modern Tanzania, the most common tongue is Swahili, alongside various local languages and English. In Swahili, two prefixes are used to denote people from a particular ethnic group – one for the singular, and one for the plural. A different prefix is used for languages. See the Ethnic Groups section on pp. 310–12 for further detail. For clarity, I've stuck with the names of ethnic groups in their basic form throughout.

I've not edited or changed the words used in historical primary sources, even though some language may be disturbing to modern readers. I have, however, done my best to avoid unnecessary repetition of offensive words. This is not to diminish the depth of colonial perversions but out of a writerly belief that we must let some words die without overlooking the ideas those words represent. My choices haven't always been straightforward given the challenge of agreeing upon consistent idioms to replace centuries of bigotry – a process which unfurls at a different pace in different parts of the world. Certain words are perceived differently in the UK than in English-speaking countries elsewhere, while translations of this book into other languages make those nuances more complicated again. If any offence is caused, I take full responsibility in line with my intention: to better understand what happened, how recently those events occurred, and how words (then and now) bear liability.

The same stands for my picture choices. Some images may be difficult to face, but it's also important to look human cruelty straight in the eye. Because if nothing else, the themes in this book have made me confront numerous issues around othering that are so much a part of writing in English – a language entwined with (and struggling to extricate itself from) the roots of colonial thinking. 'As for "ideology,"' the British economist Joan Robinson remarked, 'it's like breath: You never smell your own.' Stitching this story together has meant unpicking multiple assumptions and narrow points of view, starting with mine. To help guide me, I kept a warning pinned to my conscience – an essay by the late Kenyan author Binyavanga Wainaina, who offered outsiders his tongue-in-cheek advice on how to write about Africa. 'Establish early on that your liberalism is impeccable,' he wrote. 'Keep your descriptions romantic and evocative and unparticular ... mention near the beginning how much you love Africa ... Elephants are caring, and are good feminists or dignified patriarchs.'

For anyone who has watched the little yellow biplane bank off the Oloololo escarpment in the movie *Out of Africa*, or has seen water shimmer pink as startled flamingos take wing, the clichés Wainaina pilloried can be hard to avoid. But Wainaina was a satirist, not a censor. The truth is I *do* love Africa. I *do* think it's beautiful. I *do* think elephants are caring. I think they're some of the most extraordinarily moving creatures on Earth, while their diminished populations stand as shameful testimony to our collective human greed. By the late nineteenth century when this book's story begins, elephant numbers were so eviscerated by the ivory trade, hunters supplying foreign demand had to travel beyond Lake Tanganyika into Congo to make any significant gains. Yet only twenty-five years earlier, this stretch of country had stood for 'Regions unknown!' to inquisitive Europeans, a kind of promised land. These are Joseph Conrad's words, taken from an essay written in the last year of the novelist's life. He was describing a map in a childhood atlas from 1852, and a vow he'd made to his school friends that one day he would get there.

For Conrad, it was an ambition cut short. Following the European 'discovery' of Lake Tanganyika in the late 1850s, he pencilled in the outline of the lake where the blank space on his old map used to be. By 1890 when Conrad eventually travelled into the African interior himself, Congo was King Leopold's private colony. Conrad experienced the stark opposite of the idealized space he'd imagined as a child. 'It had got filled since my boyhood with rivers and lakes and names. It had ceased to be a blank of delightful mystery – a white patch for a boy to dream gloriously over. It had become a place of darkness.' Instead of wide-eyed adventure, Conrad reinforced the opposite trope: universal criminality and impenetrable forest. His 1899 work, *Heart of Darkness*, conjured an enormous metaphor which ever since has associated Africa with horror. That reputation sticks to the entire continent, as Wainaina reminds us, and the influential Nigerian novelist Chinua Achebe before him. Conrad was 'a thoroughgoing racist', argued Achebe in the 1970s, a white author who didn't give any African a name.

But the evocative lure of the continent that first tugged at Conrad's childhood dreams endures. So does the power of place when I'm standing on Lake Tanganyika's shores. That's the other part of this story: the tantalizing sense of infinite strangeness as I lie awake, fearful and attentive to the scattered sounds of night; the gentle waves, sucked and sieved by the thick quartz sand; the heron triggering alarm calls in the drape of tangled forest behind. That's when I wish that more of life could be perceived like this, taking me to a place – however brief, however close to the edge of uncertainty – to make me believe something beautiful might still exist outside our ugly human history.

1

Prologue to an Adventure

'I wouldn't be at home if I were at home. Everywhere I find myself seems to be nothing but a resting place between places that become resting places themselves.'

—Dylan Thomas,
Letter to A. E. Trick, Summer 1935

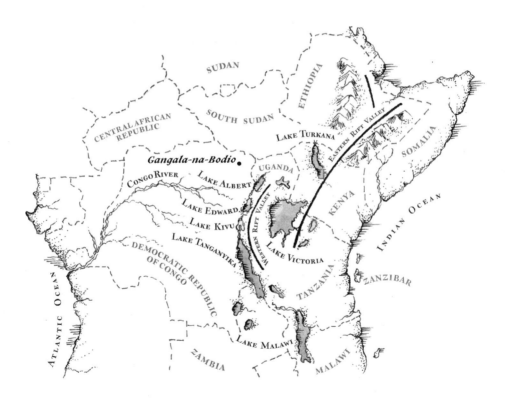

I LIVE IN A DORSET valley which falls away from a high horse-shoe ridge down to the English Channel. The landscape is arresting in its stillness, crowned with a run of Iron Age hill-forts where the poet William Wordsworth used to stride out to clear his head when he borrowed a house nearby. I walk these hillforts often, making my way home through the beech-wood alleys and sunken lanes. From my parents' old farm, the route weaves down the valley's steepest sides where there's still evidence of medieval strip lynchets – a kind of fretting, or terracing, wrinkling the land.

Not so long ago, I found myself walking this valley obses-sively, sometimes for up to six hours a day. I was stuck between pandemic lockdowns, between finishing one book and trying to settle on another. So when a friend offered me a way out of my fug – a man who suffers from the same problem as me: 'shiftless, rootless, hedge-diving restlessness', as he wrote in an email exchange – I took him up on it. He said I could borrow his cottage in Donegal for a change of scene. He described it as the wildest place he knew, in spite of a career working in remote forests in equatorial Africa. His father had bought it in the sixties on a patch of tilted Irish ground with a connection to Dylan Thomas. In 1935, the poet had come to this same treeless cliff to shake off his worsening alcoholism. Thomas had rented a donkey shed nearby made just about habitable by an American painter a few years before.

My friend's cottage was a cut above, with a view of giant sea stacks shaped like Gothic spires poking out of the Atlantic swell. The fridge was a wooden box attached to the outside wall. The bath ran the colour of thin coffee, the water drawn from a peaty brook which kept threatening to spill its banks. Sheep splotched with dye grazed outside; sometimes, when the weather was fierce, they took shelter in the lee of the cottage porch. At night, I dried my clothes on the pipes of a turf stove and read by solar lamps and candles. My mornings were stirred awake by the sound of Ocean FM as the obituaries were being read: the iambic lilt of the elegy, the names of the newly dead, the condolences and announcements of upcoming wakes.

For Thomas, his Donegal trip felt like a holiday, until the picturesque began to fail him. 'I find I can't see a landscape; scenery is just scenery to me,' he wrote to a friend. Disturbed by Ireland's violent colonial history and mass emigrations, he turned increasingly melancholic. Sometimes he would shout into the nearby mountains, only to have his voice bounce back at him. 'The dead Irish answer from behind the hill. I've forced them into confessing that they are sad, grey, lost, forgotten, dead and damned forever.' It was in Donegal that Thomas also began writing one of the stranger stories of his career. 'Prologue to an Adventure' described a winter's night walking through a city with the devil by his side. Written between the two world wars, Thomas's surrealist allegory evoked a moment in time 'before the West died.'

Thomas was living in 'a funny dimension' on this Atlantic edgeland, and so was I. I scrambled down the cliffs to a nearby storm beach. I walked in heavy wind across the headland, balls of bog cotton quivering in the mizzling rain. I could see the creep on every side – ripples of green velvet slipping from the bedrock. I poked around a village abandoned in the mid nineteenth century when Ireland lost around a quarter of its population to the famine of the 1840s. As the wet days stretched out ahead of me, I dug into my friend's bookcases for something new to read. That was when I found a nineteenth-century map of Africa's Great Lakes tucked among the spines, which drew me into a line of thought that had nothing to do with where I was.

Maps have that effect on me. They take me out of myself as much as they suggest a way into somewhere or something else. Maps seem empty where there's desert, and then you zoom in closer and discover a lost ocean in the Sahara. Story is written into the place names – a Valley of the Whales, a Place of Floating Seashells. The same with water, in the way maps are largely wordless where there's a great sweep of blue. The A T L A N T I C has plenty of space to spread out in noisy capitals across an ornamental globe. The P A C I F I C has even more, while Lake Tanganyika in the middle of Africa is so long and narrow, you sometimes see the letters stacked vertically, like a streak of lightning. Go deeper into the charts used by mariners, and the detail intensifies in the mud and broken shale, in the sticky ooze of the ocean floor. Questions lurk in each notation. Magnetic anomalies. Isolated dangers. Reported, but not confirmed. ED (meaning 'existence doubtful'). †unexamd (meaning 'unexamined'). Maps are much more powerful, more multi-dimensional than they first appear.

> *I like maps, because they lie.*
> *Because they give no access to the vicious truth.*
> *Because great-heartedly, good-naturedly*
> *they spread before me a world*
> *not of this world.*

The map I laid out on the table in Donegal covered a swathe of Africa's Great Lakes to reveal the complex, interconnected *dot dot dot* of inland waterways that pool in a line through the middle of the continent. As my finger followed the veins of water, I found myself being pulled north towards the watershed of Africa's two big rivers, the Congo and the Nile. More significantly, the map dragged me back into some strange history I'd encountered on a journalism assignment a few years before. In 2015, I'd journeyed up the line of Great Lakes, flying from Lake Tanganyika over the flank of the Rwenzori Mountains – for centuries, their remoteness was evoked in their other name, the Mountains of the Moon. The lakes shone like spills of glossy ink. Hippos looked like stepping stones spread across the water, pirogues like scattered matchsticks. I was slowly working my way north to a national park called Garamba in northeast DRC to cover a story on an ambitious conservation initiative to rehabilitate one of the continent's most important habitats for elephants. To help with safe passage for the final leg, I was met on the Uganda–DRC border by Mr Oddo, a local fixer clad in an immaculate suit printed with Heineken beer bottles. As I waited to get my passport stamped, the heat of the day thickened. The flies got dozier, the officials even slower. With my papers eventually cleared, I left the town by another small plane, this one operated by a missionary organization. When I'd used their services before, the pilot had put his hand to the Bible and read a prayer before we took off.

We banked right, flying up towards one of the biggest gold mines in Africa, then struck out northwest for Garamba, where the savannah began to bloom green beneath our wings. The landscape was scored with looping rivers, which wound so lazily I couldn't tell the direction in which they flowed. For a few days, I worked at the park headquarters, then, using the same small bush plane, flew to a place nearby called Gangala-na-Bodio. It turned out to be the location of a semi-derelict training school for African elephants dating back to the early twentieth century when Congo was a Belgian colony. I was familiar with the notion of working elephants in Asia, but in Africa? I'd never heard of such a thing.

On our approach from the air, Gangala-na-Bodio appeared as an island of palms in a rippling grass sea. When we landed, I picked my way towards the former training school through the bony roots of trees. As I walked into ruined buildings, between broken signs and clumps of bougainvillea, a young girl looked on warily. In a white broderie anglaise dress and matching bonnet neatly tied beneath her chin, she appeared like a ghost as she followed me into a clearing cut with blades of sunlight. This was where the elephant tethering stones stood, arranged in two rows with the military precision of a Brussels boulevard. Fan palm seedlings frilled the ground, sprouting up among the stones and hoops for fastening chains. I found it affecting – the idea that it wouldn't be long until nature took over completely, the seedlings bursting like giant shuttlecocks from the fertile earth to swamp this pocket of history for good.

A local man in mirrored sunglasses came up and explained how the clearing was once used for colonial parades. More recently, Gangala-na-Bodio had functioned as a lair for Joseph Kony, a former Catholic altar boy turned Ugandan warlord. Kony and his child soldiers had moved on from the area before I visited, but the threat of kidnapping endured. The man said locals still couldn't risk travelling more than a few miles from where they lived, with other active militia groups spilling into the DRC from neighbouring Uganda and South Sudan. As for the captive elephants, they'd long since died or departed – an absence which seemed profound given the wild populations that used to thrive in these grasslands, when herds a thousand elephants strong would move through the landscape like 'a solid grey army on the march'. But after Congo gained its independence in 1960, new waves of political violence meant ivory poaching expanded. It swept in from every direction, including from the sky, with elephant carcasses showing evidence of having been shot in the back from helicopters. It was only from the vantage point of the missionary plane that I'd managed to glimpse any elephants in all the days I spent in the region – a skittish breeding herd fleeing through the grass with their young. Their behaviour showed the habits of the hunted; they trumpeted and flared their ears.

Elephants photographed from the missionary plane during my 2015 visit to Garamba.

They looked vulnerable and scared, their tails stiff like fixed antennae.

When I got home to England from Donegal, I started looking into newspaper archives for stories about Gangala-na-Bodio under the Belgians. The more I searched, the greater my realization that there was something significant in the backstory to this haunting European avenue cut out of the jungle. I was curious to know more about the bond between these animals and their trainers, known as mahouts, and how patterns of subjugation were enforced. I wanted to understand how the idea of this training scheme had first come about. So I got back in touch with the Belgian conservationist who was managing the park when I'd visited. He'd collaborated on a book about the region with some details about the elephant school. He'd also tracked down an old photograph of Gangala-na-Bodio's parade ground, with the elephants in hobble chains lined up in two tidy rows.

The parade ground at Gangala-na-Bodio.

I read about how Gangala-na-Bodio was once run to military calls and bugles, with a Belgian cavalry officer overseeing up to a hundred African mahouts. I found a colonial-era film that revealed the process by which Congo's young elephants were captured in the wild, a half-grown calf lassoed and lashed with ropes to a tree. Another report described the young elephants – 'little fellows standing about five feet' – and how they 'scream with rage when they are tied to the lines'. To tame the elephants, the mahouts used the 'chicotte' – a knotted whip made out of hippo hide, which colonial soldiers also used to torture forced labourers to increase Congo's rubber harvests.

It turned out there had been various attempts at the same idea in different regions of the country. In 1899, an Elephant Domestication Centre was opened at Api, about two hundred and fifty miles west of Gangala-na-Bodio. By 1904, it was presided over by a Belgian soldier called Jules Laplume – a man described as 'lean as a cudgel', 'more of a trapper than an officer', possessing 'angelic patience'. Laplume was assigned as many local Azande elephant hunters as he needed in order to start catching juvenile elephants on the Bomokandi River. His method was to ride into the savannah on a horse. When he found a good breeding herd, the men would start stressing the elephants by firing gunshots into the air to separate an elephant calf from its mother. The men would then run after the baby elephant and bind it with ropes to a tree. If the mother continued to protect the calf, she would be shot. This approach was later adjusted to make use of habituated elephants, which were employed as decoys on capture expeditions. Soon elephant catching was being described as 'one of the new industries on the Congo'. Another school was then founded in the mid 1920s at Gangala-na-Bodio. At first, the

trained recruits were largely used for cultivating fields. Soon
'elephantdozers' were being used to construct the Route
Royale – the Belgian portion of the Great Central African
Highway – and the new colonial railways. Even local missions
found a use for elephants. At Buta, three hundred miles west
of Gangala-na-Bodio, an ad hoc operation was set up by missionaries, successful in large part due to the mission's wildlife
expert, Brother Joseph Hutsebaut. A kind of Doctor Dolittle
character, he was among the first Europeans to successfully
raise an okapi in captivity. I got in touch with Hutsebaut's
descendants, who explained how their ancestor had cared for
elephants captured by locals. His work wasn't commercial,
but I found images of elephants from other sources hauling
timber for missionaries.

By the late 1950s, Gangala-na-Bodio's elephants were decorating Belgian Congo banknotes and stamps. They were also
being marketed for tourism. A few years later when Congo's

Elephants ploughing in Congo during the colonial period.

The main boulevard in Buta in the 1930s with a young elephant being ridden like a horse.

Brother Joseph Hutsebaut with his first elephant, Ndjoku, whom he kept from 1918 to 1940. He hung this photograph on the wall in his bedroom.

independence was declared, South African writer Nadine Gordimer travelled on a paddle steamer up the Congo River. She didn't much care for her fellow passengers – Europeans who 'looked as if they were carved out of lard' – but she was fond of the captive elephants she rode at Gangala-na-Bodio, which by this time were being used for wildlife safaris. She liked watching the elephants gather down by the river at tea-time for a daily bath, 'four great stubby feet waving in the air.' Then in January 1961, Patrice Lumumba, Congo's first legally elected prime minister, was assassinated in a plot later impli-cating the American and Belgian governments, his body dissolved in sulphuric acid. That summer, Congolese soldiers mutinied against their former overlords. Not long after Gor-dimer's visit, 'all news from this remote corner of the Congo ceased'; '[t]he few white people in the district fled to the Sudan, and I imagine that the Belgian commander of the station – the only white man there – must have been among them.' Any information about what was happening to the ele-phants started to fall away. But for me, there was something about Gordimer's account which stuck. I couldn't shake off her descriptions of the songs she'd heard among the African mahouts, how the melodies evoked the soothing drone of Hindi lullabies originally used to tame elephants in Asia. The African trainers had learned the songs from the Ceylonese (Sri Lankan) mahouts Laplume had originally brought in to assist with the schooling. This historical connection prompted me to examine my lazy assumptions about what distinguished the African and Asian species – and the dogma I'd somehow absorbed that the African elephant was untameable.

I knew there were differences in the way they had been commodified – Asian elephants for captive work, African elephants for their ivory – but was there a true disparity in the species' potential for being tamed? Or was it just the history of human exploitation that told a myth about difference? The Carthaginian general Hannibal crossed the Alps with an army of African war elephants in 218 BCE, which showed that trained African elephants were in use more than a thousand years before the school at Gangala-na-Bodio came into existence. If the African elephant was in fact no more difficult to tame than the Asian, then was my assumption part of some deeply entrenched prejudice? In 1868, in a war the British fought in Abyssinia (now Ethiopia), forty-odd elephants were shipped from India to Africa to carry British artillery guns over the mountain passes. Five elephants perished, their bodies riddled with galls and sores, throats half choked by the unrelenting tug of heavy loads. The reason the army had to rely on Asian imports, posited a British commentator, was because 'the Africans have no notion what to do with an elephant at present but to kill and eat it.'

I began to understand why the Belgians had wanted to train elephants to extract Africa's resources, but I was also becoming increasingly curious about an odder, earlier story hidden in that narrative, in the seeds of Congo's elephant training schools planted decades before Gangala-na-Bodio was established. It was one of those slivers of history repeated across sources with a suspicious confusion of names and places, which made me think no one had looked into what had really happened when, in 1879, King Leopold II of Belgium settled on a seemingly bizarre idea: dispatching four Asian elephants and their mahouts from India, a region with a tradition in working elephants, to Africa, which did not. What exactly was Leopold trying to achieve on a continent with abundant elephants of its own? Why did he need to take the trouble of putting these animals on a ship bound for Africa? In 1879 the number of African elephants was estimated at between twenty to thirty times the figure it is now. The elephant stood as a popular synecdoche for the entire continent, and had done since at least the early eighteenth century:

> *So Geographers in Afric-maps*
> *With savage-pictures fill their gaps*
> *And o'er uninhabitable downs*
> *Place elephants for want of towns.*

Leopold's aim was to reach Lake Tanganyika – then a threshold of Congo's so-called 'Ivory Frontier' – and start an elephant training operation, using the Asian elephants to test a new form of transport in the race into Africa's interior. The expedition niggled away at me on numerous levels, including an interest I've always had in stories that disappear in the margins.* Leopold's elephants felt as if they had the potential to unravel the beginning of a colonial story with far-reaching effects. The 1879 expedition was part of the preamble to the 'Scramble for Africa', which resulted in decades of violent European rule. And while the era of colonial governments may have passed, the looting is ongoing, just with different

---

* I like footnotes. They're the narrative underdogs that can't quite find their place in the dominant record. They're also where a richness of nuance often resides. At their best, they can provoke a diversion or encourage a slightly shifted gaze, to say something bigger than their diminished position might first imply. Footnotes can also break a story's flow. For this reason, all but two footnotes in this book have been relegated to endnotes – see pp. 317–79.

nations making a neocolonial run on what's left of the resources. Interested in the messier swirl of how history resonates in the present, I started to think Leopold's expedition could open a window into how nineteenth-century European expansionism remains tightly bound with topics of enduring consequence: racism, resource extraction, wildlife extinction. The long tail of empire remains a dominating feature of current affairs – the push and pull of cause and effect, of then and now. In retracing the journey of Leopold's elephants, I could see a vehicle to perhaps explore some of those dynamics.

'A touching tale, if all were known', remarked a missionary who had stumbled on the elephant story at the end of the nineteenth century. He described Leopold's parade as a 'strange prodigy' of men carrying an agenda they didn't fully understand or, in their duplicity, didn't choose to disclose. 'Stuck high on the elephant's back, you have four white men who symbolize the coming struggle for supremacy', the missionary continued. I felt a beckoning in his line *if all were known*, as if there was more story to uncover. The missionary's account drew me into the absurdity of the entire endeavour, manifested in the image of Europeans on top of Asian elephants marching into the heart of Africa to inspire and demand obeisance. I was interested in how a symbol could come to mean so much – how the historical, imaginative and political dimensions of Leopold's elephant expedition converged with and contributed to the Europeans' 'invention of Africa'. And what of the four animals who carried this story on their backs? Were they loved or abused, willing or terrified? I wondered what they'd seen travelling through Africa – a wildlife Eden? – and what had since disappeared. I was curious to hear the local stories from the regions they traversed.

I've always liked elephants, and the silent dignity they project. In their company, I feel all sorts of emotions, ranging from fear to awe and affection. When I first walked with them in the wild, it changed my perspective: the things *we think* make us powerful, as intellectual beings, are rendered irrelevant. But that humbling experience is easily forgotten. I belong to an industrialized, technologically organized society so divorced from nature that it's harder and harder to feel instinctive connections with animals. It's as if the scientific approach is all that matters, even if science may eventually tell us what our hunter-gatherer forebears knew before we created organizing hierarchies; that elephants are more than biological automata. I wanted to interrogate how and why we've come to treat animals in the ways we do – and how much cruelty we've got away with. 'A robin redbreast in a cage', wrote William Blake in 'Auguries of Innocence', 'Puts all heaven in a rage.'

As summer turned to winter, I began exploring various archives in London. Among the missionary reports and consular records, I found buried mentions of Leopold's elephant schemes. What was becoming clear was the extent of the 1879 expedition's ambitions, entangling Scottish shipping magnates, anti-slavery campaigners, German zookeepers and American businessmen. Among all the names, I noticed a man given the moniker 'Lord of Tuskers' – an Irishman called Frederick Falkner Carter whom Leopold had hired to lead the expedition. Yet Carter's name had been almost completely forgotten.

I pinned Carter's portrait to a rogues' gallery on the wall of my office – my aide-mémoire detailing who I needed to keep track of as I reunited people to story, and story to place. I've been making displays like this for years, ever since I started training to be a journalist in the 1990s. I would rip out leads in newspapers, and tape them on to my apartment wall where they would yellow in the sun. I'd layer them up and place the clippings side by side – sometimes purposefully, usually haphazardly. Positions would alter. Lines of enquiry would multiply and fizzle out. New connections would sparkle attractively, or confoundingly, to reveal a logic or unlikely dissonance. My husband, who thought they looked like evidence boards in murder investigations, called them my serial-killer walls.

I drew a red line tracing Carter's beginnings. He was born in Kilkenny, Ireland, in April 1841. Aged fourteen, he joined the British merchant navy. In 1863, he moved to Mesopotamia, which is now Iraq. He found work with the Euphrates and Tigris Steam Navigation Company, owned by some enterprising childhood neighbours of his mother's called the Lynch brothers. With the Suez Canal linking Europe to the Indian Ocean, the Persian Gulf was no geographical cul-de-sac, but an increasingly relevant node in the rapidly expanding global trade routes. Though my chronology of Carter's career was only one line among many, it reinforced a bigger nineteenth-century phenomenon: in the Age of Empire, it was possible to travel freely (if you were British, often with a 'contemptuous ease') because of an unprecedented flourishing in the broadening bonds of trade and communications. As the internet has been in my lifetime, so the steamship was in Carter's – a dramatic development in speed which fed Europe and America's booming capitalist economies. The Indian Ocean before steam, wrote one of the Lynch brothers, was 'ayam al-jahilieh' – a phrase normally used to describe the absence of light before the arrival of Islam.

On the same map, I marked the traditional ivory and East

African slave trade and caravan routes of the 1870s on which all travellers depended – 'Arab'-controlled* trails that ran in and out of the coastal ports. I put a red pin in the main 'slave nests' on the edge of the Sahara further north, and sketched the shadowy trade in human lives leading out towards the Persian Gulf, where the enslaved worked in harems or diving for pearls. The numbers were staggering to me – over thirteen centuries, more than 9.8 million Africans were shipped as enslaved people to Arabia, various Indian Ocean islands and the Indian subcontinent, and a further 4.1 million were shipped across the Red Sea, yet attention has been focused on the much better-known transatlantic trade to the Americas. I highlighted the Suez Canal in blue. When it opened in 1869, this leap in infrastructure reduced a six- or seven-month journey from Europe to India via the Cape of Good Hope to a matter of weeks. Submarine telegraph cables were enabling faster communications. In 1870, the first Indian Ocean telegraph was established, connecting Britain to Bombay and Calcutta (now Mumbai and Kolkata); another line, linking Europe to South Africa via the port of Aden, was inaugurated in July 1879, with messages reaching Brussels from Zanzibar in as little as three hours.

As I surveyed the research in front of me, I knew I'd need to go to Belgium to understand Leopold's motivations for commissioning the elephant expedition. I wondered if I'd

---

* I use the word 'Arab' with caution throughout this book, as the trade was heavily tied up with Swahili communities because of centuries of mixed blood along the Indian Ocean littoral. Though other Africans were also complicit, 'Arab' became the default signifier for the eastern trade in enslaved people. This was also because of a European habit of demonizing the perpetrators (Muslim Arabs were the traditional enemy of Christian Europeans). The moralizing Europeans relied on this oversimplified narrative to help them gain a foothold in African affairs.

ever get to the Tigris River in Iraq where Carter had first made his name. As I began to pin my office map with the rough route Leopold's elephants had walked, my husband said something which felt like a blessing. 'I guess you'll be gone for a while,' he remarked. He knew my restlessness better than I wanted to admit it to myself. This was my chance to become immersed in a journey again, in the cut and thrust of unfamiliar towns, among the hot tin roofs, the smells of dry earth, and the push and shove of boda-boda motorbikes.

Plans were falling into line. In readiness, I packed a copy of George Orwell's essay 'Shooting an Elephant.' It describes how a British officer was called out from his police post in Burma (now Myanmar) to dispatch a marauding, man-killing elephant, which he shot 'solely to avoid looking a fool' in front of a gathering mob of two thousand Burmese. Orwell's

Logging elephants in Katha in 2018, in the same Burmese forests where a young George Orwell worked for the imperial police. Each evening, I'd watch the elephants bathe as the mahouts sang to them.

chilling account isn't just about a botched execution, the elephant 'dying, very slowly and in great agony'. It is a story about an Englishman's failure as a moral human being – an admission of complicity with an imperial system young men joined without questioning its depravities – and the glimmerings of self-awareness. This journey was something I wanted to take on not because it was going to be easy, but precisely because of an unease with my ignorance about the colonial story in Africa. I hoped I could follow Leopold's elephants to discover more about what had really happened: how European imperialism had unfolded on the African continent, and the effects on its people. This was always going to be about more than the historical fate of four pachyderms from India. With the 1879 expedition as my narrative thread, I could piece together a journey map to guide my enquiries into historical erasures. The path the elephants took would be my passport into a region's oral memory. My sources would expand across time and place, which appealed to the traveller in me. But before going any further, I'd need to understand Leopold's motivations. For that, I'd have to start with the nineteenth-century archives in Belgium.

2

Shopping for an Elephant

'. . . no, I don't care about silence for its lack of everything but for what it says about everything.'

—Ignacio Ruiz-Pérez,
'Blind Poet'

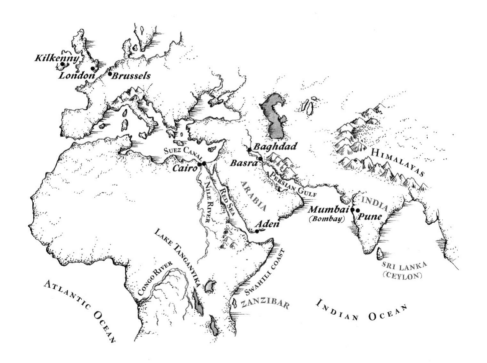

I T WAS A CRISP spring day when I arrived in Brussels to explore the colonial records. In the stark Flanders light, everything seemed to have its ordered place: the chocolatiers in the Galeries Royales Saint-Hubert, the bright chimes of church carillons sounding across the rooftops, the city's business people hurrying to appointments in tailored woollen coats buttoned up against the wind. I occasionally encountered graffiti the authorities hadn't had a chance to wash away – *Racist! Criminal! Smash the Patriarchy!* – but otherwise the city appeared as if it were just as King Leopold II had intended when he'd used the extreme wealth amassed from Congo to beautify his nation.

From 1885 to 1908, Leopold formally held Congo as his private possession, commanding a swathe of Africa eighty times the size of Belgium. He called himself the country's 'proprietor' before he was reluctantly forced to sell it to the Belgian state in 1908 – in large part because of revelations of extraordinary human rights abuses – but not before Leopold and his people had been significantly enriched. Between 1889 and 1908, the tusks of around ninety-four thousand African elephants from Congo were shipped into the Belgian port of Antwerp alone, to meet the demand for ivory objects, from piano keys to dildoes. Over the same period, exports of rubber from Congo exploded by a thousand per cent. In 1903, at the height of the rubber boom, Leopold imported the modern-day equivalent of over half a billion euros' worth of this stunningly profitable commodity. By the outbreak of the

First World War, Belgium had become Europe's fifth largest economic power.

To find my bearings with all this history, I walked the tight grid of government offices, palaces and avenues of pollarded limes. I lingered at the door of 10 Rue de Namur, where Leopold's right-hand man for African affairs, Colonel Maximilien Strauch, ran the king's various Congo schemes. The park nearby was studded with familiar icons of Western culture, including emperors alongside classical gods. Among the statues, there was one of Narcissus, the hunter from Greek mythology who perished beside the pool where he stared at his own reflection. Standing by an emptied pond, this stone Narcissus didn't have any mirrored image to admire. He was also missing a hand, which made me think of Leopold's Force Publique, a terrorizing gendarmerie who routinely chopped off the hands of the Congolese if rubber quotas weren't met. Close to the statue, there were two marble feet – just the feet, as delicate as a child's, on another broken plinth. The park map said it was Hermes, the Greek god of roads, commerce and thieves.

I headed out towards the ring road to see where Belgium had hosted the 1958 World's Fair – a kind of giant trade show for industrial nations to display their achievements. This was the same year the microchip was invented, passenger jets started flying across the Atlantic, and a US nuclear submarine passed for the first time under the North Pole. Belgium, however, had different ideas about what constituted 'progress'. Part of their propaganda as the host nation included what was known as the 'Kongorama' to demonstrate Belgium's 'civilizing' impact on Congo. Designed by the Ministry of Colonies, this 'human zoo' included nearly six hundred Congolese men, women and children the Belgians had rounded up in the 'deepest forests of Kasai and the mountains in Urundi'. Their role included re-enactments of Congolese village life. Among the 'exhibits' on show, which visitors could observe from behind bamboo fences, were some of the African mahouts from the Gangala-na-Bodio training school for elephants.

Six decades previously, Leopold had presented the Congolese in much the same manner. His earlier 1897 'human zoo' had created such a sensation, it attracted more than one in four Belgians as visitors. It was staged at the former royal hunting grounds of Tervuren, outside Brussels, which is also the location of the Royal Museum for Central Africa, a neoclassical palace Leopold originally commissioned to impress potential investors with his various Congo schemes. The museum still holds one of the world's largest collections of African artefacts.

As soon as I stepped into the atrium, I encountered placards outlining a contemporary agenda that, among other things, instructed visitors on the difference between law and morals. 'The collections that the AfricaMuseum [sic] preserves and curates are the legal property of the Belgian federal state, but the moral property of the countries of origin', read one of the notices. It wasn't the museum's business to decide on ownership and restitution, read another sign, but the Federal State Security for Science Policy. I wandered through the rooms, past polished niches occupied by statues of eminent Belgians on pedestals, and busts of King Leopold. In life, his physical presence was overbearing – a commanding six feet tall, despite being born a puny baby, and with such a large nose his mother considered it a deformity. He was his parents' least favourite child, showing a proclivity for violence early on, as well as a ruthless intelligence. 'Leopold is subtle and sly', his father had once confided to a minister; 'he never takes a chance.' He compared his son to a fox he'd watched dip its paw into the water of a stream trying to work out where to cross it, 'and then, with a thousand precautions, very slowly made his way across. That is Leopold's way!' I paused to look at trays of jewel-coloured beetles, aquariums swimming with fish from Lake Tanganyika, a pickled elephant foetus from Garamba and rare ceremonial masks. In this weird mix of exhibits, there were frequent prompts to make it easier to identify recent curatorial attempts to contextualize the challenge of lumping Victorian taxidermy, colonial plundering and a history of murderous atrocities under the same roof. But however the exhibits were put together – and this is true of numerous collections all over the world – scholarly, even apologetic curation couldn't displace a fundamental problem: much of what I was looking at was 'acquired' on profoundly amoral terms.

Some of that history was lurking in the Stanley Archives – a white pavilion next door which held a significant collection of colonial-era documents. In the hush of the pavilion's library, I struck up a whispered conversation with another researcher. He earned his living as a hotel receptionist on the night shift. By day, he came here to read.

'If people want to know more about colonial history in Congo, it exists,' he said. 'It's here in this room. But as you can see, we're not many. There are only three of us.'

I left the pavilion to explore the adjacent park, passing dog walkers who slid like shadows between the trees. Among French-style parterres with beds as neat as pin cushions, I came across another statue of Leopold, this one commissioned as recently as 1997, featuring three Congolese warriors in loincloths and the king. It was an image of a man who, over

Congolese brought to Belgium at the first of the 'human zoos' – an exhibition held at Tervuren in 1897.

This 1930 photograph shows the graves of the seven Congolese who died of pneumonia and influenza in Belgium in the run-up to the 1897 'human zoo' exhibition. Ekia, Gemba, Kitoukwa, Mpeia, Zao, Sambo and Mibange had originally been buried in unconsecrated graves reserved for suicides.

a period of twenty-three years, was responsible for the deaths of an estimated ten million Africans. In other words, the year this statue went up, the atrocities committed under Leopold's regime were already widely known, at home and abroad – and had been for close to a century.

My days passed slowly in Brussels as I built up the research I needed to piece together Leopold's march to empire. 'I am gathering proof and documentary evidence which ought to convince my fellow countrymen of the desirability of overseas expansion,' Leopold wrote as early as 1861, when he was still known as the Duke of Brabant. 'Check out the history of Venice, Rome and ancient Greece,' he insisted. 'There is no complete homeland without possessions and without activity overseas.' I wanted to take a look at his early travel diaries for insight into the genesis of his imperial ambitions prior to securing Congo, so I made an appointment at the Royal Palace, where some of Leopold's private papers were kept – the ones that survived his obliteration of incriminating evidence when in 1908 he signed over his Congo 'Free State' to Belgium. 'I will give them my Congo,' Leopold told an aide, 'but they have no right to know what I did there.' The Royal Palace furnaces burned for eight days. Among the documents spared were the journals Leopold kept of his world travels before his accession in 1865, including a tour to survey Queen Victoria's possessions in Ceylon, India and Burma.

It was on these travels to Asia, lasting from November 1864 to the following May, that the young Leopold saw the Suez Canal under construction, in which he became an investor. He stopped off at the port of Aden, the so-called 'Coal-hole of the East' at the northern rim of the Indian Ocean (which by now was being called 'the English Lake'), where

An original unpublished pen-and-ink caricature, of Leopold on top of an elephant, which I found in the Royal Palace archives. It was tucked among an odd assortment of Leopold's papers which included a passionate love letter from an American stalker who caught a glimpse of his towering frame on a seaside vacation.

he would have seen fleets of British steamships getting repro-visioned. From Aden, Leopold then travelled on to Kandy in Ceylon where some of the most 'holy' elephants in Asia reside, the animals still functioning as part of the regalia of a sacred dynasty. Once a year, the biggest tusker is given the task of carrying a casket containing a relic of the Buddha's tooth on a procession through the city. It's an important symbolic role, given that, historically in local politics, whoever holds the tooth also holds the power to govern the country. Leopold was travelling through territory where wild elephants flour-ished. There was also a lively indigenous industry around their capture. Wild herds would be driven into a wide-mouthed stockade. Each elephant's trunk was then bound to one of its forelegs to stop it lashing out. Its front and back legs would be tied together to reduce its stride. Fastened to a strong tree, it would be denied food, water and sleep until it started to submit to its keeper, who would use a metal goad to establish dominance. And then it would be 'baptized', as another European traveller described the process, in a centuries-old system of subjugation. With local variations across the region, these techniques ensured a reliable supply of elephants for work – a potential Leopold witnessed in full, from how elephants could be used as transport animals to how they were also exploited as symbols of imperial power.

When he visited Bharatpur in India, the dazzle of empire was everywhere. Leopold's Indian host arrived on top of a gilded elephant, accompanied by fireworks and a royal collec-tion of leopards. In the jungle running up to the foothills of the Himalayas, Leopold was entertained on a lavish three-day tiger hunt using fifteen elephants bedecked with brocaded saddles, or howdahs. Riding on them felt like 'sitting on a ship', remarked Leopold in his diary. The animals made the forest 'crack open' before him, filling Leopold with admiration for how the elephants used their trunks to force the hunting party's passage through the challenging terrain. With the sun rising over the mountains, Leopold was covetous of everything he could survey from his elevated perch – 'a splendid spectacle', with the snow-capped ranges stretching far behind. But if this trip was showing Leopold how elephants could thrash their way through roadless bush, it was also only a sideshow to his real motivation: discovering how a colony paid, with his travel journals including copious notes about how the British Empire worked – the trains, the opium profits, the tea plantations. It was no surprise that by the time he returned to Belgium he was increasingly desperate to acquire a colony for himself. He shopped around, looking as far afield as Fiji and New Caledonia. But it wasn't until the mid 1870s that Leopold identified a dawning opportunity, drawn by talk in European geographical societies about Congo's 'unspeakable richness'. 'I intend to find out discreetly whether there is anything doing in Africa', Leopold confided to one of his statesmen at the end of 1875.

Except Leopold wasn't the only interested party. All the major European geographical societies were already dispatching explorers into the African interior to map its 'blank spaces' and catalogue its resources. In order to deflect any suspicion about his venal motivations, Leopold needed to move first and present himself as the European king who wanted to 'save Africa' from itself. That part would prove easy enough, for in the same papers declaring Africa's commercial potential – news literally being delivered to the king on a plate each morning, in papers ironed by his valet – there was an even more dominant narrative: the time had come for 'civilized' peoples to step into the moral vacuum Africa evoked in the European mind, and stop the slaving taking place under the 'Arab' yoke.

It was the perfect cover. By the late 1860s, slavery had been widely abolished by various countries behind the transatlantic trade, including Britain, France and the US. Flush with Christian purpose, the abolitionists were starting to pay attention to the opposite side of the African continent, to the run of murky 'Arab' trading lines. The story was hot with lurid detail. The European explorers who had first gone in search of the source of the Nile – one of the biggest geographical questions of the century, which held the public spellbound with books, betrayals, libels and suspected suicides – had described the depravities of the slave caravans they had encountered on the road. These explorers were celebrities back home. They drew attention to themselves with all sorts of memorable flourishes, from Richard Francis Burton, who wore silk-embroidered Persian slippers and rimmed his eyes with charcoal, to Dr David Livingstone, whose revelations about the slaving violence were so shocking his writing inspired a generation of missionary-adventurers to answer his famous call 'to heal this open sore of the world'. When his bestseller *Missionary Travels and Researches in South Africa* was published in 1857, Livingstone complained he couldn't leave his house without being mobbed. At his funeral in London's Westminster Cathedral, one of his pallbearers was a formerly enslaved African, Jacob Wainwright, who'd walked over a thousand miles across Africa, where Livingstone died, to deliver his corpse back to England. Devotion like Wainwright's was all the proof the evangelizers needed of the 'civilizing' impact of their Christian Saviour.

Jacob Wainwright standing with Livingstone's coffin in London, 1874.

With God as both lure and punishment, Leopold could therefore 'save' Africans both from enslaving each other, as well as from the Arabs, whose faith was an easy target among Europe's Christian majority. He could ride on the back of the public mood, of Europe's sense of moral conviction fuelled by a run of expanding racist ideologies, including the enduring myth of Jean-Jacques Rousseau's 'noble savage', or the idea that certain nations must 'progress' to avoid extinction. Then there was Social Darwinism, and the pseudo-scientific theory of 'race betterment' or eugenics. In one version or another, all these notions were being endorsed in the work of the so-called 'White Heroes in Africa', who, even after the Nile's source was 'discovered' in 1858, used their adventures to turn the 'Dark Continent' into a kind of mirror reflecting Europe's 'superior' civilization. If Leopold could harness this phenomenon, he could bring public support into his sphere of influence. That was the idea when, on 12 September 1876, Leopold finally seeded his Congo masterplan: the Brussels Geographical Conference, billed as an international forum, and 'a high moral intervention' hosted at the city's Royal Palace. Instilled with the 'spirit of charity', the conference would shine a light on territory that only recently had been regarded 'as empty and as bare as that of the Pole' – 'in a word, to pour upon it the treasures of civilization', according to the king's flamboyant invitation.

Leopold's stage management included specially chartered trains. Under a steely northern sky, his guests pulled into Brussels in hissing clouds of steam, before proceeding to the palace in a clatter of carriages met by fawning royal footmen. Leopold even scheduled ships to bring his guests to Belgium – a *Who's Who* of white-bearded geographers and scientists, as well as some well-known abolitionists, leading explorers from Russia, France, Germany and Britain, and even a number of Americans sympathetic to Leopold's vision, some of whom were seeking to dispatch back to Africa the men, women and children recently released from plantation slavery. Leopold invited influential business people, including the Scottish shipping magnate William Mackinnon – a man as powerful as the Musks and Zuckerbergs of our time – who was already investigating the idea of building roads into the African interior. The conference needed to appear a truly international endeavour, a meeting of the decade's power brokers in their stovepipe hats, pulling wisely at their beards as they debated the map of Africa and all the opportunities it sequestered. Conspicuously absent from the proceedings were any Africans.

New marble staircases were built for the occasion. Rooms were lit up by seven thousand candles, and palace suites decorated in sumptuous gold and crimson damask. As discussions drew to their conclusion, Leopold announced the founding of the International African Association, or IAA, with himself as president, on a mission to 'civilize' Central Africa. To achieve this, the IAA would need to develop a line of communication running from the Indian Ocean to the Atlantic across the middle of the continent. They could then think about a line running from north to south, with Europeans working together 'instead of leaving every man to hunt for his own needle in his own bundle of hay'. As the British explorer Samuel Baker remarked in a letter to Leopold, 'military trading stations should be established in a continuous chain that would afford both a moral and material support'. What everyone was talking about was laying a cross over the African continent, with Lake Tanganyika at its heart. It was an ambition 'worthy of this century of progress', Leopold declared; 'the current is with us'. 'Need I say that in bringing you to Brussels I was guided by no egotism? No, gentlemen, Belgium may be a small country, but she is happy and satisfied with her fate.' By the time the banquet dinners were over and the last trains had left, Leopold had his guests exactly where he needed them, clutching a gilt-edged portrait of him as a parting gift.

To put his vision into practice on the ground, the king turned his attention to hiring men for the IAA with the right talents and reputation. He made enquiries about the British military hero Charles Gordon, who, at the very moment Leopold was hosting his lavish feasts in Brussels, was crawling along the banks of the Nile about as far from the pop of champagne corks as anyone could possibly get. 'A horrid "end of the world" place this', Gordon confided in his diary, describing the dense jungle, thick creepers, gloomy silences and clouds of mosquitoes, which he fended off by chain-smoking Turkish cigarettes. Gordon, who had a strong grasp of remote logistics, was engaged further north than the line Leopold was planning, establishing a run of anti-slaving stations as part of a complex British–Egyptian relationship. But if Gordon could be persuaded to switch loyalties to Leopold, his experience would be perfect for the role. He'd already proved himself as capable with Africa's river systems as he was negotiating with chiefs, sheikhs, pashas, kings and shifty European diplomats. But Gordon was also a loose cannon. He shared with the British explorer Richard Burton an 'impolitic habit of telling political truths'. The busybodies at the Royal Geographical Society in London were constantly trying to exploit Gordon's celebrity for parties. 'I say leave me alone, to rest. If they want people to eat their dinners, they have the poor', Gordon wrote to a friend. And he had no time for armchair missionaries (and wasn't afraid of telling them): 'You are bigots. Whether it be the churchyard, or the temperance question, or any other, you do not think of the other side.'

Assaulted by a barrage of letters, Gordon soon got fed up with the IAA's overtures. On his next leave in Europe, he didn't want to see 'any of the men who worry about Africa'. He yo-yoed between belief in empire, which had made him a household name in Britain, and occasional doubt: 'Am I a tool to delude the Blacks into submission . . . Am I a tool to obtain some favour from our Government.' Leopold had drawn a blank, so in December 1877 he instead dispatched the first IAA expedition to Zanzibar with three Belgians and one Austrian, none of whom had any significant Africa experience. They left with orders to get a base built inland, but it quickly turned into a debacle. Two of the men didn't even make it off the island. Perhaps it was the strain of the voyage, or shock of the climate, but they were dead almost as soon as they arrived.

Leopold clearly needed more expertise on the ground, so turned his attention towards the explorer and journalist Henry Morton Stanley. Born in January 1841, and raised in a Welsh workhouse, Stanley had absconded to sea as a cabin boy on an American ship bound for New Orleans. He fought for the Confederacy in the American Civil War, was captured, switched sides, and eventually wrangled work as a newspaper-man for the *New York Herald*. He made his break in 1871 when he famously tracked down Livingstone after the missionary-explorer got 'lost' somewhere in the middle of Africa. After his Livingstone scoop, Stanley then returned to the continent to complete a three-year crossing of Central Africa in 1877. 'The [Congo] River is and will be, the grand highway of commerce,' Stanley declared to the expedition's media sponsors, the *Daily Telegraph* and *New York Herald*. In a letter sent to Belgium's ambassador to London, Leopold stressed the urgency to making a more decisive move: 'I do not wish to miss the opportunity of our obtaining a share in this magnificent Afri-can cake.' In January 1878, he sent two of his most trusted associates – a Belgian called Jules Greindl, and a Florida busi-nessman called Henry Shelton Sanford – to secure the services of Stanley, who was as flattered by Leopold's overtures as he was offended that the British, already wrapped up in ruling a quarter of the world's population, didn't seem to care for his recent revelations about Congo's riches. Stanley, who had a fragile ego at the best of times, was feeling vulnerable. His American fiancée had abandoned him during his long absence. He was also still struggling with the stain of a British newspaper story about a massacre he'd allegedly ordered on

Lake Victoria. All these factors made him susceptible to Leopold's persuasions, which were also underhand: Stanley's hiring would be for a side arrangement to the public IAA mission.

Stanley would be employed by a shadowy venture called the Comité d'études du Haut-Congo, for which Leopold had gathered various private investors. The explorer would be entering Africa from the west, not the east, and signing up to a five-year contract to secure land deals and build trading stations on the Congo River. 'In a word, we are going to attract as little attention as possible,' wrote Greindl, in an increasingly complex series of schemes, with Leopold now acting as puppet-master-in-chief. It was turning into a strategy of smoke and mirrors. The more successful the IAA proved building 'hospitable and scientific station[s]' on the eastern approach to Lake Tanganyika, the better it would be for Leopold while he worked on this secretive commercial agenda with Stanley in the west. Except Leopold's first, lacklustre IAA expedition hadn't done this plan any favours when news reached Europe of the Belgian death toll before even leaving Zanzibar: the expedition's leader, Captain Louis Crespel, and his doctor, died within ten days of each other. '[There's] a feeling of – what shall I call it – something approaching to derision,' Stanley remarked. Leopold knew he couldn't risk any further reputational damage. To keep his 'philanthropic' mission burnished, some more pomp was required on the eastern side of the continent – a public gesture that framed Leopold as the royal figure behind a grand crusade.

Around this time another new idea was developing in Europe's geographical circles: perhaps working elephants could be utilized on the age-old eastern caravan routes to extract the region's resources? Using elephants as transport was hardly absurd compared with the French suggestion to Africa's access problem, of creating an artificial sea by flooding the Sahara. Heated conversations bounced backwards and forwards between the scientific elite, with the notion it was high time to exploit African elephants for more than just their ivory. But the idea was also derided; most people assumed the African elephant couldn't be trained like the Asian. But then news arrived that Gordon had just completed a low-profile Nile expedition with five Asian elephants (sent many years before to Egypt as a gift by the British government), as well as a pet African one. If these creatures were able to shoulder two hundred and seventy kilograms each, as Gordon's had done, that would be the equivalent of hiring nine porters, who were not only constantly at risk of disease, but often deserted their loads. If elephants could withstand the deadly bite of the tsetse fly which felled horses and cattle south of the Sahara, there'd be less need for Europeans to depend on the existing caravan mechanisms, which were largely run by the coastal Arabs. For Leopold's purposes, an elephant expedition was something European public sentiment might get behind: original, mythic, grandiose. This was also the 1870s, when elephant mania was popularized by stories like Jumbo's – an unusually tall elephant which became one of London's most well-known attractions. Each month, a new elephant story was making splashy headlines, including hysteria over American circuses coming to Europe, with big tops capable of accommodating up to ten thousand people. Elephants were exotic currency in nineteenth-century Europe, bringing the faraway closer.

Leopold made another move. Colonies, he once said,

weren't made by sitting around. One had 'to watch for the favourable moment . . . to see them in a hurry for it's rare what they represent.' The king's associates solicited Gordon again, to see if he'd attempt an elephant expedition from the east coast, but he refused. Gordon didn't know of any captive elephants in Africa that Leopold could buy, but he did give some detailed advice, including the load a single elephant could carry, and recommended rates of pay for their keepers. He warned Leopold's men about hiring Indian mahouts, whom Gordon didn't trust, and described how the Africans ran in fear from the sight of his tamed beasts. For Leopold and his proxies, the hunt was now on to find the right animals, and the man to front it, which, by March 1879, was closing in on the Irishman Frederick Carter – a tip-off that came via Leopold's deepening relationship with the Scottish shipping magnate William Mackinnon. This former grocer's apprentice had by now built a global shipping conglomerate with the world's largest cargo-carrying capacity. Mackinnon had interests in India, the Persian Gulf and increasingly in coastal Africa. He was a literal link in the chain Leopold needed for his plans to materialize.

As for Frederick Carter, he had already built a name for himself as a gifted navigator. His work on the rivers of Mesopotamia had helped establish critical trade links with the Gulf's much bigger networks across the Indian Ocean. In the 1860s, a single Bombay steamer might have come to Basra once every six weeks, but by the late 1870s, it was common to see up to twelve steamers loading from the same wharf in front of Carter's house in Maaghil (or Margil), which is now part of Basra's city sprawl. Carter introduced night sailings to Baghdad – a first for the region, carrying lucrative cargos of wool bound for France, dates for America and England, and grain for Bombay. Under his captainship, the steamers' passenger decks were packed with customers: Arabs from the Gulf and the desert inland, Jews from Baghdad, Muslims on pilgrimage to Karbala.

By 1879, Carter's home had acquired a reputation among European tourists. His house guests, including naval officers who used his home to recover when they fell sick, described the elegance of his bachelor quarters, and his beautifully tended garden. They talked about Carter's affection for his English assistant, an affable, soft-spoken man called Tom Cadenhead a few years younger than him, and Carter's Arab valet, Mahomed. 'Our genial host seemed equally at home in the serious, the sentimental, and the comic,' wrote one of Carter's visitors. Travellers who enjoyed his hospitality described how Carter would take his harmonium, and play Irish ballads until dawn broke over the river. 'The hours of the short night sped rapidly away, and before we were aware of it the morning light streaked the eastern horizon. We adjourned to the garden below, and in the wide reclining chairs once more enjoyed our coffee under the spreading branches of the great mulberry tree.' Carter kept lions as pets, allowing them to roam as they pleased both in his home and on the deck of his steamer. They were part of his riverside menagerie, which included birds, several monkeys and two large English dogs. As a sideline to his maritime work, Carter was also procuring Mesopotamian species for zoos across the British Empire. He'd shipped another of his pet lions, a six-month-old male cub called Rashched, 'tame as a dog and gentle as a lamb', to the Calcutta Zoological Gardens.

This Mesopotamian life was all a long way from the 1840s

Kilkenny of Carter's birth where the streets had smelled of corpses. 'One might suppose [Kilkenny] to be dead,' wrote a visiting English journalist reporting on the decade's famine. Each July, the people changed colour, commented a Kilkenny diarist: 'Buímhís ("yellow month") is its proper name in Irish. It is a suitable name, for the fields are yellow, and also the faces of the paupers are greenish yellow from the black famine, as they live on green cabbage and poor scraps of that sort.' In 1845, blight took out over a third of Kilkenny's potato crop. The following year, more than ninety per cent of the next crop was destroyed. By the end of the decade, one in four Kilkenny residents depended upon workhouse relief. Mass graves were being dug inside the workhouse walls because the cemeteries couldn't cope, with more than half the corpses children. While hunger (and a lack of opportunity) drove the mass exodus for England and America, the other path out of this dismal decade was into the expanding workforce of the British Empire. This was the path two of Carter's elder brothers took when they abandoned Ireland to work on the Indian railways. Empire would eventually give Carter his chance too, with Mesopotamia a place to escape the trauma of his beginnings.

His mother – the daughter of a Protestant rector in County Mayo, raised in a simple country house with a piano and a bay horse for her father to do his rounds on – had died when Carter was nine, while giving birth to her ninth child. Two other children predeceased her, leaving six. Within twelve days of her death, Carter's father, a county surveyor working on the Kilkenny turnpikes, put the family home on the market. He took to the bottle. Carter grew up in foster care, with an aunt called Mrs Johnstone living in Hertfordshire in

England. Meanwhile back in Ireland, the family's fortunes hit rock bottom when Carter's father went on a four-day drinking binge. During a visit to see his favourite prostitute, Carter's father placed a double-barrelled pistol in his mouth and blew his brains out in the bed of a Dublin brothel. In a lurid multipage report published by the *Kilkenny Journal*, the attending sergeant observed he'd died with a rather sad expression on his face. The coroner said it was a fit of delirium tremens, his suicide the result of a 'temporary insanity'.

Did it matter to Leopold that Carter had no experience of Africa? He'd travelled widely since the age of fourteen, working for the British merchant navy, where he quickly rose through the ranks. 'His experience as a sailor and officer in all parts of the world furnished an inexhaustible fund of anecdotes, some of which were located in New York, Savannah and New Orleans', remarked one of Carter's houseguests in Mesopotamia. For Leopold's scheme, Carter's strongest credential was his fluent Arabic, which would help with passage along the Arab-Swahili trade routes. He was clearly forthright, yet at the same time a proven talent at handling sensitive relationships in hostile environments. In Mesopotamia, which was a land of complex tribal constellations with almost half the population nomadic, Carter had managed to negotiate with the shifting interests to keep river piracy relatively under control. 'The Arabs round Bussorah grew to regard him as a kind of father', wrote a fawning British journalist; Carter 'identified himself with their interests in every possible way, and learnt much of their modes of thought and ways of living. He was as welcome in their tents as they were in his bungalow, and he settled their disputes and kept their turbulent spirits in order. Altogether, the strange influence he acquired over them is best expressed by the title they gave him, that of the "White Sheik" [sic].

These successes, at least as they were perceived by his fellow men of empire, had positioned Carter as a kind of de facto British official in Basra. But when an attempt was made to elevate his status into a formal appointment as vice consul, there was a problem. The consul in Baghdad hadn't sought permission from his superiors. Carter's promotion held for a few months and was then humiliatingly retracted with accusations of nepotism. So in March 1879 when Carter was summoned for an interview with Leopold in Brussels, it's easy to see why Carter said yes. A personal invitation from a European king was an improvement on shooting game in whirling sandstorms on the banks of the river Tigris. Like Stanley, Carter was a determined man with an injured ego. Also like Stanley, Carter knew his best chance to put his past behind him lay in empire. The lives of these two men – born within three months of each other in 1841, both fathered by drunkards who suffered from delirium tremens, both setting off abroad as cabin boys, both physically strong and commanding leaders – had begun to move in tighter parallel.

While Carter was being wined and dined in Belgium, Leopold and his proxies were pushing ahead and shopping for suitable elephants with a new urgency. Unless animals were found immediately, the expedition would lose its window to make meaningful progress towards Lake Tanganyika before the monsoon rains came in. If they missed the dry weather between May and November, the whole expedition would have to be delayed until the following year. Meanwhile, the shipping magnate William Mackinnon was getting word from his men on the ground: the region's trade was picking up, which meant higher demand on the transportation network. Competition was also growing for new commodities, with a hot market for gum copal used to varnish coaches. There were signs of the coastal communities going 'rubber mad.'

Leopold would need ready-tamed beasts if the expedition were to catch the travelling season. There were none to be had in Africa, while in India and Burma elephant prices were running double to what they were a few years before. In Europe, there were one or two dealers in exotic wildlife who might have been able to help. So Leopold's associates turned to a menagerie in Hamburg which had almost twenty years of experience importing African elephants. Five had been recently trained, but for one reason or another, the stock went to Berlin Zoo instead. They tried London's Zoological Society, visited the elephants at the city's Alexandra Palace, and stopped by Charles Rice's premises, which claimed to be the largest importer of animals in Europe. But Rice only had one available African elephant – a three-year-old no bigger than a horse. Meeting dead end after dead end, Leopold's men even started hustling England's travelling circus troupes for elephants – anything to get the show on the road. By mid April, it was decided that since suitable African elephants weren't forthcoming from European menageries, Carter would use trained Indian animals instead.

Telegrams criss-crossed at breakneck speed, between Glasgow (where part of Mackinnon's shipping empire was headquartered), Brussels and India. Within days, four animals were secured from the Indian government's stud at Pune, which was where the British Raj retreated each monsoon when the muggy heat of Bombay became too much.

An 1872 menagerie sale, London. Bringing these wild animals
into line, declared the London Evening Standard, *was simply a*
case of putting keeper and creature into the same cage for a few weeks
with a hook and a couple of thongs made from rhino skin. This was
how the London Zoological Gardens' prize elephant, Jumbo, was
disciplined: 'The one beating has lasted so far for the rest of his life.'

In the 1870s, George Sanger's British circus performed all over
Europe, including Belgium. His caravan ran two miles long and
included twelve 'ponderous performing elephants'. This picture shows
Tiny the elephant holding Sanger's grandson.

After a brief hiccup over who would pay the pensions should the elephants' Indian attendants die (Leopold conceded that he would bear this cost), two male and two female elephants were marched the hundred miles from Pune to Bombay to board the *Chinsura*, a steamship Mackinnon had readied for departure. On 7 May 1879, the cargo was packed, including new elephant trappings and fittings, twelve experienced mahouts and assistants, as well as sufficient food and water for the elephants' twenty-five-day oceanic crossing. Carter, meanwhile, was on his voyage from Europe, heading for the rendezvous in Aden. From there he'd sail with the elephants for Zanzibar where, with his valet Mahomed in attendance, Carter would start outfitting the expedition with local supplies and porters. It had been a strangely impetuous few weeks. The hurry had been so great that Carter had only been able to take with him part of the expedition's equipment. He'd been reassured that a thousand cartridges and twenty-three kilograms of gunpowder would be following behind.

Amid all this busyness, the duplicity of the Belgian king with his two expeditions – one secret under Stanley's command, the other public under Carter's control – went unsuspected. Rather than the buckshot Carter was sent off with, Leopold had by this time arranged for significant military supplies to be shipped to Stanley at the mouth of the Congo River, which were loaded on to a ship near Ostend. It was essential, Colonel Strauch noted, that 'nobody would ever know the nature of this shipment nor the name of the recipient'. The die was cast for Leopold's game of cloak-and-dagger machinations, with the bigger, more sinister picture still unknown to anyone outside Leopold's inner circle. Meanwhile, Carter was brimming with pride as details of his royal commission started to be fed into the European media. In the news rattling down telegraph wires, the White Sheikh from Kilkenny was about to join the race for a continent.

3

The Paris of East Africa

'I was careful not to make a sensation of danger; but future travellers ... will do well not to think that, when about to explore Central Africa, they are setting out upon a mere promenade.'

—RICHARD FRANCIS BURTON,
Zanzibar: City, Island and Coast

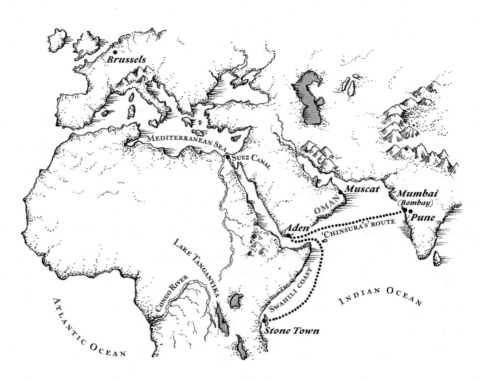

I T WAS SEPTEMBER WHEN I arrived in Zanzibar to pick up
Carter's trail – a pit stop for both of us before heading to
the mainland where, all being well with their sea passage,
Carter would disembark his elephants for the onward journey
to Lake Tanganyika. It was getting to the end of the long dry
season, a world away from the wet English autumn I'd left
behind. On the flight from London, I'd fallen in and out of
sleep, wondering how the elephants must have felt, how bleak
and strange their journey as waves broke against the *Chin-sura*'s lightless hold. In Zanzibar, I booked into a cheap room
near a narrow skirt of beach not far from the waterfront in
Stone Town, which was the island's capital in the nineteenth
century. I woke up each morning to the call to prayer. I drank
coffee to the drone of a Catholic radio station, Radio Maria
Tanzania, spilling from a neighbour's doorway. I watched fer-ries come and go from Dar es Salaam. They moved so hard
and fast, the fishing boats had to dart out of their path, the
dhows with their lateen sails scattering like birds.

Once Carter arrived in Zanzibar, there would be diplo-matic matters to attend to, as well as meetings with the island's
caravan logisticians who would outfit the expedition. There
would also be a practical challenge to solve. Carter needed
advice on how best to land the elephants at Dar es Salaam,
where the winds were so foul for nine months of the year,
boats couldn't use the harbour. For me, Zanzibar was my
chance to access an important collection of nineteenth-century records held in the island's National Archives. I

wanted to research as much history as possible before I took a boat to the mainland to pin down final logistics with two people who'd agreed to help me on the journey: an experienced Maasai naturalist called Rem with a vehicle good for off-road driving (a rugged Toyota 4×4) and Wolfe, the son of my friend from Donegal, who was raised in Tanzania. Aside from all the interpreting and permit negotiations needed to access certain territories, Rem would be responsible for equipment, including camping kit, sleeping mattresses, tarpaulins, cans of extra fuel, drinking water, spades and spare parts in case we broke down. Wolfe would be responsible for map reading, including tracking modern cartographic details on to the old, which would enable us to follow the elephants' route as accurately as possible. My focus would be on finding sources to better understand the past, which was history I could smell the moment I arrived.

The island's story oozed from every pore: from the strips of orange peel drying in pools of cobbled light, from the oily heads of cloves and fattened peppercorns sweating in the heat, from the buttery chapatis, the charcoaled meats sizzling on streetside barbecues, the briny mangroves, and the silver fish drying on the shore. It was a story of migration, of different people and their cultures, arriving on Arab dhows travelling with the trade winds. From around November to March, the *kaskazi* blows from the northeast across the Indian Ocean. Before the advent of steam power, this was long enough to sail from India to Zanzibar. From around May to September, the *kusi* travels the other way. Both winds pass over the top of the Indian Ocean where the monsoon's tail glances across the Dhofar escarpment in Oman to turn the desert's rocky edge-land a pale grass green. Then there's the in-between season, the *tanga mbili*, meaning something like 'between two sails'. It happens twice a year when the wind direction is about to shift. In the old days, the lull anticipated the arrival of new information. You couldn't quite know what might happen next, with the change of wind so influential that the decisions you made six months ago might be outdated by the next run of dhows. The in-between season carried an indecisiveness, a volatility.

But if I could smell Zanzibar's story the moment I arrived, I could also hear it in the sounds bubbling up through the narrow backstreets of Stone Town, in the puttering rise and fall of voices drifting down its passageways. Swahili, a singsong mix of Arabic and African Bantu languages, stems from the Arabic word *sawahil*, meaning 'coast'. Those maritime origins surface in the fluid syntax, in the jaunty upwellings of 'y's and 'z's, in the suffixed 'a's and 'i's as light as the surf, in the liquid vowels spilling out of the windy *mausim* root of 'monsoon'. Even the word 'safari' has the breeze blowing through its origins. It comes from the Arabic *safara*, which means 'to journey'.

In the nineteenth century, Zanzibar was politically dominated by the Omani Arabs, who for almost a millennium had been dealing in East Africa's ivory, gold and enslaved people. Some of the newcomers intermarried with coastal Africans, contributing to the Swahili mix of Afro-Arab identities. Others moved further inland, but by 1840 their dealings down the so-called 'Swahili Coast' had expanded to such a degree it made sense to move the Omani court from Muscat to Zanzibar. To facilitate a reliable supply of cloth and beads for bartering, Indian merchants opened commercial houses on the island as well as at stations along the same caravan routes Leopold's elephants needed to travel into the interior. 'When you play the flute at Zanzibar', ran a popular saying, 'all Africa, as far as the Lakes, dances.'

When the British explorer Richard Burton visited the island in 1856 on his journey to find the source of the Nile, he described Africa's last public slave market, which was still doing a brisk trade. Men, women and children were being sold for the price of a donkey, or less. The weak and dying, marched hundreds of miles in chains and wooden neck yokes, were being left to rot on the shore. The town was filthy, diseased – a scene Burton described as a pageant of moral decrepitude evoked in a Brueghel-esque panorama infected with his own racist tropes: Indian burghers resembling 'happy, well-to-do cows', Gulf Arabs with 'a greedy, cut-throat stare', Europeans with 'blanched face' and absurd clothes that were far too tight for them. There was a half-dead Irishman ensconced in the British consulate. Zanzibar was the diplomatic posting nobody wanted. When another English officer was about to be appointed to the same position, he chose to shoot himself in the head instead.

But by the time Carter and the elephants were headed for Zanzibar in the late spring of 1879, Burton's graphic descriptions were falling out of date. Among Europeans, Stone Town was being heralded as the 'Paris of East Africa'. An Anglican cathedral was going up, on the exact spot where the last slave market had stood only a few years before. There was a thriving church mission a few miles from town, whose men were employed to build a new road for the ruling Omani sultan, Barghash bin Said, whose trading monopolies were increasingly under threat. In 1873, the sultan was forced to capitulate to a British anti-slaving treaty (a staggering act of double standards from Her Majesty's government given this role of self-appointed policeman followed so closely the era of British slave-keeping in the Caribbean). On the other hand, Barghash knew how to hide hypocrisies as effectively as any of his European contemporaries. ('The people of Zanzibar as a whole can do nothing, not even clip their whiskers, without the servants and the slaves they own,' another sultan admitted some twenty years after the treaty's signing). Barghash also understood how to exploit the jealousies festering between meddling foreign agents trying to get in on the ivory trade. Stone Town was in a state of flux, but under Barghash it was also being increasingly cut up according to a dangerous hierarchy of ethnicities as a means of control: Arab here, European there, with ghettos of Goan, Cutch and other Indians. The Africans were still being kept at a distance, in slums across the creek.

Despite the anti-slaving treaty, or perhaps because of it, Sultan Barghash kept his greatest challenge close: the abolitionist John Kirk, a tenacious, straight-talking Scotsman who had worked as expedition naturalist and physician for Livingstone, and who in 1879 headed up Zanzibar's British consulate. Kirk's silhouette at his harbourside window was familiar to everyone who passed through Stone Town. He made it his business to keep a sharp eye on the winds of opportunity sweeping in and out of the same beach where these days tourist dhows now loiter, their skippers trying to drum up trade. Kirk noted the ships leaving Zanzibar carrying rubber, gum copal and a superabundance of ivory. He also noted the goods coming in, including shipments stuffed with European breech-loaders and vast amounts of gunpowder.

Stone Town merchants, with the ivory marked up for shipment. In the latter part of the nineteenth century, up to thirty thousand elephant tusks were being shipped out of Zanzibar every year alone.

Four porters carrying a piece of ivory in Zanzibar – of a length now rarely seen.

An ivory shipment being sorted at the Royal Albert Dock in London in 1926.

An American billiard ball dealer, each ball cut from African ivory.

But Kirk wasn't the only snooping diplomat. A visiting missionary remarked how all the island's foreign consuls would amuse themselves by tracking the town from telescopes. The sultan had a powerful one too, pointed out a British traveller, 'and thus often becomes acquainted with facts not intended for his eye'. But Kirk was much the best noticer, his meddling so significant that the American consul came up with a phrase for it: 'Kirkism'. '[Kirk] has got to be a perfect snob', he complained, 'the greatest gossip maker in the place'.

Each day, Kirk scribbled his observations into leatherbound diaries, which were dominated by information on custom-house returns, and the changing values of trading goods, including the going rate for rhino horns. Now and again he'd describe the everyday lives of Africans, and the filthy table manners of visiting explorers. '[T]erribly vulgar, provincial and selfish ... a gross eater', wrote Kirk about the Royal Geographical Society's newest hire, a Scottish geologist called Joseph Thomson, who was passing through Stone Town that same spring of 1879 as part of a British expedition to Africa's Great Lakes, including Tanganyika. Kirk's diaries also included notes about Leopold's curious consignment of Indian elephants, about which Kirk held all manner of knowing opinions shared with the Belgian king. In February 1879, Leopold sent Kirk a monogrammed snuffbox 'to let you know the price I attach to the benevolence you show to the diverse efforts that are being carried out to bring civilisation into Africa'.

In Kirk's opinion, Leopold was on to something: the transport problem along the caravan trails needed fixing, and maybe the African elephant could be trained in large enough

numbers to make a difference. The demand was certainly building. In 1879, more steamships were powering into Stone Town's
harbour. In May, a regular service started running between
India and Zanzibar, which was changing the region's depend-
encies on wind. By the end of the year, a cable would connect
Zanzibar to Europe for the first time – technology greeted with
a message of congratulations sent down the wire from Leopold
to Sultan Barghash. For Stone Town's expanding expat community, this new connectivity meant life was also starting to look
like a comforting facsimile of home, with games of lawn tennis,
bands, golf, polo, a monthly book club and a steady supply of
European goods. Although Carter may have left Brussels for
Africa in a hurry, his poor preparation wasn't going to be a
problem. Stone Town in 1879 had almost everything a European might need to equip a mainland expedition.

Almost everything, that is, aside from the 'right' ward-
robe, which had to be shipped from home. A 'free-and-easy
suit of Tweeds and pith hat', recommended the Royal Geographical Society's man, Thomson, who endeavoured to dress
like a gentleman even if Kirk thought he ate like a pig. French
sunglasses were essential, and a floppy, broad-brimmed 'wide-
awake' hat, recommended another of the explorers. Most
British travellers, however, relied on advice from Francis
Galton, the English eugenicist and Nile explorer, whose *Art of
Travel* was a popular how-to guide for geographers, missionaries and others 'who have to rough it'. (Stanley thought less of
Galton: 'I am told he has twice written about the Art of Travel.
I think it strange that such an accomplished Master of the Art,
did not succeed in reaching the Lake.')

Galton's tips ranged from the required roominess for a
tent, including expedition furnishings with 'the most show

for their weight', such as rugs and dinner services. He advised on the value of fireworks to impress locals, heavy bullets needed to bring down an elephant, opera glasses for hunting, how to lift a sarcophagus from an Egyptian tomb and, last but not least, how to smuggle jewels by stitching them under your skin. Stanley, whose kit list was the one Carter and his Belgian colleagues followed, was even more particular on the recommended attire. He advised a flannel suit paired with a white head covering which gleamed in the African sun. This was the peaked tropical hat of Stanley's own design with vents in the high brim and a gauze veil to keep off the mosquitoes.

As for professional navigational tools, they were most reliably sourced in Europe, and included a prismatic compass, sextant, artificial horizon, sounding line and pedometer. Decent medical supplies also needed to come from home, though a British missionary gave specific advice on a good Stone Town opium dealer just in case visitors were caught short. 'A simple, commonsense cookery book' wouldn't go amiss either, and one or two of the new bestselling travelogues (Carter packed *Across Africa* by a British naval officer called Verney Lovett Cameron, who'd recently completed the first ever European traverse of equatorial Africa from sea to sea). Tents were a point of national pride. For Carter, the Belgians provided a tall, double-roofed contraption. This was in contrast to the squat tents used by the British, which were too small to stand up in – a hangover, perhaps, from the no-frills Livingstone, who favoured 'a small gipsy tent, just sufficient to sleep in' with a horse rug for a bed. Once again, Stanley had his own custom-made solution: a double-clothed American drill tent, which he outfitted as if it were an English drawing room, with a bearskin and portable writing table.

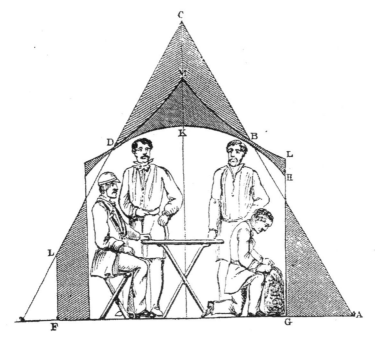

Francis Galton's diagram on the 'roominess' required in a tent.

Left: *A nineteenth-century design for a mosquito net.* Right: *Stanley modelling the 'Stanley Cap' of his own design, made by A. J. White at Jermyn Street and St James', London.*

'Armed with my experience,' Stanley boasted in a letter to the Belgians, Leopold's hires would have an easy job of it. To reach Lake Tanganyika and start some station building, Stanley recommended a caravan of sixty armed men, and another forty-three porters, who should be paid nothing but food until they made it to Tabora, which was an Arab-Swahili trading hub roughly two months' march into the interior. Before setting out, it was critical all hires were inspected for 'rupture, ulcers, dysentery, or whether they are slaves, or eaters of opium.' A major share of the luggage needed to be apportioned to barter goods for paying the local transit tax called 'hongo.' The bales also had to be correctly packed with various cloths, beads (in pinks, blues and browns) and bags of cowrie shells. 'Fashion was as dominant among Central African tribes as among the belles of Paris or London,' remarked Thomson, who was forced to take command when the Royal Geographical Society's original leader died just six weeks into their journey. 'Each tribe must have its own particular class of cotton, and its own chosen tint, colour, and size among beads.' The Europeans also needed their own gunbearers – between one and three per person – who could double up as 'tent-boys, waiting or messenger-boys.'

With all these recommendations, Stanley said his kit list would be sufficient to keep the caravan going for three years, 'without stinting yourself or men of any of the necessaries of life.' What he made no mention of was the plain truth, conceded by Thomson, that 'no caravan ever goes up the country without a number of slaves in the porters.' Stanley, however, kept the best local talent to himself. When he swept into Zanzibar in April just a few weeks ahead of Carter's arrival to pick up provisions for his Congo commission, he snaffled all the most experienced caravan professionals: sixty-eight of them, including Livingstone's former caravan leader, Abdullah Susi. Stanley then stuffed his steamer with an abundance of luxurious provisions, including gifts from the sultan, six bullocks for meat, and other delicacies. To top it all, his logistics were shrouded in a strange, hushed veil of secrecy.

Kirk already loathed Stanley, and had done for some time, because of a spat that went back to Stanley souring his reputation with Livingstone. The fact Stanley now shared nothing of his onward plans infuriated Kirk: 'I gather from what [Stanley] does and does not do that he has come here for no other object than to collect men to help him in carrying out some trading scheme up the Congo from the West Coast to which I think he means to convey the men he engages here.' It bothered Kirk that Stanley also had a Belgian crony by his side – a dandyish lieutenant called Oswald Dutalis, who'd been tasked by Leopold with getting things ready ahead of Carter's arrival. ('I am to coach [Dutalis] up in the "art" of exploration,' Stanley wrote to one of Leopold's American associates.) Kirk was mortally offended that Dutalis was falling under Stanley's influence rather than his. It put Kirk on edge that Dutalis had chosen to avail himself of the hospitality of the French and American consuls in Stone Town, and this despite Kirk's communications with the Belgian king and his proxies. 'If Stanley is to be the guiding spirit of the whole, I must keep things well in hand,' Kirk noted in his private correspondence, determined to protect British influence. Kirk didn't like the fact Stanley was having conversations with the sultan that he wasn't party to. He accused Stanley of trying to 'make mischief' for the British, and was frustrated that he couldn't break Dutalis's silence. '[Dutalis] says he does not know to what part of Africa he is to be sent,' complained Kirk. 'This is a funny way of doing business if true, but I think he knows more than he tells and knows no doubt something of Stanley's ultimate plans, with which he may be somehow associated.'

Kirk was right to be suspicious. As the elephants sailed for Zanzibar in the *Chinsura*, Stanley slipped out of Stone Town in the steamship *Albion*, chartered by Leopold. The plan was to travel the long way round to Congo by way of Suez and meet up with the secret gun haul the king had arranged. When I plotted Stanley's journey and timeline on my office wall, I could see it clearly: somewhere off the desolate edge of Somalia, Stanley would have passed Carter and the elephants coming the other way.

The view from the rooftop of where I was staying in Stone Town overlooked the heads of coconut palms, washing lines and a warren of stairways. The waterfront lay beyond. Each morning, I'd wake up listening to other early risers moving through the entangled streets, to the unlocking of the bakery opposite, and the patter and coo of pigeons breaking from their slumber. Then I'd make my way across town to dig into information held at the Zanzibar archives about the *Chinsura*'s arrival.

It was my favourite part of the day, when the sunshine wasn't yet too piercing and the powdered walls of Stone Town were soaked in a pale pink light. Schoolchildren hurried along in clacking flip-flops, the girls gliding through the chalky streets in flowing white hijabs. On Fridays, the madrassas filled up with boys reciting the Qur'an. They were dressed in spotless kanzus – long white robes traditionally worn in Tanzania – and embroidered skull caps. There was a musician

I saw more than once, carrying a pear-shaped oud, or lute, strapped like a turtle shell to his back. He seemed to me a symbol of everything gracious about this town, with its crooked alleys too narrow to pass through without giving way to a stranger walking the other way.

The neighbourhoods felt connected, the community's mixed heritage evident in the way the churches and needle minarets stood side by side, and in the long stone benches where Zanzibaris would gather later in the day. I got talking with a music producer who explained how Stone Town had a rhythm derived from the island's multicultural history. He introduced me to Siti Amina, a singer-songwriter and women's rights advocate who was exporting Zanzibar's identity to the rest of the world. She talked me through the cultural osmosis evident in the sounds of the island's traditional taarab music with its Arabic scales, and how, in the nineteenth century, the dhows brought change, from Yemen, Somalia and India. The image of the boats made me think how these days any gentler experiences of time and space are compressed into the twisted arc we watch grow across the screen in the flight map on the back of the airline seat in front of us. With the speed of getting from one place to another, we no longer absorb each other's nuances at the pace of a weather pattern. We come and go too fast.

I savoured those morning walks. Palm fronds trembled like ostrich quills. Lattice balconies splashed shade on to the alleys below. At a plastic table pulled up outside a nineteenth-century Omani-style house, four Arab men listened to their friend who'd recently returned from Muscat, where familial connections remain strong. In the decrepit Majestic Cinema, a Denzel Washington movie played to an audience of two, and down on the beach there were girls in bikinis and women in fluttering abayas. I was letting 'Fantasy Zanzibar' dominate my impressions, even though I wanted to resist the notion Stone Town was something out of the *Arabian Nights*. It's an exoticizing impulse which has pulled in numerous anglo-phone authors before me, including Stanley, who declared Stone Town 'one of the fairest gems of Nature's creation.' (Burton was less flattering: a good way to murder an unwanted wife, he ventured, was to let her breathe a few months of Zan-zibar air.) The more time I spent here, the more the sights, sounds and smells conspired with the spirit of place to endorse the versions of Zanzibar I'd arrived with, the surface so intoxi-cating it concealed the difficulties of the island's inter-racial culture born of numerous inequities – and the schisms seeded in the ethnic ghettos of nineteenth-century Stone Town, which exploded into a violent revolution in 1964.

I'd read about these bloody events, how the coup was accompanied by pogroms enacted against the Arabs by the islands' ethnic African majority. I'd been warned that people still didn't talk about what had happened, so I relied in part upon the novels of the Zanzibar-born British author Abdul-razak Gurnah, who'd fled Stone Town as a refugee. Yet the exoticizing habit lingered when I tried to switch gears in the island archives looking for mention of Leopold's elephants. I sat under the lazy beat of the building's ceiling fan, reading the letters and official records. The Arabic manuscripts looked like they were written in crushed diamonds, each sparkling letter suspended in the hardened loops of a glossy gum. Every folder was a millefeuille of the 1870s written on fragile paper in faded ink – records of events that threatened to disintegrate in my fingers as if they'd never happened. Among them, the deeds of freedom given to enslaved children without a known parent or a remembered name.

I stayed in Stone Town for longer than I perhaps needed to. I'd eat my lunches in a Swahili canteen, then in the late afternoons when the heat got too much, I'd nip round to a slippery wharf where a boatman would pick me up for a ride to a local sandbar. When I was done for the day with my research, I did little more than lie in bed, piecing together sources about Carter's voyage, with a salty breeze blowing through my room.

The first stage of Carter's Mediterranean sailing had comprised long, luxurious days of reading, deck-walking and fresh seawater baths, savouring sweet oranges and meals at dinner tables dressed in roses. It's possible that it was on this journey that Carter also had his photograph taken for a professional visiting card. All that survives of the original image is a pen-and-ink copy published by the London media. It depicts a young man in his thirties with a confident gaze and a dashing crown of hair in a neatly oiled parting. He sports a well-groomed bush of mutton-chop sideburns, which connect with a bristling moustache. It's a classic, half-heroic studio pose, the image originally created by a Swiss photographer in an Algiers studio better known for peddling erotic pictures of topless Arab women.

By the time Carter had squeezed through Suez and reached Aden, the heat from 'the burning blasts of an African sirocco' was insufferable. Carter took lodgings at the port's Hôtel de l'Europe, along with a few Africa-bound missionaries, including a nattering Dr Joseph Mullens, secretary of the London Missionary Society. 'Oh! The glare, the furnace heat; the burning winds!' complained Mullens. 'We were all upset.'

A pen-and-ink drawing of Frederick Carter, published in 1880.

Mullens was on his way to Zanzibar with two missionary underlings, William Griffith and Dr Ebenezer Southon. They were waiting to join the *Chinsura* for the final leg of their voyage, with the ship now on its way to Aden from Bombay with the elephants. Even the indomitable Carter was laid low by the Aden weather, which made the news of the *Chinsura*'s arrival into port welcome for more than just its unusual cargo.

The ship was brand new and well appointed – for passengers, not for elephants. The space was cramped, the animals penned side by side in the dingy hold. But at least the *Chinsura*'s state-of-the-art steam power would allow for a relatively quick journey south to Zanzibar, and Carter, always at his happiest with an audience, enjoyed his companions. The missionaries gossiped enthusiastically about the Africa adventures that lay ahead, with Stanley's past exploits a lively topic of conversation. 'Maps and plans and books of travel were strewn about on all sides,' reported the *Times of India*. This provided a pleasant distraction from the rough waters of the Indian Ocean now the monsoon was blowing a gale. One by one, the *Chinsura*'s passengers succumbed to sea sickness. 'Ship-tea, bad enough at all times, became unbearable,' complained Mullens, 'and the puffs and odours, which came up at times from the hold, containing the elephants and two hundred tons of onions ... We had simply to bide our time, "to suffer and be strong"; aided thereto by hard mutton chops, bone curry and the "bouquet du <u>Chinsurah</u> [sic]" in general.'

The weather deteriorated. The animals' health worsened from being cooped up for too long. They hadn't been given a chance to stretch their legs in Aden – a disembarkation attempt would have caused unnecessary delays and complications – which meant their joints were creaking sore and worryingly swollen. By the time the *Chinsura* pulled into Stone Town's harbour on 27 May, the elephants' rations were used up, and they were in desperate need of nourishment. It was also the worst season of the long rains anyone could recall. But the weather wasn't going to dampen moods. This was the day the Europeans most looked forward to – a ship bringing news from home. And this mail day was especially exciting. The patricians of Stone Town had already picked up on rumours there were elephants on board, which meant there was an even bigger crowd than usual.

The harbour pilot led the welcoming party – a well-known Zanzibar character nicknamed Admiral Bucket who went about in a black jacket, golden petticoats and scarlet fez, accompanied by a couple of pet monkeys. Jostling around the *Chinsura*'s gangway were the French consul and some Catholic missionaries, who pushed their way to the front on the sultan's boat to get a view of the *Chinsura*'s cargo. Also present was the Belgian lieutenant, Dutalis, whom Stanley had been tasked to train up in anticipation of Carter's arrival.

With the *Chinsura* moored in front of the British consulate, the passengers disembarked. The missionaries checked into yet another 'Europe' hotel furnished with the trappings of home, while Carter took Kirk up on his gracious offer of a comfortable bed in the British consulate's guest quarters. Once more, the elephants had to continue languishing inside the ship for a few more days while Carter organized himself before sailing on to Dar es Salaam. He had a diplomatic meeting to attend with Sultan Barghash, guided by the peacocking Dutalis and the inquisitive Kirk, who wanted to know everything. Although the British consul had been expecting Carter's arrival, Stanley's recent manoeuvrings had made Kirk suspicious of any expedition tied to the Belgians. The number of men employed by Leopold's new International African Association and their lack of clarity was starting to look a bit too shifty for Kirk's tastes.

Somehow Carter's elephant assignment had dropped out of the IAA's control and was now marching exclusively under Leopold's flag. The king's purported mission, to be advancing into Africa hand in hand with Christ and other 'civilized' European nations, seemed to be quietly changing. The earlier Belgian expedition dispatched by the IAA – the one Stanley had mocked for its premature fatalities – had since fallen under the command of Lieutenant Ernest Cambier of Belgium. He was making painfully slow progress inland in order to build the first station on the eastern side of Lake Tanganyika. In addition to this, Leopold had dispatched a second IAA expedition under another Belgian military captain, Émile Popelin, who was ordered to go to Nyangwe, where the ivory was best, on the Congo side of the lake. Popelin's caravan and Carter's elephants would take slightly different routes but the plan was that they would converge in the interior, to benefit from strength in numbers. The fact Leopold now had four different active caravans (if Stanley was included) 'wandering like lost sheep in the wilderness' agitated Kirk.

Kirk at least had a potential ally in the Irishman Carter, whom Kirk hoped was on the 'right' side of empire to protect British interests. With that in mind, Kirk was quick to host dinners for the new arrival to impart his seasoned advice. For not only was Kirk familiar with the inland caravan logistics, but he also knew a little about captive elephants, having briefly kept a juvenile himself. If elephant training schools were going to be part of any game plan for improving the transport problem in Africa, then Kirk wanted to exert influence. He claimed he knew where the best concentrations of wild herds could be found. To Kirk's mind, Carter was also clearly capable, unlike Leopold's other hires, who included a self-important sergeant sent from India with the *Chinsura* to aid Carter with elephant husbandry in spite of knowing no more about their behaviour than was contained in a handbook. It wasn't going to end well, Kirk warned: '[the sergeant] has joined in order to write a book and cut out Carter, so far as I can see he knows nothing of elephants, is supposed to be an Arabic interpreter, and cannot make himself understood. I gave him a lecture and it has done him good, but there will be trouble with the man.' As for the preening Dutalis, he soon proved a dud when he proudly set off for the mainland, shooting game from the hammock in which he was carried, only to lose his nerve within a few miles of the coast. He fell sick, and turned for home. Dutalis was a hopeless explorer, depicted in one of the most amusing character sketches of the entire 1879 expedition roster, a man 'full of infinite graces and smiles, charmingly dressed, and quite irresistible with the ladies, especially when he let forth his soul in passionate song.' I knew I'd seen the portrait of him somewhere before. Dutalis came straight out of Chaucer's *Canterbury Tales*. He was the Squire, who dressed lavishly, sang enthusiastically, was new to the crusades, and thought women the object of his brave and romantic deeds, which included telling fanciful stories set in distant 'heathen' lands.

It was my last day in the Zanzibar archives when, in the margins of a mission diary, I found mention of mail day and the *Chinsura*'s arrival. Carter's name was also noted, along with news of the four elephants. Squashed into the bottom of the same day's entry was a memo about two children, enslaved by the Arabs and 'redeemed' by the Mbweni mission a five-mile walk from Stone Town. The diary's author was Bishop Steere, who headed up the Universities' Mission to Central Africa (UMCA) – a solemn man with a lipless grin and chinstrap beard whose image I had stuck on my 'serial-killer' wall back home. In 1879, he was a familiar face in Stone Town, walking everywhere dressed in a white coat, black trousers and pith helmet and carrying a white umbrella. From breakfast to noon, Steere worked on various Swahili translations, including proverbs, hymns and the liturgy, believing the best way to win Africans to his Christian God was to speak their language from the pulpit, 'rarely pausing to begin a new train of idea, never at a loss for a word, and never changing one', as a contemporary remarked. Steere ran a busy printing office, which included supplying fancy menu cards for the sultan's dinner parties. The new cathedral Steere had designed in Stone Town – the one with its altar symbolically positioned on the spot of the last slave market – needed to be completed by Christmas. Meanwhile, construction was also under way for the mission's Church of St John.

Month after month, new European mission recruits were landing in Zanzibar, with the most recent arrivals brought by the *Chinsura* proving a distraction to Steere. Because not all of them, it transpired, were cut out for the holy calling. 'They have all studied medicine as well as theology,' observed a fellow passenger on the ship, 'and to judge from the formidable array of deadly weapons they carried with them, they must also have graduated in the art of war.' Only six weeks before, Steere had hired a fresh-faced Cambridge graduate called Lionel Rankin. But as soon as the *Chinsura* pulled into port, Rankin promptly quit the Mbweni mission to join Carter's royal parade. Steere was put out. He was determined this elephant kerfuffle wasn't going to divert him from the much graver job at hand, to prepare for the ordination of the first Black East African deacon. 'The importance of this step can hardly be overrated,' he said. The deacon's name was John Swedi, a formerly enslaved man who'd joined the mission in 1864 when he was granted his deeds of freedom by the sultan as a political concession to the British abolitionists.

I dug a little deeper, hoping that Steere, who was a prodigious diarist, may have been nosy enough to have picked up on other elephant gossip. I hoped he might have met Carter over a dinner table with Kirk, that his curiosity would have got the better of him. So I decided to visit the former mission where, in 1879, convert numbers were swelling, with Mbweni being described by foreign visitors as a picture-postcard village with mango trees the size of English oaks. But I could only find its ruins, some of which were in the grounds of a beachside tourist hotel. So instead I made for the mission's Church of St John nearby. The colour of milky tea, it had been built from rugged limestone, which gave it the appearance of speckled ostrich leather. It had a tin roof, arched windows with glassless slits, and two locked wooden doors studded with bronze spikes in the traditional Omani style. I explored the churchyard where villagers had planted cassava and papaya trees. Clothes were hung out to dry on toppling headstones. In a shaded corner, I saw an old man with his hands in a plastic bowl full of washing.

His name was Peter Matthew Sudi, born 10 October 1934 – 'on Wednesday', he added, 'at 11 o'clock'. He was the church sexton, and his job was to ring the bells three times a day, as well as 'cleaning, sweeping, everything really'.

Peter was eighty-seven, slight and sinewy. He opened up the church with a giant brass key to reveal an interior simply furnished with a marble altar brought from Italy, and a font where the new converts were baptized.

I told him about the elephant story I'd come to track down, and how, when the *Chinsura* arrived in Zanzibar, Bishop Steere was busy making a deacon of a formerly enslaved man.

'That was John Swedi', said Peter. 'One of his sons married my aunt.'

I said something about being stunned by the connection across such a long reach of time.

'I lived with him when I was a child, in 1940. He died four years later, in 1944. I remember his funeral. People were crying, singing.'

A bird flickered through a window slit, turned a circle

above our heads, then rested on the altar where I watched its tremulous breast twitching as it caught its tiny breath.

'John Swedi belonged to a tribe from southern Tanzania. He was taken as a slave by Arabs when he was eighteen and brought to Zanzibar. John Swedi spoke about his past. He wrote things too.'

'Where are they?' I asked. 'The things he wrote?'

'I lost it all. Long ago. I was young, and John Swedi was very old. He was a little bit deaf, and he couldn't walk properly. He'd been badly treated by the Arabs.'

I asked Peter what he looked like.

'He was tall, slender, and wore a kanzu in the Arab style, with a big leather belt and sandals. His face was wide. He had black, kind eyes.'

We both watched the bird flit from the altar into the eaves.

'He was a committed Christian who loved to sing. He is buried here – I'll show you his grave – and he lived in Mbweni. He helped build this church. It was built by freed slaves under the supervision of Bishop Steere. The bishop's picture. Have you seen his picture?'

We talked a little about why I'd come. He told me that London's Royal Geographical Society had given a sword to one of Livingstone's African attendants who'd helped carry the doctor's dead body back to the coast from Lake Tanganyika. When the men returned to Stone Town from the funeral at Westminster Abbey, a British clergyman in Stone Town sold the sword to buy land for an Anglican graveyard. I traded Peter's footnote in history for mine about the Irishman, Carter.

'Irish, you say?'

Peter Sudi standing inside the Church of St John in Mbweni holding a portrait of Bishop Steere.

'Yes, Irish.'

Peter started to sing, his soft voice floating into the space where the bird was still hiding:

> *In Dublin's fair city*
> *Where the girls are so pretty*
> *I first set my eyes*
> *On sweet Molly Malone!*

'I've known that song since the 1940s,' he said. 'A sister from Ireland used to sing it. She was one of the nuns who taught me. I listened to her when I was a child, when the mission ran all the way from here to the sea.'

Peter shuffled into the vestry to rifle through some papers. He wanted to find the registers of birth and death, of marriage and baptism, pulling out evidence of lives that were so long gone and far away they had sometimes felt like fictions to me. He talked softly, muttering to himself as his fingers ran down the records until they rested with a satisfied pause on John Swedi's name. He talked about the very first missionaries, including a cousin of the Victorian novelist William Makepeace Thackeray. He showed me scribbled signatures, including his wife's. Peter married her in 1963 – a golden year before Zanzibar was turned into a bloodbath with the revolution. They'd had many years together, but he still missed his wife terribly. He also mourned his eldest daughter, who had predeceased him. With each register, he conjured people back into a place and time I'd been worried was too distant to be retrievable. His gentle revelations felt like proof of how each life is tethered to much bigger events: in Peter's case, the slave trade, the power of the Christian missions, the violent progress of European colonialism, the island's bitter revolution and the enduring domination of Islamic political power in Zanzibar. At the crux of his free-flowing stories – of this portrait of a young man newly married and full of optimism for a future – was the devastating reminder that he'd also lived through a ban on speaking about the past. Within a few weeks of the 1964 revolution, Zanzibar's president abolished the teaching of history in schools. It was an order that endured for more than thirty years, into the late 1990s, purportedly to help heal the ethnic divisions perpetrated by the islands' various colonialists. What wasn't mentioned was the political expediency of enforced forgetting; the new president needed to smooth over those very divisions he'd relied on in his rise to power with inflammatory 'race-baiting'.

I embraced Peter Sudi warmly, and explained that the next day I'd be leaving for Dar es Salaam. He encouraged me to make the most of the travelling that lay ahead, his words reinforcing my desire to weave written history with stories told by living people. 'In the world of Herodotus, the only real repository of memory is the individual,' wrote Ryszard Kapuściński, the Polish journalist and author who travelled across Africa with the works of the ancient Greek historian tucked in his pocket. 'In order to find out that which has been remembered, one must reach this person. If he lives far away, one has to go to him, to set out on a journey. And after finally encountering him, one must sit down and listen to what he has to say – to listen, remember, perhaps write it down. That is how reportage begins; of such circumstances it is born.' There was work for me to do, a past to untangle. Peter Sudi's story had reminded me how power relies on the construction of false narratives. As the nineteenth-century French scholar Ernest Renan remarked, to build a convincing myth, nation builders need to get their history wrong. It helps keep a lid on things, for a time at least, if people are persuaded into forgetting their stories.

4

Sink or Swim

'A brief description of a road tells us how to read the present moment but also all the past moments in the story and all those still to come.'

—George Saunders,
A Swim in a Pond in the Rain

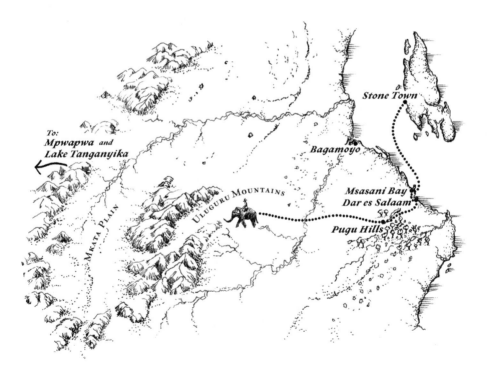

I T WAS THE LAST day of May when the *Chinsura* finally left Stone Town and pulled up to the edge of Msasani Bay on the African mainland. Some forty miles to the north lay the trading settlement of Bagamoyo, where the largest Arab-Swahili caravans would converge at the beginning and end of their journeys to Lake Tanganyika. The different caravans – a single one might number up to three thousand people – would gather around campfires on the edge of town, the glow casting ghostly shapes across the wooded groves that ran up to the water's edge. Even today, Bagamoyo has a beach lined with trading dhows bouncing in the surf. In the hum of busyness, it's as if the pulse of the caravan routes hasn't changed, just the nature of the commodities flowing out of the continent, this ongoing scramble for resources a reminder of how 'the history of humanity is the story of supply chains'. The Silk Road. The Salt Road. The Ivory Road. Men relay goods in and out of the ocean at Bagamoyo, loading up boats with palm oil, forest wood and sacks of charcoal. The surf is easily ridden by nimble dhows, but neither then nor now would this stretch of the Swahili Coast have been suitable for a steamship carrying four adult elephants.

For this reason, and to keep out of the way of Bagamoyo's Afro-Arab caravan rackets, Carter decided to follow Kirk's advice, and disembark the elephants in the sheltered waters of Msasani Bay instead. These days, Msasani is a suburb of Dar es Salaam, but in 1879 it was a thick scrub of jungle running up to the shore in a soft horseshoe curl. Carter planned to get the

elephants off the ship with the sling-and-pulley system they'd used to load them in Bombay. It would then be a day's walk to Dar es Salaam, where Carter could gather his caravan and the last of the provisions. From here, Carter would strike west through the fertile Pugu Hills and Uluguru Mountains, then pick up one of the main caravan trails at the new Anglican mission station of Mpwapwa about a hundred miles into the interior. He'd aim to meet Leopold's second IAA caravan there, which was being led by Émile Popelin. With no elephants in tow, Popelin would be following the tried-and-tested Bagamoyo route.

Carter's path was unusual, but there was some sense to it. Kirk's local botanizing had convinced him the Pugu Hills would provide reliable food and water for the elephants. It was politically expedient too. The elephant fanfare would bring favourable attention to a new road the Scottish shipbuilder Mackinnon had already started constructing out of Dar – 'the first in savage Africa', wrote a British journalist in 1879. Mackinnon was a man everyone, from Kirk to Leopold, wanted as their ally. Not least, he'd helped procure the Belgian king his elephants and their free passage from Bombay.

Kirk's advice proved helpful to Carter. Msasani was indeed a good place to land the elephants, with a silky stretch of water that puckers rather than surges in bad weather. There was also enough depth for a big ship to get relatively close to shore. When I visited, the mellow ease from Kirk's century seemed to have held out into mine. Fishermen sat around in armchairs with popping springs, waiting for the changing tide. Sails were spread out on the creamy sand while seabirds picked at fishbones and the blushed husks of prawns. A couple of traditional boat builders chiselled at wooden planks.

Children swung on the mooring lines, playing hide-and-seek in upturned skiffs. Their splashing was the only thing that broke the water's surface, which was like a pink mirror to the sky.

The *Chinsura*, on the other hand, sailed in under a bank of heavy clouds. What had been planned as a glittering launch for this new era in African 'civilization' soon turned into a sodden farce. It was a terrible day to attempt a landing. Sheet rain drenched the Europeans who had come in from Zanzibar to watch the show from the deck of the sultan's steamer. The audience had to sit out the deluge while Carter went ashore with Kirk in a small boat to figure out an approach that wouldn't risk snagging the *Chinsura* on hidden sandbanks. 'Indeed, [Kirk] could not have been more solicitous for our success if the whole official management had lain on his own shoulders', observed an unnamed journalist in the *Times of India*.

Carter's navigational expertise put him in his element. He decided the west side of the bay was too difficult because it was fringed with jungle rising straight from the tideline. The east side of Msasani Bay looked more promising, where there was at least a small fishing village. But the swim for the elephants would be long – more than two miles, reckoned one eyewitness. They'd have to sail the *Chinsura* closer, and even then, it was unclear if the elephants would swim the distance. 'No one could exactly say', reported the *Times of India*'s correspondent. 'I had myself never seen them do more than flounder about like buffaloes in shallow rivers'. With daylight hours diminishing, landing this unusual cargo was a conundrum that, as Mrs Kirk remarked, 'led them all to fussing'.

Plucked from a lazy life in a balmy Indian hill town, the elephants were bewildered by their change of situation. Before they were selected for their Africa assignment, they had been living peacefully in Pune at a British military garrison occupying a wide riverine plain. In this leafy cantonment, the elephants would graze between the barracks, colonial bungalows and parade grounds. In Pune, their days were passed among 'wonderful orange-blossomed goldmohr tree[s]'. The elephants' work wasn't much more than ceremonial, with the pattern of their lives only occasionally disturbed by bursts of fire in the shooting ranges or the crack of balls on cricket bats.

When the British artist Edward Lear spent a 'monsoon sojourn' in Pune in 1874, he fell for the town's cuckoos and the ornate temple architecture – 'all quite remarkable for picturesque beauty, and very surprising to me, who have so continually heard that "there is nothing to be seen at Poona". He especially fell for the elephants and sketched at Pune's general post office, where the animals, utilized to deliver mail, were tethered in the shade of banyan trees. There were 'elephants no end', he observed, especially in old Pune on the opposite side of the Mula-Mutha River, which was where the animals were taken to be washed. Ganesha, the elephant-headed Hindu god, was the family deity of Pune's Maratha dynasty. Even today, the crooked lanes in the old town are studded with elephant shrines and temples. There is a model Ganesha for sale on every corner, made out of wax, plastic or silver plated and bought as souvenirs by Hindu pilgrims. More than any other city in India, Pune's elephants have a history of being beloved, worshipped and thoroughly spoiled.

Edward Lear, depicted in one of his doodles, with a mahout holding a parasol above his head. Lear's Italian assistant, Georgio, rides on the elephant's rump.

It would have therefore been a shock to Leopold's four new purchases when they were walked in unrelenting heat to Bombay in one of the warmest months of the year. The journey took about a week, following a similar route to the new railway already shrieking its way between Pune and the coast. Arriving in Bombay at night, the elephants were then immediately winched on to the *Chinsura* – a chaotic endeavour, with everybody tendering every kind of advice, reported the *Times of India*: 'The crowd shouted and jostled about, until the poor beasts got quite out of control of their mahouts. There was a general stampede. The crowd flew helter-skelter on all sides.' One of the four elephants, held too long in the sling, was injured in the process, the elephant so traumatized it refused to lie down when it was finally stuffed with the cargo of onions into the *Chinsura*'s hold for its journey to Africa.

An elephant from India being hoisted from ship to ship at Middlesbrough docks on her way to London Zoo. The system used here in 1930 wasn't much different to the one in 1879.

Memories of that debacle resurfaced in Msasani Bay when the first elephant was winched over the ship's side – a manoeuvre 'anxiously debated', this time with Kirk's advice prevailing. There was no knowing how things would go. An average female Asian elephant weighs around three and a half tonnes, a male at least a tonne more. For weeks, they would have had to deal with the lurch of the ocean. Their normal eating pattern is twelve hours of steady feeding a day. On the *Chinsura*, they'd become stiff, sore and undernourished on bad, thinning rations. There was a very real possibility the animals wouldn't be able to swim to shore, putting an end to the expedition before they had even set foot on African soil.

The first elephant to make the attempt was Sosankalli, or 'Budding Lily'. The smallest of the four, she looked particularly vulnerable as she was lowered into the water. She trembled in every limb, her freckled ears flapping with distress at both the strangeness of her circumstances and the separation from her stablemates. On her back was Luximor, described as the pluckiest attendant brought from India. The hope was that after her confinement at sea, Sosankalli would see the shore and make a swim for it. Instead, she paused, panicked and trumpeted, and in the heavy monsoon rain, spent forty-five minutes trying to scramble back on board the *Chinsura*. In all the terror and confusion, Sosankalli dunked Luximor so badly, he barely escaped drowning. As her strength began to falter, the only sign of life was the occasional appearance of her trunk snatching for air. 'She must sink or swim now', wrote one of the observers. 'I was fast losing all hope.'

Carter worked out an emergency system of ropes strung between the elephant and a small boat to steer her to the beach. When that didn't work, the boat crew tried dancing

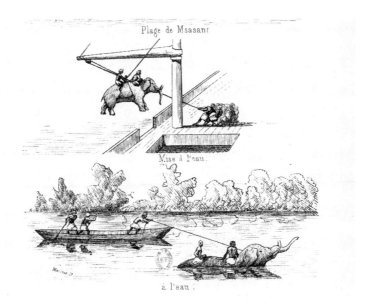

These sketches by the Belgian Military Cartographic Institute show the unloading of the elephants in Msasani Bay.

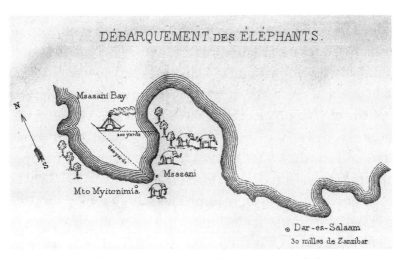

This map was drawn in response to observations made by Dr Théodore Van den Heuvel, a Belgian explorer who witnessed the disembarkation.

and singing to lure her away from her friends. It took another four hours of coaxing for Sosankalli to finally drag herself on to the African mainland, where she was rewarded with cakes made with sugar, rum and Pune spices – an elephant favourite.

With three more elephants to go, and the hours of daylight running out, attention turned to Pulmalla, or 'Flower Garland' – a stately female whose previous career had been carrying dignitaries up the wide stone elephant stairs to Pune's Parvati Temple. She was the oldest of the four, and the only riding elephant among them. The two tusked bulls were called Naderbux, or 'Wonder-Inspiring', and Sundar Gaj, 'the Beautiful Elephant' – an animal 'in the prime of elephant life', remarked one of the missionaries who'd travelled on the *Chinsura* from Aden.

After careful consultation with Carter, the ship's captain was persuaded to edge the ship closer to the land. Using a new rope system attached to a tree trunk, a smaller pilot boat was pulled into shore, which in turn towed the swimming animals. With rain still falling heavily, Pulmalla, Naderbux and Sundar Gaj swam with their trunks sticking out like snorkels. But when they finally reached solid ground, Sundar Gaj bolted into the jungle. His mahout bailed out, claiming the brushwood was too thick. And that was that: the sultan's steamer turned back for Stone Town with a crowd of Europeans soaking wet and full of story.

For Carter, it was an inauspicious start. It took three days to capture the intractable Sundar Gaj, using the two female elephants as bait. Only then was Carter able to break camp at Msasani Bay, and pull the expedition together to walk south to Dar es Salaam, which in 1879 wasn't quite the 'Haven of Peace' that its Persian-Arabic name was meant to evoke. Nor was it the city of palaces dreamed of by the sultan's brother, who'd tried to make a mainland entrepôt of Dar in the 1860s when he started building a new port town on this coastal belt. In 1879, Dar was in reality 'an infected spot' featuring little more than tenantless houses, unsightly ruins, and warehouses running with snakes and rats. This was where the elephants and their mahouts were forced to linger for the next month, while Carter finished his preparations.

If you fly into Dar at night, you will see the lights of cargo ships blink on the water like fireflies. The roads radiate out from the port as bright yellow spokes. Against a cloudless sky, the glowing lines are mesmerizing, but they also conceal the city's noisy, complex human scale. Arrive in Dar by ferry from Zanzibar and it's possible to get a little closer to this pulse. The ferry glides in through the harbour's neck past a thick line of waiting ships, the cargo containers stacked so high they look as if they might topple in the roll of passing wakes. But drive into the city by car, and you're in the thick of it, in the sweating, swirling whirls and eddies of the second-fastest-growing city in Africa. Dar is one of the major lines out of the continent connecting the rest of the world with raw materials from DRC, Rwanda, Burundi, Malawi, Uganda, Tanzania and Zambia. The energy shows in the flash of neon casino signs, in the surge of people trying to make something of the opportunities, including Egyptians, Indians and Chinese squeezing through the streets of the busiest neighbourhoods.

After booking into a hotel near the hustle of Dar's main ferry terminal, I walked along the harbourside thoroughfare where barristers in polished Oxfords and stark white jabots were coming and going on official business from the city's

High Court. As the temperature climbed, fruit bats swarmed into Dar's few remaining trees to roost out of the heat. I ventured down to the Kivukoni fish market where I picked my way among buckets full of ruby lobsters and baskets of brain-grey octopuses. Steamed in plastic bags with tandoori spices, the tentacles shrank into tight red rosettes. At first, the market looked like chaos, with cigarette vendors clicking stone tiles in their palms to draw attention to their wares. But the closer I looked, the more a system began to reveal itself.

Scores of wooden boats – 'Strong Boys', 'Street Boys' and even one called 'Covid-19' – were coming into shore and out again as deliveries came and went, but the ropes never got tangled. Men in chequered headscarves waded waist deep into the sea to fetch pails of fish. There were filleters, ice carriers and women stirring vats of soup with yellow chillies bobbing among the fish cheeks. Tiny dagaa were being auctioned on open tables where hundreds of hands reached out to buy the silvery fish, which, in spite of the commotion, didn't slip from the slimy dealing surface to the floor. I noticed an old man standing on a high wall with a plastic bucket tied to a line of knotted rope. He was selling seawater to men washing fish guts down the drains – a job he'd been doing for the last forty-eight years.

My phone rang, summoning me to a meeting at the Ministry of Information to secure my press card – necessary red tape for safe passage in a country where journalists have historically had a difficult time of things. When I'd first started plotting my African travels in 2020, I'd been naive. John Magufuli, then president of the country, was still in power. I'd been warned that going into remote areas might arouse suspicion. When I began to make enquiries, the Ministry of

Information wanted to send a full-time minder to keep an eye on my reporting. Even without that problem, it would have been an impossible expense, given I would also have had to pay the government minder for the pleasure of his assistance. Then Magufuli died, which made things a little easier for me. But the country's silencing habit was still a concern. It reached back to when the former schoolteacher Julius Nyerere became the first leader of an independent Tanzania in 1961.

Coming after the hierarchies of colonialism, it was easy to see why Nyerere's ideas took hold. He delivered the stabilizing effects of a strong, state-controlled narrative. Nyerere's socialist agenda reorganized the country's geographically dispersed tribal groups into 'Ujamaa villages'. He collectivized agriculture and dismantled old hegemonies, which encouraged a shift in identity: under Nyerere, citizens described themselves as Tanzanian first, not Nyamwezi or Gogo or any of the other hundred-and-twenty-odd ethnicities within the country's borders. This proved successful in tempering any tribalism that might have flared up in a country emerging from the abuses of colonialism. But the policy also fostered a culture of suspicion towards any challenge to 'familyhood', which is the meaning of the Swahili word *ujaama*. The strength (and sacrifice) implicit in that idea endures. Nyerere, who died in 1999, is widely loved as the 'father of the nation'. He is even being billed as a candidate for Catholic sainthood, which speaks to the ongoing regard in which he's held. In modern Tanzania, Nyerere's influence also means self-censorship remains significant. It's a way to uphold the values of the nation's 'founder' and why, seventy years after independence, a community tale-telling habit still endures.

Julius Nyerere in Dar es Salaam. The crowd is celebrating the announcement of a date for Tanzanian independence, which was set for December 1961.

At the Ministry of Information, I was led into an airless room at the back of a concrete building with long, empty corridors and a towering atrium. When I arrived, there was another journalist in the office, who introduced himself as the editor of one of the largest Pentecostal newspapers in Tanzania. I told him what I was up to, and with a wide grin and a notebook of telephone numbers, he assured me his network of pastor-reporters would help me. He and the government's media officer talked enthusiastically about my plans, eager for me to like their country. From the range of our conversation, I reckoned the journalist might prove useful, with friends in remote places. Even in the short time I'd been in Dar, I'd noticed frequent reference to the divine. 'In God We Trust' was emblazoned on the crumpled backs of buses, 'Mr Confidence' on the fronts. Roadside hoardings were decorated with the faces of celebrity preachers, including an American whose website promised all sorts of miracles – 'Jesus has the power to heal and deliver what doctors cannot help with or explain!' I knew I'd need all the support I could get, including any shortcuts the Almighty might provide. It was with that in mind that I talked for some time with my new acquaintances about a God I had no intention of including in this journey, except that he kept reappearing.

I left the ministry, triumphantly furnished with my Tanzanian press card, and went in search of a bookshop to pick through the shelves for something that might help me on the road. Instead, I was confronted by all sorts of curious imports. *Why We Want You to be Rich: Two Men, One Message* by Donald J. Trump and Robert T. Kiyosaki; *Business Secrets from the Bible: Spiritual Success Strategies for Financial Abundance*; and *Sell Like Crazy: How to Get as Many Clients, Customers and Sales as You Possibly Can.* In a section packed with second-hand romance novels, there was a book called *Jackie the Ravenous Pest.* But there was no useful travel information. Instead, I left with just a small English–Swahili phrasebook. Under 'Amusements' the first line was '*Nataka kuona ngoma za kienyeji*', meaning 'I want to see native dances'. Under 'Lodgings': 'Can I get a maid?' Under 'Religion': 'Are there any Catholics here?' When I looked for the publisher's details, I discovered it was a phrasebook for English-speaking missionaries printed as recently as 1999.

On 2 July 1879, more than seven weeks since leaving Pune, the elephants were finally mustered for their overland journey west from Dar es Salaam with the blowing of antelope horns, the crack of guns and a *rum-tee-tum* on a drum in the ritualistic performance that accompanied all departing caravans of any size. The party was a curious medley. It included Carter and his new second-in-command, the mission dropout Lionel Rankin (by this time, the self-important sergeant who'd travelled with the elephants from India had been fired – for insubordination, ineptitude, or because he was just downright annoying, it's not quite clear). There were six mahouts, six other Indian attendants, ten Zanzibaris, eight soldiers, four guides and over seventy porters – more than a hundred people in total. Each elephant was loaded with five hundred kilograms of equipment. 'Accompanied by the people of Dar es Salaam shouting', the Belgian flag led the vanguard. Except it was a flag unfamiliar to everyone, including Carter's caravan porters used to marching under the fading blood-red insignia of the sultan of Zanzibar.

I left Dar on a bright September day with my two new companions, Wolfe and Rem, who had secured all the gear as planned. I had my notes tucked into the collection of books I'd brought. As we drove out of the city to pick up the road which ran past the airport towards the Pugu Hills, I kept one eye on the cityscape rolling by, the other on the history of the road built by Mackinnon, for whom the pathway to empire was clear. Mackinnon may have backed Leopold's elephant mission, but he also knew the most efficient access to Africa's resources required a more reliable thoroughfare. In the rainy season, the coastal region was sometimes so thick with sprouting vegetation, caravans would sink out of sight, according to travellers, and a route would literally have 'to be felt for'. But nor did Mackinnon's ambitions bear easy fruit. Sometimes it was as if his road didn't want to be built, complained the Europeans, the ground putting forth an 'extraordinary growth of grass and seed which is only too willing to resent this interference'. And then the monsoon arrived and washed away whole sections. The road 'seems better to travel alongside of rather than on it for most of the way', remarked Kirk, who groused about the calibre of Mackinnon's British engineers. 'The difficulty is here again to find men fit for Africa'. Mackinnon's hires were spending all their time 'bird, beetle and butterfly killing'. Not used to the African climate, the men often fell sick. To make matters worse, the coast's Zaramo labourers would frequently desert. They said they could hear the sound of drums beating inside the rocks, that spirits would kill anyone who meddled with them, which was why, every few weeks, Mackinnon's Road was rerouted. It's a traditional Zaramo belief system that still exists. At the end of Dar's new Tanzanite Bridge, there's a very old baobab. When the bridge construction began in 2018, the bats and owls took flight. 'Our ancestors were leaving', a Tanzanian journalist explained to me – and people were unhappy about it.

Carter, however, made no complaints about Mackinnon's Road, or at least any he was going to share with his benefactors, even if there was one section where the going was so soft one of the elephants sank to the root of its tail. 'I cannot tell you the obligation this expedition and myself owe to your East African Road', Carter wrote to Mackinnon. '[I]t's like the king's highway; there is no part of it along which you could not drive a dog cart'. Bogs and flattery aside, the elephant caravan was being corralled into relative order as it marched on towards the green shadow of the Pugu forest. Leopold's dream was in motion, declared Rankin – 'a triumphal progress, all the numerous villages emptying themselves to see the strange procession pass.'

My exit from Dar was the opposite. We'd chosen a terrible hour, in the thick of a weekday-morning traffic jam. The city moved past us like a slow-moving filmstrip. We passed modern shopping malls; the Tanzania–Zambia railway intersection; bus depots; the 'Chinese Experts Cemetery' (for Chinese employees of the different rail, road and mining companies); ornamental garden statues of zebras; and second-hand clothes suspended from the branches of neem trees. Whenever the traffic stopped, street vendors slipped between the trucks like water, their arms held aloft where the spaces were too tight. The young men pushed into pockets of opportunity, each of them trying to find gaps in the networks of supply and demand. They all sold something different: footballs, ice cream, avocados, chef hats, cotton buds, battery chargers, underwear. There was the smell of meat on charcoal, hot pumpkin samosas and burning clutches. Someone squeezed juice from sugarcane into a plastic cup. Another man picked up the used stalk thrown on to the road, and sucked on whatever remaining sweetness he could extract. The catchy melodies of Bongo Flava rolled out of the city's minibuses. The songs combined with police sirens and the toneless blast of train horns. I closed the car windows to keep out the dust, but it still seeped through the gaps to cover me in a pale film that would cling to me for weeks.

We pressed on towards Ukonga Prison. Now a maximum-security jail, this was originally the site of Carter's first camp after leaving Dar on his march inland. It was here that the elephant party spent two days jettisoning non-essentials, reducing the weight to about thirty kilograms per porter.

They repacked the bales of trading goods, including the clothes, beads and guns that would be paid in tolls to local chiefs, and made for the Pugu forest.

Rankin was full of excitement at the emerging landscape, which even today is referred to as the lungs of Dar. 'The scenery, with its low irregular blue hills in the eastern distance, and its near hills and dales, recalled Yorkshire to one's mind', he wrote in his expedition report. The mood was upbeat, buoyed by Kirk's reassurances that Pugu had abundant water for the elephants. These days, however, those streams don't flow as they used to. The polluted Msimbazi River can no longer supply the water needed by the city's population, with urban migration trickling into every chink of available space between the hills and the port. As we started to rise above the sprawl, fires smouldered in a rubbish dump where diggers glistened in the distance like bluebottle flies. It didn't look to me like the jungle Carter's expedition had encountered – and clearly hadn't for some time.

In 1879, the Zaramo used to crop copal and rubber from the forest, which they traded on the coast: small amounts, benefiting a modest population. As the colonial administration tightened its grip, it exploited the forest more ruthlessly to provide a rapidly expanding Dar with fuel and timber. Today, Pugu's diminishing forest and the exploding city are pushed up hard against each other, the boundary drawn with a startling clarity. Various conservation measures have been put in place, but it's not enough: Pugu is one of the oldest forests in the world, a hangover of a lowland coastal ecosystem with staggeringly high rates of endemism. Over thirty per cent of its plant species are found nowhere else. As we closed in on the hills, we started to see charcoal in nylon bags on the back of bikes heading for Dar, the sacks in piles almost twice as tall as the seated drivers. The rougher the road, the more frequent the spills where these precarious balancing acts came undone.

A few miles short of the Pugu town of Kisarawe, we turned on to a red-earth track leading into the forest to find the camping spot where Carter took a bath that drew a crowd of villagers. But our coordinates were muddled, and we ended up in the grounds of a boys' boarding school instead. I got chatting to one of the students, telling him how Leopold's elephants took fright at the unfamiliar jungle.

'You ever seen an elephant here?' I asked.

He shook his head.

'Just dudus.'

'What's that?'

'Grasshoppers. Insects.'

Rem went to the local town to find someone who could guide us into the seams of the landscape Rankin had described in detail. His expedition diary recounted how Sundar Gaj, the stubborn male, kept trying to flee, despite the spiked iron bracelets clapped on his legs to restrain him. The only way he could be held in check was via the entreaties of Sosankalli, the female who'd been the first to swim to shore. She would fondly rub her head against him, encouraging him over tricky fords and bogs, but even that was fraught with difficulty. Sometimes Sundar Gaj's greater weight would drag Sosankalli into his rebellion, the elephants blundering backwards in a mess of legs and chains.

Rem found us a guide: a Zaramo forest ranger called Nassoro Saidi Jaswa, who said he was familiar with the elephant story. Someone I bought two oranges from at the roadside said the same. 'The Zaramo like to gossip,' added a young ranger called Joseph, who joined the conversation with a half-smile. 'They're talkative people.'

Nassoro was an older man with smiling eyes which made him appear constantly amused. He took us into the forest along a narrow path where exposed roots made the trees look as if they were walking. We passed under curtains of vines, some of the creepers described in the nineteenth century as 'thick as a man's thigh, gnarled and twisted, binding the tree-trunks as with bands of iron', into leafy alleys where blue monkeys called to mark out their territory. Sometimes we had to crawl. A line of stinging Matabele ants marched across our trail in single file, hissing as they went. They were robbing eggs from a termite mound. Rem explained how the ants kill the termite leaders at the entrance, and take the young, their glossy backs loaded with the termites, which they bury alive.

'If you see the ants carrying baggage, it brings you luck,' said Rem.

Nassoro pointed out a rubber tree. Against the murmuring of the city in the background, he explained how he used to collect the sap to make balls to play with when he was a child. Everything in the forest has a purpose, he said. There are poultices for sprains, bitter-tasting medicines for toothache, and others to cure illnesses caused by the local bad spirit, Mweneembago. Hanging from the canopy was a woody endemic vine – the colour of chocolate, curled like a kudu horn – and another which he slashed open to reveal a goblet of drinking water.

'This forest is with us from birth to death,' said Nassoro, snapping a leaf stem to reveal water droplets. 'We put these into the eyes of newborn babies; it helps them to see clearly. Pugu is our forest. That's how we know it.'

Nassoro took us to a place where he'd encountered a huge snake five times before, its girth about a foot in diameter. He explained how the Zaramo were mostly Muslim, but they also held on to a traditional belief system anchored to the spirits. He talked about two ways of knowing – one indigenous, the other Islamic – and the origins of the place name 'Kisarawe', from the Zaramo *tenda uharawe*, which means 'do and leave'.

'But the outsiders didn't pass through; they came and stayed', he said.

We disturbed a cloud of butterflies feeding at the mouth of a cave. In the cool earth, there was evidence of offerings: clothes, coins and perfume bottles.

'This cave is for healing', said Nassoro. 'The Zaramo come to pray for rain. In the old days, we used to bring sick people here, but the traditions are changing. The most important thing is you're not supposed to ask for everything'.

'It's our greed that's the problem', remarked Rem.

'It's because we don't listen to local people who know better', said Nassoro.

Joseph, the younger ranger who'd tagged along, showed me a tree, like a giant fig, which made a hollow sound like a drum when he struck it.

'If you bang it once, it tells the other people you have an emergency and need help. If you bang it twice, it means you're under attack. If you bang it three times, you're telling people there's a celebration. The tree can speak. The bigger and older it gets, the louder its voice in the forest. The voice spreads out over the land until all the Zaramo can hear'.

Nassoro hadn't heard the story before. He said traditions were getting confused by a younger generation who could no longer speak the local language.

Nassoro Saidi Jaswa, photographed at a café in Kisarawe close to the spot where Carter and the elephants camped.

It was dusk by the time we made it to a clearing cut out of a bamboo thicket. We grilled some beef on a fire and shared a few beers. The men talked about a national soccer fixture coming up. A friend of Joseph's joined us – a girl called Erica-neema, who chatted to me about how Zaramo women love music and sex. Her grandmother explained everything to her, she said; in Zaramo culture, the older women tell the next generation how to make men happy. In the old days, women would educate their daughters from the time of puberty until their marriage day, in a period of seclusion sometimes lasting up to three years. Ericaneema worked in healthcare, analysing data for patients living with HIV. She wanted to win a scholar-ship to improve her education, but as a woman, she said it wasn't going to be easy. It helped that the nation's new leader was female, she said, even though that was more by accident than design when, a few months prior to my arrival, Magufuli died and his female deputy, Samia Suluhu Hassan, was constitutionally pushed into the role.

By the time we turned in for the night, the bats had settled. I listened to the train to Zambia passing somewhere in the distance, between the sounds of spitting embers, the bamboo creaking and electronic music rolling out from a bar. The bushbabies' eyes flashed in my torchlight like blinking stars. I turned it off and looked up through my tent's thin mesh of mosquito netting, which was the only thing separating me from the sky. In India, the Assamese, who have a long tradition of working elephants, call the Milky Way 'the elephant road', as if it were the path to heaven. I wondered how foreign the wildlife in these hills must have sounded to Leopold's four Asian elephants used to the sound of bazaars, the clash of festival cymbals, and the worshipful hum of priests paying homage to Ganesha in an Indian monsoon with the rain beating down on temple roofs. I could soon hear a gentle flutter of snoring from my companions. I checked the zip on my pop-up tent was tightly closed. I needed time to get used to the rustle of small animals moving through the trees. When the train sounded its horn, the hollow noise seemed to hang in the air, making me think of the giant fig which used to speak. Here was a city growing and a forest retreating; and a man called Nassoro who believed all the knowledge we'd ever need to save our species was right here, girdling the city he also feared would soon swallow the forest up.

5
Miss Kisabengo

'Everything flows, but in flowing, it undergoes transformation. So it is with memory.'

—Ryszard Kapuściński,
Travels with Herodotus

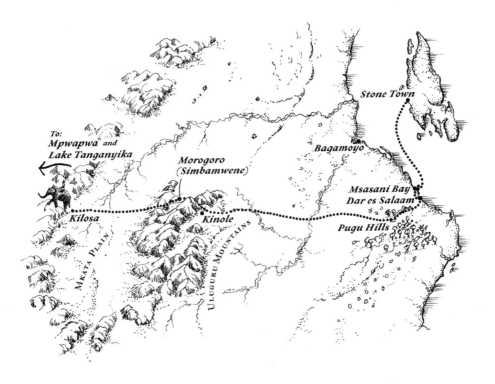

As WE DROVE WESTWARDS from Pugu in the direction of the Uluguru Mountains, Rem, Wolfe and I were three travelling companions getting to know each other gently. We talked about the abundance of animals we'd taken for granted in our different childhoods, with the easy flow of conversation reminding me why I liked road trips. There was a pliancy to the back and forth, in the rhythm of alternating talk and silence.

Wolfe grew up on Lake Tanganyika. When he was small, his mother was always scared he'd be stolen by a leopard. Wolfe remembered how sometimes chimps would come down to the beach where they lived, and how he'd take a canoe out on the lake to paddle among the hippos. I talked about growing up in the 1970s in rural Scotland. After school in spring, I sometimes joined my father when he was doing work on the farm. I'd scoop handfuls of gloopy frogspawn from the pond for my fish tank. In the days that followed, I'd wait patiently for the little black apostrophes to break out of their glassy bubbles, their heads swelling with the encroaching season. I'd fish for sticklebacks and minnows from the stream with a cheap plastic net on a long bamboo pole. I remembered someone I used to call 'the moth man' – an acquaintance of my father's, who visited us with a light trap. When he opened his contraption in the morning, I was mesmerized by the hawk moths, a fluttering of stripes and fuchsia pinks, which I had no idea existed in the damp Scottish landscapes. But as I grew older, the rarer these encounters became. Maybe I'd just stopped noticing, distracted by other things. Maybe it was Britain's diminishing biodiversity passing me by. Because I hadn't seen a stickleback for years. Or frogspawn. Or a hawk moth.

Rem said it was the same for him. His children didn't encounter what he had done growing up, and wildlife populations had radically declined since his boyhood. A distancing was setting in – a kind of national malaise. Elephants felt like relics to Tanzania's expanding urban population living a long way from the country's national parks. Conservationists across the wider region were suggesting wilderness areas might need fencing off because of increased human–wildlife conflict on the margins of protected land. It wasn't just Dar es Salaam that was exploding, said Rem; Tanzania has one of the fastest-growing populations in the world. In the 1930s, author Karen Blixen described a herd of elephants 'pacing along as if they had an appointment at the end of the world'. Now there's no longer the space to roam, despite a third of the country falling under some kind of protection. Elephant corridors, which are those long stretches of country necessary for the animals' seasonal migrations, have narrowed to the point they've almost stopped functioning altogether. The government is building underpasses for elephants to prevent them from being struck by traffic – a stark image of the collision of past and present.

We talked about tipping points, how in the flow of living it can be hard to identify the moment in time when we can no longer hold on to an accurate memory of what's already gone. Elephants remember too, said Rem. They return to where their kin have died, to touch the bones with their trunks. Memory helps them survive in the wild. The matriarchs can recall the exact locations of limited water sources across huge distances and will use those remembered paths to educate their young. Elephants also recall the killing fields where poachers made an ambush. That old saying – 'an elephant never forgets' – has some truth to it, said Rem.

Our conversation bumped around with the car. Rem dodged cattle on the road, their horns curved like sickle moons. Wolfe plotted and replotted our route on a digital GPS system to map the smallest details of Carter's journey, lining up mistranscribed place names from the nineteenth century with contemporary locations, identifying landscapes by the inflow or outflow of a river, a forest or a rocky outcrop flagged up in the archives. Meanwhile, I dipped in and out of the 1879 expedition notes. By this point in the journey, the two female elephants, Pulmalla and Sosankalli, were turning into everyone's favourites: they were softer, smaller, gentler than the males.

Only the females could calm Sundar Gaj when he went into musth – a hormonal surge that makes bull elephants more aggressive and unpredictable. Carter nicknamed him 'Old Musty'. The mahouts called him 'Must Wallah'. He was proving 'very troublesome and unmanageable' according to the reports sent back to Europe. It turned out Sundar Gaj often had to be worked in chains in Pune, and it was much the same in Africa. Bull elephants prefer to be solitary. Only female elephants naturally live in herds, in strongly bonded family units. It's why working female elephants were traditionally used by mahouts to capture and calm new animals – and why they were so important to Leopold's agenda. 'The feline caresses begin, together with compliments, playful trunk movements, joyful murmurs and deceptive frolicking,' remarked one of the king's men about elephant capture in India; the 'female traitor' would work through a whole range of 'enchanting seductions' before she moved away to play the same tactic on another male. In the midst of the trickery, the mahouts would place a slip knot around the legs of captured males, and fetter them to trees where they would 'weep and moan like children' – a training role Pulmalla had pulled off so well in Pune, it had earned her the nickname Delilah after the biblical prostitute who deceived Samson. Womanly wiles aside, Pulmalla was appreciated by Carter for her steadfastness in the face of growing challenges. Ten days in, and the tsetse flies were beginning to bite, blood trickling down the animals' flanks. For Carter and his companions, the journey was also beginning to get more uncomfortable. The slimy water was so bad, remarked Rankin, they couldn't even get through a cup of tea. The expedition was forced to make river crossings by canoe (one of which capsized) while the elephants floundered about in the water. Where the currents were too swift, the porters made tree bridges, which took up the best part of a day.

As the caravan trudged west towards the Kingani River Valley, we tried our best to follow Carter's daily coordinates noted in Rankin's expedition journal. In the nineteenth century, this was 'splendid, likely-looking game country', according to Rankin, teeming with wildebeest, zebra and giraffe. I wanted to compare these two views of Africa – mine and Carter's, set one hundred and fifty years apart. But the links wouldn't hold between my journey and the elephants' passage across a starkly unrecognizable land. There were none of the murmuring pigeons or brightly coloured parrots Rankin had described. When we were eventually forced to take a route a little north of Carter's line, we passed a desolate settlement called Picha ya Ndege, or 'Picture of a Bird'. I was struck by the notion of this emptied symbol, of an image divorced from its referent. Was this all that was left of the Africa Carter's expedition had observed? A picture of a bird? Would that be the future of the elephant – a disembodied sign telling a story of twenty-first-century extinction?

Ancestors of the modern elephant used to roam all over the globe. There were Mediterranean dwarf elephants, and Columbian mammoths on the coast of what's now California. While the species of elephant that once thrived in the Sahara is long gone, Chad's isolated Tibesti Plateau has rock art depictions of these creatures dating to around twelve thousand years ago, when the Sahara was still green. Images of fabulous pachyderms started to spread into Europe with the writings of Herodotus and Pliny. Descriptions began to reach the shores of Britain, of strange, trunk-snouted animals grazing the plains of Libya and Mauritania. Medieval bestiaries depicted creatures that lived for three hundred years, and

Early European natural history compendiums portrayed elephants based on travellers' fantastical hearsay.

The Siege of the Elephant, *a sixteenth-century engraving possibly derived from a lost painting by Hieronymus Bosch.*

images of elephants with webbed toes. Their only mortal enemies were believed to be dragons, but otherwise they were so formidable, they could be ridden into a siege and prevail.

These days, the only two extant elephant species in Africa are confined to dramatically narrowed geographical areas. Yet we used to depend on elephants to survive. Elephants and their relatives literally forged new landscapes. Where they walked, people followed the paths the elephants opened up, leading early humans to food and water. If a hunter killed an elephant, the entire community benefited. People used every part of the animal, including the meat. They celebrated its spirit in rituals and masquerades, which invested the hunter with the powerful essence of the animal killed.

Now we only take their tusks – and the numbers are hard to digest. At the start of the nineteenth century, there were up to twenty-six million elephants in Africa. That number currently sits between four and five hundred thousand. In Tanzania alone, there were around a hundred thousand elephants in 2009, but within five years that number had halved. It's now very rare to see great tuskers of the size common in Carter's day. To date, the record for a single tusk currently sits at over a hundred kilograms for one more than ten feet in length. At the peak of the poaching scourge in the late 1980s, average weights fell to a pathetic three kilograms per tusk. Only two-thirds of a tusk is even visible on an elephant. The rest is embedded in the socket – tusks are incisor teeth – which is why, to take all the ivory, the animal must be slaughtered. It's also why an encounter with a poached elephant is a scene of mutilation you can't unsee: the bloody hollows in the head, the leaden deadness of the trunk, the calf nosing its mother's teats, refusing to abandon her corpse.

Even at the time Carter came this way, there were no more elephants to be found in this swathe of coastal country we were traversing out of Pugu. It had already been stripped of its ivory stocks. Modern tests on nineteenth-century piano keys used to locate the sources of historical ivory indicate how far west the elephant slaughter had penetrated – an expansion which peaked in the second half of the nineteenth century when ivory carvers in Europe and North America got pickier. Because of a reputation for whiteness and quality, there was a spike in demand for the tusks of female African forest elephants, found much deeper into the Congo Basin. This pushed traders into the so-called Ivory Frontier west of Lake Tanganyika. Meanwhile, in the United States, which had become the world's biggest consumer of ivory, whole towns were given over to processing the tusks, including Ivoryton in Connecticut, which supplied ivory to America's booming piano industry. But the soaring value of the raw material wasn't always clear to the local African communities. In remote regions, traders found tusks thrown into the bush, where they rotted. People were using the ivory as fencing for their homesteads. As late as 1886, there was a story of a missionary able to swap a tusk for a tin can.

A 1989 ivory burn in Kenya, from stocks confiscated from poachers by government game wardens. Tanzania's government chooses not to burn ivory confiscated from poachers. In 2012, they wanted to hold a sale of more than a hundred tonnes of their stock to Japan and China with the argument the funds could be fed back into conservation. But in 2013, universal outcry forced them to withdraw their proposal.

Tusks in late nineteenth-century Zanzibar.

African tusks on the back of a cart in Deep River, Connecticut, on their way to the Pratt, Read & Company piano factory. From 1870 to 1890, the manufacture of these instruments nationwide multiplied at 1.6 times the rate of the American population; by 1910, that rate had increased fourfold.

It had been a long day of driving when we finally approached the Uluguru Mountains in the falling light. A strong line of hills rose ahead of us in a single graceful wave, a sharply drawn rim running along a north–south axis with a saddle-like dip at their waist. Everything seemed to sweeten as the sun sliced across the land: the earth reddened and the greens intensified, dipping the scene in jewel-like dollops of colour.

I'd been looking forward to getting here. The Ulugurus contain one of the last surviving relics of a broken chain of ancient forests scattered over the Eastern Arc Mountains, which stretch from the Taita Hills in Kenya to the southern-most Udzungwas in Tanzania. Tens of millions of years ago, these mountain forests extended from east to west across the continent. With climatic and geological shifts, they were reduced to a few isolated patches, of which the Ulugurus are one. Today, the mountains' reputation for an almost freakish endemism outshines even Pugu. There is an Uluguru antelope so elusive it was reportedly only photographed for the first time in 2003.

Leopold's caravan was in rhapsodies at the picturesque landscape punctuated with breast-shaped peaks, 'each crowned with a nest of huts? Rankin described secret valleys enclosed by hills where 'the inhabitants could, I think, forget in time that there was a world beyond them? After the aggressions of the spear-carrying Zaramo people with their 'Van Dyke beards', the elephant caravan was met with a much more gentle reception. 'The people crowded together among the tall corn to look at us, but rushed away on the least movement of the elephants', wrote Rankin. There was a surfeit of splendid streams running straight from the mountains, 'pebble-bottomed and clear as crystal? There was food everywhere, including wild cherries and shimmering fields of grain. This was the paradise the Europeans needed to dream was possible, even in Africa; without it, they would have nothing worth 'saving? Here was a pocket of something they could depict as Eden, populated by nameless 'natives' the Europeans could evoke with paternal benevolence. The hills were 'abodes of peace and plenty', the land glittering with flecks of 'gold-dust? It all felt so easy, as if they could just walk right in and take it.

Stanley had painted a similar image of the Ulugurus when he had passed through in 1871, laying the foundations of an expanding myth that Western writers would turn to as their ambitions to possess the continent enlarged: 'I look back upon the scene with pleasure, for the wealth and prosperity it promises to some civilized nation, which in some future time will come and take possession of it.' The delusion endured. In the 1930s, the essence of East Africa was still being presented as a kind of promised land the white 'civilizers' were predetermined, or at least entitled, to occupy. 'Where a man feels at home, outside of where he's born, is where he's meant to go,' wrote Ernest Hemingway of his big-game hunting expeditions in *Green Hills of Africa*. 'Up in this high air you breathed easily, drawing in a vital assurance and lightness of heart. In the highlands you woke up in the morning and thought: Here I am, where I ought to be,' wrote Karen Blixen in *Out of Africa*. Except no one had invited them in – something Stanley and the British explorer Verney Lovett Cameron, whose book Carter was carrying, were both reminded of in the Ulugurus, when they reached the town of Simbamwene in the northern shadow of the mountains.

When Stanley visited Simbamwene, it was a walled town with fortifications he described as sophisticated as anything he'd seen on his travels, with stone walls pierced with holes for musketry, corner towers and thick, studded doors. More or less occupying the site of present-day Morogoro, it was built by Kisabengo, a charismatic 'robber and kidnapper' with an army of people fleeing from slavery. By the time Stanley visited, power had passed into the hands of Kisabengo's daughter, Pangiro. Stanley nicknamed her 'Amazon Simbamwenni' and treated her with disdain. He described her army following his caravan as if they were children running after the Pied Piper of Hamelin, literally dancing to his tune. When she demanded the hongo transit tax that was due to her, Stanley refused – a miscalculation he was to regret when she seized his goods and took his men hostage. Two years later, when Cameron passed by the same settlement, he also haughtily dismissed 'Miss Kisabengo', as he called her: 'We marched past with colours flying, and altogether disregarding the demands of its present ruler.' Despite being a subject of the mighty Queen Victoria, Cameron wasn't going to pay homage to any African equivalent: '[Miss Kisabengo] possesses the will, but lacks the power, of rendering herself as obnoxious as was her robber sire.'

Such total scorn for female power at even the highest levels of African society was only one aspect of how women were regarded by nineteenth-century European travellers. Although the records of Carter's elephant expedition described just an occasional 'squat and ill-favoured' woman encountered on the road, it would have been unusual for females not to have been part of the caravan. Women were, as one missionary put it, 'supernumeraries', because they exceeded what was deemed necessary. Yet many of the caravans at this time were attended by 'slave concubines'. 'Caravan marriage' was common too, especially among the Nyamwezi people, whose wives accompanied their husbands' on their cross-country journeys. Several explorers were also suspected of siring children on the road. Others were complicit in different ways. 'Her figure was far from being attractive', wrote Joseph Thomson about a woman who had attached herself to his caravan. 'I therefore determined to give her a chance, so the drum was beat to call the men together. Before they all assembled, I gave her a yard of cotton to hide a few of the more glaring defects, and in this bridal dress she was offered in marriage to whosoever would have her.'

Some travellers admitted women were critical to a caravan's success, but only in as much as they served men's needs.

They cooked, carried food and beer, and washed clothes. 'It gives great life to the party,' remarked Galton in his *Art of Travel*; 'a woman will enjoy a long journey nearly as well as a man, and certainly better than a horse or bullock.' They were also good for 'hearsay gossip,' remarked Galton, adding: 'it is in the nature of women to be fond of carrying weights.' Richard Burton openly regarded women as the travellers' playthings: 'All the chiefs of the caravan carried with them wives and female slaves' – 'tall, bulky, and "plenty of them"'. He described the 'frightful morals' of an enslaved woman called Sikujui, or 'I Don't Know You'; she 'disordered the caravan by her irregularities,' for which she was eventually cast off in western Tanzania for the price of 'a few measures of rice.' For most of the explorers, it was all too much. 'I looked at the skies, and I looked at the ground,' wrote Thomson, who ran away and hid his head under a blanket to avoid the sight of dancing African women, and their large 'mammæ'. For one Belgian traveller, an attempted seduction by an African chieftainess was so shocking, he remarked of her reign that 'future historians would be wise to write only in Latin.' The subject was simply too indecent to be described in the vernacular.

We turned off the main road on to a rough track. On each side, squat spikes of sisal grew in ordered rows. As we drove down a tunnel of moringa trees, a Verreaux's eagle-owl swooped towards us, its wings caught in the last of the gilding sun. We slept off the journey at a local homestay, then the next day met a birding guide called Charles Masunzu in a noisy streetside café on the edge of Morogoro. He'd agreed to show us the Kiroka Valley on the Ulugurus' eastern flank, which would pick up the route Leopold's elephants had walked.

Charles was busy preparing logistics for a Pentecostal pastor's upcoming 'crusade' (Charles's word) into the mountain villages. People came and went, he said. They always had. Morogoro was a crossroads where there was a long history of tolerance towards outsiders. Charles explained how, in the late 1960s, Morogoro became a base for South Africa's anti-apartheid leaders. The exiled African National Congress party, or ANC, used the Ulugurus to train their supporters in guerrilla warfare when Morogoro granted them refuge and political asylum. In 1969, the town hosted a critical conference focused on armed struggle to counter white supremacy across the continent, attended by revolutionaries from Mozambique, Angola and Rhodesia (now Zimbabwe). 'There are no limits to the cowardly and dastardly crimes of the imperialists and their agents,' announced the ANC's leader, Oliver Tambo. In Nyerere's Morogoro, Tambo felt he could speak more freely.

We planned our route with Charles in the café as Turkish engineers started coming in for lunch. They were building a new railway across the middle of the country. Charles looked over my notes, nodding at Carter's problems with the jungle. The expedition made slow passage through the foothills, along a footpath just wide enough for men to travel in single file, but not suitable for the elephants. 'My roads had to be 12 feet x 10 feet to let the co[mpany] pass,' complained Carter. The hill country was impossibly steep. 'No loaded animal save an elephant could have accomplished them.' 'Picture to yourself what difficulties I have had to contend with on an unknown route with caravan and elephants,' Carter moaned in a private letter to his friends in Mesopotamia. 'I have cut down enough wood to build the whole of Brussels, and made as many bridges over valleys and swampy ground as would bridge the Thames.'

Charles patted his belly, pleased with all the eating we were getting done as we plotted our course for the week. He talked excitedly, with a gentle stutter. He wasn't as fit as he once was, he warned me. The iron in the Uluguru soil – had I noticed how red it was? It was used by pregnant women all over Tanzania to prevent morning sickness. I was curious if this story had anything to do with the Uluguru cave Burton described, which women used to visit to improve their fertility. Plenty of those, said Charles; the Ulugurus had a number of sacred sites. We would camp near the village of Kinole, and meet the leader of the Luguru people, Chief Kingalu Mwanabanzi, who lived by the mobile tower. Charles started tapping at his phone. He said he knew someone who knew someone who could get hold of him.

The next day, we set out with our tents, roll mats and food for a few days to explore the hills. We stopped at a cave close to Carter's route, where a crowd of men seemed to come out of nowhere the moment we arrived. We were rare visitors, but from the heated discussion, it was clear we could advance no further. An elder explained why. Inside the cave, there was a rock shaped like a woman. It was missing a breast because a white woman had stolen it long ago. He said the foreigners had built a church close by, but one day the missionaries were almost beaten to death by invisible sticks. After the desecration of the rock, the cave's spirit drove the intruders away.

We passed a village called Kisauke, meaning 'Because of a Woman', the name apparently derived from an adulterous scandal. We walked into jungle striped with *Sterculia appendiculata* trees, their bare trunks the colour of bleached bones, and climbed a path that wound up through clumps of wild bananas and begonias, where branches were festooned with trumpeting moonflowers and leathery seed pods. In the leaf-mould, which smelled strongly of cloves, we caught a glimpse of an acid-green boomslang snake. Close to the Mvuha River, which the expedition had followed, I watched a man pan for gold in the water. A little further on, we came upon a group of men covered in wet, red mud, pit-digging the banks with spades. They explained how a few of them were graduates in forestry conservation who couldn't find government jobs.

'The first time we found a piece of gold, I cannot tell you the feeling,' said one of the men. 'Once you touch gold, you can feel how powerful it is, even when you close your eyes.'

'The colour of gold is very strong,' said one of his friends. 'When you see it in the earth, it's a shining yellow, like a sun in the mud.'

We hiked further to find Chief Kingalu, who was waiting for us in a clearing beneath the mobile tower. Sitting next to him in a semicircle of plastic chairs was a younger woman with long braided hair and a cream dress printed with lilies. There were two other elders present as witness to events – a traditional quorum system to help protect the people's collective rights – and in the shadows, a lizard with turret eyes, which held its pose throughout.

Chief Kingalu looked at my nineteenth-century maps of the region. He made sense of Rankin's mistranscribed villages to help me track the elephants' journey as they passed through his people's ancestral lands. He was the fifteenth chief, he said, but in 1879 it would have been a different kinship line in control of the area. In Luguru society, if there's no daughter, the chieftainship passes into another branch.

'You mean son,' I remarked.

'No, I mean daughter. Since women give birth to the child, they are powerful in our culture. Women hold the clan. A mother divides the land between her daughters. If she only has sons, then it goes to her sister's family.'

'So a baby girl is a blessing?'

'You're bringing something valuable into the house.'

The elders explained that female clan power still governed his people's relationship with land. The traditional inheritance system was a way of stopping men from marrying outside the Luguru community.

There was a recipe, explained one of the elders, using medicine from the forest that made it easier for women to conceive girls.

I wanted to talk about it with the only other woman in our gathering – the one in the lily-printed dress, but she wouldn't look me in the eye.

'Bibi,' said Charles. 'We address her as Bibi. We can't know her real name. She is the chief's wife. No one in the village ever speaks her name. If she wants to say something, she will speak later, through someone else.'

I tried to draw Bibi's attention, but she continued to look down at her hands. I was intrigued by the paradox of a culture which empowered women – Bibi was their queen – while also rendering them so invisible that the most revered female in their society was effectively silenced in the company of strangers. The men continued to talk over my questions as if neither of us were there. When a chicken startled me and I nearly broke the leg of my plastic chair, she smiled at me briefly, but that was about as far as we were going to get. The chief talked instead about how, during the colonial period,

the mining of mica and garnets in the mountains had undermined the traditional system of land rights. Then under
Nyerere's Ujamaa policy following independence, other Tanzanian ethnic groups had started migrating into the area.

'Tanzania is all shuffle, and shuffle is good,' said Rem.
'Rwanda has two dominant tribes. Kenya is dominated by
about five. Tanzania has more than a hundred and twenty and
is dominated by none.'

Rem was descended from pastoralists – Maasai nomads
who moved around in pursuit of seasonal grazing. The
Luguru, on the other hand, were settled people who relied on
small-scale farming. They depended on a sensitive symbiosis
with the forest that had been undermined by the rapid com-
moditization of the land. Chief Kingalu stood up and showed
me where the line of old-growth forest used to be – a significant distance below us – and where that boundary had moved,
far above the village. He described the wild animals he remembered from his childhood. He estimated that in his lifetime
alone a quarter of the forest had gone, and this despite formal
protection for about ninety square miles of the Uluguru
Mountains.

'Some of us still worship the trees,' he said, 'and we still
mention our traditional gods by name. Even though we are
Christian and Muslim, we haven't lost that connection.'

I asked Chief Kingalu if he was hopeful about the future.
He paused and stroked his chin.

'In the Uluguru Mountains, our streams never run dry.'

We packed up to drive west across the Mkata floodplain. We
were heading to the old Arab caravan town of Kilosa at the
mouth of the Rubeho range, which is another of the relic

forests of the Eastern Arc. When Stanley had come this way to find Livingstone, he had made his Mkata crossing in the wet season when the plain turned into 'one vast lake, a small Tanganyika'. '[The] horrors ... left a durable impression on our minds', wrote Stanley; 'the animals died from this date by twos and threes, almost every day, until but five sickly worn-out beasts remained'. Occasionally there would be an island where the caravan would camp, 'nested like Noah's dove', but otherwise the land was 'as level as a billiard table', forcing Stanley and his party to walk through water up to their armpits. Where the plain wasn't flooded, the soil was like a black slick of oil.

For Carter, the Mkata crossing proved more straightforward. Like him, I was travelling in the dry season, which meant the ground was as hard as stone. But what I didn't see were any of the giant elephant footprints, 'half as large again as those of our animals', which Rankin had observed. An Irishman we'd met in Morogoro had described building roads across Mkata. 'Sometimes we'd be cut off by the rains for a week, but the variety in terms of landscape, wildlife, geography, ethnicity – it's one of the most significant places to live on this continent. If you love Africa, you will love it out there.' He said Mkata still functioned as a migration path for elephants between the Mikumi and Ruaha national parks, but a couple of years ago a bull elephant had been struck by a cargo train. The rhinos had disappeared. So had the African wild dogs he'd seen in the 1990s. The only animals I spotted were skinny cattle, which milled around security checkpoints for the new electric railway. The crossings were presided over by bored Maasai men wrapped in red shuka blankets. Plastic bags snagged in thorn bushes. The land was overgrazed. I'd read about rising tensions between the farmers and pastoralists, which, to my eye, looked like fights for dust. Mkata's cattle herds were expanding, instigating competitive land right claims and violent clashes. Whenever we stopped, Maasai men on motorbikes asked what we were up to. I'd been warned there had been killings in the neighbourhood in recent years, especially on Mkata's periphery in the fertile run-off of the Rubeho Mountains. I didn't want to hang around, but it turned out we'd underestimated the time it took to travel from Morogoro to Kilosa, and we'd need to break the journey for a night. As dusk began to creep up on us, Rem negotiated a camping spot with some elders. He found a location on the edge of a cattle corral presided over by a Maasai woman called Nunu.

She and her five young children brought us fresh milk and helped light our campfire. Nunu's father had nine wives, she said; her mother was the fifth. Nunu was one of between forty and fifty children all with the same father; she wasn't quite sure of the final count. When I pushed a little harder, Rem said it was unlucky for Maasai people to put a number on anything, especially cows. Nunu explained that her husband was away because he was staying with his other wife. Was Nunu jealous, I asked. But my question didn't quite translate. I told Nunu that, in my culture, women didn't generally like to share their husbands. She said Christians said the same when she was growing up, but in her opinion, I was missing out. She talked about how Maasai wives stuck together and raised each other's children as their own, how in her culture the bonds between women were the strongest of all. When Rem got up to deal with a Maasai man who had swooped in on a motorbike, Nunu ignored them. Instead, she leaned in closer to show me a clip on her mobile phone of an African dance troupe she admired. With a flourish that made her children giggle, she imitated the dancers beside the fire. She wanted to look at the pictures on my phone. She was interested in everything – my sons, my thatched home back in Dorset, the photographs of my father's sheep in a British landscape under snow. When Rem returned to translate, I explained more about Carter's caravan snaking across Mkata with Pulmalla at its head, and Rankin's description of Sosankalli pulling the caravan's donkeys over the rivers using a rope tied to her trunk. We talked about the women who were part of the nineteenth-century caravan culture – the supernumeraries written out of history – and she shrugged, as if to say there was nothing new under the sun. Before heading off for bed, Nunu tied a bracelet she'd made around my wrist, of tiny white beads. I gave her some shillings for it; the jewellery was her way of making money in a world still controlled by men.

6

Big With Blessing

'The white man is very clever. He came quietly and peaceably with his religion. We were amused at his foolishness and allowed him to stay. Now he has won our brothers, and our clan can no longer act like one. He has put a knife on the things that held us together and we have fallen apart.'

—Chinua Achebe,
Things Fall Apart

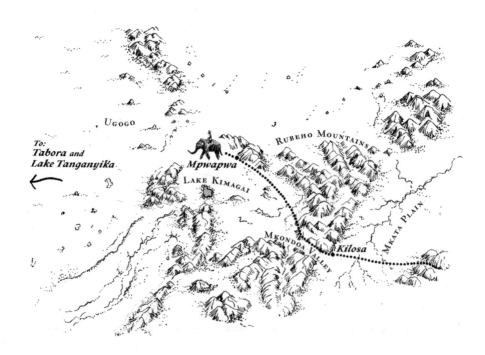

WOLFE AND I WAITED to catch the 'Up Train' at the old railway station on the edge of Kilosa, located on the edge of the Mkata Plain and the Rubeho Mountains. Rem split, taking the long way round the hills by car. The plan was to reconvene on the other side of the Mkondoa Valley, which runs through the middle of this rocky spine, and drive together to Mpwapwa. This was because the train more or less followed the elephants' original line through the tightly folded hills, whereas the higgledy-piggledy mountain roads did not. As a meeting place, Mpwapwa was also significant to the historical journey. It was where Carter was instructed to wait for Leopold's other expedition being led by the IAA's Émile Popelin, who was making slow progress on the caravan route from Bagamoyo. With strength in numbers, Leopold's two parties would then travel as one to take on the hinterland – stark and arid territory where the hongo tax ran infamously high.

It was early in the day when we pulled into Kilosa. Hour by hour, a small crowd began to expand under the awning of the train station's single platform. As the sun climbed higher in the sky, people arrived on foot or by bike to squash into the narrowing pool of shade. There was a hand-cranked iron water pump, a crackling tannoy system amplifying a slow drone of occasional announcements, and various hand-painted signs – 'Parcel & Luggage Office', 'Booking Office, I, II & III Class' – suspended from their hinges. The station master sat in his office behind a heavy wooden desk. He still knew how the colonial-era signalling system worked, which included a tool

The station master at Kilosa photographed with original German and British signalling tools behind him.

that looked like a stringless badminton racket used to wave the 'Up Train' and the 'Down Train' along the line.

When Carter came through Kilosa, the settlement was dominated by Arabs loyal to Sultan Barghash in Zanzibar who used Kilosa as a funnelling point through the mountains to control the caravan trade. The elephants struggled with the hilly terrain – a landscape Burton described as the 'Pass Terrible'. So did the men who constructed the Central Railway Line, later built under German rule, which followed the same route. Local people were forced to labour without wages. Attempted desertions were punished with beatings. In the Mkata marshes, around a hundred men died each month. The Central Railway took ten years to complete, but by 1914 a track nearly eight hundred miles long was running all the way from Dar es Salaam to Lake Tanganyika. Then just two years later, the railway was turned into a battleground when the First World War expanded into Europe's colonies on the African continent, embroiling German East Africa, Belgian Congo and the British East Africa Protectorate (now Kenya). When the war finally came to an end, the German Kaiser was forced to cede his African colony to the British, which is perhaps why neither nation talked about this railway as the significant feat of engineering it really was. The British didn't build it. The Germans surrendered it. As for the indigenous population, you won't find any obvious recognition of those who lost their lives constructing or defending it. In fact, in the whole of Tanzania, I encountered only one memorial, the Askari Monument in Dar es Salaam, for the one hundred thousand African soldiers who fought and fell for a European war.

At the peak of its construction, around twenty thousand Africans worked on the Central Railway.

Europeans travelling on the Central Railway in 1914.

The Central Line was a relic, said a railway enthusiast who'd joined the conversation I was having with the station master. The newcomer, who wore a leopard-print trilby and smelled strongly of cinnamon aftershave, was pleased I'd come to Kilosa with an interest in its story. 'The German system was once beautiful,' he said. 'Now the new railway is being built and our passengers will be taken, this piece of history will go to sleep.'

We talked about how in 1879 Leopold's elephants had travelled through Kilosa on more or less the same path as the trains.

'Elephants? From India? We have elephants too,' he said, cocking his head.

I mentioned a conservationist I'd interviewed a few weeks earlier, who explained how the Tanzanians were building special tunnels so the elephant migrations wouldn't be impeded by all the new roads and railways.

'Tunnels, for elephants?' he said. 'Trains hit elephants. That happens in this country. Elephants walk where they like when they like. They don't read signs.'

It wasn't long after noon when a slow groan started hissing down the rails. Before the train had even come to a standstill, fruit and vegetable sellers approached the carriage windows with buckets of oranges, papayas and bananas. While they traded with passengers, we climbed on board and settled into our seats. Then the train rolled out west in golden light, which made it feel as if we were drifting through honey. The route curled along the Mkondoa River, threading through the neck of a pinched valley. In those places where the landscape flattened out into a longer view, farmers were putting their onion bulbs out to dry – a collage of copper balls as finely polished as doorknobs. In the canteen car, the kitchen crew stirred potato fries in boiling vats of blackened fat. The cook shouted above the snap and grind of couplings bouncing above the rails. Beers were ordered. Radio played through the train's loudspeakers. A girl pushed her head out of the window, which made her hijab putter, loosening some hair. I dozed in and out to the gentle thump and clunk of iron, to flashes of children waving from the fields, sometimes perilously close to the tracks, and the occasional glide and screech of a buckle on the line. At some point, I must have fallen asleep because the next thing I remember, I was being woken up by the slow passage of a train moving in the opposite direction. The effect was hypnotic. Faces shimmered past, eyes pressed to the windows, until I couldn't quite tell which one of us was in motion. My judgement was off, intensifying the sensation of not perceiving things quite as they really were. When I caught my reflection in the glass, I thought about the pitfalls of writing about a country and a past from the outside looking in, sitting in a train compartment, making notes on faint impressions, my limiting perspective boxed into sedentary observations. It was a point of view with a long history in this part of Africa, in the way Europeans travelled in largely passive comfort.

Travelling on the Central Line from Kilosa. The railway was originally built to transport cargo from sisal, tea, cotton and coffee plantations to East Africa's ports.

A few weeks before Carter came through the Rubeho Mountains, he'd been preceded by Dr Joseph Mullens of the London Missionary Society, who'd travelled with him on the *Chinsura* and complained about the stink of onions and elephants coming up from the hold. To spare himself the discomfort of walking in Africa's 'long, rank grass', the ageing Mullens relied on an iron chair made in Zanzibar to carry him along the caravan route inland. Eight porters divided into two teams of four were appointed as his bearers. The chair was slung between two bamboo poles hefted on to the men's shoulders. Eventually the contraption's weight compelled one of his colleagues to rig up a camp chair as a replacement. From thereon in, all ran 'smoothly and harmoniously', reported Mullens's assistant. The experience was 'like a huge picnic', he recounted; 'The men did their work willingly and cheerfully, and though the poor, dear doctor was generally tired out, and a little late in getting in to camp, a cup of cocoa or tea and a little rest sufficed to restore him to his wonted health and spirits.'

Mullens was not unusual in his choice of transport. Europeans often elected to be carried through East Africa, which was another reason this elephant business was important, given pachyderms might prove to be a better vehicle. In 1858, Burton was conveyed in a hammock in order to cross a large swathe of territory after suffering partial paralysis. In the months before his death in 1873, an ailing Livingstone was fed, nursed and carried like a babe in a cot. When a group of British missionaries asked for permission to bring their wives to Africa, they designed a contraption to be hoisted by four men, walking one behind the other. The conveyance was intended to protect ladies from the 'annoyances' of vegetation that snagged European clothes, including the high wet grasses which 'soak one to the skin even when the sun is shining'.

Among those female travellers, perhaps the most memorable was Annie Hore, who in 1882 travelled from England to join her missionary husband on Lake Tanganyika. A team of sixteen men took it in turns to wheel her in a padded wicker bathchair, which was fitted with two long poles for lifting the chair wherever the terrain got challenging. While the coir fastenings and bamboo ensured 'a pleasant springiness', she complained about the waterproof awning: 'I could see nothing of the country, or people, only the dark forms of our own men, and, dimly, the clumps of bushes and trees gliding by.' Her young son, meanwhile, was carted beside her in a wheelbarrow, which could be easily rigged to a bamboo pole. 'Though always carried, I endured my own particular kind of weariness, and often longed for the relief of a walk', she said, insisting she was by no means a profligate traveller: 'indeed we had no gilt tent-knobs, or fancy portmanteaus or canteens.' All in all, she considered her journey to Lake Tanganyika a grand success, '[which] was, I think, notwithstanding its difficulties, the quickest on record by any European.'

A photograph on display in the National Museum of Tanzania in Dar es Salaam, with the following caption: 'Transportation before construction of Railway was very difficult.'

A photograph from the Zanzibar National Archives. It has no source details or caption, but the message is clear: nineteenth-century European visitors literally travelled on the shoulders of Africans.

Female missionaries being carried in hammocks.

Single-wheeled rubber carts later became popular with Europeans in settlements where there were smoother paths.

At least Carter was walking alongside his men, as he wrote to his old friend Tom Cadenhead. He didn't take to riding Pulmalla, unlike Rankin. Carter's valet, Mahomed, also opted to use Pulmalla wherever possible, though she wasn't always an armchair ride, complained one of her passengers, even if lounging in the padded howdah on her back was better than walking up to one's chest in grass. At least she was reliable. In new and unfamiliar terrain, Pulmalla didn't take any risks. She would test whether it was safe before putting her whole weight on the ground. She was experienced, used to carrying dignitaries through noisy city crowds. If Rankin's story was to be believed, Pulmalla had even carried the Prince of Wales through Pune when he'd visited India just four years prior to Leopold's assignment.

With other members of the expedition begging for a ride, Carter was determined not to add to Pulmalla's burden. He was growing fond of the animals, impressed by their endurance. His letters revealed a deepening affection for the elephants, except for the bolter, Sundar Gaj, or 'Old Musty', who was continuing to cause trouble. In the missives he sent to his friend Cadenhead, Carter described walking up to ten hours a day on foot. He was determined to set a strong example. Sometimes Carter led from the front, sometimes from the rear of the caravan, 'keeping the ball always rolling'.

'I have got my men in such splendid order and they have such implicit trust in me that they would follow me to the devil', Carter wrote to Cadenhead, even if 'everything of course has to be done with my own hands'. But not all of Carter's caravan hires were following him as dutifully as he claimed. Within the same twenty-four hours as he penned his boast to Cadenhead, Carter messaged Belgium in a furious scribble. With one or two exceptions, Carter considered every Indian in his entourage 'useless except to ride the elephants', either being 'old men with all the infirmity of old age upon them or young men and boys without experience'. The mahouts had to be 'nursed and looked after like babies'. They were a burden, not a help, refusing to make their own fires or cook their own food. Occasionally, they even took the meal prepared for Carter's own table. Carter's increasingly erratic outbursts included accusations that the Africans were 'stupid brutes' – words that poisoned my own relationship with a man I'd first hoped might rise above the prejudices of his time. I'd initially felt sympathetic towards Carter since travelling to Ireland to find the lost biography of his childhood. I'd booked into a pub on the edge of 'the Continent', as Carter's parish in Kilkenny used to be known. With snow falling outside in thick doily flakes, I'd wandered around his family's old neighbourhood, including the Kilkenny Union Workhouse, which had been turned into a shopping mall and bowling alley where tourists now take self-guided tours of the 'Famine Experience'. I'd come across these particular letters only later in my research, and they repulsed me, making him complex company to travel alongside.

What surfaced in Carter's correspondence was also his growing sense of loneliness. 'I cannot tell you how often I have longed for you to help me', Carter wrote to Cadenhead. In another letter sent just twelve days later: 'From what I have written home about you I think the King will be sure to give you the chance of coming out just as I stand now'. What was becoming clear by the time Carter had covered just two hundred miles of the journey, was that he was in too deep with this expedition, and he needed help from someone he trusted. 'It's downright hard work, lots of hardships to be endured and lots of difficulties to be overcome without one hour of pleasure of any kind'. But Carter had set his goal, and he refused to concede failure. That was the imperial way, the position Orwell's colonial policeman had upheld when he shot the elephant simply to avoid looking like a fool. 'There is a great future in store', Carter reassured Cadenhead. '[W]e may both together be leading a caravan of 100 or 200 elephants across the Dark, very Dark Continent, as there is not the slightest doubt that elephants are the baggage carriers for Africa. Railways must be far distant as hills and mountains cover the country.'

Rem was waiting for us at the station on the other side of the Rubeho Mountains. Together we drove into Mpwapwa, which sat at a bend in a river, and at the feet of some low-lying, brush-covered hills. In the late 1870s when the elephants came through, the British were nurturing ambitions to turn Mpwapwa into one of the most important mission stations in Africa – a 'centre of light for the lakes around'. On the drive in, I'd noticed some graffiti scrawled on to an ochre wall: 'AFRICA HAS GOT NO REMEDY'. It seemed ironic, to be met by such a godless message in a God-obsessed town pricked with church spires, including an Anglican cathedral.

'You brought us Christianity, dropped it yourselves, and left us with the guilt,' said Rem.

By 1876, the Church Missionary Society, or CMS, had settled on Mpwapwa in a deal with the local chief: a present of cloth as 'a token of purchase' in order to open a kind of refugee centre for formerly enslaved people, and anyone else, for that matter, the missionaries could convince about Christ's redemption. In the missionaries' version of events, the Mpwapwa chief said he 'hoped they would stay for a hundred years'. Slavery had been officially outlawed, but it was still prevalent, with the Arab-Swahili caravans now marching 'out of sight' and 'in the dead of night'. 'So far as I can learn, few ivory caravans arrive without bringing slaves,' Kirk remarked; 'Before reaching the coast towns the slaves are scattered among the plantations, so that all trace of them is eventually lost.' Kirk may have been exaggerating things in order to help justify increased European meddling on the continent, but the fact was the brutality of the trade endured. Meanwhile, on the ground, God's work wasn't an easy calling, complained Mpwapwa's brethren. The escapees they took in always risked being recognized and snatched back if they strayed too close to the caravan camps nearby – reports which only hardened Christian resolve and fed collection boxes in Europe. Africa '[is] a cloud which is "big with blessing"' promised the CMS's impassioned secretary in England, as if Africans were desperate for salvation, as Livingstone, Stanley and Leopold had all argued for some time. But it would take a certain kind of fortitude to carry out the work. When local food supplies ran low in 1877, the first run of CMS missionaries abandoned Mpwapwa. By the following spring, fresh recruits found nothing left of the mission except a pile of rubbish.

These new hires were Dr Edward Baxter and Joseph Last – two Englishmen in their thirties. After purchasing a good stock of fowls, sheep, goats and oxen, they began to cultivate twenty-five acres of land for coconuts, pineapples, cassava and bananas. Things started out well, but day by day, their livestock was picked off by hyenas. The houses the two men built disintegrated as quickly as they were put up, owing to the ravages of termites, which ate through the wood. 'I should not be surprised if in a year or two the straw roof covering the whole were to be bodily carried off by a gust of wind,' bemoaned Baxter. The missionaries rose with the dawn and were so tired by dusk that they could barely summon up the energy to report their successes. They were running a two-hundred-strong workforce, many of them formerly enslaved people from Zanzibar. At Mpwapwa, the converts were given gardens to grow food, but how 'free' they really were was another matter. 'With all I made one agreement, which was, that they would not be allowed to return to the coast again, but that they should make their permanent home at Mpwapwa,' wrote Last. His personal entourage included twelve-year-old Faida, 'a slave boy . . . given to me' by one of the coastal Arabs. 'On the road, he was always with me, carrying any little thing I might want; here he does little odd jobs about the house, and always attends school every day, as well as the services and meetings.' In addition, the missionaries employed locals to harvest grass for thatching, but before long, the mission ran out of cloth to pay them. The brethren needed to find other ways of winning over the population. The first Mpwapwa missionaries had attracted attention with their concertina playing, while lessons from colleagues at other missions had shown that magic lanterns, barrel organs and portable printing presses could also help nudge people towards adopting the new religion. In Mpwapwa, the penny-pinched missionaries made the most of Baxter's cabinet of medical potions, and a few coloured illustrations of the scriptures. 'I can often tell a story to the Waswahili with a picture whereas if I had it not, they would not care to listen to me,' wrote Last.

A picture of the crucifixion of the kind commonly distributed by European missionaries. The photographer is unknown, but the image is from East Africa, circa 1910.

Souls were beginning to turn, with Sundays in Mpwapwa given over to teaching hymns in Swahili using Bishop Steere's new translations. Among the most committed members of the growing congregation was Kanganiza, Mpwapwa's star convert, who would often speak about his plans to get to heaven; Songoro, who was the mission's chief carpenter; and a girl called Trouble, the daughter of a formerly enslaved woman who'd managed to escape the Arab–Swahili caravans.

When Carter trudged into Mpwapwa at the beginning of August 1879, Baxter was away, leaving only Last to entertain him. Last was '[a] man of robust and virile personality' who was glad of Carter's jovial company. Last had also been having a tricky time of late with a funeral to officiate. Three weeks prior to Carter's arrival, old Dr Mullens had made his last sombre procession through the African bush – this time not carried in his iron palanquin, but in a coffin. A suspected cold had spiralled into death 'from exhaustion' twenty-nine miles shy of Mpwapwa (the official medical report said his death was caused by 'inflammation of the rectum'). The doctor was laid to rest in the mission's new burial ground, shaded by bright mimosas. Words from the Holy Writ were spoken. A temporary marker was made from a piece of mahogany with an inscription painted on it. There were plans to add a head-stone later.

As I walked along the river where Carter's elephants would have been watered by their mahouts, I lingered in the shade of the oldest trees – spreading figs, which also appeared in nineteenth-century drawings of the settlement. I went to find Mullens's grave, and was led to a scrubby hillside by two young men, who said they were direct descendants of the first Africans 'saved' by the mission. While they weren't entirely sure whose names were carved on the three headstones hidden in the thorns, they were pretty certain they were the earliest foreign graves in Mpwapwa. The inscriptions had worn away, so I went to meet an elder, born in 1934, who I'd been told held Mpwapwa's oral history. His name was Tito Habeli. We sat on plastic chairs in the neatly brushed yard beside his house, with chickens scratching at our feet.

'This was a big trading town, where the Arabs exchanged cloth for ivory, and the Nyamwezi porters brought alcohol to trade too. You're on my father's ground,' he said. 'It was famous in those times.'

As a young man, Tito had worked as a 'houseboy' for the British on a sisal estate. He later got a job as a bus conductor in Nairobi, then moved into politics with Tanzania's independence.

'During the First World War, the Germans kept an important headquarters in Mpwapwa for their troops. Near the roundabout in town there was a bunker where they stored bombs and ammunition.'

Tito pointed to the side of the road.

'There used to be a tree there. German soldiers used to hang their hats on it. They came to get wax from the honey hunters, pombe and peanuts. Passing Africans had to salute the German hats on the post. If they didn't, they'd be beaten.'

He described the palanquins used to transport the Germans.

'You had to sing a song as you carried it. The song was called "Cry Like A Donkey". If you didn't, or couldn't sing the song, you were whipped.'

I asked what was left of the old mission. He gave me a

couple of contacts, and described what Carter and the elephants might have seen – stories told to Tito by his elders.

'There's a well where slaves used to stop and drink water. Near the big fig tree. That's still there, the fig. The well is there too, but I'm not sure if there's any water left.'

I left Tito to meet Sylivester Chamwela, a teacher and senior member of Mpwapwa's St Paul's Church.

'Once everyone knew Mpwapwa's name,' said Sylivester. 'Our cathedral was the Canterbury of Africa. They call it the mother church of Tanzania. But we're forgotten. We have no church papers. They're all in your country, in England. I've been to Bognor Regis, twice, which is enough. If I returned, I'd go to Buckingham Palace, to ask for our history back. Not copies, but the originals. Land ownership has become very important in the last ten years. It's the source of all rights.'

Sylivester drew three printed sheets of information from a plastic sleeve – it was all he had to share with me on Mpwapwa's official Anglican past – and invited Wolfe, Rem and me to join him at church the following day. He instructed me to buy a full-length dress. It was very important I dressed correctly for the Sunday service, he said. When he asked if I could sing, I mentioned that Wolfe was the musical one. So it was decided: Wolfe would join the Sunday choir, and for that it was agreed he'd also need to buy a smarter outfit.

We left for the market, where Wolfe found a primrose-yellow shirt with pearly cufflinks, and I bought an ill-fitting dress embroidered with rose buds. Rem, it turned out, had packed more appropriately than both of us. The following morning, we walked to St Paul's, passing a parade of women singing on the street. Mpwapwa's Catholics were on their way to worship, carrying plastic chairs on their heads. The procession was trailed by children in nylon dresses in white so clean they had a silver gleam, like fresh meringues. On the other side of town we could hear the Pentecostals turn up their speakers to broadcast their electric guitars, in screechy twangs that ricocheted through the town. Mpwapwa was so noisy, it was as if everyone were trying to drown the other out with the volume of their faith.

'Sunday is a happy day with us here', wrote Last to his superiors in 1879; 'we have much to make us so, and to remind us of scenes at home – abstinence from work, the bell ringing, the people coming and going to church'. It gave him great satisfaction to see his congregation assembled in their Sunday best: 'The men and boys, in their clean white coats and trousers, on the one side, and the women, in their gay cotton clothes on the other'. His descriptions fell into line with the Anglican service I attended that morning: the sexes more or less separated on either side of the church, with girls in ankle socks, women in dresses and hats, boys in waistcoats and men in polished black shoes as shiny as beetles. The catechism rolled into song, led by a choir swinging and swaying in satin baby pinks, with Wolfe falling into tune with his usual good-natured enthusiasm. When the collection came round, it felt like an auction. A woman gave ten chicken eggs, for which someone else offered money. A suited man stood up to announce a cash donation, and was warmly applauded. A newly painted hospital trolley was trundled up the aisle. It was a gift from the Lutherans for coffins, declared the Reverend Canon Robert Chiteme, to spare the men's shoulders. Nearly everyone took the Eucharist, except for a few women.

'If you're a convert and polygamous, wife number one

can come to church and take the Eucharist; the other wives can still attend, but they can't partake,' explained Sylivester.

As the service drew to a close, the reverend urged everyone to speak to God all at once. 'Throw out your words! Don't just expect your leader to pray for you. You must speak to him direct!'

The congregation rose up in a wave of noise. They spoke. They sang. They wept. 'They always go on too long,' said my neighbour, half under his breath.

When the service was over, I chatted with Sylivester at the church doors. Then we went for some lunch and cold beer, and talked about how when Carter arrived in Mpwapwa, Last had been caught up in a moralizing spat with his colleague, Baxter, who was absent in Zanzibar. Baxter claimed that the mission supplies Last had purchased were unnecessary. Among them: fifty pounds' worth of gold-fringed cloths, six bottles of sherry, three bottles of brandy, twenty pints of stout

Community elder Tito Habeli.

Teacher Sylivester Chamwela.

The Reverend Canon Robert Chiteme at St Paul's.

The choir outside St Paul's posing for a photograph.

and three umbrellas. Baxter was 'more and more astonished' at Last's growing expenditure. Baxter's censorious implication to his mission superiors in England was clear: Last was extravagant, and a sot to boot.

'I never was a drunkard or a tippler,' insisted Last in his eight-point defence. 'I do not wish to say that wine and spirits are necessary as a beverage, but I think the majority of Church missionaries will agree with me in saying that there are many cases in which they are.' He passionately argued for the gold-fringed cloth. 'The Royal Elephant Expedition has a large box of such things for presents,' he insisted. He conceded to only one error of judgement, which was the fault of his sweet tooth. To make up for it, he agreed to use his personal funds to reimburse the CMS for three jars of confectionery, but that would be it. The problem was that Last had 'no idea whatever of faring differently from what he would at home', complained Baxter, which was precisely what made Last such a welcome host to Carter. The two men immediately hit it off, with Last sending off eulogizing letters to Europe in praise of the 'White Sheikh' and his remarkable pachyderms. Last wrote with such conviction, in fact, that his seniors were soon calling for 'two or three of these wise beasts' of their own; 'think what a help the elephant would be on a missionary tour'.

For his part, Carter was grateful for Last's supply of fresh milk and vegetables, as well as the comforts of his personal hut, described as 'a delightful nook, 800 feet above the valley'. He was waited on by the mission's cook, Majwara. Enslaved as a child, Majwara had been enlisted by Stanley as his gun carrier. Majwara had then looked after Livingstone in his final days. By his early twenties, he was said to have walked a staggering ten thousand miles in the service of Europeans. But by 1879, Majwara had apparently hung up his boots, and settled down for a quieter life in this emerging mission town.

Yet even these relative luxuries weren't enough to assuage Carter's homesickness for Mesopotamia, which he described with painful resignation in letters home to Cadenhead. 'I often think of Maaghil and wish myself there but what a difference of life. There I vegetated like a cabbage and here I have more downright hard work than would be good for a dozen men'. Writing from Last's mission hut, Carter's old home would have felt as if it belonged to another lifetime: wide verandas, interiors cooled by fans, foreign produce imported from England. He dearly missed his garden, which was planted on the edge of a palm grove. In the evenings, he'd listen to the barking of jackals and the splashing of his courtyard fountain. 'Well-arranged and comfortable', his garden smelled of roses, orange and lemon trees, and the delicious perfume of yellow-blossomed acacias. According to an American journalist who visited Carter before he left for Africa, Carter joked it even featured fig trees taken from the biblical Garden of Eden located a few miles upriver.

But Mesopotamia might as well have been on the moon now to Carter, who was beginning to have doubts about Leopold's commission. He worried that Popelin's entourage, which had left Bagamoyo a week after the elephant party had set off from Dar, was now running hopelessly late for their planned assignation in Mpwapwa. As Carter waited for Popelin's arrival, he killed time writing a run of official letters to allay some of his misgivings by proclaiming the elephant experiment already 'a complete success' – so much so that he wished he were crossing the whole continent alone with his party of mahouts. For twenty-three days, the elephants had been covered with tsetse fly, and yet they'd resisted its disease. '[We] have passed through a country unknown, untraversed previously by a white man and unsurveyed', he boasted to the Scottish shipping magnate Mackinnon. He described the challenging topography, the 'mountains and incessant hills alternate with boggy valleys, and dense thorn jungles with swamps and steep banked streams and rivers'. The elephants were magnificent, he declared, 'carrying loads of about five hundred kilograms under conditions very different to those obtaining in India; the various questions attaching to the problem of "the Indian elephant in Africa" has [sic] been solved and the elements of doubt cleared up'.

With his letters dispatched, Carter set off on a trip to

nearby Lake Kimagai with Sundar Gaj and Naderbux. The two males were the caravan's strongest weight bearers, and Carter wanted to collect some long grass to make rope. Carter duly loaded up the bull elephants then sent them back to Mpwapwa while he stayed on to enjoy the lake's charms a little longer. The lake looked promising for some sport, with geese, cranes, and even eagles 'with wattles like a turkey'. From correspondence with one of his brothers in India, it was clear that Africa's big-game shooting was among the lures which had drawn Carter to Leopold's job offer in the first place. Hunting was something Carter had made a habit of on the river Tigris, shooting from his steamer's bow. 'There is an almost constant fusilade [sic] of guns and rifles from the deck,' wrote one of his former passengers. Birds, antelopes and boar all fell to his gun, but in time, it became a running joke that Carter would slow the steamer for nothing less than a Persian lion. In one memorable day, four were shot without an officer ever leaving the deck. The species was rendered extinct in Mesopotamia just forty years later.

But while Carter was enjoying his leisurely break on Kimagai's shores, a very different scene was starting to unfold in Mpwapwa. As dawn broke on 13 August 1879, there were whispers of a catastrophe. A servant woke Rankin with the news: Sundar Gaj wasn't moving. When the elephant had returned from Kimagai, he'd eaten his usual meal of leaf boughs prepared by the mahouts. At three in the morning, Old Musty had been standing, but just two and a half hours later, the elephant was dead. There was no sign of any struggle. A subdued circle gathered around the animal. Difficult and curmudgeonly, but also seemingly invincible, Sundar Gaj had dominated each step of the expedition so far with his larger-than-life temperament. And now he lay in a broken grey heap.

Rankin delivered an urgent message to Carter. While they waited for their leader to return, Rankin ordered the tusks to be removed, the feet amputated – perhaps taxidermied for a commemorative stool or champagne cooler – and a grave immediately dug. The first two tasks Rankin personally performed ('our porters could scarcely be compelled even to lend their knives', he remarked). Over the course of the next two days, Sundar Gaj's body was hewn to bits, his wrinkled skin stabbed until it could be peeled back, and the elephant's huge heart extracted, prodded and weighed. Carter arranged for the tusks, each measuring just over three feet in length, to be forwarded to Belgium for Leopold's attention – 'a souvenir of the death', reported a British newspaper, 'of the first elephant in the praiseworthy attempt to civilise and develop Africa, in which so many noble lives have been sacrificed'. Stripped of his glory, all that was left of Sundar Gaj was a legless, toothless stump of carrion, bubbling with flies. His remains were buried in a grave measuring twelve feet long, ten feet wide and eight feet deep.

Carter quickly took to writing his way out of this worrying turn of events. He claimed it was death by apoplexy – a stroke of some kind. Kirk rallied support, and reported back to Europe that although he was grieved by the news, it was no reflection on the expedition's early successes. Leopold should blame the Indian government, wrote Kirk, which had 'behaved very meanly'. They'd not only provided substandard elephants, but then charged Leopold for the animals when it had been assumed they would be gifted. Kirk recommended that Leopold's expedition should begin catching and training African elephants at once – 'just <u>for fear</u> of any accident happening to the Indian ones.'

Rankin, who was responsible for the post-mortem, came to a different conclusion about Sundar Gaj's demise. Lifting the animal's heavy heart from his body – fourteen kilograms in weight, and some sixteen inches in length – he found no trace of visible disease. Sundar Gaj, he insisted, had died 'a victim of too-herculean labours and of an insufficiency of food.' Perhaps, Rankin suggested, the shocking change from a white bread diet enjoyed at his comfortable elephant stable in India had been too much for him. Perhaps he'd been over-worked by Carter's demanding marches. However mighty Old Musty had first appeared, he'd carried weights over double that which an elephant was reasonably capable of, up and down hills which by Carter's admission only a few days ear-lier were 'like the side of a house.' In the time it had taken to reach Mpwapwa from the coast, the elephant, 'fat and round at starting', had lost so much flesh that his backbone stood up six or seven inches from his flanks.

The British newspapers attached little credence to Rankin's analysis. They were also mostly unsympathetic in their reporting of Sundar Gaj's passing: 'It had been the most difficult to manage of the four, and was therefore the easiest to spare, for though of course a loss to the expedition, yet as it never could be turned, having made up its mind to do a thing, it made up its mind to die, and succeeded.' As for Carter, he was fed up with Rankin's unwanted opinions and his inexperience. He'd already marked him out in a letter to Cadenhead as 'such an ass that I cannot trust him with the simplest thing.' Carter's relationship with his Indian attend-ants was also continuing to deteriorate. When six of them broke rank and returned to Zanzibar from Mpwapwa, Carter picked up his pen again in a flurry of letter writing. He insisted to his superiors that all was well, that Sundar Gaj's death was barely a blip. But privately in his letters to Cadenhead, he was more affected. He was worried about further desertions, and the very real threat of another elephant dying so soon into the journey. He needed the Indian mahouts to stay faithful to him, because if this experiment proved a success and a training school were to materialize, the mahouts were the only ones with any knowledge of capturing wild elephants. 'I dare not leave my camp,' Carter wrote to Cadenhead. 'I know if I do something is sure to happen.'

Only in Cadenhead did Carter continue to confide anything of his real feelings, including his growing dread of giving up authority to the IAA caravan led by Popelin. If they were to advance into the interior as one party, a new pecking order would be established – and it had already been determined by Belgium that Popelin would take precedence. This worried Carter greatly, because two days after Sundar Gaj died, Popelin was carried into camp in a hammock, and a month later than promised. He was ill with fever. Popelin's second-in-command, the Belgian expedition doctor Théodore Van den Heuvel, wasn't looking much better. He rode in behind on a donkey; his head drooped pitifully. 'I fear Popelin's gang will spoil mine,' Carter wrote to Cadenhead. 'And Popelin's short marches will not suit me.' Popelin had turned into a ghost of the man Carter had last seen at the coast. He no longer bore any resemblance to the military strongman variously described by his Belgian compatriots as a tall and robust 'son of the north,' a 'warlike' professional soldier with muscles 'made of steel.' Carter worried that he now had two invalids to deal with, as well as the calamity of Sundar Gaj.

'These men should never have been sent', Carter complained; 'they are not fit for African hardships'. He nursed Popelin, feeding him chicken soup, cornflour mixed with wine, and liberal quantities of Last's contentious port supplies. Meanwhile, Van den Heuvel was threatening to quit, 'disgusted with the whole thing'. If Popelin should die, the command of both caravans would fall on Carter, which would mean taking on responsibility for an extra IAA enterprise from which this elephant commission was meant to be distinct. Carter was losing confidence in Leopold's murky ambitions. He'd been told to keep moving west to Tabora, where new, more specific orders were expected to arrive by the time he got there. But to Carter's mind, it was all so haphazard. 'I have no instructions where to go or what to do when I get there', he complained to Cadenhead. His hongo supplies for paying transit taxes were running low because of the delays. He was heading into remote territory where the prices would only get higher. '[I] feel like a ship without a rudder or mast', fretted Carter. 'I don't know no more [sic] than the man in the moon'. One thing, however, was clear. It was a 'fearful mistake' to mix the expeditions: 'had I been on my own account I would have been half way across before now'. Meanwhile, some of the busybodies in Zanzibar keeping tabs on the expedition had little confidence in his suitability for the job. '[Carter] has given out word that the people here may not be surprised to see him back to the coast in less than six months, implying that he will throw up his contract if he likes it or not', the American consul had already written to Stanley. 'I think he is a "muff" and talks too much', the consul remarked in the same letter. But Carter wasn't a man who gave up easily, despite all the behind-the-scenes back-stabbing.

At the beginning of September, Popelin's health turned a corner, which allowed Carter to finally prepare for their combined departure. He entrusted his correspondence to the mailman, including a gracious letter to the mission authorities in London about Last's good character, and his hospitality. But who knew when it would reach its destination or any return mail might arrive? The further Carter proceeded inland, the more unpredictable the system. It took around sixty days for letters from Europe to reach all the way to the lake, with erratic drop-offs at the stations between. First, the letters would be packed on to one of Mackinnon's mail steamers to Zanzibar via Aden. There, they'd be transferred into mail bags and given to trusted runners or mailmen, who'd take the letters in a kind of relay, stopping at one caravan settlement, then the next, and so on until they reached Lake Tanganyika. Once there, they'd pause long enough to pick up the outgoing replies and reports, then turn for Zanzibar again in the same relay in reverse, to send and receive the next batch. The runners travelled more quickly than a caravan could, but there was no question that 'the mailmen [ran] the gauntlet every journey'. Thieves targeted the mail routes in search of easy pickings, which was why the runners travelled in groups of up to five men as a deterrent.

Worrying news about shifting ethnic rivalries was also travelling up and down the caravan road, with increasing threats of violence towards Europeans. Over the last few months, there had been a wave of unsettling tensions washing through the interior after a deranged French clergyman and explorer, Abbé Michel Debaize, had ordered two Africans to be shot, and their wives sold. The victims' chief was Nyungu-ya-Mawe, who was determined to seek vengeance. He ordered his men to kill the next white man they encountered. Sure enough, in December 1878, a twenty-four-year-old mission engineer, William Penrose, was murdered on the very trail where Carter was now headed. A mailman travelling back to the coast reported the grizzly scene: the skin was stripped from Penrose's face like a skinned rabbit, and his mutilated body surrounded by ransacked books. Back in Zanzibar, a concerned Bishop Steere remarked that all were watching 'how far the example may spread'. By the time Carter was on the move again, everyone's nerves were jumpy. '[F]or now having attacked and killed one white man they will not be so slow to attack Europeans again', warned one of Mpwapwa's Christian brethren. It was hard to get a handle on which places, if any, were going to be safe to pass through. It was into this fresh uncertainty that Carter – confidence badly knocked and plans askew – was set to venture. 'Our troubles will begin at Mpwapwa', Rankin ominously predicted. He was right, not least in relation to his own role in the expedition. Rankin, it turned out, would be journeying no further. Carter dismissed him, and in a persuasive attempt to get his splintering expedition back on track, he made another appeal to Brussels. There was no more room for error. Tom Cadenhead was the only man for the job, and Carter would appreciate it if the king of the Belgians could dispatch him forthwith to Africa.

7

Acacia horrida

'Mmoja anapokimbia asipigwe na mvua mwingine analilia tone la maji.'

('While one runs in order not to be caught by rain, another cries for a drop of water.')

—EUPHRASE KEZILAHABI,
Dunia Uwanja wa Fujo (World, the Court of Chaos)

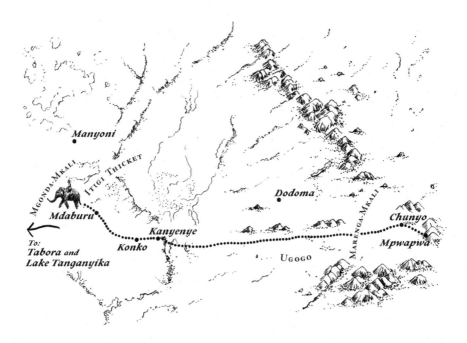

IN THE AUTUMN OF 1897, after gold was struck on the Klondike in northwestern Canada, my English great-grandfather rode out from a cattle ranch near Edmonton to try and make his fortune. It was late in the season. The weather was beginning to grow cold, and there were occasional light flurries of snow. He travelled with three American companions, eight pack ponies, a Winchester rifle, a tin billy for tea, a Dutch oven for making bread, a goatskin coat and a few light mining implements. But the snowfall was heavier than expected, which made the ground treacherous for horses. When his companions wanted to sit out the winter with some fur trapping, my great-grandfather split. He sold his share of the ponies for sledge dogs and hired an indigenous guide instead. His progress quickly picked up – he had more than a thousand miles to travel – but the weather deteriorated. When supplies got dangerously low, he suggested they might eat the dogs instead. That was when his guide refused to go any further. My great-grandfather returned to the ranch on Red Deer River, then not long after left North America for Africa where another gold rush was beginning to glint in the South African veld.

I was brought up on the family story that my ancestor was a pioneer – a word which implies something bigger than its pedestrian etymology denotes. 'Pioneer' comes from the sixteenth-century French military *pionnier*, meaning 'foot soldier', which is derived from the Old French *paon*, meaning 'pawn'. As it turned out, my ancestor wasn't particularly suited to the prospecting business, and much like his Yukon sojourn, he left Africa not long after he arrived, returning to England to farm. But despite his failures in the gold-prospecting business, his diaries reveal a belief that he would somehow pull it off. It was the spirit of Britishness in the Age of Empire – an astonishingly short window between 1876 and 1915 when a quarter of the globe's land surface was cut up into colonies controlled by a half-dozen nation states. To be a 'pioneer' was to belong to the same arc of ambition driving the European men I was following to Lake Tanganyika – everyday foot soldiers fuelled by a spike in imperial exceptionalism. They were seizing their chance on every new horizon, chasing opportunities that were wide open because of where and when they were born. For Stanley, this included the Ugogo country that lay beyond Mpwapwa. 'I looked at this land and people with desiring eyes,' wrote Stanley about the hinterland. 'I saw in it a field worth some effort to reclaim.'

I was travelling under a different sky. The landscape felt so bare, it was as if it had been shorn to its stone foundations. Confusion prevailed as we pulled out of Mpwapwa in search of a place called Chunyo, where caravans would fill up at the last spring before the dreaded Marenga-Mkali, or 'desert of bitter waters'. The Chunyo water was notoriously noxious – 'extremely offensive to the palate', according to Stanley. Carter's elephants refused to drink it. After Chunyo, the caravan then had a thirty-mile march through a vicious covering of brittle thorn. The dread was in the name: *Acacia horrida*. The brush was as sharp as needles, the branches meeting at shoulder height, where the thorns could pierce a human eyeball. 'If I were to speak for a month you could not understand what a thing <u>African</u> jungle is,' Carter wrote to one of his old friends in Mesopotamia. 'I never thought the human frame could have stood such lengthened and hard work without water.' Carter's caravan men worked day and night to cut a trail wide enough for the elephants.

As we drove from Mpwapwa and tried looking for Chunyo, I got myself in a muddle. I couldn't find a trace of the spring where hundreds of thousands of enslaved Africans had been forced to take water on their passage to the coast. I also couldn't find any *Acacia horrida*. The landscape was denuded – a hard rind of earth, where the turn of our wheels threw up clouds of light-spangled dust. There were none of the rhinos Stanley wrote about, not even a rock rabbit scuttling over the stones. When I interfered with Wolfe's map reading, we ended up getting even more lost, with a two-hour detour and some agitated backtracking through a barren run of hills fading out into a concertina of diminishing blues and greys. Rem couldn't disentangle the muddle either – he suspected the missing thorn thicket was simply a case of deforestation – so I called one of the elders I'd met at church in Mpwapwa.

'I know what you're trying to find,' he said. 'It used to be all forest. Even in the 1980s, I remember some bush and elephants. Now there's nothing. What remains is just a story.'

We took a line west by northwest across a level stretch of land in the direction of Tanzania's capital, Dodoma, through arid territory the local Gogo knew how to survive in ways that Carter and his contemporaries did not. In the Marenga-Mkali, Carter began to suffer a run of hallucinations. Under the sprinkled stars, he imagined himself in the arms of his foster mother, drinking streams of cool water on a warm day back home in Hertfordshire. It was early September. In England, the apple trees would have been laden, the wasps feeding drunkenly on the bounty. But it was also a fever dream. Carter was in the grip of extreme dehydration. Either that, or he'd dosed himself with too much morphine from the expedition's medicine chest. On the caravan road, European travellers reached for quinine and arsenic 'much like pepper and salt' at the evening meal. Laudanum helped a racing mind to sleep. 'Wine is generally helpful,' advised one of the Belgian expedition doctors. 'Residents at the coast or in the vicinity of the coast can and must resort to it.' The supplies Carter now had access to in Van den Heuvel's abundant medicine chest included the usual uppers and downers, as well as all sorts of potions another traveller remarked he dared not even touch.

The African caravan members weren't faring well either, and they had none of Carter's remedies. They 'looked as if they would not live an hour,' said Carter. But it was the Indian mahouts who seemed to suffer the most. The head elephant keeper collapsed. Another man died soon after. Carter panicked and buried the body secretly in the shadow of his tent at night. Had the story leaked out, there would have been accusations of witchcraft from the Gogo medicine men. Unexplained burials were regarded with fearful suspicion, with the graves of foreigners the worst of all.

By the time Carter's caravan staggered out the other side of the thorny scrub, Pulmalla, Sosankalli and Naderbux had gone without water for a remarkable forty-two hours, and they'd survived thirty-one hours without food. For most of that journey, the elephants had been carrying over four hundred and fifty kilograms each. They'd also had to help fell trees. They were mourning their companion, Sundar Gaj, who'd been buried where he'd died, under the Mpwapwa figs. 'A wonder of endurance,' declared Carter, who was keen to keep the mood heroic after the recent disaster with Old Musty. Perhaps Carter simply didn't know what a suffering elephant looked like. When they're emotionally disturbed, elephants cry (experts say it's unusual to see tears in wild elephants, although it's common among those kept in captivity). When one of the herd is sick, elephants will treat the illness with different bark, leaves and clay. They form specific, preferential bonds, and look after each other, including adopting elephant calves that aren't theirs. Elephants refuse to abandon their sick or dying family members. They communicate via an infrasonic system inaudible to the human ear, and show an unusual capacity for empathy. Grieving elephants throw dust over the bones of their deceased. Distressed elephants, removed from their social groups, can suffer from chronic anxiety, and have even been known to commit suicide. They are selective eaters, but if they're starving, they'll eat anything. This forced march of Leopold's elephants went completely against their natural instincts.

Wolfe turned up the music in the car for what was going to be one of our longest days on the road. The temperature outside was running at more than thirty-five degrees centigrade. The ground looked like the earth was shedding its dead skin, the shadowless plain covered in dried curls of soil. Then the landscape started to change into another version of monotony: hundreds of shiny baobabs sprouting in an expanse as wide as it was deep. It made me think of English parkland, of a grove of mature oaks, except there was no tinge of green. The baobabs' leafless branches were stunted, their silver trunks like swollen candles melting in the heat. Rem said the trees, some more than a thousand years old, made terrible firewood, which was probably why they were still standing. The giant baobabs felt as if they were the only almost-living thing left, unsettling in their beautiful but lonely existence sizzling on the plain.

The plain of baobabs on my journey from Mpwapwa to Dodoma.

Rumbling onwards through the day's rising temperatures, I talked with Rem about the human impact on the landscape we were traversing, and how it had changed between Carter's time and our own. Eking out a livelihood had never been easy in Ugogo's drought-prone country, but by all accounts, it also wasn't like this, as if life were over and it wasn't going to come back. The Gogo people traditionally cultivated patches of ground until the crops failed. They would then relocate in step with the invocations of their rainmakers, moving between kinship settlements to beat the erratic weather and locust invasions. Famines came and went. Ugogo's history was a dramatic narrative of human survival intensified by the degradations the nineteenth-century caravan industry inflicted on the local environment.

A standard Ugogo crossing from Mpwapwa to the Arab-Swahili town of Tabora – as the crow flies, some two hundred and fifty miles – took about a month for a caravan to walk. Much of that time was taken up with negotiating hongo, with caravan numbers running up to an estimated half a million travellers every year, necessitating significant supplies of food and water. A missionary who came through in 1878 described a scene that could have been the aftermath of a modern music festival: 'The large plain, not unlike a dirty bare common in England, is horrible with the filth and refuse and ashes of many caravans.' On the main routes, Ugogo's cultivated ground was soon exploited beyond its carrying capacity. The rainy season, from December to April, was called 'the hunger period', when the seed was still in the ground and travel was hardest. This was when the Gogo people held even more negotiating power with passing caravans over access to their food and wells.

'One would think there was a school somewhere in Ugogo to teach low cunning and vicious malice to the chiefs, who are masters in foxy-craft', complained Stanley. He likened the Gogo to the Irish – 'clannish and full of fight' – accusing them of being greedy and avaricious. Yet all that travellers ever gave them in return for crossing their territory were coloured beads and bolts of cheap, machine-produced cloth. 'A tax on thirst' was how Ugogo's hongo was described by another of Leopold's men, which was a bitter cost to swallow when by the end of the dry season the last of the well-water was more like a 'foul porridge'. 'Nothing but wholesale robbery', chimed in an Irish missionary. Only Dr Ebenezer Southon, another of the missionaries who'd sailed on the *Chinsura* with the elephants, saw it a little differently.

Southon conceded that the Ugogo hongo was 'a kind of water tax' but only because the commodity was so scarce. The people had to make extensive excavations to obtain it. 'Hence, they would value it highly', remarked Southon, 'and as a passing caravan uses a large quantity of water, it is but reasonable to suppose that the Wagogo would make them pay for it.' Southon thought the Gogo people were anything but the cheats he'd been led to believe by Stanley and his ilk: 'they would be glad to see us gone, for they were afraid we should drink all their water.'

Rem explained how the demonization of the Ugogo transit tax was taken much further when the German colonizers banned hongo altogether. The Germans redefined its purpose as extortion. What once gave people an income for their surplus food and rainwater harvesting, started to mean bribe. The exploitation of Ugogo's land and people continued under British rule until they were left with a ravaged, semi-arid land, and no right to charge for what remained of their resources. Then came a run of devastating famines. By the 1960s, a stereotype was fixed: the Gogo were the beggars of Tanzania. Nyerere tried to repair some of that damage with his Ujamaa policies, but this infertile ground couldn't cope with the dense pockets of habitation created by collectivization. Trees were harvested for charcoal. Desertification picked up pace. The diminishing returns resulted in a wave of migrants who left for Dar es Salaam and elsewhere.

As we drove westwards, a new gash opened in front of us through the plain where the Dar–Dodoma railway was being constructed along the old caravan route. Workers were filling wire gabions with stone. In the middle of the road, there was a man walking barefoot. He was wrapped in a woollen blanket. For a moment he turned in our direction, trying to rub the grit out of his eyes, his face as white as an eggshell from the dust. With the cloth pulled over his hair, he looked like he was wearing a shroud. I watched his weary silhouette disappear in my wing mirror. As he walked among the abject baobabs, the space between us pulled further apart. With the man dwindling to a speck behind me, the road ahead expanded into an even wider span of bulldozed ground. The silver baobabs were replaced by corridors of pylons marching in the direction of Dodoma. The powdered earth turned into a slick of asphalt. Beside it, the new train line began to look more complete. Dodoma emerged ahead of us – a city encircled by giant kopjes, the granite boulders shimmering in the heat 'like a burial site of the Titans' one of Carter's contemporaries remarked.

When Carter came through, he travelled on a route a little further south of where the modern city now stands. I wanted to spend a night here to meet an elder who could help me trace some of the smaller Ugogo villages noted in Carter's account. I was also intrigued by the very idea of Dodoma as the nation's capital. In 1974, it was chosen by Nyerere, its location in the middle of the country intended not only to foster greater inclusiveness but also to shift power away from Dar es Salaam and the coast, and a history of foreign interference. But it wasn't easy for Tanzania to turn its back on history. Africa needed new technologies, which was how China began to assert its influence over Tanzania in the 1970s when it built the railway from Dar to Zambia. That relationship endures in the Belt and Road web of power China is using to tighten its economic grip on the continent at large. Over the last twenty years, it's estimated that China has pumped more than a hundred and twenty-six billion dollars into African countries, giving the Chinese a controlling influence over trade and numerous government loans in a continent-wide sweep, with Tanzania one of the larger beneficiaries. But if I found that relationship interesting, this layer of neocolonialism was also elusive. The closest I could get to any Chinese ex-pats who might talk about it was to eat in the restaurants they might favour on my journey between Dar es Salaam and the lake. It was why I'd chosen the China Garden restaurant at the New Dodoma Hotel for my meeting with the Gogo chief. It felt like an important landmark, the sort of place where government deals might be discussed in VIP lounges over the clink of ice in whisky tumblers. But my luck wasn't in. At the time of my visit, business was quiet.

The Gogo chief, Henry Mtemi Mazengo II, arrived wearing a red fez with a black tassel, and carrying a black stick, which denoted his authority. After we'd settled in the restaurant with my route map laid out in front of us, I asked him about the word *Gogo*.

'It means "log", because our people are stubborn. When travellers passed through this territory, we would be sitting on a log waiting for them. It was a kind of joke, but also true.'

We talked about how the last trees in Ugogo were being felled to make way for small farms.

'This is the world,' he said. 'We've gone past what we used to need.'

Wolfe pulled out our maps. Chief Henry studied the coordinates of Carter's expedition and helped us identify the name and location of another of the thorny forests that lay ahead of us – a landscape which, according to Chief Henry, remained in some parts just as Carter's expedition notes had described it. Chief Henry traced his finger across the different settlements to explain the current boundary of this unique ecosystem, which he also said had been diminishing for some time, with some of the old territory now allocated for big-game hunting. He said we needed to head for the Itigi Thicket, which was previously part of the Mgonda-Mkali, or 'fiery plains', and the next step in Carter's journey towards Lake Tanganyika.

We hit the road again, queued in traffic jams where there were building works, and wound up our windows to avoid choking on the dust. Elsewhere we drove along new roads that glistened with hazy mirages. Wolfe played Bongo Flava. I made call after call until someone eventually put me in touch with a professional safari hunter with rights to one of the hunting blocks close to the Itigi Thicket we hoped to reach the next day. The hunter said he wasn't in the area, so couldn't grant me permission to enter his concession, but yes, the main caravan trail used to run right through it. He said the local game wardens still found nineteenth-century slave shackles in the ground.

We kept on going, making for a town called Manyoni, where we planned to rest for the night. While Rem navigated the stop-start traffic, I scrolled through pictures on the hunter's website. In a 'Trophy Gallery', a white woman wore a freshly shot leopard around her shoulders. Dead lions were slumped on termite mounds. Sometimes a hunter held the mane, raising the lion's chin from the ground. I remarked to my two companions that it felt like a throwback, as if we'd never left the nineteenth century. Then Rem said something he hadn't mentioned before. When he was a young man, he'd worked as a gunbearer for another big-game hunter, a European, operating in central Tanzania.

He talked about how the tourists shot almost everything except wild dog, rhino and giraffe. They would make soup from the animals' tongues or tails. The main client would usually eat the fillet. Sometimes they'd eat the heart 'to show they were the king'. They would break up and boil the bones for the marrow, which the local people mixed with medicinal

On his 1909 East African safari, the former US president Theodore Roosevelt shot 296 animals, including nine lions. He was assisted by a team of 250 porters and guides.

An elephant shot down, Rutenganio, Tanzania, circa 1898–1914.

A 1908 photograph of the British governor of Uganda, Sir Hesketh Bell, surrounded by hunting trophies. By this time, big-game-hunting safaris were considered a fashionable pursuit for foreign visitors.

'Untitled hunter, trophy room #VII, Dallas, Texas, 2011', from the series 'Safari Club' © David Chancellor.

roots. 'Africans might keep the kudu horn,' said Rem. 'It can be used like a whistle. But we don't have a tradition of taking hunting trophies to hang on walls. Only foreigners do.'

We continued westwards to Manyoni – a highway town and trucker stop beside a wide road carrying goods from the lake regions to the coast. Manyoni had a frenetic energy to it, functioning as both a confluence in the centre of the country and a threshold to the remote western region. The smoke from café kitchens combined with the black belch of exhaust fumes. Drivers with bloodshot eyes picked over charred chunks of meat, and chips fried in beaten egg. It struck me that Manyoni's identity seemed to be defined by everything it wasn't, as if people were saying they'd rather be anywhere but here. It was a sentiment expressed in the roadside hoardings: Paris, Santiago Hotel, Caspian Café, Hotel Nile Falls, Paradise Lodge.

We turned in for the night, but any hope of sleep eluded me. Outside the bars of my hotel window, trucks kept rolling past, their cabs pulsing with the light of neon bulbs. Every few seconds, the bed shook in my pink hotel room, which was furnished with a Bible, a tattered mosquito net and a broken lock (a friend told me how, in her experience, Manyoni lodgings came with a communal jar of Vaseline and a sign that read 'Strictly No Prostitution'). When a tyre blew on an articulated lorry, it sounded like a gun going off. I peeked out from behind the curtain. A sex worker hustled for business, as delicate as a broken bird. She was drunk and trying to cross the road. The traffic noise drilled holes into my head until my skull felt like a beehive. The mechanics lining both sides of the highway welded through the night. The circular saws continued spinning. The blue sparks kept flying. I lay in bed listening to the muddle of voices caught up inside Manyoni's slipstreams of supply and demand – cogs in an age-old system, where individual lives felt as if they'd been hollowed out until they'd become as dispensable as burst tyres.

The next morning, we departed early to rejoin Carter's coordinates. On 23 September 1879, he rallied his caravan party for a 6.30 a.m. departure for Kanyenye, a small settlement to our south. In Carter's time, Kanyenye was significant – another Manyoni, where caravans stopped for supplies. The people kept large cattle herds and well-tended crops. But the hongo also ran notoriously high, earning the local chief his nickname 'the Croesus of the Ugogo'. It was a stage of the journey Carter was dreading. The financial health of his expedition was gnawing at his confidence. He'd already complained in a letter sent from Mpwapwa that the Belgians' agent-cum-banker in Zanzibar was refusing to advance him any money, or resupply his stocks of cloth for trading: '[S]tranded in the middle of Africa without an agent – manslaughter is a mild name for it.' He was almost halfway through his original hongo budget, and there was still no reassurance from Brussels that more financial support would be forthcoming. From correspondence passing between Leopold and his right-hand man, Colonel Strauch, it was clear the costs of the elephant enterprise were intended to be kept in check, especially now Stanley's expedition was beginning to bear fruit on the other side of the continent. For it was around this time that Stanley was making his first promising deal in Congo on Leopold's behalf. At Vivi, a hundred and fifteen miles up the Congo River, Stanley had persuaded five African chiefs to sign an agreement for a new trading station. Leopold would pay a monthly rent of two pounds (the equivalent of about three hundred pounds today), in addition to a one-off sum of thirty-two pounds (around five thousand pounds today), with both deals settled in cloth. It was the beginning of one of the most brazen land grabs in history – and with all eyes on Carter's elephant expedition to the east, no one except Leopold's inner circle in Brussels had any clear idea it was even happening.

Rem slowed down to point out our first sighting of the Itigi Thicket. Not long after, he pulled over to talk with two passers-by. They were Sukuma herdsmen, who cut striking figures against the dull grey thorn bushes flanking the road. The taller of the two sported an Arsenal football shirt and a jaunty pork-pie hat decorated with beads. His companion wore a beaded neck choker. The men were returning from making a

A 1900 photograph of a thorn thicket in Ugogo with a path cut through it. The German photographer Walter Busse, who captured this image, wrote how dismal the landscape looked: '[T]he ground, the bark, the twigs, even the lizards and monkeys seemed grey – the only evidence of life amidst a frozen deathly stillness'.

cattle delivery – a bride price for their sister. They accompanied me into a roadside patch of thorn – a tiny relic of what used to take caravans days to traverse, which I wanted to see for myself. In Carter's time, these briars caught at the bare soles of the caravan men. The thorns would also have been a constant source of distress to the elephants' feet, tenderized by the journey and having to carry heavy loads. The thicket was astonishing, as cruel as barbed wire, each stem reaching above my head. Among the harpoon spikes were scarlet flowers whose fragile stamens looked like coloured sparks flung from a Catherine wheel, or spots of blood.

In the next village, where we stopped to buy chapatis and fresh tomatoes, I got talking with an old woman, born in the 1930s. She said her name was Eda Mpwepwe.

'The thicket used to be very serious,' she said. 'I would pass through it, but on the edge. Now new people are coming who cut down the trees. They leave it empty. They leave us with a Sahara Desert.'

A small crowd of children had gathered to listen in. She arranged them so that they were seated in the shade, then went back to her house to fetch some pages from an old German book she kept under her bed. Though it was written by the Europeans, she said it was her most precious possession because it recorded her clan's lineage. Eda explained that, aside from the tree felling, the biggest threat to her community was wild elephants: 'There used to be lots of animals, including buffalo. Now there are only elephants – too many elephants – which raid the crops.'

I was struck by the fact this was the most I'd heard about the living animal since starting out in Carter's footsteps from the coast.

Gogo chief Henry Mtemi
Mazengo II.

Sukuma herdsmen on the edge
of the Itigi Thicket.

Eda Mpwepwe holding her clan
history.

Wildlife officer Kanunga
Namayan Marau.

'The size of an elephant's memory is our biggest challenge,' explained a wildlife officer called Kanunga Namayan Marau, who had joined the conversation. 'They memorize their old roads, their old tracks. Their migration routes pass through the farming plots where people now live.'

Kanunga explained how locals demanded compensation when their crops were destroyed. The villagers sometimes made revenge killings of elephants when the animals trespassed outside the hunting blocks and other protected areas the people now had to live alongside. Expanding communities were being compressed into increasingly vulnerable, smaller parcels along the fringes, especially now there was a new problem on the horizon: artisanal gold mining.

'Everywhere we're seeing digging on our patrols,' said Kanunga. 'People coming with headlamps and shovels from more than three hundred miles away. Is this area going to be protected in the future for mining, or for big-game hunting? I suppose the government will have to decide which has more value.'

Perhaps it was dread of the Kanyenye hongo that had taken Carter's eye off the ball, but on the very day the caravan started out for 'Croesus's' settlement, the remaining bull elephant in Carter's expedition began to show worrying signs of lagging. Naderbux was the animal Carter had come to rely on for carrying extra weight. His keeper said it was an attack of rheumatism caused by a cold, that Naderbux had been sickly before he left Bombay. He said the elephant had been for sale for months before Leopold took him off the Indian government's hands.

Carter decided to split up his men. He ordered Naderbux's baggage to be removed, and arranged a private escort for
the elephant under the command of his Arab caravan leader,
two mahouts and three soldiers. Naderbux could then travel
at his own pace behind the rest of the party and recover his
health. This would allow Carter to get ahead to negotiate the
upcoming hongo with 'Croesus.' But in the late afternoon,
after a long day's march spent worrying about his rheumatic
charge, Carter received a message from down the line: Naderbux's strength was deteriorating quickly. When Carter
hurriedly retraced his steps to join the rear party, he arrived
three hours later to find Naderbux lying crumpled on the
plain.

'His legs are folded under him in a very peculiar way,'
wrote Carter; 'his head rests on his tusks, and with mouth
wide open, he breathes heavily and noisily through his trunk.'
The elephant's stomach was 'rising and falling like bellows at
a forge.' Naderbux's usually limpid eyes were dull, as if they'd
retreated into his skull. The elephant was so weak that his
trunk coiled lifeless on to the ground – 'an inert mass of cold
flesh.' Setting his ear to Naderbux's ribs, Carter took note of
the elephant's heaving sides: '[L]ying down next to it, one
feels that the body is agitated, as if a large mechanical hammer
is working inside.'

Naderbux remained immovable for over five hours, the
pale pink flesh of his mouth gaping like an open wound.
Hyenas whooped with the encroaching gloom. Vultures circled overhead. In last light, as Naderbux lay surrounded by
faeces and urine in his hopeless distress, Carter asked his
mahouts whether there was any chance of recovery for 'the

poor lost beast?' When he got his answer, Carter made the call: '[T]he matter is obvious, I rid him of his ills with a shot.' The account brought Orwell's story back to me: 'It is a serious matter to shoot a working elephant – it is comparable to destroying a huge and costly piece of machinery – and obviously one ought not to do it if it can possibly be avoided.'

We don't know where Carter aimed his bullet; the placement differs based on the shooter's position and the angle of the elephant's head. Today's hunters are recommended to aim for the ear gusset, which gives a line into the back third of the brain – the part that controls breathing and motion. Shoot an elephant there, and its back legs will go down first, then it will just drop. A shot to the front of the brain – the part that controls logic and reasoning – is much less effective. Then there's the worst-case scenario: faced by an elephant that's trying to make its escape, the hunter should aim for a hip joint or the tail end of its spine first because an elephant can't run on three legs.

Carter, who had proved himself an amateur surgeon in Mesopotamia, no longer had Rankin in his personnel to perform the bloody autopsy. He sawed off the tusks for delivery to Leopold in Brussels. With the pace of the caravan's advance now of utmost importance, there wasn't going to be time for any deeper investigations. The keeper's revelation that Naderbux had been a poor purchase in the first place was going to have to suffice as an explanation. Besides, Carter needed the story to be just as the mahouts had claimed, that Naderbux was sick before he'd even left Pune. Perhaps Carter could also blame the delay in Mpwapwa which he'd railed so hard against. The millet stalks the elephants now relied on for food had lost their nutrition. Perhaps it was the recent diet of wild figs and rushes, or even the Ugogo water, 'so saturated with lime and impurities that it alone would be enough to kill an elephant', wrote Carter to his Belgian superiors. But even before Naderbux's death, Carter's style of management had started to be scrutinized as the root of his expanding problems. Leopold's man Strauch suspected Carter was 'a bit feverish and a bit demanding of mahouts and Indian servants'. If the elephant keepers had not been left so diminished from their marches, perhaps they would have been better able to care for their charges? Strauch suggested that Mackinnon should give Carter some 'friendly advice on how he should deal with staff'.

It was past midnight by the time Carter returned to camp. Had it been daylight, Carter noted, 'Croesus' would have claimed the ivory. But despite his best efforts to keep Naderbux's death a secret, the news trickled out. 'Croesus' sent his men to enquire 'how [the elephant] had dared to die in his territory without asking his consent'. He demanded someone from Carter's party consume a portion of Naderbux's flesh to prove that the elephant wasn't poisoned, which would mean yet another day's delay. By now, the caravan was over halfway to Lake Tanganyika, with exact details of where Carter needed to travel to next expected to be waiting for him in Tabora at least three weeks' march away. The seasonal rains would also soon arrive, making the going more difficult again. Carter was concerned about the lack of wild elephants to catch, which meant that the bigger ambition of a training school was looking increasingly remote. The situation was the opposite to the abundant herds everyone had been expecting. To make matters worse, it was evident from the tusks coming down the trading lines to the coast that the pace of ivory hunting in the interior was also going against them. If Africa's elephants were to be harnessed as the continent's 'civilizing' tool, it would have to be done fast, cautioned Carter; 'in a country like this, where there is no law to protect the elephant, like in India, these animals will be destroyed before long.'

Meanwhile, back in Brussels where news of Sundar Gaj's death was breaking, there were whispers about Carter's ability to pull off his commission. There was talk of going to George Sanderson, a specialist elephant-catcher based in India, though the cost of his hiring was prohibitive – fifteen hundred pounds a year just for him, which was four times Carter's salary. It was suggested that Leopold should cosy up again to his original first choice, Charles Gordon, and offer him 'the top management of elephant-related businesses'. But Leopold and his associates had wasted time with Gordon's flip-flopping conscience before. '[Gordon] is different from all the other men,' Mackinnon reiterated. 'If he doesn't like it, no amount of salary will tempt him to undertake it.' Kirk meanwhile continued to recommend finding suitable Africans to replace the Indian mahouts, insisting that it would be sensible to get a training strategy up and running as soon as possible. This chimed with Carter's complaint, that 'there is not a single mahout of Bombay' brave enough to get within a mile of a wild African elephant. But Mackinnon also now worried Carter would fail in 'wild elephant capturing experience if left to himself'. It was clearly critical to secure a level-headed second-in-command for him as soon as possible. Perhaps they should consider this English assistant Tom Cadenhead for whom Carter kept asking. '[A] quiet sober minded looking man of about 30 but hasn't anything like the physical vigour Carter has,' wrote Mackinnon; '[t]hey know each other thoroughly I understand and have been accustomed to work together so they are sure to agree and the one may help to tone down the other a little.'

Carter was feeling pressure from every direction. He was two elephants down. He was about to enter another vicious thorn thicket. The cost of provisions was going up with every day's advance further west, and Popelin was pulling rank, which not only wounded Carter's ego but made caravan management much more complicated. Most worrying of all, they were approaching territory that fell under the influence of powerful warring inland chiefs the likes of which Carter hadn't yet encountered. With so much on his mind, including a creep of self-knowledge about the ridiculousness of his situation, Carter sought to take back some control. A day of sport would be just the thing to retrieve some of his natural optimism.

At the threshold of the Mgonda-Mkali, not far from the settlement of Mdaburu, Carter took up his Winchester rifle – 'the truest little weapon I ever fired out of.' He shot a giraffe as it ran at full gallop, 'and, to my great delight, bowled him over', the animal falling 'like a huge minaret tumbling down'. He boasted about shooting so many hippos, the final numbers 'do not count.' When he took down another giraffe, it was a female measuring some eighteen feet in height, nursing a calf. Except Carter's aim was off. The bullet hit the animal's hindquarter so it died slowly, falling first into 'a very drunken trot, then a walk'. With the hunting over, the caravan devoured the giraffes' milk and blood, leaving Carter to enjoy giraffe soup. 'And very good it is', remarked Carter, 'like good beef.' When I retold this story as we drove towards Tabora, Rem remarked how, these days, the giraffe is treasured as

Tanzania's national animal. No one is allowed to kill one unless an exemption is granted by the president. As for elephants, they can still be legally hunted in parts of present-day Tanzania under special licence. As I watched the plains moving past our car window, I noted in my diary that we'd seen no elephants yet on the route Carter had taken, and already we were more than a month into our overland travels. Carter had spent close to three months on the same road, yet he too hadn't encountered a single elephant in the bush – and he'd *literally* hunted for them. This wasn't the parallel I'd been expecting with Carter's experience, nor Stanley's, who it turned out also hadn't seen elephants by this point when he'd come this way in 1871. As we kept on pressing west, the absence was beginning to haunt me. For Carter and everyone watching his advance, no one was ready to admit the dawning truth: expertise wasn't the only problem with Leopold's vision of elephants walking nose to tail down the trading lines; it was a simple lack of animals to catch and train.

8

The Land of the Moon

'. . . it is the drama of human endeavour that will be the thing, with a ruling passion expressed by outward action marching perhaps blindly to success or failure'.

—Joseph Conrad,
Geography and Some Explorers

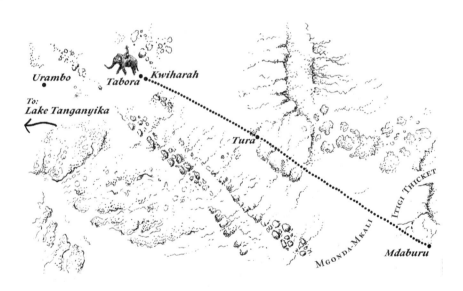

I HAVE A PHOTOGRAPH OF the landing strip from the last time I came to Tabora, when the small plane I was using needed to be refuelled. I was headed inland to report an anti-poaching story in a remote part of western Tanzania. While I sat and waited for my ride under the windless shade of a frangipani tree, Tabora had seemed to me little more than the sound of dry earth beneath the hurtling wheel-roll of a bush plane. But this time around, deep into my journey following Carter's elephants, I realized Tabora was far more interesting than it had first appeared to me.

In the nineteenth century, Tabora was considered one of the most significant towns on the inland caravan trails, in the kingdom of Unyanyembe, or Unyamwezi. It was the heart of 'moon' country, an image derived from the name of the people who traditionally dominate this region. The Nyamwezi, or 'People of the Moon', made up most of the long-distance, wage-earning workers on the caravan routes between the lake and Bagamoyo, with up to twenty thousand Nyamwezi a year travelling to the coast as porters. In other words, Tabora was once the navel of one of the greatest journeying cultures in East Africa. The Nyamwezi defined themselves by the places to which they ventured. 'A young man is looked upon as a milksop until he has made at least one journey down to the coast,' observed Bishop Steere; 'when he has, he is proportionately proud of it, and often takes back a new name in honour of his visit.' Pride in voyaging was imprinted in the Nyamwezi lexicon. Newborns were named after the position of the stars or the different phases of the moon.

It was this notion of moons – of being a long way from the familiar – which appealed to me when I made a return visit, this time following Leopold's elephants. I hoped for some uplift after the derelictions of Ugogo, some glimmering of enchantment. Stanley thought Unyamwezi 'a romantic name', as exotic as Istanbul or Isfahan to the foreign ear. 'Why is it called the country of the moon?' a missionary had asked a local chief. 'O[h]', he replied, 'I suppose it is because the Wanyamwezi worship the new moon; they fire off their guns nowadays, when they first behold it, but formerly there used to be great ceremonies and many rites observed on such an occasion.' To outsiders, Tabora felt remote and alluring. For the nineteenth-century science fiction writer Jules Verne, Tabora was where three Englishmen in a balloon landed on their journey to Central Africa. In his story, the Nyamwezi thought the balloon *was* the moon until the real one rose in the night sky.

I was in a good mood. The journey from what remained of the Itigi Thicket had been easy, following a smooth, new road. Every now and again, we'd encountered people selling fresh tamarind. Because of the changing season, the landscape had been getting greener. The mangoes were fattening, and soon the fruit would be as heavy and smooth as cricket balls. Wolfe's playlist had also improved now he'd abandoned any attempt of persuading me about the merits of singeli, a genre of breakneck electronic music from Dar es Salaam. From our vehicle's windows, the view expanded into a gentle contour of rocks etched against a pastel wash of sky. Up ahead, metal roofs glared like quicksilver in the sun.

For Carter's caravan, the approach to Tabora involved fifteen days of cutting their way through the 'cruel prickles' of the Mgonda-Mkali, which in places formed 'a vault bristling with spikes' above the elephants' heads. Hyenas prowled among the thorn bushes, trying to snatch porters while they slept. The country that lay between the thicket and Tabora was also in 'a horrible state of war' – 'a frightful den of iniquity and sin and the only place up here where Englishmen are not welcome', wrote an anxious missionary. Indeed, it's a miracle that any letters from the elephant expedition survived. In 1879, this section of the mail system kept breaking down, the precious missives left to rot in the open. The land was scarred with looted villages. In addition to the carcasses of hunted rhinos, there were the bleached skeletons of porters. The bandits would launch ambushes on passing caravans, mercilessly dispatching 'the stragglers and the cripples', wrote Cambier, the leader of the first, stumbling IAA expedition, who, not long before Carter, had travelled through the same region to set up a station at Lake Tanganyika.

It was only when Carter's caravan reached a stop called Tura, around eighty miles shy of Tabora, that he could sleep more easily. Soon he'd be getting news from Brussels. The Tabora landscape was also providing the elephants with more nourishing fodder, the fresh grazing doing Pulmalla and Sosankalli so much good that, within a few days, Carter declared the elephants were in better condition than when they'd left the coast. This opportunity to recuperate also gave Carter time to organize himself before making his entry to the famous Arab town of the interior. He wanted to give the right impression, to arrive 'in proper style', to borrow Stanley's phrase. The attention Carter won at Tabora would, after all, be reflected in the reports other travellers would inevitably deliver to the coast. 'His energetic face, his male voice, his physical vigour reminded me of the face of the famous Burton with whom Mr. Carter has several points of resemblance,' wrote an admiring Belgian who'd already encountered Carter and his elephants. Like Burton, Carter spoke Arabic 'admirably'; the Arabs on the road 'take him for one of their co-religionists'.

We settled into a hotel called the Orion, a Tabora landmark constructed around 1914 for the German Kaiser as a hunting lodge. Built close enough to the station to hear the train, it was suggestive of another place and time: a grand cream portico, broad verandas, rooms with high ceilings and an antique red postbox at reception. The Kaiser, it turned out, never made it this far before ceding his African territory to the British. Queen Elizabeth II never visited either. But in 1956, Princess Margaret came on an official visit, and spent a night at the Orion. Her arrival was greeted by a gathering of over forty thousand people. They staged a mock battle in her honour, with toy rifles, spears and shields, while Margaret looked on in her sunglasses, a sky-blue shantung silk dress and a dainty cornflower hat.

After emptying my bags of all the dust that had built up over the last few weeks, I headed out to Tabora's market. I needed to replace my worn-out shoes. I also wanted to absorb what Tabora had once stood for, to go deeper into a trading confluence most outsiders still fly over if they come this way at all. A boy in a bright white kanzu returning from his midday prayers offered to show me around. He was polite, precise, proud of his town. The main streets were wide and straight, flanked by low-lying buildings. There were echoes of

Omani architecture in the run of shopfronts, in the skyline marked with candy-coloured minarets. We meandered along shaded alleys, which fanned out in a labyrinth of stalls selling everything from live chickens and dried fish to flimsy footballs and Chinese electronics. The shoe stall was stacked with European and American brands – another world's spillover. A teenage boy squatted beside a bowl of soapy water, using a toothbrush to remove the grit from the sole of a Nike high top. There was a languid hum of conversation – nothing garrulous, just easy talk between people in a town small enough for faces to be familiar. And then a bus pulled into the station, and the tempo changed. Before it had even come to a complete stop, porters swarmed around the arrivals. Wheelie bags were passed out of bus windows, and children too. Taxis honked as roof racks were packed and unpacked in a noisy scrum.

I compared my experience of Tabora with the records of the 1870s. Back then, the market was busy with Swahili and Indian traders, and filled with the smell of hashish and clothes perfumed with sandalwood worn by the men from Muscat. 'A second Zanzibar,' wrote a European missionary. Goods cost five to six times what they might at the coast, but at least there was plenty of food, in the heaps of rice, sorghum, sugar cane, sweet potatoes and grapes that the Nyamwezi cultivated. But in 1879, Tabora was more than a land of milk and honey for replenishing caravan stocks. It was a major geopolitical hub in the path I was following, a vortex of African, Arab, Swahili, Indian and European interests.

By the time Leopold's elephants arrived, the closure of Zanzibar's slave market might have impeded Tabora's Arabs, but the business in human chattel was by no means over. Behind the surface abundance of Tabora and the other larger

Arab-Swahili settlements on the caravan road – including Ujiji to the west, and Bagamoyo to the east – there was a grimmer reality. Nineteenth-century European travellers described how traders still kept up to three hundred men and women to run each household. The enslaved would 'waddle about or rattle along with four or five fathoms of chain'. The clean facades and neat verandas screened 'a mass of dirty back slums ... a steaming mess of cesspools scarce hidden from the eye'. The other side to Tabora's wealth was the profits from ivory, with the biggest merchant of all the Arab-Swahili dealer and slave trader Tippu Tip.

Tippu Tip, pictured on the right. He was said to have earned his nickname from the 'tip-tip' sounds made by the fifty thousand guns at his command. His heavy-lidded eyes had a twitch to them, which was why he was also called 'the Blinker'.

One of Tippu Tip's ivory camps at Stanley Falls, in Congo, where he also served a brief stint as governor after Stanley recommended his appointment to Leopold in 1887.

In Tabora, the seemingly unstoppable flow of lucrative resources had created a knot of uneasy alliances. Through the early 1870s, the region had been marked by bloody Arab and Nyamwezi rivalry, guerrilla tactics and periods of parlous all-out war. By 1879, tensions had calmed a little; Tabora's Nyamwezi chief Isike had allied himself to Abdallah bin Nasibu, leader of the Tabora Arabs. But there were still some powerful interests at play, principally two other Nyamwezi chiefs, Mirambo and Nyungu-ya-Mawe, who were broadly responsible for the regional wars earlier in the decade. Mirambo's kingdom 'of ill defined limits' lay to the west of Tabora. Nyungu-ya-Mawe's territory lay to the east and south and included the 'fiery plains' the elephants had just passed through. Both men wanted a bigger share of the caravan trade for themselves – and they were prepared to make on-off-again alliances to get it.

In 1876 when Stanley met Mirambo, he'd expected the so-called 'Maker of Corpses' to be a 'terrible bandit'. He found instead a slight, handsome, soft-spoken teetotaller who stood a little under six feet tall. Stanley described him wearing a fez and carrying a scimitar. Others depicted him in a gold-embroidered Arab coat. Later reports described the chief in a traditional loincloth with a patched white jacket given to him by a missionary. He wore it slung nonchalantly over his shoulders, paired with a wisp of blue cloth tied rakishly around his forehead like 'a vulgar cattle keeper'. 'There is a large mixture of "don't care" about him and a reckless look which tells of a life of continuous daring and ever-changing fortune,' observed the British missionary Dr Ebenezer Southon, who in 1879 was busy settling into Mirambo's capital, Urambo, with permission from the chief. But Mirambo was also a brilliant military tactician, which was what Stanley meant when he called him 'the black Bonaparte'. Like Napoleon, Mirambo expanded his territory at an extraordinary pace. His gift was being nowhere and everywhere all at once. 'No one could tell in what district he would appear next; today he was at one place, yet yesterday he was forty miles south of it.'

In every new region Mirambo occupied, he'd appoint a ruler, then marry or kidnap a relation of theirs to ensure loyalty. He commanded a lethally effective army of disciplined fighters, or ruga-ruga, who were well armed with a combination of traditional weapons and plundered European muzzle loaders. His favourite soldiers were adolescents. '[Boys] have sharper eyes,' Mirambo had once told Stanley, 'and their young limbs enable them to move with the ease of serpents.' His men were almost fanatical in their mission to prove themselves. In return, Mirambo ensured the rewards were great, including the right to marry and accumulate wealth. 'Mirambo is the only man I fear very much,' commented another of the British missionaries; '[he] professes to be the friend of English men but it is only to make power for himself and make himself stronger.' At the peak of his career, Mirambo's rule extended over about fifty-five thousand square miles, reaching west, north and south of Tabora. 'Every passing year seems to draw nearer that desirable time when the inhabitants of Unyam-wezi shall be in one language, customs and religion,' wrote Southon. 'Mirambo is for the time being the most important man in Nyamwezi land,' observed Bishop Steere in 1879, 'but it would be premature to regard him as the head of a settled Kingdom.'

Chief Nyungu-ya-Mawe on Tabora's eastern flank had an equally fearsome reputation, although the details that have passed down to us are fewer. One-eyed and small of stature, Nyungu-ya-Mawe also commanded a ruthless army of ruga-ruga, which functioned as a hit squad of mercenaries. Many of them were enslaved people recruited from wars and caravans. He would refer to his men as *mapimpiti*, or 'logs' in the local language. 'Pile on more logs!' he'd shout, as he summoned his fighters. In grisly descriptions relayed by various travellers, his men wore 'ghastly finery', including caps made of human scalps, belts strung with human guts, and necklaces of his vic-tims' teeth. There was strict discipline in the ranks, with capital sentences swiftly issued to those who stepped out of line. Booty was meticulously shared among warriors and dispensed by Nyungu-ya-Mawe on a pro rata basis for bravery. Like Mirambo, he ruled with acute political intelligence, dividing his territory into different provinces led by lieutenants who adopted names such as 'Kafupa Mugazi' ('Spitter of Blood') and 'Kania Vanhu' ('Defecator of Men'). These deputies would police the territory and gather ivory for forwarding to Kiwele – Nyungu-ya-Mawe's headquarters in a country once richly endowed with elephants.

On his approach to Tabora, Carter had managed to dodge Nyungu-ya-Mawe's men – a stroke of luck, most probably due to fighting further south. Carter's explanation to his Belgian benefactors, however, was a little different: Nyungu-ya-Mawe had hidden himself deep in the interior along with his 'gang' because he'd learned that a European, 'accompanied by several elephants carrying cannons', was advancing to avenge the death of the British mission engineer, Penrose, who'd been skinned like a rabbit. Carter mocked the African chief in his letters for thinking his water pumps were heavy artillery. He claimed the announcement of the elephants' arrival was so awesome to the African mind, it was enough to purge the forest east of Tabora of all the ruga-ruga who 'infested' it. In reality, Carter was missing one of the most significant manifestations of indigenous East African power in the run-up to the 'Scramble'. In 1879, this swathe of country represented one of the last moments pre-colonization when two gifted African leaders almost bound together a huge, politically complex region. I was no longer seeing Tabora as dusty moon country, but a critical pivot in the way major history had been told, and silenced. Mirambo and Nyungu-ya-Mawe in particular had much more depth and agency than commonly ascribed by Europeans to nineteenth-century African figures of authority – a concept articulated as late as 1965 by Hugh Trevor-Roper, Regius Professor of Modern History at Oxford University: 'Perhaps in the future there will be some African history to teach. But at the present there is none, or very little:

there is only the history of the Europeans in Africa. The rest is largely darkness . . . And darkness is not a subject for history.'

The Orion hotel was more comfortable than any of us had anticipated. So we decided to rest for a few days, which would allow me to build a more complete picture of the town's former significance. I needed time to visit the Arab-style tembe, which was the house where Carter had stayed in the village of Kwiharah on Tabora's outskirts, courtesy of the Arab governor. For Carter, this pause in his journey was also a chance to take stock of his situation now that a clear message via the caravan mail system had reached him. Carter had direct orders from Leopold to go ahead and identify a good location somewhere between Tabora and the lake for an elephant capture and training school. 'Mature a plan of elephant stud,' instructed the king. It would make sense if the school was in easy proximity to the more permanent encampment Cambier was now building on the shores of Lake Tanganyika.

Each day, I wandered through Tabora looking for links binding past and present, exploring an easy, leafy town where the trill of bicycle bells was louder than the sound of cars. But my discoveries were disappointing. There were no memorials to the African experience of slavery, which was the trade that had helped secure Tabora's economic ascendancy in the first place. Aside from two suites in the Orion named after Mirambo and Nyungu-ya-Mawe, I came across no further mention of either of these two chiefs. The Arab history felt absent too, despite some of the Arabic trading names on shopfronts, buses and road hauliers. Slumping into a seat at the back of a restaurant which only served chips, I worried that the closest I was going to get to nineteenth-century Tabora was the conversation I'd had with a security guard in the Uluguru jungle. In Tanzania, it's customary to greet your elders with the Swahili word *shikamoo*, a term of respect I'd been using for weeks. The guard, who was from Tabora, told me it was an Arab word meaning 'touching your leg'. It evoked bowing to the oppressor, while the Arab response, *marhaba*, meant 'good', reinforcing the implied submission. The guard said *shikamoo* now carried a bad connotation among Nyamwezi people who knew their history in porterage on the caravan trails.

We drove out to the site of the tembe where Carter had stayed – a long, flat-roofed, terracotta-coloured bungalow hidden in a hamlet of homes at the end of a weave of unmarked tracks. In front of the tembe stood one of the largest mango trees I'd ever seen, with a parked motorbike taking advantage of the shade. I thought of Carter's arrival in the last days of October, and the expedition's two remaining elephants, Pulmalla and Sosankalli, resting under its canopy just like this.

'If that tree could speak', I remarked to Rem, 'what would you ask it?'

'I'd ask it to tell the truth', he said. 'How were the Africans treated?'

The tembe, now a small museum, was where Livingstone spent several months in 1871. 'On my honor [sic], it was a most comfortable place', Stanley wrote of his visit later that same year; '[o]ne could almost wax poetic'. He described the bungalow's thick mud walls, the kitchen shed and his personal quarters, which he furnished with an oxhide writing desk. His Arab hosts were well stocked with supplies, from spices, jellies, wine, sardines and salmon, to gold watches and

Persian carpets. 'This was real, practical, noble courtesy, munificent hospitality, which quite took my gratitude by storm.' The British explorer Verney Lovett Cameron also had flattering things to say about the constant stream of milk, gifts of fowls, eggs and goats, and 'dishes of well-cooked curry, far beyond the attainments of our own *cordon bleu*.'

For Carter, the Arab governor's welcome was just as he'd hoped from the culture he knew from Mesopotamia. He no longer had reason to complain in his letters to Cadenhead about 'bad food and in small quantities … What would I not give for a loaf of white bread, a potatoe [sic] and a chop or piece of beef. Oh Lord the thoughts of them make me so hungry that I have to eat a hunck [sic] of black dough.' He could finally take a break from his bush diet of pickled zebra tongues and salted giraffe steaks. You ate whatever protein you could get on the road, which for Livingstone had included an elephant's foot – 'a whiteish mass, slightly gelatinous, and sweet, like marrow.' In Tabora, however, it was a different story. There was always good butter. Honey was readily available, bound in bark containers. Carter was also among people with whom he could easily converse, including a new friend to drink with: a young Irish missionary called Charles Stokes who'd been passing close to Tabora when he'd heard rumours of Leopold's elephants. Easily distracted from more godly pursuits, Stokes set out to meet Carter at the governor's tembe, where the fellow Irishmen were delighted to make each other's acquaintance. In Carter's company, 'the fun never flagged for a moment.' With Stokes, Carter struck up an instant friendship of the kind he was well known for back home, entertaining with 'unusual brilliancy.' Carter also now had an opportunity to tell his story, and with two Indian elephants in tow, it sounded much more glorious than being the son of an Irish drunk who'd blown his brains out in a brothel. We all have a habit of reworking our pasts, recasting our motivations, blanking out the grey days and family histories we might prefer to forget. Carter was no different. In Tabora, his African adventure – retold in Stokes's letters home – was all about heroics.

Rem peeled off to find someone to open the museum. While Wolfe and I passed the time talking, I thought of Stokes and Carter trading memories in this very spot, of the Ireland they'd both put behind them. As the folk saying goes, 'In Ireland long ago there were good times, not your time nor my time but somebody's time.' I pictured Carter's pride at how his life had been transformed. '[T]his historical *tembè*, redolent with the memories of so many travellers in Central Africa' functioned like a monument to the titans of African exploration, wrote a British traveller shortly after Carter had passed through. The pedigree of the visitors' book would have tickled Carter's ego, his name now coupled with those of explorers like Burton whose fame had encouraged him to sign up to this commission in the first place. It's a story that is still hard to shift, which was evident when the museum's caretaker arrived and told tales of Europe's 'discovery' of Africa in more or less the same way as I'd heard them before, about the 'good' Christian explorers. In the rooms where Carter ate and slept, there were facsimiles of Stanley's *New York Herald* reports, a few iron shackles and a drawing of the tembe's fruit orchards. The cumulative effect began to seem more like an ode to European incursions than a challenge as to why the explorers had sought the hospitality of the slave traders they were meant to be here to expose. When Rem pointed this out, the

The museum at Kwiharah occupying the same site as the Arab tembe where Carter stayed. The caretaker is opening a display case to reveal an explorer's map.

caretaker nodded; he understood perfectly some of the European hypocrisies on show. I thought of Rem's line again, about what he'd ask the tree if it could speak. *I'd ask it to tell the truth. How were the Africans treated?*

I wondered if perhaps there was something relevant to my hunt in Tabora's Catholic archives. The first of the White Fathers – officially known as the Missionaries of Africa, founded in 1868 by the French Archbishop of Algiers – arrived here the year before Leopold's elephants. So I knocked on the door of Kipalapala seminary – a white, colonnaded building festooned in pink bougainvillea. The rector invited me to join a singing lesson with the trainee priests, then redirected my

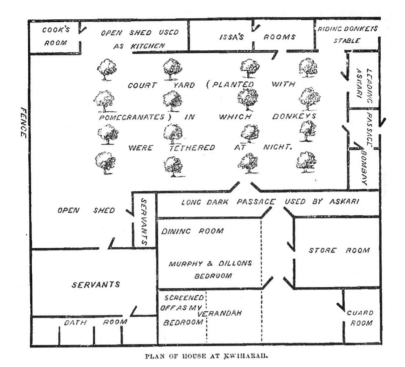

PLAN OF HOUSE AT KWIHARAH.

Cameron's plan of the Kwiharah house and orchard.

enquiries to the Catholic Church headquarters in Tabora's town centre. I'd noticed its neatly swept premises before, next to the spire of St Theresa's Cathedral. Nuns crossed to and fro with wimpled heads and tidy shoes, heels clacking on the paved courtyard. When I did as the rector advised and sought their help, one of the senior sisters told me that, before asking her for anything, I should dress appropriately (I was wearing trousers that Rem said looked like pyjamas). Another nun told me to come back when she'd had a chance to seek permission from the archbishop. I pushed harder, despite the sister's sartorial reproaches. Telephone calls were made. More calls tinkled on mobile phones. Finally, a cheery, sympathetic nun from Uganda let me into the archives for a couple of hours under her careful supervision. I understood why, given how history can be stolen. In Zanzibar, listed archives had gone missing. Among nineteenth-century papers I'd encountered in London, it wasn't uncommon to see letters with an explorer's signature torn off (usually Stanley's), which was the result of autograph hunters in pursuit of memorabilia.

Tabora's early Catholic records turned out to be thin on Leopold's expeditions but abundant in tales about slavery. Among the material – which included an impassioned tussle with an African bishop who refused to send his archives to Rome – there were allegations about forced labour at missions, and numerous German-issued 'Certificates of Freedom'. The local names of the enslaved included 'Lupande', which the letter writer translated as 'a piece of cloth'; 'Mlekana' meant 'a woman separated from her family'; 'Nyanzila' meant 'the one who makes a path on the road with her feet'. There was a 1913 note about an enslaved woman called Maria Wantiho who had only fifteen rupees to her name, which wasn't enough to buy her freedom (her value was fixed at forty rupees, according to a letter to Tabora's magistrate). And some 1922 correspondence from a British official informing Tabora's White Fathers that the government wasn't going to issue any more 'Certificates of Freedom from Slavery': '[They] have all been told by me that they are free to do as they please now ... [to] remain with their late master, or otherwise.' These redemption schemes, which included compensation fees paid to former slave owners, had been active in East Africa since the 1870s. Yet still the trade endured. In a letter from 1924 – more than fifty years after the treaty designed to end slavery in the region – a British official asked the mission for more information about two enslaved children who'd been sent to him to deal with.

'Can you tell me anything of their history?' he enquired.

At 8 a.m. on 28 October, Carter assembled his caravan outside the Kwiharah tembe with unusual good humour. Not since leaving Dar es Salaam had the elephants been dressed in their scarlet and black trappings brought from India. The intention was to walk into the heart of Tabora as a grand procession. It would be an act of diplomatic pomp to foster Arab–European relations, and a PR stunt to burnish not just Carter's ego, but Leopold's reputation too. It was a function Pulmalla and her mahout, Bonheti, were used to from their ceremonial work in Pune. Bonheti had Pulmalla kneel to the floor to be mounted by the party's four Europeans: Captain Popelin, the feverish Dr Van den Heuvel, a well-barbered Carter and his irreverent new friend, the Irish missionary Charles Stokes. The Arab governor refused a seat on Pulmalla's back. By Carter's admission, this was probably a good thing. The burden of four men was already 'much too heavy a load for the poor old lady'.

Off they went to the beat of the caravan's drum, with Pulmalla tailed by a riderless Sosankalli. At every Arab home the Europeans passed, they were presented with 'more than was good for us' wrote a rueful Carter, who took his fill of the sugared vermicelli, cakes and tea. Curries were presented in abundance, on china plates. The elephants were given treats too, earning delicacies with each party trick they performed, which included bidding 'salaam' with their trunks at the gates of the biggest Arab homes. As the day wore on, the crowd expanded, drawn by the elephants' bright livery and the howdah carrying four men in polished boots, but most of all by the strange sight of elephants behaving as obediently as donkeys. For Carter, the reception was nothing short of jubilant – 'hundreds and hundreds of men, women and children shouting, screaming and laughing'. 'It was a day never to be forgotten by the people of Tabora,' he reported back to Brussels, seeding a quote widely repeated in Belgian newspapers. Leopold was thrilled. 'Good news for elephants!' he messaged Strauch. It was just the kind of story the king needed to deflect any meddling attention from Stanley, to whom new funds were being funnelled all the time. While Carter was putting on his show in Tabora, Stanley's advance up the Congo River was about a hundred miles along. Having negotiated a treaty with the chiefs of Vivi, Stanley was now putting pressure on the king's purse strings as he enacted plans for the station he needed to build, comprising houses, stables, blacksmiths' stores and a two-thousand-square-foot garden. 'The place looked so devoid of grace and completeness without,' said Stanley, whose extravagances and slow progress were now agitating his benefactors.

Meanwhile, Tabora's hearts and minds were being won for Leopold, or so claimed Carter. 'News of the elephants have gone right through Africa,' he wrote to Strauch. Carter recounted a story of a man who told everyone how the elephants would just lie down and beg 'the big master' for more weight – 'one of the thousand exaggerated stories floating about regarding the power of the white man over the elephants'. In his letters home, he wanted everyone to understand how the sight of trained elephants seemed like a miracle to the Nyamwezi, that the sensational concept of these animals being ridden was something Africans hadn't ever encountered before. The expedition had 'already given more of a footing to Europeans than the thousands and thousands of pounds spent up to the present in trying to civilise the country. The Africans say as Europeans can make elephants obey them they can do anything.' It was a messianic symbolism that Carter encouraged Stokes to communicate in correspondence with his London superiors: 'Capt. C. asked me to write home to you on the subject and I hope you will make the matter public.' No matter that two of the Indian elephants were already dead. From the outset of his journey, Carter had hoped that Europe's mastery of the continent would date from "'the year of the Elephants".' 'The spectacle of the elephants tamely and docilely obeying the will of a white man appears to have struck the imagination of the people of these countries,' Strauch wrote to Mackinnon. 'It to them has caused an impression analogous to that experienced at another time by the natives of America at the sight of the guns of the Spaniards.' Here then, an explicit indication, not of trade, not of civilization, but of conquest – a grand statement that assumed Africans were too moonstruck to exercise their own agency.

Perhaps because he was so caught up in the pageantry, Carter was oblivious of the ironies. His Arab-friendly expedition relied on the very slave traders Leopold declared his explorers were marching forth to suppress. Carter completely ignored this double standard when he wrote to Brussels with news that Sultan Barghash of Zanzibar had ordered local authorities 'to place themselves and all they had at my disposal.' He boasted about how easy it was for him to arrange the purchase of a piece of land for Leopold's men to build a new base at Tabora that Van den Heuvel could oversee. Carter, whose fluency in Arabic had now pushed him back up the expedition pecking order, seemed under the impression that everyone wanted him here in the middle of Africa, as an emissary for a powerful foreign king. There were even rumours that the mighty Mirambo was sending an embassy to Carter, along with fifty elephant tusks, to persuade him to settle in his country.

But Carter was being played. His belief that Mirambo was in thrall to this elephant parade was as dangerous as his mocking of Nyungu-ya-Mawe for thinking the expedition's water pumps were cannons. Carter's affection for Arab culture also didn't take account of the venal realities in Tabora. 'All the Arabs up here have an idea that I am come as English consul to Central Africa,' he wrote to Strauch – a misconception Carter relished given the humiliation of his short-lived tenure as vice-consul in Basra. The Tabora Arabs might have tolerated Carter with his close ties to their language. They might have offered food, shelter and gracious welcomes. But the goodwill extended no further. Tabora's traders didn't like the Europeans with their brash assumptions of superiority. Their new religion and stance against slavery made them a threat to profit margins. Tabora's Arabs already had enough of a problem keeping ruga-ruga off their ivory without these newcomers hustling for a share. As for all the rumours of a hearty African welcome, the fifty tusks from Mirambo never did materialize.

There was a miasma lingering over Tabora – that 'bad air' regarded by Europeans as the cause of malaria. 'Sleepy fever' was also prevalent, from the bite of the tsetse, and it was affecting Carter's men. Over thirty of them were laid up with illness, lying among the scattered trees surrounding the tembe. Then a grim prognosis from the expedition doctor indicated that another of the mahouts was going down, this time with stomach cancer. But the nuances failed to travel some four thousand miles to Strauch's office on Brussels' Rue de Namur. Leopold was buoyed up by the fact Carter's advance was progressing at a quicker pace than Stanley's. With only a couple of hundred miles to go before the elephants reached Lake Tanganyika, the project's relative successes justified the hiring of a new second-in-command. With some progress to show for his investments, Leopold was finally willing to pay out for the back-up Carter had been pushing so hard for from the start: his friend, Tom Cadenhead, who'd been at Carter's side on the river Tigris in Mesopotamia.

On our last evening in Tabora, I headed back to our hotel, passing the town's high-walled boma – a Swahili word for 'homestead', also used for colonial garrisons. The boma in Tabora had a hulking profile dating from the first German administration. During the First World War, they had moved their headquarters here from Dar es Salaam because of the risk of naval attack by the British. This remained the status quo until 1916, when the colonial army of the Belgian Congo advanced into German East Africa and annexed Tabora. When the continent was cut up once again by Europeans in the aftermath of the Kaiser's defeat, the British began building colonial bungalows on Tabora's Ulaiya – or Europe – Road. They added staff quarters, borders blooming with white lilies, and well-watered lawns. They planted flame trees, which were always scattering their crimson petals. Children played in the gardens. Dalmatians lazed on the grass. Africans, however, weren't allowed to walk down Europe Road unless they had deliveries to make.

Under the veil of twilight, I picked my way among some

of the semi-derelict buildings in the old colonial neighbourhood. For the most part, I kept my back to the German boma,
which I found unsettling. It stood on a slight incline as an
eerie projection of power, its heavy presence emphasized by
the long shadows of dusk and an alley of mango trees narrowing to a vanishing point. Then came the swell of evening
insect life, and the song of a rainbird – the hubble-bubble
rising and falling. As the light petered out, I was spooked by a
marabou stork standing beside a broken window, the floor
strewn with splintered glass and purple jacaranda blossoms.
At an old German hospital, a painted red cross was peeling off
the wall. I picked up a hollowed egg, its shell as thin as paper,
which must have fallen from one of the weaverbird nests.
Normally this would have fired up Rem's naturalist's instinct,
but he seemed unusually disconnected. As I pulled back a
door drooping from its hinges, I could sense him retreating
from the work I wanted to do; he simply wasn't interested in
the grubby corners of Tabora's colonial past.

'You're poking around a history the Africans are happy to
give up on,' he said. 'Why should we keep it? What for?'

We went back to our hotel, where I got talking with a
British woman who'd known Tabora for many years.

'There used to be quite a scene,' she remembered. The
town once had a Gymkhana Club – for as long as the Europeans had been here, there'd been a gymkhana tradition – and
an eighteen-hole golf course. But those days had gone. She
described how tobacco and sisal had once brought foreigners
this far west. So yes, she'd known other Europeans in the years
she'd lived in Tabora. But she was among the very few who'd
stuck it out. Not enough for them to do, she suggested with a
half-smile.

*A German colonial officer takes a leap on the back of a tame
zebra in German East Africa, circa 1910. The idea of riding zebras
across Africa was suggested by a French geographer in the 1870s –
another fanciful solution to the transport problem in Africa.*

I peeled away for dinner in the hotel garden, where I got
talking with a group of American missionaries who said they
worked with some kind of 'saving' Africa NGO. 'Saving Africa
from what?' I wondered. I listened to a white woman describe
why she was taking her children out of their school in another
part of East Africa to be educated in a classroom where there
were more white people. She was drunk, but the sentiment
underlying her words was ugly and real. As the night pro-
gressed, I talked with a big-game hunter who was on his way
to a swamp in western Tanzania to bag a sitatunga – a rare
marsh-dwelling antelope with striking spiral horns. Wolfe
and I had discussed it often on this trip, how sometimes it felt

as if the colonial times weren't over at all, as if the surface politics had changed, but not the attitudes of the old guard still stuck in their ways. But that evening something inside me shifted. On this journey, I was learning that we're all prone to self-deception, and will convince ourselves it's the only truth. We become more entrenched in our views by way of defence. That's what Orwell's 'Shooting an Elephant' is really all about. Every one of us is beleaguered by misapprehensions of one kind or another, but some of those self-deceits are more extreme, more psychotic, more fanciful, more deliberate, more hateful, more seductive, more demagogic, more venal, violent and dangerously ideological than others. But what also makes us human is our conscience, of which self-criticism is part. We can listen to our conscience or choose silent complicity with an uncomfortable truth. In his 1992 Saharan travelogue, *Exterminate All the Brutes* – an original meditation on Conrad, Leopold's Congo and the Holocaust – the Swedish author Sven Lindqvist remarked: 'You already know enough. So do I. It is not knowledge we lack. What is missing is the courage to understand what we know and to draw conclusions.'

In the Orion's ill-lit bar, two staff in white shirts lingered in front of a run of bottles that looked as if they hadn't been poured in a while. There were signs on the blood-red wall, including pub rules about the bar being a good place to hide from your wife. In a corridor off the lobby, there were noisy African grey parrots in cages, and two amorous tortoises in a scrubby enclosure nearby. When I turned in for the night, I could hear the mocking call of the caged birds and the slow *pah-pah* of the copulating tortoises panting with an asthmatic wheeze. I pulled the curtains across my wire-meshed window. After I'd lowered the mosquito net before settling down to sleep, I found I couldn't get comfortable. The ceiling fan slapped the air in a slow, heavy beat, drowning the sound of the tortoises outside. Everything was beginning to taste and smell a little bit different. The rain was coming. The season was about to change.

9

Chief of Chiefs

'Let me tell you more about the voice that my mother gave me. First it was oral. All languages are oral. The literary always mimics the oral. At night and around the fireside, this voice reached me in the form of stories. We were told that stories went away in daytime. Where did they go? We didn't know. Fortunately, they always came back in the night, after all the chores of the day.'

—Ngũgĩ wa Thiong'o,
'African Literature . . . Says Who?'

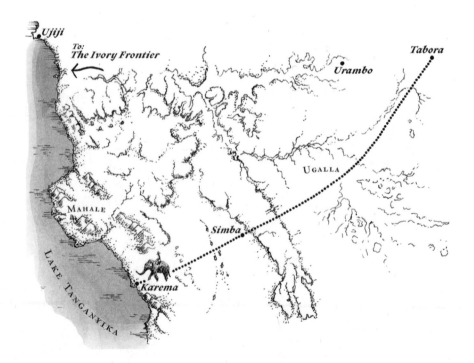

O N 5 NOVEMBER 1879, a week after the elephant parade through Tabora, Carter's caravan left the tembe at Kwiharah to complete the final two hundred miles to the lake. Popelin's expedition doctor, Van den Heuvel, was staying behind to get started on a new IAA station. As for the rest of Popelin's caravan, it had left Tabora a couple of days ahead of the elephants. With the power struggle between Carter and Popelin worsening, they agreed that two smaller travelling parties would be more flexible than one large one.

Both men were following the latest instructions received in Tabora. They were to join Leopold's IAA man Cambier, who had left Bagamoyo sixteen months earlier for a lakeside village called Karema (a journey which took Cambier 'about a year and a half in what two months ought to have seen finished', sniped Kirk). Popelin's task was then to proceed from Karema to the ivory honeypot of Nyangwe in Congo, while Carter was to focus on wild elephant capture within a reasonable distance of Cambier's location.

From Brussels' point of view, the outlook for all these projects was looking positive in spite of the two dead elephants. Cambier had successfully signed a deal with Karema's 'miniscule potentate', in the words of Leopold's chief propagandist, for a 'few hundred acres with the authorization to settle'. As a result, Leopold's IAA ambitions were becoming more precise. Meanwhile, the king and his cronies were also tightening the framework around Leopold's other developing interests on the continent, including at Vivi where Stanley was finally constructing his first river station. In one of his most cunning moves yet, Leopold persuaded the international subscribers of his Comité d'études du Haut-Congo to dissolve the committee paying out for Stanley's Congo explorations. It was a deal Leopold presented as a chance for them to cut their losses (he would repay their original investments) when in fact he just wanted Stanley's Congo gains all for himself. In the Comité's place, Leopold established the International Association of the Congo – a newer, even more shadowy organization, which deliberately carried a name easily muddled with the International African Association, but free of its pesky 'philanthropic' constraints.

In fact, by the time Carter had started out from Tabora for this final stage, Leopold had his men better lined up than they had been for months: Stanley in Congo; Cambier at Karema; and Carter's and Popelin's caravans both advancing to the new IAA station at Lake Tanganyika. The two female elephants, Pulmalla and Sosankalli, were also well rested for the last push. The next part of their journey would take a line through a fan of seasonal caravan trails that shifted with the rains, the movements of the wild elephant herds and the hunters who tailed them. It was decided that the party would head south by southwest, avoiding Mirambo's capital of Urambo in favour of making quick progress. Carter would then skirt the edges of Ugalla, a region far less trodden than the road to Ujiji, which was the most significant Arab-Swahili town on the lake. Another advantage of this southerly route was that Carter would pass through Simba, a settlement of around three thousand people named after an eponymous Nyamwezi chief. There was hope Simba could be the right spot to start some elephant capture work since this was where Stanley had reported seeing his first large herd on his 1871 journey to the lake. The beginning of an end lay in sight. 'It's a triumph,' reported Brussels' newspapers. Hopes were running high that the African transport problem would soon be a thing of the past as the Asian elephants employed to start a training school continued to prove immune to the tsetse.

But there was a counter-narrative which everyone except Kirk was still missing: the scale of Nyamwezi power. It was a reality Cambier's party had disregarded on almost every level, from mismanaging hongo payments to putting porters in chains. When Cambier had visited Mirambo's capital the previous year, it had turned into a political disaster. He was 'practically kept ... as a prisoner' for three months, reported one of the missionaries, and his goods held hostage. When Cambier told Mirambo he wasn't fond of noise, and asked him to tone down his song and dance, Mirambo branded him a fool. Before long, Mirambo had confiscated Cambier's gun as if he were a child. 'There is Cambier not yet at Ujiji rustling up in a fright at Mirambo who laughs at him,' remarked Kirk. 'Other men go to Mirambo and find him an honest fellow but he must be met by a man.' When one of Cambier's party had started measuring human skulls adorning a village entrance, accusations of witchcraft began to circulate. Omens began to proliferate. When Cambier eventually got going again, he described earth tremors 'preceded by a noise comparable to that of a heavily loaded cart rolling rapidly.' The locals explained what was happening. 'They told me that it was the soul of a long deceased Sultan that passed underground and that his passage announced the imminent death of an important personage.'

But not all responsibility for deteriorating relations with the Europeans could be laid at Cambier's door. The situation was exacerbated by a Swiss trader called Philippe Broyon – a mercurial character born in the Rhône Valley who had joined a boat in Marseilles and ended up in Zanzibar. He quickly learned several local languages, and cut deals with African chiefs as their European interpreter. By the time Carter showed up, Broyon was regarded as one of the best-travelled caravan specialists in the East African interior. He made Mirambo gunpowder and helped sell his ivory at the coast. He married an African woman, whom Broyon liked to claim was one of Mirambo's daughters. He even signed his letters 'Philippe Broyon-Mirambo.' But Broyon got greedy, and after pocketing the money from one of Mirambo's ivory runs, he ramped up relationships with various missionary organizations to transport church supplies inland instead. An incandescent Mirambo sent a party of men to confiscate everything in the next caravan Broyon organized, which left the missionary in the advancing party, a young Yorkshireman called Arthur Dodgshun, almost destitute. The strain of the whole encounter was such that Dodgshun died just a week after finally reaching Tanganyika. 'There never seems to be any "last words" before death amongst African travellers,' wrote an LMS colleague who tended him on his deathbed, 'but Dodgshun was <u>ready</u>.'

A polite letter was sent by the mission to Mirambo distancing the organization from Broyon's actions and asking for their possessions to be returned. But while Mirambo may have been willing to de-escalate this particular situation, he was famously sensitive to any slights. Thanks to Broyon, all foreign flags were now held in suspicion, bordering on enmity. The fact Broyon was Swiss added to the increasing muddle of European nationalities, which at times were as confusing to Africans as the Nyamwezi chiefdoms were to Europeans. The antipathy was in no way surprising, said Kirk. Mirambo was 'grossly ill used if not cheated by Broyon', and between this and Cambier's naivety, everyone on the caravan road was now dealing with the consequences.

But it would be too simplistic to think Mirambo was only motivated by injured feelings. Mirambo wanted to understand the Europeans he was beginning to see so much more of. In fact, it was in order to help patch up the Dodgshun affair that he had given permission for another missionary, Dr Ebenezer Southon, to settle at his capital in August 1879. Before long, Mirambo made Southon a blood-brother – a traditional ceremony in which a few drops of blood were exchanged between the men, rubbed on with butter – just as he had with Broyon and Stanley before him. Having lost his conduit into European affairs with Broyon, Mirambo now nurtured Southon as his interpreter. Southon's skills as a surgeon also proved useful in digging bullets out of Mirambo's men. Mirambo even talked about sending one of his sons to England, to train as a doctor. The respect seemed to go both ways. In Mirambo, Southon found a man with 'an intelligent desire to know and understand things'. '[Mirambo] handles a new thing as thoughtfully as a skilled mechanic,' remarked Southon, describing how Mirambo would watch him repair his musical box; 'He appeared to weigh well every word.' Southon also showed Mirambo how to write his name – a

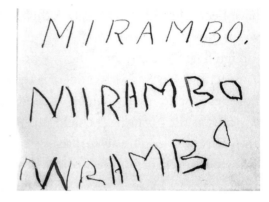

Top left: *The only known surviving photograph of Chief Mirambo. There are numerous reports, however, of his sartorial flair, which combined elements of Nyamwezi, Arab and European dress.* Top right: *Mirambo's first attempt at writing in September 1879. Southon wrote the top line of Roman characters on an envelope, which he described Mirambo copying 'fairly well' underneath.* Above: *Nyamwezi porters on the caravan route.*

signature that survives on a matchbox-sized piece of card in a London archive.

We left Tabora early, the town washed in a watercolour sunrise, having been joined by an old friend, a naturalist called Richard Knocker who had wanted to see Ugalla for some time. I'd worked with him before in northern Tanzania, and still had my notepads full of his colourful aphorisms. 'Lions have their own myth but elephants up close, it's something spiritual.' The hornbill is 'a pick-axe with a brain.' The blister beetle is 'the Ziggy Stardust of the bush.' As the sun lifted, clumps of bright white cloud hung suspended in the pale blue sky. The road was smooth, at least at first, with new asphalt stretching out west in a slick, oily sheet. As always, we wanted to keep close to Carter's coordinates, even when they were awkward or unclear. With Wolfe plotting the route, we soon wound south by southwest, hitting rougher road as we started to penetrate the wilderness region of Ugalla. Until very recently, access to the heart of this ecosystem had been limited to big-game trophy hunters. But my luck was in. Just before I'd arrived in Tanzania, the authorities had flipped Ugalla's protected status into a national park for tourists – the kind who carry cameras, not guns.

With nowhere to stay, we'd have to camp. So I got in touch with Ismail Omari – a Tanzanian conservationist newly assigned as Ugalla's head of anti-poaching. Ismail said he would help guide us through the area. He mentioned he could also connect me with a Nyamwezi chief who could tell me some history. He added that the chief would expect a gift for sharing his knowledge, so Ismail suggested we should buy him a goat. I also had with me

Southon's rare nineteenth-century account of the wider region based on numerous interviews with Mirambo – an unpublished history, which reads like reportage, peppered with detailed observations about a landscape even less travelled now than it was in 1879.

We pulled off on to a local road and wound past tobacco farms, rice fields and village shambas, or farming plots – country 'royally prolific in vegetation', according to Southon. We were being pursued by clusters of black tsetse that stuck like hot tar to our closed windows. The fly thrives in the dry, crackling miombo – a nutrient-thin native woodland held together with tap roots nearly as deep as each tree is tall. After a few hours of journeying, we reached the Ugalla River. Travelling in convoy with Ismail and three armed rangers, we followed the meandering line of water. A canoe darted out of our view like a dragonfly – a local fish poacher, said Ismail. Hippos snorted their surprise. The river expanded and uncoiled into a ribbon of loops, pools and oxbows, then widened in the open flatlands, studded here and there with salt licks and pom-pom-headed Borassus palms. Tall termite nests looked like giant snorkels poking out of the sandy loam.

The landscape was instantly recognizable from Southon's descriptions. Open-billed storks with nutcracker beaks picked at mussel shells on the riverine beaches where crocodiles were sunning themselves on the sand. On the far edge of the river plain, there was an acacia forest with a high browsing line being clipped by giraffes. I took a photograph, but my motion broke the spell. When one of the giraffes spooked, the whole herd fled, their slow canter falling into a kind of syncopated rhythm with the scattering of antelope. The effect was mesmeric. Birds took flight. The sky shimmered. More animals joined the gentle panic rippling across the plain. We kept our distance, watching the commotion rise and fall away as the animals returned to their grazing. Impala tails ticked like metronomes in the dappled shade of the jackalberry trees. Young warthogs darted through the grasses, their tails stuck up like the aerials on radio-controlled toy cars. Rem sparkled with whispered insights. Did I know palm swifts slept on the wing? That they glue their eggs to palm fronds to stop them being blown about in the wind? Then a creature appeared, looking as if it had just stepped out of Narnia, with a blazed face and flexed neck, like a horse held tightly on the bit. Its backward sweep of horns was drawn sharp against the sun. It was a glorious black sable antelope bull – the first my friend Richard had seen in over a decade.

In a few weeks, everything would change. The rains would soak into every inch of this thirsty ground, the water turning the termite towers – some reaching back hundreds of years before even Carter came through – into little islands of life in this seasonal floodplain. White tide marks circled the trunks of palms. When the levels rose, the grazing trails radiating out from the hippo pools would be rubbed away. Ismail explained how people had used this land for millennia, living on it lightly, making their own paths which came and went with the rains. It was only under the colonizers that communities were pushed out to make 'protected' wildlife areas, which included designating land for a big-game hunting industry for foreigners. He showed us a riverside glade where those hunters' kills were butchered and skinned. There was just enough left of the camp's infrastructure to identify a trail of scattered bones. There had been a plan for us to sleep in the same location, but Ismail said he didn't care for the ghosts. He didn't want to think about what had been shot when there were so few animals left. He was against hunting, despite the counter-arguments that the high fees were meant to go back into the conservation of remote wildlife areas where mainstream tourists would never go. He explained how big-game hunting was allowed in almost a third of the country – including on the other side of the river we were following.

We found a hippo's skull with its incisor teeth removed. Ismail said poachers took the teeth for traditional amulets in the belief it made them invisible in the bush. Locals also collected latex from strangler figs to trap wild birds. In addition, there was pressure on the landscape from Sukuma pastoralists who were slashing and burning bush in search of new grazing. When Ismail first arrived, he said there had been trouble with a violent criminal gang, the Sanjo, nicknamed the Lost Boys; for some time, the Sanjo had been living inside the protected area, which was against the law. Like the ruga-ruga of the nineteenth century, they smeared their bodies in animal fat, which the Sanjo believed offered protection from bullets. They had also acquired a sinister reputation for killing albino people, whose body parts they allegedly used in rituals.

We put up our tents in a puddle of green forest where birds with brightly coloured neckties flitted through the leaves. We then cooked dinner in the shade of a 'rhino-rib' tree, the bark evoking the animal's thick grey hide. Around the camp-fire, our pace slowed. The fire flickered. We listened to branches snap as animals moved through the night. A troop of baboons shook the canopy above our heads. I worried about the venomous black mamba snake that had crossed the track in front of us earlier in the day.

Each evening, we followed more or less the same routine. We drew in closer, the conversation loosening around the fire, our talk broken by natural silences when an animal's alarm call ricocheted through the forest. As a salt-white moon began to swell over the river, we recalled what we had seen each day, and what we hadn't. The moon's borrowed light dipped us in a silver glow. It was beautiful and serene, but I was also haunted by what was missing – insights into how the landscape had changed, which I was able to glean from experiencing the region side by side with Southon's records. There simply wasn't the same abundance of mahogany and teak that Southon described. We encountered numerous flowering plants – in Southon's words, 'exceedingly beautiful' with 'exquisite perfumes' – but some of the lagoons were choked with an invasive water hyacinth. Like Southon, we could hear the 'woo-u' of hyenas – 'something like maniacal laughter . . . slurred, in a peculiar manner.' But we encountered no lions, which used to be common. The locals believed the lion's fat was a preventative against being bitten by a tsetse, wrote Southon. The lion's claws were filled by the Nyamwezi with magic powder and worn as amulets, while the lion's heart was 'the sole property of the reigning king and by him alone it is eaten.' As for rhinos, they were already on their way out in 1879. 'King Mirambo told me that a few years ago they were plentiful,' wrote Southon, 'but since the people got guns they hunted it so much that now it is rare to meet with one unless far north.'

On our last night, we all fell under the spell of a master storyteller – a ranger called Baltazary Gitamwa Boa. He talked about his childhood, remembering how he'd learned not to fear wild animals: 'Sometimes when I was young, I'd see a leopard sleeping close to get warmth from our fire. I realized we could be together.' He was bemused by Carter's story: 'It is not our culture to ride on an elephant's back.' As we shared meat cooked over the lick of flames, Baltazary talked about his father, who had twelve wives and fifty children, and was a traditional healer. The clan 'rainmakers' could make it rain, but Baltazary's ancestor could also make it stop. 'Nowadays people say to these healers: if it's true, then why don't you people stop the floods in Dar es Salaam? Even the government could pay you!' As if on cue, the sky began to spit, and everyone laughed.

Left: *Baltazary Gitamwa Boa, one of Ugalla River National Park's conservation rangers.* Right: *Ismail Omari in Ugalla River National Park.*

In 1879, the rains were also beginning to put pressure on Carter's journey. He needed to hurry up, to take the most direct route possible to Karema. But speed was denied him when, two days after leaving Tabora, Sosankalli's eyes started to water with fat, gloopy tears. Two days after that, a white film began to stretch across each orb. Within hours, Sosankalli was completely blind, stumbling with every step she took. Carter ordered her loads to be removed. But when he questioned his mahouts about her health, they had nothing to report: Sosankalli was eating as usual.

The caravan ground to a halt as Carter ordered a rest day for Sosankalli. Pulmalla was doing fine, so perhaps that was all it was – a funny turn for Sosankalli that would improve if Carter took things a little slower. The following day, finding her in much the same state, Carter had his men carry Sosankalli's load to the next camp, where again, the expedition was forced to delay. This time, the pause seemed to do her good. Carter judged that she was well enough to continue with a quarter of her usual baggage. A couple of days later, Sosankalli's full load was hauled on to her back. Then the rains arrived in another deluge. Fever and dysentery raced through the ranks, affecting the whole caravan, including Carter. For two more days, there was no breaking camp in the pouring wet. The fires smoked and died. Food was impossible to cook. By the time Carter started up again, the caravan was a bedraggled mess. Then the rains closed in once more at Simba, which was the settlement where there had been such high hopes for making a grand impression, to persuade the chief that Simba was just the place for a training school for elephants. 'It was the first time I had seen these animals in their native wildness,' wrote Stanley of his encounter with a herd of elephants nearby, 'and my first impressions of them I shall not readily forget. I am induced to think that the elephant deserves the title of "king of beasts".' Sosankalli's arrival looked piteous by comparison. She entered Simba with pus flowing from her ears and inflamed patches on her head. Her mahouts administered medicine brought from India, but the pus continued to accumulate. Carter needed to get to Cambier's station at Karema as soon as possible. With no news reaching him yet as to whether Cadenhead would join him, he was struggling without the support of a second-in-command. At least Sosankalli was still eating. The road had 'forage in abundance', remarked Carter, but Sosankalli could barely hold her own bodyweight. Still blind, she was weaving along 'like she [was] drunk'.

We met up with Ugalla's Nyamwezi 'chief of chiefs' in some sun-dappled woodland on the edge of the park. His name was Lindyati Finulla, and he came with six elders. They included his two spiritual protectors, who laid out various herbs, and a man called Hamisi who introduced himself as the clan's historian. They were accompanied by a black-and-white goat on a rope I had given them the money to purchase. The piebald colouring, said one of the chief's men, symbolized our meeting: of Black and white, African and European.

The chief wore his royal regalia. His seashell headpiece denoted the Nyamwezi history of trading with the Swahili coast. It was strung together with leather made from a lion's skin. 'A cap like your monarch wears,' he said; 'I'm the thirtieth chief wearing this crown.' On his right leg, he wore a jingling seashell anklet. 'Wherever I step I show the boundaries of my territory,' he explained. He had two bracelets, one woven from the hairs of an elephant tail, the other in

Chief Lindyati Finulla flanked by his two spiritual protectors. The chief sits on a small throne.

twisted brass, which in the past would have been made from elephant hide. He also carried a stick and a fly whisk made from a cow's tail.

We passed some time in small talk, the men speaking between themselves in the Nyamwezi language.

'It's important to our rituals,' said Chief Finulla. 'We have always been identified by our language, our traditions and our heroism.'

I thanked them for letting me travel through their ancestral land, and told them about the animals we'd encountered, including the black mamba.

'We sent it to greet you,' said one of the spiritual protectors.

I showed them copies of my nineteenth-century maps, which they started to analyse.

'This is the route the people used to pass through at this time,' said Chief Finulla. 'Most of the dominant Nyamwezi leaders were allies.'

The elders talked at length about the complex allegiance between Tabora's Chief Isike (who was related to Nyungu-ya-Mawe), Simba, Mirambo and a number of other Nyamwezi leaders I hadn't come across in written records. They said their culture needed greater recognition, and that they wanted their five spiritual sites inside the park's boundaries to be protected in perpetuity, and their people's long-term access assured. They said it was important people were made aware of their rights. Their story belonged to a growing movement of indigenous voices speaking out against 'fortress' conservation policies in other parts of Tanzania. In the north, the Maasai were being ruthlessly, forcibly evicted from their ancestral land, their homes razed and cows confiscated. Leaders had been arrested, people shot, journalists silenced – all in the name of landscape and wildlife conservation, and the money that could be made from safari tourists. I understood that the animals needed to be protected as a national natural resource, but from a historical point of view, the fortress conservation model was riven with hypocrisies. In creating the first national parks in Africa, the Europeans had essentially fenced out locals in favour of foreign ideas about 'wilderness' protection and big-game hunters. It was also the nineteenth-century Europeans who imported the guns that shifted the balance so dramatically, from local 'bush meat' poaching to mass killing. In 1860, Richard Burton wrote that more than thirteen thousand muskets a year were passing through the hands of a single European trading house in Zanzibar. By the late nineteenth century, the trade in guns was assuming even greater proportions, reported a British official: 'Unless some steps are taken to check this immense import of arms into East Africa the development and pacification of this great continent will have to be carried out in the face of an enormous population, the majority of whom will probably be armed with first-class breech-loading rifles.'

I told Chief Finulla the story of Cambier's first encounter with Simba in Ugalla more than a century ago, and how the chief was accompanied by 'a troop of about three hundred elephant hunters, armed with old large calibre flintlock rifles.'

'It is true, it is true. We were the best elephant hunters in East Africa,' said the historian, Hamisi. 'When our hunters killed an elephant, and it fell to the ground, the tusk that hit the ground first was given to the chief as tribute. The upper tusk the hunter kept for himself. Before it was completely dead, but lying on its side dying, we would put a ladder against the flank, and the hunter would climb up with our spiritual protectors and spear it again in its heart. Then the hunter would lay his ear against the elephant's body and hear the animal's death call' – he mimicked a long haunting groan – 'and that was when the hunter would take on the strength and power of the elephant.'

When I asked him to repeat the sound, it was as if a colossal weight was somehow pressing in on the air. I could feel it spreading like storm clouds – the death call of the elephant reverberating through wilderness where I'd seen none. The thought troubled me. I'd gone from the euphoria of nights sleeping under the Southern Cross to feeling exhausted. I was struggling to keep up with the three-way interpreting, between

Nyamwezi, Swahili and English. After a couple of hours, I started to pack away my map to draw the interview to a close.

'You have to work hard for a story in Africa,' said Rem, who was acting as my interpreter, along with Richard. 'Maybe that's why your explorers just wrote about themselves.'

Rem urged me to be patient. The Nyamwezi people's sophisticated social habits were shaped by their long migrations on the caravan paths. Times may have changed, explained Rem, but something of the Nyamwezi's relationship with outsiders endured, including the rituals and requisite manners. You don't rush a Nyamwezi meeting. You pay proper respect.

The chief's spiritual protectors laid out a cloth for their bottles and herbs. They sang a song. They blessed our safe passage to the lake. One of them sprayed something from a phial and cast it in a circle around our gathering using Chief Finulla's whisk. The men tied the forelegs of the goat. They nimbly turned it on its back, and with one smooth slice, they cut the animal's throat. I watched the blood pool in a vivid red, then disappear into soil as hungry as blotting paper. As the blood dispersed, I thought of Carter's sick elephant struggling to make her final traverse from Simba to Karema – every march now reduced to only a few hours. But the season was moving faster than she was capable of. The going was getting treacherous through the last of the marshy plains. And then, at long last, came the view Carter had been waiting for. On 12 December, at 9.40 a.m., he walked on to higher ground, and caught a glimpse of shimmering blue. 'Thank God!' wrote Carter. 'My elephants got to see the Lake! . . . A sense of completion.'

On the morning of 14 December, Carter rallied his caravan one last time for the final push into Karema. But at 4 p.m., just two hundred yards from their final destination, Sosankalli stopped, her hind legs shaking. She lay down, breathing heavily. While her mahouts tended her, Carter looked on. The smallest and pluckiest of Carter's charges – the first to swim to shore at Zanzibar, the one who'd coaxed her male companions through bogs and over streams – had finally given up. Carter couldn't understand it. Until recently, Sosankalli had seemed in good condition. She was plump and well fed. She'd been eating, in fact, just a very short time before falling. 'A strange thing,' he remarked. How could this have happened when he'd taken such 'great care of her,' making short marches when necessary and dallying twelve days in this last stage to let her rest.

Two hours later, Sosankalli quietly died.

Another elephant lost. Another swarm of flies bubbling over pus and carrion. Another reach for an explanation. The mahouts attributed her death to a mysterious condition specific to elephants called 'aghin baho,' which Carter interpreted as an infection of some sort, the symptoms beginning with inflammation of the eyes, followed by a skin rash. The whole caravan was distressed. Carter grew despondent. He was making his most important entrance yet, under a gloomy sky, in a state of abject hopelessness. Dreams of four healthy elephants marching triumphantly into Leopold's lakeside fort had vanished within sight of Lake Tanganyika. I pictured Pulmalla tenderly pushing at Sosankalli's corpse with her trunk. She was now the only elephant left to make the last march to the water's edge, her gently domed head and speckled trunk as out of place in this far-off rift as the three uniformed Europeans. Instead of a jubilant celebration that should have attended the caravan's arrival at the IAA's first station on African soil, Cambier and Popelin gathered around to shake their heads at the tragedy of Sosankalli, the 'Budding Lily' of Leopold's elephant expedition. Carter was ashamed by the encounter, because it was also the first time he was meeting Cambier. 'I'm very sore about her loss,' said Carter; 'all of that was for naught. She is dead.'

10

Fish Without Number

'Certainly it's good to question why anyone would choose to place his professional compass out there on the edge.'

—Barry Lopez,
Embrace Fearlessly the Burning World

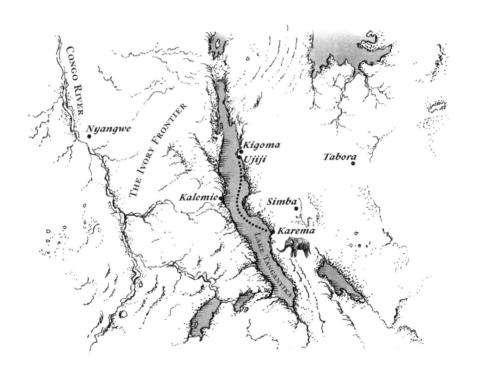

WE THREADED OUR WAY through a patchwork of rice and maize fields crisped to burnt paper, past clumps of tall, reedy grasses and the entrance to Karema's new port. The security guard wouldn't let us in, but the reason was self-evident in the sound of blasting dynamite I'd mistaken for thunder. A major construction project was under way. Tanzania was developing Karema on Lake Tanganyika as an economic gateway to the DRC. Soon a new road would be coming, connecting Karema in a smooth line of tarmac to the Indian Ocean, where another ten-billion-dollar investment was being talked about by Tanzanian politicians, this one potentially involving the Omanis and the Chinese. There were ambitions to make Bagamoyo the largest port in East Africa, capable of handling twenty-five times the amount of cargo currently running through Dar es Salaam – new trading paths layered on the old, just as Leopold had envisioned back in 1879 when he'd conjured up the idea of elephants taking the place of human porters.

We followed the road which ran along the edge of Karema's cemetery. Thinking we were Chinese engineers, children ran up to our windows with shouts of '*nǐ hǎo*', Mandarin for 'hello'. There was a shop with a boombox playing amapiano, a teenage boy dancing alone outside, and the sour smell of piglets grazing in piles of rubbish. The route we'd been following for the last two months was finally narrowing to a single sandy street, which petered out on a beach where fishermen were fixing their nets on upturned pirogues. Rem drove on to the sands, where the three of us got out and stood on the eastern shore looking out over the water.

The air tasted of sweetness when I was half expecting salt. Out on the lake, some of the boats were powered by paddles, others by swollen lateen sails made from fertilizer bags sewn together. The silhouettes of canoes moved across the stillness like puffs of thistle seed, the spores too light to settle. A rocky peninsula to our left marked the bay's southern limit. The bay's northern rim was flatter. This was where the port construction was under way, the work hidden behind a new breakwater. At our backs, there was a bright pink guesthouse. On the top of a small hill, there was a Catholic church flanked by a convent occupying a walled courtyard. This was the site of Leopold's first station on Lake Tanganyika, before it was handed over to the White Fathers in 1885, the original batch of converts made up of five hundred men, women and children newly 'redeemed' from slavery.

'Karema,' said Rem. 'Big name, little place.'

'The word means "torture" in the local language,' said a man we got talking with. His name was Josephat Zongwe, who said he was of Congolese descent. 'Maybe it's because of all the rocks. Or because of the history when Karema was a back route to the slave trade. Or because the first missionary found it torture to convert us. To understand Karema, you have to understand it as a melting pot between Tanzania and Congo. Our people are all sisters, brothers. Only water divides us.'

It was Stanley who had recommended Karema to Leopold as a good place to build a station. By Stanley's estimation, it was just a three-hour boat journey across to the Lukuga River, an outflow of the lake that eventually fed into the

Congo River, which could ultimately link Karema to the king's schemes on the west side of Africa. Only later did it transpire that Stanley had made a spectacular muddle of two local place names. The more appropriate location Stanley had meant for the first IAA station was called Massi-Kamba, which lay some twenty miles to the south. 'An atrocious blunder,' railed the Scottish explorer Joseph Thomson, who visited Karema a few months after Carter's arrival while scouting Tanganyika's eastern shore for London's Royal Geographical Society; 'The great civilising station ... may be described as situated on a hill inaccessible from the lake, surrounded by a marsh and a great uninhabited jungle, the favourite haunt of clouds of mosquitoes.' The locals said it was cursed with an evil spirit, which could only be allayed by a local priestess. To silence the woman's night-time howls, the community demanded constant payments of cloth from the Belgians.

The lake was a landscape unlike anything Carter, or I, had ever encountered. I'd read various nineteenth-century descriptions of Tanganyika's storms, of 'the cloud masses joined together like the closing of a skylight in a vaulted roof', about the waterspouts and pillars of water that sometimes came out of nowhere and barrelled across the surface like a 'vast, glass-like cylinder.' Sometimes the people woke up to a shoreline scattered with a black substance 'like bitumen', as if volcanoes had spewed from some hidden underwater fissure. Wolfe had recounted stories about his lakeside childhood, describing bruised skies, white lightning, three-metre waves and clattering, skin-numbing rain. Another friend who'd sailed around Tanganyika had talked to me about the lake in the language of an obsession, how the water appeared blue-black from a distance but had a startling clarity up close. He explained how the orographic winds worked, generated by the sun heating up the water and the energy of evaporation, until eventually they might trigger katabatic winds to swoop in from the higher ground. When those two phenomena were funnelled through the lake by the trade winds, chaos would erupt, in blistering electric storms. On days like those, Congo was no longer visible on the far shore, but the notion of it remained, hidden behind the shifting veils of extreme weather.

I walked along the beach past two women washing clothes in the shadow of a swollen hull, the planks like the expanding pleats that form the throat of a gulping whale. A carpenter was caulking the wood in cotton fibres and coconut oil to waterproof the dhow with the same technique described in nineteenth-century accounts. The dhow was being built for shipping rice and maize between Karema, Congo, Zambia to the south and Burundi to the north. I stopped to talk with a group of men disentangling their nets. They described how their boats went out in pairs – they used the term *kipe*, a local word meaning 'togetherness' – with the nets slung between them. There were superstitions about fishing, they said. It was a bad omen if you found an owl, or someone sleeping naked in your boat. Someone else explained how, in the most violent storms, the fishermen would retreat into the safety of a bay, and the ghosts of white people would sometimes appear. 'You don't know where they've come from and you do not see them again,' he said. 'There are strange things in Lake Tanganyika. All I can tell you is there are creatures, and you can't avoid them, because God put them there.'

As we talked, a young girl played in a wet dress on the top of a drowned palm a few metres out from shore. She stood balanced on the tree stump, her shoulders thrown back like a

Degas ballerina. Rem explained how, over the last few years, Tanganyika's water levels had been rising and eating up the treeline, forcing people to move their homes. Environmentalists said the problem was a combination of global warming and deforestation because the trees could no longer absorb the run-off. Seismologists said it was because of plate movements in the East African Rift, gradually unzipping the region apart. Others argued it wasn't climate change but a climate cycle. In 1879, the Royal Geographical Society's explorer Joseph Thomson was mesmerized by a fringe of dead trees, 'killed by the recent rise in its level', the stumps 'standing out in the lake', and evidence of 'a sudden lowering'. Another traveller wondered if perhaps some 'waste-pipe of the lake' had become unclogged. Had a new outlet opened up, like the plug being pulled in a bath?

The truth is a tectonic pulse has always haunted the everyday existence of people living on the divide. From the beginning of my journey, Lake Tanganyika had felt like it was part of something bigger than the sum of its parts. With the colour of the sky now changing in front of me, I picked up a stone and cast it into the water. I imagined it trying to find a place to settle in the Rift where Africa was being pulled apart, sinking under the surface of the water but never finding the bottom. I thought of the lack of an ending, and how the events of 1879 still haven't reached their conclusion. Even today, we still haven't touched the lake's deepest parts. Tanganyika is an abyss filled with our unknowing, a place that demands you ignore the scant hydrography and accept the largeness of a world we try to pin down but we haven't yet comprehended. Etymologists say 'Tanganyika' comes from the Swahili words *tanga*, meaning 'sail' or 'roaming around', and *nyika*, meaning 'wilderness'. A fisherman told me this wasn't accurate, that these same two words denoted different species of fish found in the lake. Maybe the muddle was the point. 'Tanganyika, in the Swahili language, can be translated as "the mixture" – the coming together and mingling in the lake cavity of the waters which flow into it from every side down the slopes of its containing basin', wrote one of Carter's contemporaries. You saw in Tanganyika what you wanted to see: 'The Great Lake, the supreme goal, the Promised Land', wrote another. For Thomson, it was the kind of place where you 'dreamed of fairy things'. For me, it felt like a landscape that had the capacity to shift my thinking – a reminder that perhaps discovery can still mean something today if only we could re-see the world as an opportunity to wonder.

I turned my back on the shore where I'd imagined Pulmalla being brought to be washed by her mahout. She was grieving in her aloneness – 'the spoiled child of the station' – living about as far from Pune as it was possible to get. Meanwhile, Wolfe and Rem had managed to secure a room in Karema's pink guesthouse. It didn't have space for all three of us, so I begged a bed in the convent on the hill, which was presided over by three kind nuns. My room was furnished with a frilly mosquito net and a single narrow bed positioned beneath a crucifix. Over the next few days, I would help the nuns feed their chickens and pigs, pluck small, sweet mangoes from their courtyard orchard, and watch Sister Rebecca make her creamy groundnut soup. I loved being among women again, surrounded by the sound of crowing cockerels, the choir practising for church and the melody of the Ave Maria, which the community sang at sundown at a shrine outside the convent's corrugated-iron gates. I adored the sight of Sister

Left: *Kitumbi, a flooded community on the eastern shore of Lake Tanganyika.* Right: *Local girls playing at Karema.*

Left: *Sister Lydia Kivamba, who also worked in the dispensary at Karema.* Right: *Damage from rising waters on the edge of Lake Tanganyika.*

Lydia tipped back in her chair with her arms around her tummy to stop the rippling laughter. I liked watching her hanging out the nuns' habits on the washing line, the sky-blue cloth whipping in the wind. I enjoyed listening to her irrepressible squeals when she took a cold bucket shower each morning in the room next to mine, the sound of her humming in the garden and, in the distance, the glimmer of Lake Tanganyika under a rising yolk of yellow sun. At dinner one night, I told the nuns about Carter and why I'd travelled this far. I mentioned what I'd found in the convent's visitors' book. Between the signatures of priests, I'd spotted the name of a man called Cambier whom I could only assume had come all the way out here to trace the story of his ancestor. I told them about Pulmalla, who would have stood in the very courtyard where the sisters deadheaded the roses. The nuns nodded in polite interest, then the senior sister cut me short to say grace. She had other things on her mind. The roasted rabbit they'd cooked wasn't going to wait.

The days following Carter's arrival at Karema passed in a blur. There was the death of an elephant to explain, an exhausted Pulmalla who needed rest, and Cambier's half-built station to complete – to be made of stone, with an interior mimicking a Swiss chalet. 'This is a most fearful spot that Mr Stanley has pitched on for a station,' bemoaned Carter; 'had he ever set foot on land here, he would never have recommended it.' There was also a chronic shortage of basic provisions. A local legend claimed Tanganyika was a lake full of 'fish without number'; instead, Carter was met by stores dwindling to a reserve of Indian corn. Which was why as soon as Carter arrived, Cambier set sail for Ujiji – located some hundred and forty miles north of Karema as the crow flies – to buy from Arab-Swahili traders. Carter was left behind with Popelin as the rainclouds gathered overhead.

Nearly eight weeks passed, and Cambier still hadn't returned from his Ujiji supply run. 'You may fancy how hard up we all are,' wrote Carter after yet another meal of corn bread; 'nothing but salt to help it down'; 'when it fails we shall get rather thin.' Carter had left Brussels behind him in late spring. Now it was December, with a sparse Christmas to look forward to in the middle of Africa. We don't know if the plum pudding promised by one of the IAA committee members made it out to Karema in time, but the arrival of the new year did nothing to lift spirits. Popelin described a 'sad season' a world away from the bounteous feasts and snowstorms gusting through Belgium.

Impatient and uneasy from the lack of news, Carter took to hunting whenever possible, marching up to ten hours a day in search of game, traipsing through swamp now the rains had come in. 'You can't go through the jungle, even following the trails, without being immediately wet to the bone,' Cambier complained. Leopold's men had promised Carter a country with 'abundant elephant'. There appeared to be none. When Carter approached a warthog he'd shot, he walked into three feeding lions. His gunbearers ran, leaving him with only one loaded barrel and three 'wild brutes with fangs, beards, chests and claws dripping with blood.' He described pulling the trigger, hunching in anticipation of the lions ripping through him as he fired. 'I have faced death many times but never had a narrower escape than this.' The lions bolted, and Carter's scorching anger was unleashed: 'I felt very like putting a bullet through my cowardly gunbearers who were standing fifty yards off blue with fright and shaking all over?' His last thoughts, or so he later wrote, had been to make a trophy of the lions' claws for the wife of the IAA member who'd promised Carter a Christmas pudding.

But hunger, rewritten by Carter as a hunter's tale of daring, was only one part of station life. The boredom was worse. Carter may have been gregarious and full of distracting anecdote but, as one of his contemporaries remarked, 'if he had a fault at all, it was simply that he was perhaps a little too impulsive for the exigencies of African travelling'. Moreover, Carter was becoming feverish as he awaited new instructions to come down the line. He couldn't bear the inactivity, sitting out the wet season in this half-built station. Was he still to go and strike a deal with Simba, or move on somewhere else? Was he to go back to the coast to collect more Asian elephants to help with the capture work? He would need some new taming decoys – more 'Delilahs' like Pulmalla, traditionally used to entrap wild calves. He also needed to replenish his ranks with another batch of experienced Indian mahouts. And what of Cadenhead? Was he on his way to Africa, or not?

Pulmalla, meanwhile, was adjusting to station life with her keeper, Bonheti. The elephant was a local novelty, quickly becoming 'the only topic of conversation for people all around the lake', wrote one of Leopold's propagandists. Carter hastily arranged for a stable to shelter her from the worst of the rains – a grass roof on stilts. But Pulmalla was struggling. Female elephants have a profound need to be part of a herd. That's what makes their taming possible: of all the systems of deprivation used to break an elephant's spirit, from food and water restriction to chains and beatings, it's the isolation that finally wears them down. In Karema, Pulmalla was alone. Her draughty lean-to was a poor facsimile of her previous life in a Pune elephant stable. Though her daily marches might have been over for the time being, life at Karema came with its own challenges, including the danger of fire. The problem was compounded by the makeshift huts Carter's caravan had built, which were too close together. Frequent threats of arson from the community were enough for the Europeans to dictate that no fires were to be lit in close proximity. But that instruction was often ignored. Sure enough, a fire took hold and both Pulmalla's stable and Carter's huts were destroyed. It was a small miracle that Pulmalla escaped unhurt, but it served as a warning to all that Carter couldn't afford to lose his last elephant. The weight of that responsibility fell heavily on him – Pulmalla's survival was the only tangible success thus far in the whole experiment – which depressed his mood further.

When Cambier eventually returned from Ujiji, at least it was with an opportunity for Carter to get away too. A British missionary called Edward Hore – husband to Annie, who'd soon be joining him in her bath chair – had been living at Ujiji for the last eighteen months. Hore wanted help negotiating a land deal for the London Missionary Society with the Ujiji Arabs, and needed Carter's language skills. Hore also required assistance settling the estate of Abbé Debaize, the explorer who'd originally set out in 1878 to lead the ambitious French Scientific Expedition – a three-year mission across Africa from east to west, with a caravan of nine hundred porters. (It was Debaize who'd ordered two Africans to be shot shortly after he'd set off, which led to the revenge killing of the mission engineer Penrose near Tabora.) According to Hore, Debaize was infamous for his 'noisy harangues'. Another traveller described how he would strap a hurdy-gurdy to one of his men's backs, careful not to damage this ludicrously expensive item worth some twelve thousand francs. Turning the handle, he'd march towards his antagonist, and if the 'softening influence of music' failed to secure a suitable welcome, he'd let off a few rockets. He was a drunk, who lived on bread soaked in brandy, and in his last days, deserted by his entire caravan, walked around Ujiji firing his revolver at random. Hore, who'd given Debaize a place to stay in Ujiji when the rival Catholic missionaries refused to do so, watched over him until his eyes rolled back into his head in a final, mortal fit from suspected sunstroke. This left Hore with the responsibility of sorting through the peculiar detritus of the Frenchman's scattered caravan, including twelve boxes of fireworks.

Leaving Popelin to hold the fort at Karema, Carter and Cambier sailed for Ujiji at the end of January 1880. For Carter, the journey to this trading entrepôt would, he hoped, be a return to Arab-speaking company. Though when he pulled up on Ujiji's muddy rim, the Arabs were more openly hostile towards Europeans than they'd been in Tabora. By Hore's estimation, the de facto leader, Mwinyi Heri, was a 'pushing, avaricious, and unscrupulous' man. His strong grip on the local population allowed him to stoke fear through Ujiji that the missionary folk were going to jeopardize the slavery business in which nearly everyone, Arab and African, was in some way involved. In spite of this, Carter helped tip negotiations in Hore's favour. According to Hore, Carter's every word was 'listened to open mouthed' by the Ujiji Arabs; 'he reminds many of them of their language or customs well nigh forgotten? To express his gratitude for Carter's assistance, Hore expounded Leopold's 'excellent' vision for Africa in his correspondence home, acknowledging the Belgian king as 'a very considerable supporter' of missionary progress.

Back in Europe, that news was well received, especially when on the other side of the continent Stanley was still being slow to advance from Vivi. 'He lingers too long in the first station', complained Strauch. 'He is sometimes like a child', added Leopold. Carter, by contrast, was being seen as someone to be taken seriously, despite three dead elephants. He was clearly resilient, and his Arabic was proving a diplomatic asset. Would it be worth sending Carter even deeper into Central Africa, to the west side of the lake, suggested one of Leopold's advisors? '[W]ith his business and commercial knowledge and experience', Carter was 'very different from such as Stanley, floating and fighting down the swift flowing Congo.'

For Carter, his sojourn in Ujiji felt something like a holiday, albeit at the rough end of the caravan road. The town rang with the clanking of slave shackles – sometimes six men bound to a single chain, collared and stapled directly to the store shelves where they worked. There were gunsmiths, beggars, fishermen, well-dressed people from the coast, birds singing in the pomegranate trees, spitting snakes, and late-night conversations with the harried Hore, who complained about the African chiefs switching allegiances as often as Tanganyika's winds changed direction. Hore had been starved of convivial company. The Roman Catholics, made up of four White Fathers from Algiers, were occasionally seen wandering the streets of Ujiji. They wore long black cassocks worn over 'white night gowns', and solemn wide-awake hats tied on with silk cord chin-straps. Rather than befriend Hore, they kept themselves to themselves, waiting nervously for reinforcements to arrive from the coast.

It was the lake – the magnificent, brooding *mare incognitum* – which excited Carter and Hore more than anything over their dinner table. Hore, who'd cut his teeth on P&O cruisers, was 'the right man in the right place,' Carter asserted; '[b]eing a sailor, he can turn his hand to anything.' For his part, Hore was happy to be breaking bread with a man who shared his desire to rig up a good boat and explore the lake's southern reaches. Between them, they had little respect for the maritime talents of the local Jiji people, the so-called 'sons of the waves.' According to Hore, the Jiji would panic in a storm, only to return home and 'strut about with a little cane in their hands and boast of their sailoring.' But for the two master mariners, these nautical anecdotes were all part of the pleasure of discussion.

There was so much to take in. Hore described the 'grotesque-looking craft of the Arab merchants'; the 'small catamarans, made up of four or five trunks of the pith-tree strung together'; the twenty-five-foot-long solid-log canoes (also good for baths, remarked Hore). There was boat-building to talk about, too. Hore was converting an old slaving dhow for his missionary work, a 'piratical' ship he called the *Calabash*, with a jib, mizzen and rigging in 'English fashion.' There had been numerous moments on Carter's long African journey that had stripped him of his delusions, but in Hore's company his ambitions started to expand from training elephants to opening up the waterways of the African interior. In June 1879, a story had run in the *Times of India* about why Carter was the best man for Leopold's scheme. 'It is no secret that the rivers ... and the adjacent lakes will soon be alive with steam craft if they be found sufficiently practicable,' a British journalist remarked, recalling Carter's nautical successes in Mesopotamia. 'It is not unlikely this practical knowledge of difficult river navigation may have more to do with the ultimate service on which he is to be employed than at first appears.' Was Lake Tanganyika Carter's chance to fulfil a new calling?

As they sat talking by candlelight, the plans Carter and Hore made were detailed, and potentially much more reliable than using elephants. A modern steamer, carried to the lake in parts and reconstructed at Ujiji, was 'absolutely necessary,' suggested Carter, to keep up communication and share goods

A nineteenth-century drawing of Hore's boat, the Calabash, *taking on a storm. The waterspouts in this image are not common on Lake Tanganyika, but they do occur. One lakeside resident I spoke with described once seeing a spout rising from the lake into the clouds.*

and mail between the new European stations spreading along the shores. Carter proposed greater cooperation: Hore's mission and Leopold's IAA ought to co-invest in the scheme, which would make money by charging caravans a 'fair rate' for transport. The 'civilising effect' would be 'immense'. 'The constant visits of the steamer to the different stations would do away with the dangers to which isolated white men are now exposed from the natives'. An English officer would be in command, with a 'respectable able seaman as his chief mate'. 'I could of course fill pages as to the advantages of having a steamer', enthused Carter – a vision he hoped to make happen 'on this important inland sea before I leave Africa'.

I wanted to know what had come of all those aspirations, so after a few days of rest in the convent at Karema, I took leave of the nuns to travel to Ujiji. I said goodbye at the gates with a promise to Sister Lydia that I'd return. I made my assurances, with a sense of my own fickleness. How often do we promise friends we make on the road that we'll see them again?

To get to Ujiji, Wolfe had managed to charter a banana-yellow fibre boat. The alternative, of travelling to Ujiji by road, would have taken a couple of days of weaving north on indirect roads. So we split from Rem and the car. With the morning bell ringing for church, we pulled away from the beach, the steeple fading to a disappearing speck. Out on the water, the going was far rougher than it had appeared from land. Without the support of Rem's unflappable demeanour, Wolfe and I worried the boat's single engine might not make the eight-hour passage, and that the splashing waves would sink us.

The lake was stewing with cross-currents. Crocodiles with cream-coloured bellies basked in rocky coves. Here and there, hippos snorted and spun their ears. On the steeper contours, village paths wound up from the waterline. We passed whaleback ridges, forest-covered chines, and a peak sacred to the local Tongwe people. Wolfe had spent much of his childhood living in the mountains' shadows. He explained how the Tongwe's customary laws prohibited the cutting of large trees. They believed their guardian spirits lived with the forest's chimpanzees. We talked about the Tongwe's ritual sites hidden within the sinewy embrace of root systems stretching across the ground, one tree entwined with another, the roots knitting the forest together in a web of flying buttresses and burnished, copper-coloured bark.

It was the very end of the day when we pulled up on the beach at Kigoma, a port town connected to old Ujiji by a ribbon of churches, mosques, shops and market stalls, where we met a man called Malilo Omari Umande, originally from Manyema in Congo. A former fisherman, he was impeccably attired in a tangerine-coloured shirt. He seemed to know everything about the comings and goings of Kigoma, and said he'd act as my guide. Malilo described how in the 1980s Kigoma had functioned as a sorting house for black-market gold and diamonds. He remembered the First Congo War in the mid 1990s when refugees started coming over the lake in waves of canoes.

'I saw with my own eyes,' said Malilo. 'That is how history is understood.'

He took me to see the Livingstone Memorial that marked the Ujiji tree where Stanley famously 'met' Livingstone for the first time. Malilo, however, didn't care two hoots for the monument.

'Explorers: I don't like them,' he said. 'They come to see

what we have, our raw materials, and then, like the rest of them, their people come and take them away.'

Wanting to know if anything had ever come of Carter and Hore's dreams of steamship enterprise, I asked Malilo if he could help find what was left of one of Tanganyika's oldest boats – the MV *Liemba*, formerly the *Graf von Goetzen*, moored in Kigoma's harbour. The *Liemba* was a survivor, built in Germany in 1913, and then transported to the lake by rail in around five thousand wooden crates. In 1916, during one of the most far-flung battles of the First World War, the Germans scuttled her. In 1920, the Belgians then pulled her up from her shallow grave, but not long afterwards, she sank in a storm. In 1924, the British raised her again, this time turning her into a passenger ferry. The *Liemba* became the only ship running a transport service up and down the lake. She'd survived a century, carrying cargo, soldiers, and waves of refugees escaping Zaire in 1997 after the fall of Mobutu Sese Seko, who had seized power in a 1965 coup. In 2015, the *Liemba* helped some of the fifty thousand people fleeing Burundi's civil war. At the height of these catastrophes, she was extracting some six hundred refugees at a time, which went far beyond her intended carrying capacity.

Malilo tracked down the *Liemba*'s captain, Titus Benjamin Mnyanyi. When we arrived, the ship was moored up against another boat and a broken wooden walkway. A quartermaster was washing down the poop deck. I poked around the *Liemba*'s rotting carcass, my footsteps echoing through the rusty German ironwork. The peeling paint was the colour of custard. The lino in the canteen split under my feet. I stood in the chilly silence of the ship's groaning bowels, a place where some of the most desperate people in the world had found their passage out of civil wars in Congo, Burundi and Rwanda. On the ship's bridge, Titus showed me the 1924 glass-domed magnetic compass, which still worked, and some of the old charts. I told him about Carter, Hore and their grand visions for steamships on Tanganyika.

'The *Liemba* is the grandmother of the lake', Titus said, looking through another drawer for maps. 'She's stable, strong, graceful. She's where German, British, Tanzanian and Congolese history meet. She has fought two world wars, and has carried many people of the lake to safety.'

Titus talked about the journeys he'd made in the twenty-five years he'd sailed her, with her last voyage in 2018 before the ship was retired to her berth in Kigoma for critical repairs. He described attacks from Congolese pirates, and how the *Liemba* was too fast for any of them to catch her. As we talked, I noticed Malilo turning the ship's wheel dreamily. I asked him if he could take the *Liemba* on any journey – 'You can go to the moon', I said, 'you can go to paradise' – where would he sail?

'I'd start in Mpulungu', he said, spinning the wheel as if he were setting out from the port on the lake's southern tip in Zambia. 'I'd sail up to Ujiji. I'd go to Egypt. I'd take a left.'

'You'd go to Mecca, to perform the Hajj?'

'No. I'd go to Libya.'

'Why?'

'For turning. I'd sail to Morocco, then take a right, go to Britain. After that, America.'

'Would you want to live there, in America?'

'No', he said. 'I just want to see it. That would be enough for me. I'd like to come back here.'

*

Left: *The* Liemba *photographed in Kigoma in 2021.* Right: *Malilo Omari Umande standing at the ship's wheel.*

A rare photograph of Mimi – *one of two armed motorboats from England carried by rail, road and river to Kalemie on the western shore of Lake Tanganyika in 1915. They were used for surprise attacks on the Germans during the First World War.*

By the time Carter and Cambier left Ujiji to sail back to Karema, they'd not only sorted out the affairs of the crazed Abbé Debaize, but they'd also procured the dead Frenchman's boat. The dhow was packed with new supplies, including chickens, goats and Debaize's hurdy-gurdy. The voyage started well. They stopped on the Congo side of the lake, with a brief stay at a new missionary station called 'Plymouth Rock', where Carter was thrilled to be greeted with the moniker 'Lord of the Elephants'.

From here, Carter and Cambier then sailed for Karema, but when they were recrossing the lake, a sudden squall came out of nowhere and swamped the vessel. In the commotion of flailing oarsmen, the livestock all drowned, though the hurdy-gurdy survived. The group was forced to set up a temporary camp on the shore so Carter could fix the damage. Then a few days later, steering around a promontory of glistening rocks, a band of men started firing bullets at Carter's boat from both sides. His crew dropped into the hull for cover. Carter whipped out his rifle and 'shot one or two of the savages' (as another explorer later reported). As Africans fell on either side, Carter streamed curses at his boatmen, threatening to turn his gun on them too unless they started rowing.

Carter had blood on his hands. He'd followed the British advice to the letter – the administration of 'Bush Law', which was something Francis Galton had described in his explorers' guide *The Art of Travel*: each man should behave as 'a nation in himself'. Once Carter's boat finally pulled back into Karema, it was clear Popelin had also been making enemies. An 'intense feeling of hostility' was reported in the lakeside community. Popelin displayed 'haughty disregard' for indigenous customs. Instead, he'd continued to build fortifications, including trenches and arrow slits, to protect the Belgians in case any of the spats spilled into war. Not a single person would 'move his little finger to assist them for either love or money'. Karema's small population – ruled by a 'poor-looking elderly [chief] with broken fingers and weak screwed-up eyes that never looked straight' – only saw catastrophe in this new European presence.

Meanwhile, weeks had turned to months and still no further instructions from Brussels. Carter was feeling intensely lonely, his Ujiji adventure long forgotten. Paranoid about being regarded as a 'foreigner and outsider' by Cambier and Popelin, Carter also now felt he had 'no personal friends in the bureau at Brussels'. 'I keep myself and opinions (in writing) thoroughly in the background', he wrote. His letters to Strauch grew shorter, the subject matter focused solely on Pulmalla. Aside from his Arab valet Mahomed, Carter's only friend this far from home was Hore, who sailed south from Ujiji at the end of March, accompanied by Thomson who was by this time exploring the southern end of the lake for the Royal Geographical Society.

Carter was out shooting hippos when he caught sight of Hore's dhow sailing towards him with its English rigging. From his hunting camp on a small ridge, he hollered a 'jolly "Halloo!"'. The three men 'drew to each other like brothers', wrote Thomson. That night, they sat down to supper around a fire 'a thousand miles from the faintest trace of civilization'. They talked until dawn, Carter 'bursting with stories'. The men listened to each other's tales, Carter's often leaning towards the fantastical – 'involuntarily or by mistake', remarked Thomson.

The next morning, Carter's expanded party made its way

to Leopold's station on the back of Pulmalla. By now 'fat, strong and well', or so claimed Carter, Pulmalla raised her trunk in the familiar 'salaam' to her saluting passengers, Hore and Thomson. Advancing at a swinging pace, she deposited the men at the fort on the same hill where I'd sought shelter from the nuns.

Thomson was horrified by the miserable conditions. He accused the Belgians of an 'utter want of the most rudimentary knowledge of the geography of Africa'. Karema was clearly no place for a 'civilizing' station, he contended. To make matters worse, Thomson was met with the 'melancholy' reception of a single Roman Catholic missionary – one of three White Fathers who'd recently arrived in Karema half starved while en route to join their compatriots at Ujiji. One of the priests was quite blind, another mad. But at least they were alive, Carter confided to Thomson; Popelin and Cambier had tried to turn their backs on the missionaries, and it was only Carter's 'indignant protest' that had saved them. Karema seemed to Thomson a gathering of bedraggled misfits, but nonetheless it was a 'remarkable' party that sat down to eat together at the station that evening: 'an Englishman, an Irishman, a Scotchman, a Frenchman, a Belgian, and a German' representing five different expeditions and telling 'a sad tale of trial and utmost hardship' – as well as a love of firearms.

'The three captains', as Thomson referred to Cambier, Carter and Popelin, 'showed a strongly military tendency in their ideas': 'not one of them will ever venture half-a-dozen steps from the door without his favourite weapon'. 'They put implicit faith in their guns, holding it as an axiom that every native who meets them is thirsting for their blood, and only waiting to get them without their fire-arms to do some bloody deed? Yet Popelin, who by his own admission had already shown an affection for 'a few vigorous strokes of the cane' on his march to Karema, seemed too frightened to continue onwards, in spite of instructions from Brussels to proceed to Nyangwe in Congo. Thomson thought Popelin was labouring under the impression that 'all he had to do was to come out to Karema for a certain number of years, live as comfortably as possible' and then return to Belgium. As for the elephants, Thomson considered the whole expedition a disaster. He couldn't get past the fact that three of the four elephants had died. In his opinion, the fourth had only survived because she hadn't had to carry any loads. Surely that proved the 'utter unsuitability' of these animals? Hore, on the other hand, was impressed by Pulmalla, and thought elephants would do well in Africa as draft animals hitched to wagons. But there wasn't any consensus. 'We could find no question on which we were mutually agreed,' said Thomson. 'So we had to give up the notion of setting everybody right about Africa.' Instead, Debaize's hurdy-gurdy was hauled out of a corner to play feeble 'operatic selections' and 'old familiar airs'. Against a sky streaked with rainclouds threatening to break, Pulmalla then bore Thomson and Hore back to their tents at the edge of the lake. The next day, they resumed their voyage south, but not without leaving behind a variety of useful articles for the station. To the competitive Thomson – the same man Kirk had accused in Zanzibar of having filthy table manners – the irony was delicious. It gave him great pleasure 'to assist the members of the International Association (who are generally supposed to be stationed there to assist, not to be assisted)'.

With the visitors' departure, life at Karema once again lapsed into the boredom of the everyday. The hurdy-gurdy was pushed back in its corner, Pulmalla returned to her make-shift stable, and Carter was locked into an increasingly abject wait for instructions. Carter described earthquakes rumbling like 'distant tumbrils'. Storms came and went. As the weeks lengthened, Carter admitted being 'afraid to leave Karema for any time'. With each day that passed, he expected new orders to arrive from Brussels.

At midnight on 12 April, a glimmer of clarity finally made it down the mail lines. Tom Cadenhead was on his way. He'd left Zanzibar on 25 January. By Carter's calculation, that meant he was now twenty days from Karema. But there was bad news too. The letter explained that, instead of waiting for his friend, Carter was to return immediately to the coast to meet four more elephants and their mahouts due to be arriving from India, and then march them back inland – which would be a repeat of the terrible journey he'd only just completed. Meanwhile, Cadenhead would be expected to fill Carter's role at Karema. Now Pulmalla had proved her species could survive the journey and the tsetse, Carter was told to use the new Asian elephants as decoys to capture and train African elephants in Simba's territory. Leopold's men were apparently all on board with this new phase, although behind the scenes there were others who had hoped for much better planning. 'Do not I pray send a ship as happened before without a day's notice', Kirk wrote to Mackinnon. Mrs Kirk was less restrained in her opinion: 'I feel more savage at the poor elephants being tacked onto those helpless Belgians than I can say. They haven't a chance!!!'

Carter was stuck. He might have been told to proceed immediately for the coast, but he couldn't think about leaving Karema before Cadenhead arrived. Having persuaded his beloved friend to join him, he couldn't then abandon him. For the first time, Carter broke rank. He wouldn't proceed to the coast, as ordered. He'd at least delay things a little. But three weeks of waiting stretched into four, then four into five. The rain didn't stop. The grass grew longer. The Belgians were confined to their little fort on the hill while the pestilence, hunger and frustration intensified. Carter felt marooned, waking up each morning to a moral dilemma, colleagues who didn't much like him, distressed mahouts who didn't think they'd ever see India again, and a grieving elephant with a bad diet and no purpose. Carter chafed at his inability to manipulate the public adulation he craved. He wrote obsequious letters – '(I hope you won't think it snobbish my saying so) I have a strong degree of personal liking and respect for The King' – and complained about playing second fiddle to Cambier and Popelin in the European press: '[m]any of my friends have written to me saying they have seen several articles ... but that my name is not <u>even mentioned</u>.' After all his self-perceived successes, 'it looks like [sic] as if I were under a cloud of some sort', he thought it 'rather rough' that the 'general idea in the clubs is that my expedition was commanded by Belgian officers'. 'I feel rather disgusted with the Belgian correspondents whoever they are. Let them talk up their own men as much as they like, but not at the cost of Truth', he wrote. If Strauch wouldn't do anything about it, might someone 'put the saddle on the right horse, and let the public know the facts of the case'? After all, 'even the "old-gentleman" deserves his dice!!' Carter's paranoia was straining under the pressure, perhaps exacerbated by malaria. 'It is a most extraordinary thing how this African fever stays in one's blood', he wrote. Quinine had long stopped having any effect, and he had no arsenic, or medical help. Popelin's expedition doctor, Van den Heuvel, was still festering in Tabora. As for the dead Debaize's stash of medicines, they were useless because all the labels had been lost.

To escape the increasingly heavy atmosphere, Carter redoubled his attempts to conduct his own searches for wild elephants. He employed local parties of men to try to capture one or two calves. 'Days, and days, looking for them but never even caught sight of one,' he complained. 'People at home also seem to think that elephants are as thick as sparrows, and just as easily caught, but . . . this is very far from being the case.' He put the problem down to the ivory trade running rampant, which meant any elephants which did still exist in the region were easily spooked. With 'every man and boy being armed with rifles and guns of sorts,' wrote Carter, 'the elephants get no rest whatever.'

Carter's impatience was driving him crazy, while in Brussels Leopold was being fêted and met with applause at another meeting of the IAA. 'The results of the year 1879, as you see, Gentlemen, are brilliant,' intoned the president of Antwerp's geographical society; 'that of 1880 even richer in hopes.' Near Karema, meanwhile, news of an elephant! It had trampled to death a member of Carter's crew during a capturing expedition eight days' march from the station.

Carter needed to hold firm more than ever. '"Failure" is a word I don't believe in,' he wrote; 'success will be mine.' To Carter's mind, there was only one way of doing things, of dominating a world seen in black and white, of drawing the line dividing the 'savage' from the 'civilized'. But as Orwell would later warn in his indictment of imperialism, 'when the white man turns tyrant it is his own freedom that he destroys.'

As I read through Carter's letters, I could sense him adapting to his situation by doing what we're all guilty of at one time or another, to different degrees: we cling to our absolutes, yet become more self-delusional in a bid to keep control when a situation is running away with us. I imagined Carter out there on the edge: thin, exhausted, feverish. 'I feel it night and day coursing through my blood,' he wrote; 'my skin is always like fire.' He didn't dream of fairy things. There was no romance left to his African misadventure. Carter felt responsible for having drawn Cadenhead to this sorry place, which he couldn't wait to turn his back on. All Carter wanted was to be reunited with someone who understood him – and to take the most direct route possible to get out of this African quagmire where the grass and thorns grew so tall they now reached over his head.

11

Paradise Plains

'… when an elephant's mind is made up it is next to impossible to change it.'

—FREDERICK CARTER,
Letter to William Mackinnon, 6 August 1879

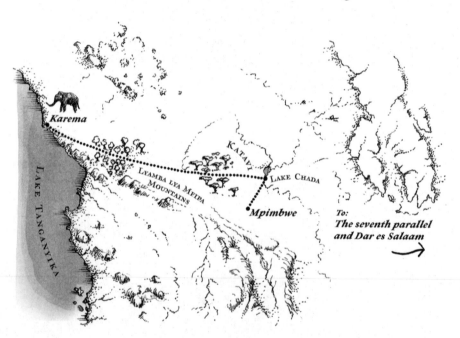

BEFORE WE LEFT LAKE Tanganyika, Wolfe wanted to pay a visit to the people he'd grown up with along its shores, so we stopped at a village called Kitumbi between Karema and Ujiji. Wolfe introduced me to a Tongwe elder and family friend called Ramadhani Nyundo, who talked about how he wished everyone had known his people's way of life before it had started to disappear. The Tongwe regarded themselves as the guardians of Lake Tanganyika's eastern forest, but they had been losing territory for some time. First came the Arabs in pursuit of slaves and ivory. Then the Christian missionaries in pursuit of souls. After independence, the Tongwe were displaced by Nyerere's Ujamaa villages, with a section of their ancestral forest, known as Mahale, designated as a national park. More recently, they had been challenged by the incursions of the Sukuma, who were slashing forests to expand their shambas and grazing pastures for cattle. Congolese fishermen had also been overstepping the border between the DRC and Tanzania to build fishing camps on the eastern side of the lake. Moreover, rising water levels had been 'stealing the land' – a phrase Hore had used. Space for the Tongwe was beginning to feel like it was running out.

'Chimpanzees build a new nest every day,' said Ramadhani. 'The Tongwe believe that if you take a twig from a chimp's nest and burn it, you will never settle in one place. We still do it – burn a twig – to put a curse on people we want to move on.'

In 1880, Carter was desperate to leave Karema, but he was

tortured by his predicament: who was he going to let down? Cadenhead, whose presence he had lobbied so hard for, or Leopold, who had given him orders to advance immediately to the coast. Meanwhile, Cadenhead was struggling with his own demons as he tried to cross the country. Like Carter, he wasn't hitting it off with his Belgian colleagues: Adolphe Burdo, hired to lead a third IAA expedition, and Burdo's second-in-command, Oscar Roger. The three men had been tasked to travel in convoy to Karema, but it had started to go wrong before they even reached Africa. They hardly spoke on the voyage from Europe to Zanzibar. In Aden, Cadenhead chose to splinter off with old friends rather than keep the company of the Belgians. In Stone Town, he stayed with the agent for Mackinnon's shipping company, while Burdo and Roger lodged elsewhere. In between banquets hosted by Sultan Barghash and John Kirk, Cadenhead was often absent – 'off to breathe the air', sniped Burdo, with 'one of his compatriots'. To compound the ill-feeling, Cadenhead, who'd been responsible for purchasing camping equipment in England, forgot to have it unloaded and packed on to the onward steamer at Aden, which meant the group had to have clumsy articles made in Zanzibar instead – including a replacement tricolour flag cobbled together for Cadenhead (representing Leopold) and a blue standard with a gold star (representing the IAA) for Burdo and Roger.

Cadenhead – young, taciturn, clean-shaven – started to show his nerves almost immediately. From Carter's letters home, Cadenhead already knew Africa was no Mesopotamian rose garden, but according to Burdo, Cadenhead was neurotic and slept with his hands tightly clenched. On the journey from Zanzibar to the mainland, the party then had to abandon their dhow two miles off the coast due to a clumsy approach – an ominous repeat of the debacle with the elephants' disembarkation the previous May. The men waded through the shallows on foot, water lapping at their chests while the porters kept dropping packages into the surf.

In Mpwapwa, Cadenhead picked up his first letter from Carter since reaching the mainland, and responded immediately, hopelessly trying to communicate 'on every possible occasion' by sending messages via the caravan mail 'so that he is always aware of my movements'. But not all the messages were getting through to Karema. Meanwhile, Cadenhead's relationship with the Belgians continued to deteriorate. In Mpwapwa, he decided to take a day out hiking with the missionary Joseph Last, which didn't go down well with Burdo and Roger. Divisions were setting in, which got worse in the thorny Mgonda-Mkali when Cadenhead fell sick and stubbornly refused help. 'My pride as an Englishman would not suffer me to give in or allow myself to be carried, or to ride on one of the donkeys,' he said. 'I had walked every inch of the way from the coast, and was not likely to give in at this stage without a struggle.'

When Cadenhead chose to visit Tabora's Arab leaders without his Belgian colleagues, tensions were inflamed. By the time the caravan was ready to move on, Burdo's retinue had taken umbrage with Cadenhead's over the amount of weight being carried; Cadenhead's men were portering half-loads, Burdo's full ones. Arguments escalated into 'terrible conflicts', reported Burdo, until it was decided it would be best if the expedition divided. Cadenhead and his entourage would travel ahead but stay close enough to lend a hand if danger should arise. But that plan soon went wrong too. Cadenhead, desperate to catch Carter at Karema, advanced too quickly. When the Belgians arrived at the next caravan stop, they found Cadenhead had already departed, having been picked up by eight of Carter's best men whom he'd sent from Karema to help. Burdo was left speechless by Cadenhead's hastily scribbled note to say he regretted not being able to assist the Belgians further but they detained him from carrying out his orders to get to Karema fast. Cadenhead was in such a rush, in fact, that when he happened to cross paths with Joseph Thomson in a forest in Ugalla, the two men lingered for no more than two hours – a brief and 'pleasant chat', said Thomson, and that was it. Thomson was surprised. Cadenhead, 'terribly pulled down with fever', evidently had trouble even speaking. Thomson was even more taken aback when the next day he encountered the Belgians on the same path. They were being led on donkeys, the men 'dressed in white clothes, military riding-boots, and a helmet, and wearing blue goggles or glasses to protect the eyes'. Both Belgians, said Thomson, carried two guns each: in one hand a rifle with the butt propped up on a thigh, and in the other hand a revolver.

It was now the beginning of June, and what had begun as a 'tiptoe of expectation' for Cadenhead's arrival in Karema – Carter's words, brimming with affection – had reached a point of 'such turmoil' that Carter had fallen seriously ill, 'to the point of worrying us', wrote Cambier. With febrile determination, Carter spent his time hunting for a bird he could shoot to give Cadenhead a proper welcome feast. Each day, he would circle the marshes around Karema for game. Carter was beside himself with sickness and worry; he'd delayed his departure for the coast by two months knowing he was flouting the king's instructions. 'This is the first time that I have not obeyed an order,' he'd repeated to Cambier and Popelin as often as they would listen. When Cadenhead finally limped into Karema on 4 June 1880 with five skinny donkeys, he was in a terrible state, 'beaten down by fever.' There was no time for any sentimental reunion, or dinners and songs with the hurdy-gurdy. Cadenhead needed nursing. Carter couldn't possibly leave him behind, but taking an invalid carried risks too. More than anything else, Carter wanted his friend by his side, not festering as a tag-team deputy overseeing one last Asian elephant at a non-existent training establishment in Karema. Besides, there had to be a better location for wild elephant capture than here or Simba. There was Wrori, for instance, which Carter had heard about from Arab traders – an elephant paradise watered by branches of the Ruaha River, with substantial herds year round ('[t]his you will understand is all on hearsay', noted Carter with caution). While Cadenhead rested in the station, Carter considered his options. Perhaps he could investigate Wrori's potential on his return to the coast. After all, Kirk had harboured ideas about Wrori too, and the Ruaha region's dense elephant population, which was protected by a far-sighted local chief.

Carter reached a decision. Now reunited, he and Cadenhead would leave Karema together as soon as possible, taking a different line back to Zanzibar along the seventh parallel – a southerly route recommended by Kirk as 'new and more direct' to avoid the 'scoundrels in Ugogo'. Not only would this course pass Wrori, but it would also avoid the live wire Mirambo, who was said to be setting his sights on new dominions. 'Wars and rumours of wars' were being bandied about, wrote Carter; tensions were rising to a point where the country between Karema and the coast was 'impassable'; 'this I mean to find out for myself, as one cannot trust to reports in Africa.' For all his disillusionment, Carter still dreamed of glory. He hoped the Belgian king would present him with the prestigious Order of Leopold, just as he had Cambier. He felt encouraged that the king had ordered a new elephant rifle to be brought to him by Cadenhead, in recognition of his work thus far. It was a shame Cadenhead had left the gun in Zanzibar in order to travel more quickly, but Carter would see it soon enough. There was also news that an engraved plaque would be sent to Carter's foster mother in Hertfordshire. '[T]he pleasure it will give her having this plate stuck up in her little cottage, will be worth to me more than the weight of the rifle in pure gold,' wrote Carter. 'She is my "all in all", and I am her "all in all".'

While Cadenhead recuperated on the same Karema hilltop as the convent where I'd found a bed, Carter packed for the long journey ahead. 'Distances on the map look small,' wrote Carter, 'but when you come to step it foot by foot under a burning sun it is quite a different matter.' Carter put his personal effects into two tin boxes. He'd already posted the collection of feathers he'd been gathering for the wives of Leopold's investors, together with a fine pair of hippo tusks he'd bagged in April ('If one could get a few tons of these his fortune would be made, as I hear hippos [sic] ivory is much more valuable than elephants [sic], being much harder and whiter.')

On 13 June 1880, nine days after Cadenhead's arrival in Karema, the caravan was ready to depart. Carter said a last farewell to Pulmalla, with whom he was leaving his chief mahout, Bonheti. The other Indians and porters would join Carter on the return journey, in a caravan of one hundred and twenty men armed with muskets. To mark the procession's

departure, the mahouts donned their brilliant costumes –
silks and jackets in dazzling colours (Carter had always
preferred to travel 'like a prince', reported a Belgian newspaper). Shots were fired and the porters sang and sounded
bugles, excited to be finally returning to the coast. Waving
goodbye, Cambier watched the caravan fade out of sight with
concern: Cadenhead was ill, Carter fevered, and both men
were disregarding their orders from Brussels. But for Carter, it
was now or never. He was determined to forge a new route
between Karema and the coast, to attach his name firmly
among the stars of African exploration. As for Popelin, he
wasn't there to see his colleague leave. Four days earlier, he'd
gathered fifty men and gone to rescue Burdo and Roger, who
were still struggling on their journey from Tabora. Despite
their riding donkeys, or perhaps because of them, the two
men were lagging some ten days' march from the station.

I planned to follow Carter's line of latitude, which ran more
or less directly from Karema to Dar es Salaam. It would be
awkward, because of a lack of roads going in the right direction. Wolfe plotted the route as best he could on the GPS map
as we sat in a café on the edge of Katavi National Park – now
one of the largest protected areas in Tanzania, running
between the lake to the west, Ugalla to the north and Lake
Rukwa to the southeast. With Carter's surviving day-by-day
diary entries for June 1880, we also had specific topographical
features to help us find our way.

'That place – Lake Chada. I know it,' said Wolfe. 'And
here – about ten miles away from where Carter camped. See
that? When I was a child, my father called it Paradise Plains.'

Wolfe's finger pulled at the GPS screen to magnify the

detail, the focus getting closer and closer until I could see the weave of lake and streams.

'When my sister and I were children, my father used to come out to exactly this spot to camp. Right there, in that patch of trees.'

So much of this journey I'd been on with Carter felt improbable, but this parallel had a satisfying synchronicity. From the beginning of our travels, Wolfe's presence had given me confidence, not least because he'd never doubted what I was trying to achieve, despite numerous diversions. He'd always related to where I'd started with this book, at his father's cottage in Donegal. The Irish–Tanganyika connection I'd made early on was a link which resonated with him. But in that moment Wolfe added the pin to our GPS map, we both

My travelling companions, Rem and Wolfe.

felt something snap into place, as if Carter's Irish ghost were rising from the grave.

For Carter, the journey out of Karema was heavy going. The grass was eight feet tall, even in the mountains, which were covered in hemp. There was difficult marsh and deserted villages, interspersed with scenes Carter described as like 'an English park'. Where the ground hardened, an unsettling echo dogged the caravan's footsteps, like the sound of beating drums. Then the landscape changed again: a well-cultivated settlement, a route following a tributary of Lake Tanganyika, and a night's camping under 'some splendid African ash trees'.

Carter, who was still ill himself, could see Cadenhead's fever was getting worse. On 16 June, the morning broke 'clear, but bitterly cold', Carter scribbled in his notes. Cadenhead was too sick to rise. On 17 June, Carter arranged a hammock to be rigged so Cadenhead could be carried. Swarms of tsetse thickened the air, 'nearly driving us mad'. The party climbed the forested Lyamba lya Mfipa mountains, rising up some fourteen hundred metres, where people had built homes along the peaks, described by a later traveller as 'like a flight of huts perched like emigrating birds'. The path then took Carter's caravan down the other side into Katavi, where scudding clouds raced across the plain. It was a landscape of abundance, noted Carter in his diary: 'lots of food for elephants ... at all times of year'. On 20 June, the expedition struck camp close to a small river outlet of Lake Chada.

As we retraced Carter's steps, our views each day were his. We followed sandy riverside tracks occupied by crocodiles sunbathing with their jaws locked open. Storks as slender as paint strokes picked their way along the banks. Pink-cheeked hippos with stubbled noses and goggle eyes burped and belched in pools. Then mine and Carter's experiences diverged when I saw a wild elephant – the first in my long journey following in the expedition's footsteps – which stared back at me with the familiarity of an animal used to safari vehicles. On a newspaper story covering the African elephant populations in southern Chad, I'd seen how the elephants' behaviour altered when humans approached the herd. The females clustered into a whirling circle to protect the young at the centre – a trait derived from centuries of killing by Sudanese ivory hunters. In Mozambique too, in an area where poaching and civil unrest was rampant, the elephants were terrified by the sound of a vehicle; they blew through their trunks in terror, throwing up dust as they charged in a mix of panic and aggression. But this old bull, who lived inside the protective boundaries of a national park, stood motionless in the midday sun, his body caked in black mud. His drawn flanks reminded me that the reality of an animal's everyday existence is much less picturesque, more mundane, than the symbolism we might attach to it. In the broiling heat, I took in the wider scene, watching vultures devour a dead impala, its teeth bared in its rotting skull, a hind leg cracked out of its socket. Then we drove on through a grove of trees, and there were more elephants walking head to tail along the side of a river. They cast a cursory glance back in our direction, nothing more, then kept on going, the infants following at a trot.

We camped on Paradise Plains under the bronze fronds of palms, which made an almost deafening rustle in the breeze. This would be one of my last nights out west, and the stars shone brightly. In April 1880, one of Hore's colleagues at the lake's Plymouth Rock mission recounted a conversation he'd had with an elder about the night-time constellations: 'pointing to one in Orion, I asked him its name. "<u>Sala</u>" he said. I then asked him if he knew any others in the Southern Cross for instance, but he said, no he only knew <u>Sala</u> and this he knew because wherever they went they always looked towards it and knew that it was shining over their country and the Waguha say "<u>Tu-bagala kwa Sala</u>" ie Let us go towards Sala, meaning home.'

When Carter struck camp in Katavi, he had little interest in star-gazing. A local chief insisted messengers must be sent to Kasogera, the chief of Mpimbwe, about twelve miles south because Carter needed permission for his caravan to advance any further across the plain. The country was unsettled. The rumours of war that Carter had first picked up in Karema were becoming 'more accentuated, more precise ... like the

Paradise Plains, in Katavi National Park.

whistling of a stormy wind, like distant blowing of a tempest', observed Burdo, who was still struggling to make his way to the lake. To ease relations, Carter would have to go and pay hongo to Kasogera, which would delay progress by a couple of days.

On 22 June, Carter ordered his caravan to march in single file for Kasogera's 'great town' of Mpimbwe. These days, it's known as Majimoto – in Swahili, *maji* means 'water' and *moto* means 'fire' – after the hot spring that streams out near the foot of a vine-wrapped tree. The water is crystal clear, tumbling between smooth rocks in a copse where, today, locals come to collect the warm water in yellow jerry cans. I went to visit the spring's source, in the company of the Pimbwe's current chief, Alex Savery Kalulu. 'This spring is the origin of our people,' he said solemnly, 'the source of all our history.' Joined by his two sisters with whom he regularly conferred, the chief pointed out the building which four days after my visit would be used to stage the annual rainmaking ceremony. 'We are praying to our spirits to protect our resources,' he said. Around us, there was a stirring of birds. Vervet monkeys picked off reddish fruits, the seeds suspended from the trees in thick, jewel-like clusters.

As Carter approached, one of Kasogera's leaders came out to show him a hill near the village where the caravan could wait while the hongo was agreed. The price was steep, but Carter settled the matter at eighteen bolts of cloth and an old French gun. Once the novelty of the soldiers' appearance had worn off – 'fine-looking fellows ... heads shaved in several fantastic ways' – Carter began to get a measure of his situation. Things were not quite as they should have been. Trees had been cut to make a new fortification around the town. His men picked up on conversations about how 'the great Mirambo' had set his sights on Mpimbwe, and that he'd teamed up with Simba and the elephant hunter Matumula to make a raid on Kasogera. 'Mirambo seems to be ubiquitous; he is everywhere and in every one's [sic] mouth,' noted Carter. He'd heard these rumours a hundred times before, but this time, there was a tangible unease.

The town was getting busier with people retreating to Kasogera's boma for cover. As Carter unbundled his caravan and settled a sick Cadenhead, Kasogera sent a messenger to Carter's camp on the hill. He claimed Mirambo was now only one day's march away. Kasogera demanded that Carter, Cadenhead and their caravan therefore move inside his fortifications for their own safety. Carter demurred, but Kasogera resisted; it was suspicious, he said, that the Europeans had arrived with all their distractions just as Mirambo and his men were closing in. If Carter and Cadenhead refused to come inside his settlement, Kasogera could only assume the Europeans were in league with Mirambo, and Kasogera would therefore need to take them as hostages. If Mirambo didn't attack before morning, Kasogera swore an oath that he would let them go.

Wondering what to believe, Carter gathered his caravan leaders. With one voice, they argued it would be madness to refuse to camp within Kasogera's fortifications for a single night. Carter's local guide, who was one of Kasogera's own subjects, insisted it was the only safe thing to do. Should they make an enemy of the chief, they'd find themselves in an extremely vulnerable position. In short, he 'could chaw us up whenever he liked'. But once inside, 'we were like rats in a trap,' worried Carter. Kasogera had two thousand armed men compared to Carter's one hundred and twenty. With those kinds of numbers, Carter was concerned his caravan might be kept hostage not for one night but a whole month. He hovered outside the gates, negotiating backwards and forwards over Kasogera's demands. Then as the setting sun lit up the Katavi plains in stripes of gold and green, half the town spilled out of the fortified gates 'yelling and screaming'. Kasogera's men had set fire to a ring of grass to create a defensive blaze.

'[T]hey really expect Mirambo and Simba's men to attack them to-night', wrote a mistrusting Carter in his diary. Observing the 'most excited state' of the townspeople, he told his men to stand to their guns. They would be safe within the town, said Kasogera's negotiator; if the two white men insisted on staying outside and were hurt, they risked Kasogera's reputation. 'A lot of bosh of this kind', said Carter, was bandied around, but by 9 p.m., 'after five hours' jaw', Carter eventually capitulated. His caravan entered the town to set up camp for the night beside the hot springs. The decision was 'sorely against my own judgement', groused Carter. 'Nothing else for it, though it does go hard against the grain to be forced to do what I know is against common sense.'

As the hours passed, the night-time temperature dropped until it became uncomfortably cold. Kasogera's men were drinking hard, filling the town with shouts and war dances. The drums were beating, and there were several false alarms. Carter was exhausted when, at 6 a.m. on Thursday 24 June, he turned to his diary: 'Sent Abdullah [sic] to sultan [Kasogera], saying we wanted to start according to his promise.' Carter continued: 'it is now 8.30 and he has not come back. Sent him word, I think it would be better for me to go and have it out in person with the sultan.' Carter couldn't bear being so reliant on a middleman for the negotiations. 'I fear much we are in durance vile until Mirambo's men beat this brute or he beats them, for he will not part with us as long as he thinks Mirambo's people are near at hand.' Stuck inside Kasogera's fortifications, Carter also now had a better grip on the lay of the land: 'Their boma is strong, but it would take about 5000 men to defend it properly as it is much too large. Outside their boma there is an earthwork thrown up right round for the sharpshooters to lie behind.' He took note of the guns: 'The men are well armed, mostly with old Brown Besses, but I saw several long Enfields also.'

Carter, Cadenhead and their caravan didn't leave Mpimbwe that morning. Accounts vary as to why. Some reported that Kasogera had fled during the night with his wife and possessions, leaving the town undefended. Others said Kasogera had refused to let Leopold's caravan leave as long as the Mirambo threat remained, trapping Carter and Cadenhead in the middle of the settlement. But by 10 a.m., ninety minutes after Carter's last diary entry, the point was moot. Mirambo's men had arrived. His flag was seen floating beside the village – a standard which 'resembled that of the English' to an uncanny degree, or so a report asserted in the Belgian media.

According to various accounts taken from survivors, an army of ruga-ruga descended on Mpimbwe, quickly crashing through the palisade, looting and killing as they went. Some two thousand men had come to battle, including Mirambo's soldiers, as well as Simba's men, and three hundred elephant hunters. At first, Carter had rallied his caravan around him with orders they weren't to join in the fighting. Carter wanted no quarrel with Mirambo. He'd told his men to remain 'impassive spectators of the struggle'; 'have no fear, he will not attack us and will not allow you to be harmed' – words attributed to Carter in the dramatized account of events which would later appear in European newspapers.

As the fighting intensified, Carter and Cadenhead watched the carnage unfold, their tents behind them, on the rise of ground close to where Mpimbwe's hot springs still gurgle out of the earth, and where there are two large baobab trees. One of the two trees still stands; it bears fruit, its branches drawn like a web across the sky. The other baobab was recently cut down, the Pimbwe claim by Sukuma pastoralists, but the felled tree's roots remain – gnarled, knotted and entwined with the survivor's. It was here that Carter held his white handkerchief and hat aloft, shouting, *'Rafiki! Rafiki!'* ('Friends! Friends!') As shots flew, Carter cried out that he didn't want to be a part of their war. But then a stray bullet fired across

The baobab that still stands in Mpimbwe. The felled baobab is to its right.

Chief Alex Savery Kalulu, with his two sisters, at the source of their sacred spring.

Carter's caravan was met by an answering shot from Cadenhead, and the melee turned to chaos. Cadenhead fell, struck by a bullet through his back. Others said it was his eye. Then another bullet landed square in his chest. Cadenhead let out a single cry, his frame collapsing like a marionette with its strings cut. Carter cradled his friend's body, unable to make sense of what was happening while the rest of his men quailed.

In the combined jigsaw of second-hand accounts by Cambier, Burdo and Southon detailing what happened next, Carter pulled out his watch and 'threw down his gun'. How true the next acts of heroism, we will never know; the contemporary European version of events would never have amounted to anything less. According to these reports, Carter told any of his men still in earshot to save themselves and try to get back to Karema. He then picked up Cadenhead's sagging body, carried him to his camp bed, and deposited a last, loving kiss on his friend's bloody forehead. With the sound of bullets hailing around the baobabs, Carter pressed his papers and diaries into the hands of his valet, Mahomed, and urged him to escape.

When Carter re-emerged from his tent, there weren't many men left to hear his furious order to fire. Most had already fled or were dead. Porters lay among heaps of shredded packages and splintered boxes, their blood running into the channels flowing from the springs. The mahouts had fallen too, their wounds streaming a brighter scarlet than their Indian regalia. When only three men were left standing around Carter, they made for the settlement's perimeter, hoping to find a hole in the defences. Instead, they found themselves pinned against an unbroken line of the fortified palisade with an army of Nyamwezi warriors fast closing in on them.

Carter lifted his Winchester rifle to his shoulder, and fired until he ran out of bullets. With only his revolver left, he continued to shoot. But they were cornered. Carter's caravan leader, Abdallah Djemallé, fell next to him. Cadenhead's headman, Abdallah-ben-Rassami, was shot too. As the ruga-ruga swarmed towards Carter, he let loose the last of his bullets before he was struck between the shoulder blades. Another bullet tore into his kidneys. With a reflexive jerk, the leader and commander of Leopold's elephant expedition crumpled, his hands falling limply from his revolver as the ruga-ruga attacked his body with spears and English guns. The looting continued. The fires burned brightly. The

palisade came down, post by post, presaging some of the geopolitical dominoes which would soon fall all over the region
and beyond. In the diplomatic storm about to break over the
trading lines, in the fizz of telegrams soon to race between
Zanzibar and Europe, in the accusations and counter-
accusations, and the widening divisions between Nyamwezi
chiefs, there was now an excuse for a change of tactics by the
Europeans. This flash of violence at Mpimbwe would give
Leopold, his allies and their competitors yet another way to
justify an 'intervention'. The dominoes would start to topple
sequentially and not so sequentially. It was now only a matter
of time before Europe's rule of law – however ugly, however
ruthless – would prevail.

12

Two Tin Boxes

'And whether it is the end of the world we are heading for now, none of us knows. That was a thought I had.'

—Tshibumba Kanda Matulu,
Remembering the Present

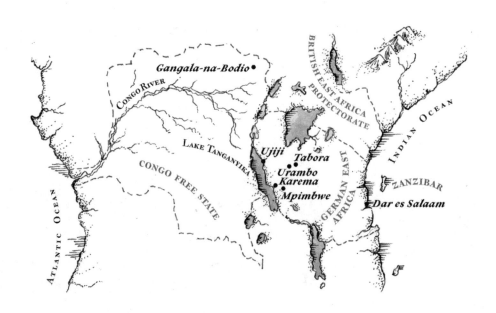

THERE IS AN OLD Indian parable about the elephant, which goes something like this. Three blind men are all trying to feel their way around an elephant in a room. One says it must be a fan (the ear). Another describes a tree trunk (the leg). A third is convinced he's fondling a spear (the tusk). The point is this: we all respond subjectively to the world according to the partial truths presented to us. The bigger picture only becomes clearer when we pull back and acknowledge our limited perspectives.

After Katavi, I took the train with Wolfe from Kigoma back to Dar es Salaam. Rem drove separately, returning to his family in the north. I had a couple of days ahead of me, to put some distance between the journey I'd just completed and flying home to England. By following the elephants' trail, I'd done what I'd set out to achieve when I'd first plotted the line Leopold's expedition had walked. Yet the journey I'd made was also profoundly incomplete.

Part of it was a writing problem that lay ahead – finding the right words for Leopold's masquerade, and the elephants' symbolic function in a story about blind ambition, violence and subjugation. 'Do you see him? Do you see the story? Do you see anything?' wrote Conrad in *Heart of Darkness*. 'No, it is impossible; it is impossible to convey the life-sensation of any given epoch of one's existence.' As the train rumbled back towards the coast, I also worried about what I might have missed. In 1910, a British male explorer wrote about how easy travel to this part of the world had become, the region ringing with 'the lisping accents of the lady traveller who is trying to write a book about Africa in a four months' tour (lapped in luxury as she passes from one hospitable station to another)'. Those words carried a sting of recognition, even though I'd never taken on this journey to prove my resilience. My anxieties weren't practical as much as they were journalistic, about getting an interpretation wrong. I knew I'd never see the proverbial elephant in its entirety, but at least I'd gained a more nuanced understanding of history by the time I returned to Dar es Salaam compared to when I'd started out. By 1914, Europe had devoured the continent to the extent that only two independent states remained: Liberia and the territory that is now Ethiopia. Now there are reckonings taking place, but also denials of responsibility. Formal colonialism might be over, the cruelties and absurdities forgotten or glossed over by the perpetrators, but the aftermath still reveals conspicuous failures of acknowledgement. The trope that the past is another country where they do things differently makes it too easy to tidy away ugly truths, to dismantle the link between cause and effect. As recently as June 2020, the younger brother of the current Belgian king made headlines with his assertion that Leopold II shouldn't be held responsible for suffering in Congo because he'd never been there.

The news of Carter and Cadenhead's deaths reached Zanzibar on 4 August 1880, and quickly sped by cable from Stone Town to Europe. On 11 August, *The Times* made a short announcement: 'Captain Carter and Mr Cadenhead, of the Royal Belgian Exploration Expedition, have both been killed by the Chief Wrambo in Central Africa. "This may possibly mean the great robber chief Mercambo."' That same day in Urambo,

Mirambo asked for an audience with his missionary friend Dr Southon.

So far, there had only been unsubstantiated rumours of how events at Mpimbwe had played out. One report said either Carter or Cadenhead, wounded in the arm, had escaped on a donkey. Another claimed that four of the Indian mahouts had shut themselves inside a hut, which the ruga-ruga burned down. There was talk that Carter had committed suicide, and his valet Mahomed had found Carter's body entwined with Cadenhead's. He'd buried both men in a shallow grave between the two baobabs. Other reports said the valet was stripped by his captors and kept prisoner for three days; he'd escaped, and managed to throw a cloth over Carter's corpse. The rumours multiplied until Mirambo was said to be on the war path with thirty thousand men. 'Contradictory talk and many different versions of the same story' abounded, noted Southon in his journal. He hoped that by letting Mirambo 'tell his tale in his own way and time', everyone would be more likely to get a fuller version of what had really occurred.

Mirambo invited Southon to join him on his veranda so he could deliver his version of what had transpired. According to Mirambo, he'd set out on an unrelated campaign when he'd received a request from Simba to help fight their rival, Kasogera, at Mpimbwe. On the morning of 24 June, the combined army began their assault. During that battle, one of Mirambo's men rushed back to tell him there were Europeans inside Kasogera's boma. Mirambo ordered they should be saved 'at all costs', but it was already too late. By the time Mirambo reached the hot springs, the battlefield was a churning mass of papers, bodies, the Belgian flag (a standard Mirambo claimed he didn't recognize), broken boxes and collapsed tents. Mirambo told Southon he was extremely sorry he'd unwittingly attacked white men, and that had he known they were inside Mpimbwe's fortifications, he would never have advanced. He said he'd only been able to save five of Carter's cases, which he'd brought back to Urambo for Southon to inspect, and seventeen prisoners, whom he would of course immediately release.

The survivors included Hames Wad Sameri – the last man standing when Carter was killed with his back against the palisade, who gave his account of Carter's final moments to Southon. Carter's Arab valet, Mahomed, was another of Mirambo's prisoners – a man Southon recognized from when he'd sailed with Carter and the elephants from Aden to Zanzibar on the *Chinsura*. 'I told him to tell me all about it and entered in my notebook his story, just as I had entered that of Mirambo,' reported Southon.

Mahomed handed over Carter's papers to Southon in their two tin boxes. 'I should have sealed up the journal at once,' wrote Southon, 'but a casual glance showed that the last page was written only about two hours before Carter died.' At the very back of Carter's red notebook was a short instruction: if the book should fall into the hands of anyone after his death, it must be 'immediately sealed up and forwarded to a certain address.' Southon arranged for his effects to be sewn inside a cloth package. They were personally carried by Mahomed to Kirk in Zanzibar in case anything further could be gleaned from Carter's final scrawls.

Snippets of that diary were released 'by the family of the late Captain Carter' to the Royal Geographical Society in London in December 1880. Whatever else was in Carter's two tins was lost, miscatalogued, deliberately destroyed, or still lies hidden in some attic. In Belgium, for instance, extracts from the same last days of Carter's diary are held in the Émile Storms inventory at the Royal Museum for Central Africa at Tervuren. When I checked online, they were mislabelled as belonging to 'B. C. Carter', a British general who commanded the imperial troops in South Africa during the First World War.

We don't know whether Carter's foster mother received her plaque from Leopold to hang up in her house, though Carter's old friends from Mesopotamia made some attempt to ensure she was looked after following his death. Leopold claimed to be 'very affected' by the loss and sent her a personally signed letter of condolence. But his words were hollow. Leopold 'treats men as we use lemons', one of Belgium's prime ministers had once remarked; 'when he has squeezed them dry he throws away the peel'. On the same day Brussels received news of Carter's death, all payments of his salary – previously sent straight to his foster mother – ceased. No lifetime annuity or pension was provided. A one-off pity payment was made by Mackinnon, who sent a hundred pounds, and that was it. Carter's old friends continued to lobby for her interests, but to no avail. 'The poor lady is very old and her wants are not many', pleaded one; she was left 'quite destitute'. As for Carter, you won't find his name on the wall of explorers commemorated in the Royal Museum for Central Africa at Tervuren. Carter was a foot soldier, who became a footnote, the White Sheikh relegated to that vast, forgotten layer of people who oiled the machinery of Europe's imperial agenda.

A few days after the sacking of Mpimbwe, survivors from Carter's caravan began to straggle into the station at Karema. The women – the supernumeraries not factored into any of the official tallies – had been captured and enslaved. 'Cruel events,' wrote Cambier to his Brussels overseers; he acknowledged Cadenhead had been admirable in his 'complete devotion' to Carter, and Carter 'a true friend.' Nevertheless, Carter had 'paid dearly for the disobedience he committed by not going to the coast immediately after being ordered to do so.' Cambier lamented the loss that was Carter's death, the 'frankness and loyalty of his character.' But Carter's skill, wrote Cambier, 'went as far as recklessness'; his generosity degenerated 'into prodigality.' Carter had left a position in Basra worth 'more than 25,000 francs,' 'for the glory of taking the lead in the elephant expedition,' and this 'without having saved a thing.' As for Cadenhead, his presence had been too fleeting on the African caravan road for anyone to much grieve – or comment – upon his life or his passing.

In Zanzibar, the news cast 'a gloom' among the British community 'with whom Carter was a great favourite.' Mirambo, however, was the bigger story. As word of the scandal spread, Southon's sympathetic defence of Mirambo became hard to square with the image of a dastardly chief who'd been terrorizing travellers for some time. Carter's friend the Irish missionary Charles Stokes was convinced Mirambo was 'a deep dyed villain.' How could anything else be expected from an African who had made his wealth from ivory and slavery, contended Stokes. With hindsight, his words were heavy in irony. Stokes would eventually set up a successful ivory trading business of his own, running Congo-bound caravans some three thousand porters strong.

As for Karema, the fort descended into panic. Cambier's 'single chance of salvation,' recommended Popelin, was to burn all the Belgian and IAA supplies so Mirambo couldn't get his hands on them. Popelin said Cambier needed to head for Ujiji. Pulmalla was the station's prize, and everyone now feared for her safety. But it turned out that within hours of Carter setting out from Karema, on 13 June, Pulmalla had fallen ill. According to Cambier, she'd started 'staggering and shaking with convulsive chills'. Nothing could alleviate her misery, not even the piles of blankets her mahout Bonheti gathered to keep her warm. On the morning of 16 June, she tumbled over, refusing all food and drink. With all the other Pune elephants dead, Carter gone and only one of her Indian handlers left to look after her, 'the joy of the small colony' of Karema – the gentle elephant who for one long year had borne the weight of a king's dream – finally gave up and died two days later, on 18 June 1880.

The public wanted answers, action, retribution. 'Any news from Karema?' asked the Belgian press. 'Every day, we are asked if we no longer receive letters from Central Africa and if we do, why we no longer publish them. We are very embarrassed to reply to the relatives and friends of our explorers, who are justly uneasy at the silence which is accorded to our expeditions.' As for Mirambo's crimes, '[T]his now opens a new phase in Africa history', Kirk remarked. There was immediate talk of vengeance. '[I]t has caused me an emotion which is only surpassed in violence by the thirst for retaliation', Strauch wrote to Mackinnon.

Kirk, who until now had staunchly supported Mirambo, was livid about how things had played out. Mirambo likely had spies in Mpimbwe the day before the battle, and 'no doubt gave the order for the expedition to set out for the purpose of the murder'. It was nonsense to suggest Mirambo didn't have a clue about Carter's presence. And Southon's defence was making Mirambo think he was now '"Boss" of the whole country'.

Differing interpretations of events started piling up but perhaps the *Standard* newspaper exposed the crux of the matter first: 'Hitherto, disease, and not violence, has been the cause of the fatality which has overtaken so many of the explorers of the Dark Continent'. Violence against any European could not be permitted to stand. Murdering the personal representative of the Belgian king was a step too far. The events at Mpimbwe gave Europeans and their Western allies another justification to get involved in 'the Africa problem', even if it was a problem entirely of their invention.

Popelin, who was cowering in Tabora where he'd fled with Burdo and Roger at the first murmur of Carter's murder, wrote how the gangs of Mirambo's ruga-ruga were 'ravaging' all Ugalla where he'd encountered survivors from the battle, including one of Carter's most trusted Zanzibari attendants. Paranoid that his own caravan would be intercepted next, Popelin decided 'there was nothing I could do except to get out of the clutches of these bandits as quickly as possible'. He wrote to the IAA headquarters in Brussels to tell them the roads to the north, southeast, east and west were in the allied hands of Mirambo, Simba and Nyungu-ya-Mawe; 'as long as these men exist there will be nothing to do'. The inland Arabs, seeing an opportunity in the wedge they could force between Nyamwezi power and the Europeans, begged Popelin to get permission from Sultan Barghash for more guns 'to make a point of reducing Mirambo, Simba and Nyungu to helplessness forever'. Popelin was getting jumpier by the day. He said he didn't have enough ammunition, claiming his journey to Congo would have to be abandoned, at least for now. When

Popelin did finally make the attempt the following spring, gunpowder wasn't his problem; a few weeks after leaving Karema for the western shore of Lake Tanganyika, he died from a suspected abscess of the liver.

Across the region, panic was spreading 'like a gunpowder flame', said Burdo. Suffering from sore feet, he opted to be carried home to the coast on the back of a donkey, on a journey that came with excitements of its own. East of Tabora, Burdo encountered his largest herd of elephants yet – more than a hundred taking water. 'They frolicked joyfully and with their trunks coming and going, falling, rising, sucking up water and squirting it through an enormous gullet sheltered by superb ivory tusks', he wrote. 'Their huge ears were wide open and their intelligent eyes shone like two stars on the forehead of a black marble colossus.' Putting his donkey to one side, Burdo slipped into the jungle with rifle in hand to take a shot at a trophy.

As for Van den Heuvel, he also made his way back to Zanzibar. Before he left Africa, he threw a punch at the British explorer Joseph Thomson in Stone Town – payback for the unflattering portrait Thomson had written of the Belgian doctor rotting in a fug of incompetence in Tabora. According to Thomson's inflammatory account, Van den Heuvel's behaviour had so upset the local Arabs that 'in a district where cows could be counted by the hundred, he actually could not get a drop of milk.'

Except for Carter's friend Stokes, who blamed Mirambo as vociferously as he could, the Protestant missionaries were determined not to let the massacre at Mpimbwe diminish the trust they had worked so hard to gain from local chiefs. The Protestants, after all, were in a race of their own against the Roman Catholics to win as many African souls as they could. Mirambo 'is not given to assassinating white men', wrote the secretary of the Church Missionary Society to *The Times*. With a view to settling the furore, Edward Hore travelled from the lake to Urambo, carrying the standard of the London Missionary Society – a white dove holding an olive branch – to give some support to his colleague Southon.

Mirambo told Hore how treacherous Kasogera had been – a false friend to the Europeans. Mirambo said he wasn't jealous of European interests in Africa; if anything, he wanted to help them obtain a footing, and had 'placed his faith thoroughly in the English'. But Mirambo was also hearing rumours that he was to be blocked from obtaining guns, that Sultan Barghash might declare war against him and that these moves were being backed by the British. If Mirambo were to face punishment for an honest accident, Hore warned that 'ghastly doubt' would set in about whom Mirambo could trust in the future. The chief, wrote Hore, was in a state of 'grieving that perhaps after all, his dear good Englishmen were not what he had thought'. Hore asked for Mirambo to be given a chance, pointing out that Europeans couldn't expect good diplomatic relations if they weren't willing to return them. 'Suspicion begets suspicion', Hore wrote. There had been the underhanded Swiss trader, Broyon, allegedly cheating Mirambo of his ivory proceeds. Then Carter, who'd gone off script and disregarded custom by avoiding Mirambo's lands on his journey to Karema when, as an envoy of the Belgian king, he should have had the diplomatic nous to introduce himself. And of course there had also been Cambier's numerous offences. Was Cambier's king the same as Hore's, asked Mirambo. Did Leopold even know how badly Mirambo had been disrespected?

Could Hore communicate the nature of these incidents back to Brussels? 'Your mtoto (subject or child) [sic] came to me and I welcomed him, I gave him a place to live, I gave him food and oxen. I said "tell me everything you want" and I was his friend,' said Mirambo. 'Cambier treated me very badly. He was a fool ... [He] built a house in part of my dominions without saying anything to me. This is not right.' If Cambier was representative of all the other Europeans, 'what shall I do when they ignore me in this way?'

It's hard to tell at what point genuine outrage morphed into political acuity. But with each run of telegrams, letters and newspaper articles, events at Mpimbwe were becoming symbolic of a much larger Africa 'problem' for Europeans: the people who lived there. Ultimately, it didn't matter whether Mirambo meant to kill Carter and Cadenhead, or not. Nor did it matter if the deaths were an accidental consequence of a kidnapping attempt by Mirambo on Carter's last elephant, Pulmalla, which was the story some of the newspapers were reporting, not knowing she was already dead. It was of little consequence if Mirambo's actual intention had been to storm Karema and slaughter Pulmalla 'with his own bare hands' and distribute her flesh among his men, as some of the rumours went. If the deaths of Carter and Cadenhead were just an accidental result of local warfare, as Mirambo claimed, then what future for Christians and commerce could there be? From here on in, said Kirk, 'the sympathy and support of the civilised world will be against Mirambo and his allies.' Law and order was needed. A show of authority was necessary, actioned without delay.

On 30 August 1880, it was announced by William Gladstone's Under-Secretary of State for Foreign Affairs in the

House of Commons that Lieutenant William Lloyd Mathews, a British naval officer seconded to work as the sultan of Zanzibar's chief of police, would be tasked with an important new mission: to set out from Stone Town and follow the mainland caravan route with a thousand of the sultan's soldiers and 'make safe for travellers those countries where they are now subject to outrage'. Mathews began pulling his army of mercenaries into line: 'a motley crew' of men 'selected from the slave gangs of former years', wrote a journalist for the *Times of India*, instructed in the 'intricacies of the goose-step'. Dressed in red caps, cropped black jackets, dark-blue frock coats and breeches fringed with silver lace, they looked like they belonged to a circus. Rifles were donated by the British government, with one lad dressed 'in odds and ends of different uniforms' carrying a sword 'as tall as himself'.

With hindsight, this rag-tag army of mercenaries is perhaps a good symbol to hold on to for the knee-jerk opportunism coming next, not just along the caravan road Leopold's elephants had traversed, but across the continent at large. What happened at Mpimbwe was by no means the crisis that either triggered or made the 'Scramble for Africa' inevitable, but it was certainly part of a growing, scrappy, semi-improvised grab for authority that was now gaining a dangerous momentum. The idea of trying to master the continent by elephant had turned into a striking example of the audacity of European desire to get a share of the African cake. There was still much more to come from other so-called 'filibustering expeditions', including Stanley's. As events unravelled in the aftermath of Mpimbwe, Stanley continued moving up the Congo River, building stations and signing treaties on behalf of Leopold.

More rapid-fire, hodge-podge plans were on their way, bank-rolled by men of influence splintering out of the original IAA mission of international cooperation to reveal much more obvious agendas, both private and national. There were new strategic allegiances emerging between Western countries, which bestowed rights on the first to plant a flag for a new trading concession. In October 1884, four Germans set off for Zanzibar under false names and with third-class steamer tickets. Within six weeks, they had twelve treaties in their pockets signed by local chiefs, giving a German company control of over fifty thousand square miles of East African territory. This formed the basis of the nation's claim to what was to become German East Africa following the 1884–5 Conference of Berlin.

Mirambo survived his 'mistake' at Mpimbwe, but only just. There was no war, which many had predicted, but old allegiances fell apart. Mirambo lost Kirk's support. Sultan Barghash enacted his promised threat on the sale of gunpowder. Using the mix-up at Mpimbwe as a pretext to punish his erstwhile ally Simba, Mirambo razed the latter's settlement, which had once been the richest in Ugalla. Southon issued a warning to fellow missionaries in his 1881 annual report about the rapidly deteriorating security. But Southon didn't get to see his hunch mature because, a few months later, he was dead. Mirambo's interpreter and best diplomatic defence was killed as the result of a freak hunting accident.

On 2 December 1884, Mirambo fell ill and died, aged forty-four. The short, one-eyed Nyungu-ya-Mawe was poisoned around the same time, though the cause of his death was never entirely clear. But his legacy endured as one of East

Africa's most powerful chiefs and elephant hunters. In 1966, Nyungu-ya-Mawe's grave was still marked with a reverential pile of tusks.

On 15 November 1881 – known as King's Day in Belgium – Karema's new station commander, Guillaume Ramaeckers, fired off a twenty-one-round volley. 'The Belgian colours float on the mainmast . . . The whole Station is decorated with flags and the garrison is jubilant . . . I gave presents to my men and lifted all punishments . . . Karema is no longer Africa, it is a Belgian land, where we acclaim, as at home, far away, the name of Leopold II. It is with real emotion that I draw these few lines. You have to be far from the country to feel how much you love it and, above all, how much you venerate the One whom, for us, is the living incarnation of the Fatherland.'

Epilogue

'The off forefoot of my donkey stands upon the centre of the earth. If you don't believe me, go and measure for yourself.'
—Arab proverb

I N NOVEMBER 2022, I visited Pune to piece together the early biographies of Pulmalla, Sosankalli, Naderbux and Sundar Gaj. I wanted to go back to the beginning of 1879 and explore the cool, monsoon capital of the British Raj where Leopold's elephants had come from. When I took a taxi from Mumbai where I'd been on another job, the driver asked if I worked in tech, since that's what Pune is now known for. When I explained what I was up to, I assumed four dead elephants would be obscure enough to keep him quiet so I could sleep on the long drive ahead.

'That's a strange story,' said the driver. 'That's a really strange story.'

By the time we'd reached Pune, the driver, Shaikh Ali Mohd Aslam, had offered to help me. The elephants deserved recognition, he said, and so did their Pune mahouts. So we worked together for the next three days. Ali went to look for what was left of the city's dwindling tradition in elephant training while I visited various historians, including an academic I'd got in touch with called Pushkar Sohoni. He'd written a paper about the translocation of animals by colonial powers.

Pushkar talked about how Pune remained elephant-obsessed, even if the only living specimens were now confined to the city zoo. In Pune, the elephant was the deity of the city's founding dynasty. In the 1890s, when Pune became a centre of political unrest against British rule in India, the elephant-headed Hindu god, Ganesha, acquired a new lease of life as a symbol of Indian nationalism. Images of Ganesha were depicted killing demons, in symbolic representations of India's fight for freedom. In the 1960s, Ganesha acquired even more political resonance as emblematic of Hindu power in post-independence India. Today, the city's Dagadusheth Halwai Ganpati temple is visited by over a hundred thousand people every year. At the heart of the shrine is a statue of Ganesha with majestic golden ears donated by a Bollywood film star.

'Elephants, if not part of our daily lives, still loom very large in the imagination,' said Pushkar, 'and when a creature moves from the everyday to fantasy, it's even more potent.'

He described the ways elephants are trained in India, and the sharp bullhook used on the thin skin behind the animals' ears to discipline them: 'If you talk to most people who don't know any better, it's an imagined bond of gentle care, but it's anything but. It's like having a knife held to your throat every day.'

I went to a horse race in the military cantonment where Leopold's four elephants were originally stabled. I visited the post office where Edward Lear had drawn Pune's elephants in the shade of the banyan trees. On the pavement nearby, there was a nineteenth-century monument called the Zero Stone, which was put in place to mark the start of future colonial surveys of the country. There was also this inscription of a poem:

> *He scans the skies,*
> *reading some far-off star*
> *by which he plots*
> *meridians and makes his maps,*

stitching a new-found world
into a patchwork quilt,
a net of metes and bounds,
so lands may know their own
and live in peace.

Between helpings of steaming pilaf I went over my notes with Ali, including the story of Pulmalla carrying the Prince of Wales to Parvati Temple. Later that day, when I was climbing those same polished steps to the temple's inner sanctum, Ali got talking with an ice-cream seller at the bottom of the hill who thought there was perhaps only one mahout remaining in the entire city. Ali tracked down an address.

The mahout's name was Tajuddin Allabaksh Mahat. He used to train elephants for the circus, and now looked after the elephants at the zoo. Tajuddin's wife was also descended from a long line of Pune mahouts. It was a profession closed off to her

A photograph of Pune showing Parvati Hill in the distance. This was taken around the time Leopold's elephants were living here.

Left: *The* garbhagriha, *or sanctum sanctorum, in Pune's Parvati Temple complex.* Right: *The view from the top of Parvati Hill, which Pulmalla used to climb as part of her ceremonial duties before she was taken to Africa. The modern city of Pune now stretches out on all sides.*

as a woman, but she was proud of her heritage. So was Tajuddin's daughter who helped with translation as we sat looking over family photographs in the front room of their home.

Tajuddin explained the relationship between an animal and its keeper, how elephants become used to their mahout's songs and how that dependency lasts a captive elephant's lifetime. He said there was an elephant at the zoo that recognized his bicycle bell in a traffic jam, his description reminding me of Nadine Gordimer's evocation of the lullabies she'd heard among the African elephant trainers at Gangala-na-Bodio in Congo. When Tajuddin talked about an elephant's capacity for gentleness, his words recalled Orwell's haunting image of the elephant about to be shot: it was grazing peacefully, looking 'no more dangerous than a cow'.

When I described the journey Leopold's elephants had made, Tajuddin agreed that Sosankalli may well have succumbed to 'aghin baho', or 'Aganbowa', which is an Urdu term for an inflammatory disease caused by overheating from an elephant walking too far and too hard while carrying too heavy a load.

'Like a cancer of the bone,' said Tajuddin. 'It causes continuous bleeding, and makes the eyes a bit blind.'

The weight limit should have been a hundred kilograms each, said Tajuddin, but Carter had loaded them with up to seven times that amount. As working elephants, they might have been used to carrying heavy loads over short distances, but only if travelling slowly, and with several breaks each day to compensate. Tajuddin's diagnosis more or less lined up with those of specialist elephant veterinarians I consulted. The animals should have been walked at night when the ground was cooler. Asian elephants have less robust footpads than the African species; they're used to jungle habitats, so East Africa's hard, hot substrates would have bruised their feet. The elephants would have needed access to at least a hundred and twenty litres of water every twenty-four hours, and should have had regular breaks to feed. Carter, on the other hand, had boasted of the many days they'd worked without food or water. The boat passage alone would have left them unfit and ill-prepared for such a major journey in a hostile habitat. Sending them to Africa under a leader who didn't have a clue about elephants or elephant medicine ultimately meant only one thing: all of Carter's elephants died as a result of maltreatment.

Tajuddin shook his head. He was sorry Carter hadn't

listened more closely to the expertise of Pune's elephant keepers, who would have known better. Elephants don't forget people who have directly helped or injured them. They are one of very few animals to also recognize their own reflection in a mirror. 'You can teach elephants anything,' said Tajuddin: 'It's a memory thing. An elephant has an extraordinary memory, better than humans.'

As I sat with Tajuddin's family looking through their albums, I could sense the mixed feelings our conversation was bringing up.

'The mahout way of life is over,' he said. 'I'm the last generation. In my opinion, animals should be free. They've been good for war, work and entertainment. I think the time for training elephants is finished.'

As the conversation wove in and out of memories held by the three generations in the room, I thought about that line from Kapuściński, the Polish journalist who wrote so powerfully about the value of oral history. 'Without memory one cannot live,' he said; '[I]t is what elevates man above beasts, determines the contours of the human soul.' I was struck by questions around who and what decides if memory is experienced by non-human animals, and who and what has the authority to determine if those non-human memories are valid. What does 'soul' really mean anyway? What can we know of elephants' experience of consciousness without fully understanding how they 'talk' to each other and their young? We're beginning to learn more about how these animals can communicate using low-frequency messages that can travel a dozen miles across the plains. They pick up the signals with their feet. Ongoing research is proving the complexity of elephant behaviour, which is affecting perceptions around moral obligations not just in relation to the largest land mammal on earth, but towards all our fellow creatures, big and small. Which begs more questions. If a large part of memory is defined by the pain non-human animals suffer at our hands, what ethical considerations are therefore owed to them? As a prescient *New Yorker* article put it: 'If animals deserved the same consideration as humans, then we would find ourselves in a world in which billions of persons were living awful, almost unimaginably horrible lives. In which case, we might have to do something about it.'

Later that evening, wandering through Old Pune's higgledy-piggledy streets, I visited the shrine of Ganesha – the one where I'd watched traffic pause so Hindus could say a prayer to the temple deity with the Bollywood ears. I went inside and left an offering in memory of the four elephants and the Pune mahouts who'd lost their lives in Africa. Wanting to honour the weight Pulmalla, Sosankalli, Naderbux and Sundar Gaj had carried in my journey, I paused at the deity to read out the names of the mahouts and their attendants from the only source I'd found which listed their identities. Which mahout was nicknamed Bonheti, I could never know. Nor could I confirm if Pulmalla's keeper, after his elephant died at Karema, ever made it safely home to Pune. Perhaps the mahouts were Muslim, not Hindu; I couldn't be sure, but I felt some sense of closure all the same, in being able to acknowledge the fact that no one is a nobody just because they've fallen silent in the historical record.

The mahouts' names were as follows: Chiragan Khan Kadurdatkhan, Kirwim Khan Hoosenkhan, Vuzeer Khan Rustomkhan, Shaik Moodier Luantbux, Syed Ahmed Wullud Yakoob, Shaik Imam Sullud Ahmed, Isuf Khan Lutikhan, Sherif

Khan Esmalkhan, Mahomed Khan Riankhan, Maria Dhura-noo, Shaik Rahimon Mahomed and Luximan Zenkuttee.

I didn't return to Belgium, though I tried to trace the tusks of Sundar Gaj and Naderbux, sent back to Brussels from Africa. I found notes about Naderbux's ivory almost going down in a Mediterranean storm with a cargo of mangoes. I also discovered a letter that said the tusks were used to adorn Colonel Strauch's office on the Rue de Namur in Belgium. Then the trail went cold.

I returned to Africa in October 2023 to fact-check contemporary sources. By chance, my visit coincided with Zanzibar's first literary festival. Before the Zanzibar Revolution in 1964, Stone Town had numerous publishers in Swahili, Arabic, English, Gujarati, French, Hindi, even Farsi. Now there were just a couple of independent presses, publishing in English and Swahili.

The headline speaker was the Zanzibar-born British author and Nobel Prize Laureate Abdulrazak Gurnah. With his translator, Ida Hadjivayanis, they were launching the first ever Swahili edition of Gurnah's work *Paradise*, or *Peponi* – a historical novel about the nineteenth-century caravan road that ran inland from the East African coast.

'Writing is a hard business,' said Gurnah in his speech. 'If you have something you want to say, then you have to – or you should – stick with it.'

I chatted with a student in the audience. Shy and unsure of himself, he was dressed in a kanzu and skullcap. He said he only wrote for himself, and not for publication. 'I still can't believe it's actually happening,' he told me. Gurnah's words, and the glimmer of a renaissance in book publishing, were giving him the permission he sought to express something hidden. Later, the student showed me some of his works, including a deeply felt love story dressed in a metaphor about computer programming. Beautiful, moving and painful, it reminded me that however we choose to tell stories, whichever way we chart our course through fact and fiction, the emotional truth that resides in the complicated recesses of our remembered experience is by far the hardest part to distil.

During my return visit to the island, I also went to meet a Tanzanian historian called Abdul Sheriff on his blossom-strewn veranda in Stone Town. We talked among the graves of his Gujarati ancestors about the 'Arab'-controlled slave trade, which he'd spent many years studying. Estimates about the numbers vary. With caution, the Canadian historian Paul Lovejoy has suggested that between 800 and 1900 CE in East Africa alone, around 2.1 million Africans were enslaved and sold through the Swahili slave markets, of which the one in Zanzibar was the last to close, in 1873. Sheriff holds a different opinion about the numbers: 'To the British abolitionists, Arabia was a convenient bottomless pit that allegedly consumed any number of slaves that their lively imagination conjured up.' In our meeting, Sheriff talked about how the research methodology needed to shift – from 'counting heads' to trying to understand how and why the slave trade developed, and the stories of the enslaved themselves. There is much more work to do on this topic. To uncover what really happened, Arab sources also need to be investigated in the Middle East.

I went to a Sunday service at the Anglican cathedral Bishop Steere had built on the site of Africa's last slave market.

It was a peaceful place away from the day's heat to sit and consider the good and bad perpetrated in the name of religion. Today, roughly sixty-three per cent of Tanzania's population identifies as Christian. More Christians live in Africa than in any other continent.

I visited Peter Sudi at the site of the Anglican mission Bishop Steere had helped establish at nearby Mbweni. Peter had just celebrated his eighty-ninth birthday, and was pleased I'd returned. He wanted to know everything about the journey I'd taken.

'There is an English proverb I want to tell you,' he said. 'What is not seen by the eye is not here in the heart.'

I asked Peter for his mailing address so I could send him a copy of this book when it was published. He said he expected he'd be dead by then, so I should send it to his daughter instead.

'I want to be buried here,' he said, as he closed the church with the same long brass key he'd used to open up the door when I'd first arrived in Zanzibar. 'My time is done. I am at peace.'

When I said goodbye to him outside, the rain was falling in thick plops on waxy leaves, and the air smelled clean and sweet.

On that same return visit to Tanzania, I spent four weeks travelling overland from Dar es Salaam to Lake Tanganyika. Since my last visit, new railways, roads and bridges had been built. The port at Karema had opened, even though the only trade I encountered was a single dhow being loaded for the eastern Congo. In May 2023, a Tanzanian journalist described it perfectly: 'Lying invitingly on the eastern shore . . . Karema Port is like a beautiful lady waiting for a proposal?' Down by the beach, more trees had drowned and new chunks of coastline had been eaten up by the lake's rising water levels.

When I pushed open the squeaky gates to Karema's convent, birds were singing in the mango trees and chickens were picking at the grass. A nun in a pristine white habit was ambling up the sweep of brick stairs to the main veranda. When I called Sister Lydia's name, she turned around. At first she didn't recognize me. Then she started to hug me, and stroke my hair. Squealing with the ebullience I remembered from the last time I was here, she suggested we should eat another rabbit. Except she couldn't go and wring its neck because the senior sister was away. Fish and vegetables would have to do instead. She ushered me into a bedroom done up with pink bedlinen, teddy bears and posters of Jesus, and encouraged me to stay for as long as I liked. She brought me buckets of hot water to wash with. She wanted me to meet 'Father-Priest', who hadn't been in Karema last time I'd visited, and to tell him all about the elephants. At church the following Sunday, I stood in front of the congregation and recounted Pulmalla's story to pews rammed with worshippers, with Father-Priest translating, and the children falling asleep.

In February 2023, I travelled to Iraq on an assignment for a British newspaper. I took with me the picture I'd found of the Lynch warehouses that showed the riverside location of Carter's home before he left for Africa. I wanted to see what remained of where he'd lived when Margil was a grove of date palms on Basra's outskirts. Now it was just another neighbourhood absorbed into the sprawl of military checkpoints, clogged canals, crumbling Ottoman caravanserais, war-torn ruins and the odd blue dome in the shape of a swollen water drop. On the Margil riverside, young men with gelled quiffs posed for photographs. Street hawkers sold balls of candyfloss. When I wandered through the dilapidated site where the original Lynch buildings used to stand, a local man asked me why I was there. I explained Carter's story, and he invited me into his home. He showed me where he and his family of ten lived in two crumbling rooms, and had done ever since he'd lost his house under Saddam Hussein's regime. Revealing his mutilated ear from when he was tortured as a political prisoner, the man recalled how much Iraq had suffered, and how recovery felt impossible. He said he thought there used to be a garden among the ruins I was poking around, but during the chaos of the US-led invasion of Iraq, even the palm trees had been stolen. A Basra historian told me the same story, that in 2003 the city was looted inside-out. 'What happened in those times? I've only been able to write about it for myself,' he said.

I narrowed my eyes to take in the riverscape for which Carter had once held such affection. Here he'd been a success, the king of the Tigris poised for greater things. Then a few years after Carter's death, a story was published in the *Times of India* mentioning a boat captain who claimed he was the one who transported Leopold's four elephants across the Indian Ocean. 'My officers and I laughed a little afterwards at the extraordinary fuss they made at home about shipping Jumbo,' said the captain. 'Our elephants, though, were failures from the first, and instead of training the African elephants they turned wild themselves, and bolted into the jungle.' And Carter? 'O[h]! He was a failure, too, so far as success goes. He died riddled through and through with assegais, and that was the end of it.' Carter's ambitions for glory had come to nothing. I'd pursued his story, not because I'd wanted to recast his march on Africa as heroic, but because Carter and his elephants had functioned as a vehicle for me to understand what was missing from the fragments of story we inherit. In Iraq, I'd tried to reimagine Carter's earlier, happier life, of how Mesopotamia used to be, when the river Tigris was so still you could 'see the Scorpion in it, star by star.' I'd wanted to reach for something evocative about the histories the river contained: the ghost of Carter's Irish song drifting across the water, the plash of an oar. Instead, my view was dominated by Saddam's scuttled pleasure cruiser showing its belly to the sky. There was no wildlife, aside from a few kerning swifts darting along a riverbank studded with headless palms. But I was glad I'd come, if only to experience the death of any lingering romance I'd first attached to that image of the White Sheikh galloping across the Mesopotamian sands.

Leopold's dream for the domestication of African elephants didn't die with Carter. As Leopold said to Strauch in early 1879: 'African business in a long-term business.' After Mpimbwe and the disruptions that occurred as a result along the caravan routes, any further attempts to train African elephants were put aside – at least for a time. Instead, Leopold focused on Stanley's line to Nyangwe from the mouth of the Congo River. Through the early 1880s, Stanley continued to make his way upriver with a thickening sheaf of treaties. In December 1882, he pitched his tent on the banks of what became known as Stanley Pool. 'The Belgian flag lies at the door of the new world', declared Leopold's propagandists. Boats were brought in. The 'iron horse' was built. The new railways enabled the efficient extraction of Congo's resources as Leopold's next crop of hirelings arrived, like 'burglars breaking into a safe'. Stanley, like Carter, was discarded by Leopold like a used lemon. The colonial agenda shifted into a new gear. There was 'no heroism, no geographical glory, just the distasteful know-ledge of the vilest scramble for loot that ever disfigured the history of human conscience', wrote Conrad.

By 1899, Leopold's Africa obsession had switched from ivory to rubber. The means of control had morphed from treaty signing to horrifying atrocities, including forced labour, torture and indiscriminate mass murder. Secure in his owner-ship and exploitation of Congo, Leopold was soon ready to start up his strange elephant experiment again, appointing Jules Laplume to open the first training school at Api in northeast Congo. This time Leopold's ambitions came to frui-tion. By 1910, a year after his death, there were thirty-five trained African elephants at the station. The operation then expanded to Gangala-na-Bodio, also in northeast Congo, which was where I'd encountered the ruins of the training school in 2015. Leopold's pet project had finally generated momentum – the captive elephants decorating banknotes, stamps and postcards as a mark of Belgian pride – which only fell apart after Congo's independence in 1960. Then in 1984, a final attempt was made at Gangala-na-Bodio to use the sur-viving elephants for elephant-back wildlife safaris. It relied on four captive animals that had survived decades of colonial and postcolonial violence. Gangala-na-Bodio's last habituated ele-phant died in 2010. Her name was Kiko; she was the daughter of Moganga, captured in 1912.

As I started to pack away the notes covering the wall of my office, I found a couple of old photographs from the first time I'd visited that old training school in Congo. In one of the pictures, I was standing in a graveyard of animal skulls: one belonged to the last northern white rhino known to have existed in the wild; the others belonged to elephants.

I also found a quote which I'd pinned to my map at the very beginning of my journey.

'The elephant is the most respectable animal in the world. In size he surpasses all other terrestrial creatures; and, by his intelligence, he makes as near an approach to man, as matter can approach spirit.'

These words were written nearly two hundred years ago. And yet?

'To ride an elephant gives you a false sense of your own importance,' Pune's last mahout had told me when I'd finished recounting Leopold's parade. 'An elephant is very high up. It's a good place to be cowardly from.'

Ethnic Groups

'Usisafirie nyota ya mwenzio.'
('Don't set sail using somebody else's star.')

—SWAHILI PROVERB

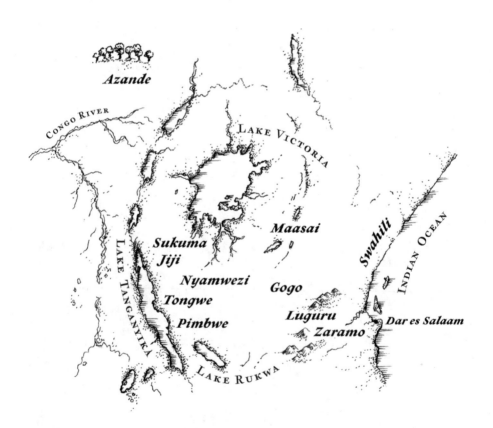

Listed below are the main ethnic groups mentioned in this book, the map opposite showing their distribution at the time of Carter's expedition in 1879. These groupings more or less hold today, although the boundaries have been loosened by urban migration, cultural integration and dispersal of traditionally nomadic pastoralist groups. The names of the groups here, and throughout the book, are given in their basic form, though in Swahili various prefixes may be used. The prefix *Ki-*, for example, denotes the language – hence '*Ki*swahili', for instance, or '*Ki*tongwe' (the language of the Tongwe people). *M-* is used to indicate an individual from a group ('*M*tongwe') and *Wa-* the people in general ('*Wa*tongwe').

Azande. Local to northeastern Democratic Republic of Congo (including the region around Garamba National Park). In the nineteenth century, they were known for their elephant hunting.

Gogo. Residing in the arid Dodoma region of central Tanzania. In the nineteenth century, they were known for charging caravans high water taxes.

Jiji. Living in and around Kigoma, on Lake Tanganyika. In the nineteenth century, their local influence was constantly challenged by Arab-Swahili traders.

Luguru. Living in and around the Morogoro region of Tanzania. They are a matrilineal ethnic society.

Maasai. Nomadic pastoralists widely dispersed over north, central and southern Kenya, as well as northern Tanzania.

Nyamwezi. One of the largest ethnic groups in northwest and central Tanzania, living between lakes Victoria and Rukwa. In the nineteenth century, the Nyamwezi made up most of the long-distance porters on the caravan routes between Lake Tanganyika and the coast. From around 1860 to 1884, they were led by the powerful Chief Mirambo.

Pimbwe. Pimbwe territory traditionally encompassed the area that is now Katavi National Park in western Tanzania. In 1879, their ruler was Chief Kasogera.

Sukuma. Tanzania's largest ethnic group, based in northwestern Tanzania. They operate a mixed economy – part pastoralist and part agriculturalist.

Swahili. The Swahili are based along the coast of Tanzania as well as parts of Kenya and Mozambique, with a culture that combines African, Arab and some Indian and European influences.

Tongwe. Living on the eastern shore of Lake Tanganyika, this ethnic group has Congolese roots.

Zaramo. Based along the central eastern coast of Tanzania, around Dar es Salaam and the Pugu Hills.

Historical Characters

These are the main nineteenth-century characters connected to the elephant expedition of 1879. They are listed in alphabetical order; not all names are in full owing to omissions in the historical record. Cross-references to individuals with their own entries are in **bold** and the following abbreviations have been used: CMS (Church Missionary Society); IAA (International African Association); LMS (London Missionary Society).

Samuel Baker. An English explorer who was the first European to visit Lake Albert – one of the northerly African Great Lakes – in 1864.

Sultan Barghash. See **Barghash bin Said**.

Edward Baxter. A British missionary stationed at Mpwapwa for the CMS.

Bonheti. Pulmalla's mahout from Pune, India.

Philippe Broyon. A Swiss trader who operated between Lake Tanganyika and the coast.

Adolphe Burdo. Belgian leader of the third IAA expedition, which left Zanzibar in 1880.

Richard Francis Burton. One of the nineteenth century's leading British explorers, who reached Lake Tanganyika in 1858.

Verney Lovett Cameron. A British explorer, and the first person to cross equatorial Africa from sea to sea, between 1872 and 1875.

Tom Cadenhead. **Carter**'s British assistant and closest friend.

Ernest François Cambier. Belgian leader of the first IAA expedition in 1878, appointed after Captain Louis Crespel died in Zanzibar.

Frederick Falkner Carter. The Irishman hired by **Leopold II** to lead the elephant expedition of 1879.

Abbé Michel Debaize. A French clergyman and explorer, commissioned in 1878 to lead the French Scientific Expedition travelling across Africa from east to west.

Abdallah Djemallé. Carter's caravan headman, most likely hired in Zanzibar at the outset of the expedition.

Arthur Dodgshun. A British missionary hired by the LMS to go to Ujiji.

Oswald Dutalis. A Belgian appointed to join the second IAA expedition in 1879.

Francis Galton. A British scientist and eugenicist who explored southwest Africa in the 1850s.

Charles Gordon. A British military leader employed in the Equatoria region (today's South Sudan and northern Uganda) in the 1870s.

Jules Greindl. A Belgian diplomat and minister of state who helped set up both the IAA and the Comité d'études du Haut-Congo for **Leopold II**.

William Griffith. A British LMS missionary who helped establish the Plymouth Rock station on Lake Tanganyika.

Mwinyi Heri. Leader of the Ujiji Arabs on Lake Tanganyika.

Annie Hore. Wife of the LMS missionary **Edward Hore**.

Edward Coode Hore. A British LMS missionary and experienced sailor, stationed at Ujiji.

Isike. Tabora's Nyamwezi chief, and a relative of **Nyungu-ya-Mawe**. He was militarily astute, resisting Arab power as well as later colonial incursions.

Kasogera. Ruler of Mpimbwe who agitated **Simba** and his allies.

John Kirk. Political agent and British consul to Zanzibar from 1873 to 1887.

Jules Laplume. A Belgian cavalry officer appointed head of **Leopold II**'s elephant training school in northeast Congo in 1899.

Joseph Last. A British CMS missionary stationed at Mpwapwa.

Leopold II. Ruled Belgium from 1865 to his death in 1909. He owned the Congo Free State from 1885 to 1908.

David Livingstone. Scottish missionary-explorer who died in 1873 in what is now known as Zambia.

Luximor. Sosankalli's mahout from Pune, India.

William Mackinnon. Scottish shipbuilder and owner, founder of the British India Steam Navigation Company, and serial investor in Africa schemes, including those of **Leopold II.**

Mahomed. Carter's valet, who accompanied him to Africa from Mesopotamia.

Majwara. The mission cook at Mpwapwa who had formerly served on **Stanley** and **Livingstone**'s expeditions.

William Lloyd Mathews. British naval officer seconded to **Sultan Barghash** in Zanzibar as chief of police.

Matumula. A celebrated elephant hunter, and vassal of **Simba.**

Mirambo. A Nyamwezi chief who ruled a vast territory west of Tabora.

Joseph Mullens. British secretary of the LMS travelling from Dar es Salaam to Lake Tanganyika.

Abdallah bin Nasibu. A prominent slave and ivory trader, and leader of the Tabora Arabs. He was often in conflict with **Isike.**

Nyungu-ya-Mawe. An African chief who by 1876 commanded a large swathe of territory southeast of Tabora.

William Penrose. A young British engineer and lay member of the CMS travelling the inland caravan route.

Émile Popelin. Belgian leader of the second IAA expedition, tasked to reach Nyangwe via Lake Tanganyika.

Guillaume Ramaeckers. Belgian leader of the fourth IAA expedition in 1880. He was ordered to relieve **Cambier** at Karema and take over the station.

Lionel Kentish Rankin. A British missionary who joined the Universities' Mission to Central Africa in Zanzibar in 1879 – a position he abandoned in favour of the elephant expedition.

Abdallah-ben-Rassami. Cadenhead's caravan headman, most likely hired in Zanzibar at the outset of the expedition.

Oscar Roger. The Belgian second-in-command of **Leopold II**'s third IAA expedition, which was led by **Adolphe Burdo.**

Barghash bin Said. The second sultan of Zanzibar, who ruled from 1870 until his death in 1888.

George Sanderson. The most notable elephant catcher of his day, based in India. He was superintendent of the kheddah capturing system at Mysore.

Henry Shelton Sanford. An American businessman and former ambassador to Belgium. He was a member of the executive committee of the IAA.

Simba. A Nyamwezi chief who ruled over a significant region southwest of Tabora.

Ebenezer Southon. LMS missionary who settled in Urambo in August 1879.

John Hanning Speke. Another of the celebrity British explorers of the day, who confirmed the source of the Nile in 1862.

Henry Morton Stanley. The Welsh-American explorer who led African expeditions in 1871–2 (the search for **Livingstone**); 1874–7 (crossing Africa from east to west); 1879–84 (laying claim to parts of Congo for the Comité d'études du Haut-Congo); and 1887–90 (a rescue mission to save Emin Pasha, the governor of Equatoria).

Edward Steere. Anglican missionary and third bishop of Zanzibar.

Charles Stokes. An Irish-born CMS missionary in East Africa who later became an ivory trader.

Maximilien Strauch. Appointed secretary-general of the IAA in 1878, and a critical part of **Leopold II**'s Africa schemes.

Abdullah Susi. One of **Livingstone**'s most trusted assistants, along with James Chuma. Susi accompanied **Stanley**'s expedition to Congo from 1879 to 1882. James Chuma joined **Thomson**'s 1879 expedition from the east coast to Lake Tanganyika.

John Swedi. The first Black East African deacon, ordained by **Edward Steere** in June 1879.

Joseph Thomson. Hired in 1878 as geologist and naturalist on London's Royal Geographical Society's expedition. He later became its leader.

Tippu Tip. Born Hamad bin Muhammad al-Murjabi, he was East Africa's most prominent slave and ivory dealer. His father was an Omani trader in Tabora, his mother the daughter of Chief Fundikira I, a famous Nyamwezi leader in the 1840s.

Théodore Van den Heuvel. Belgian doctor and second-in-command of the second IAA expedition.

Notes

Unless otherwise stated, translations from French sources are my own. For abbreviations used in archive references, please see under 'Archives' in the Select Bibliography, p. 385.

vi **'All continents are dark continents ... not empty'** [epigraph]: Teju Cole, 'Shadow Cabinet: On Kerry James Marshall', in *Black Paper: Writing in a Dark Time* (Chicago and London: University of Chicago Press, 2021), p. 121.

vi **'Better to know ... it's not over'** [epigraph]: Kunle Ajibade, 'INTERVIEW: Nobel prize winner Abdulrazak Gurnah talks about his writing life', *Premium Times*, 4 December 2022.

vi **'It was impossible to keep a real course, the path wound so'** [epigraph]: Verney Lovett Cameron, 'Journal of Lieutenant V. L. Cameron, Commander of the Livingstone East Coast Aid Expedition. From Unyanyembe to Ujiji', *Proceedings of the Royal Geographical Society of London*, 19:2 (1874–5), p. 151.

AUTHOR'S NOTE

xiv **Zanzibar:** An archipelago of many islands, the largest being Unguja and Pemba.

xiv **the African oral tradition ... European documentarians:** See Adam Jones and Isabel Voigt, '"Just a First Sketchy Makeshift": German Travellers and Their Cartographic Encounters in Africa, 1850–1914', *History in Africa*, 29 (2012), pp. 9–39.

xv **'As for "ideology" ... never smell your own':** Cited in 'Letters to the
–xvi Editor from Steven Pinker, Jonathan Gottschall, and Others', *New York Times*, 14 January 2022.

xvi **'Establish early on ... good feminists or dignified patriarchs':** Binyavanga Wainaina, 'How to Write About Africa', *Granta*, 2 May 2019.

xvi **'Regions unknown!' ... map in a childhood atlas from 1852:** Joseph Conrad, 'Geography and Some Explorers', *National Geographic* (March 1924), cited in R. Curle (ed.), *Last Essays by Joseph Conrad* (London and Toronto: J. M. Dent & Sons, 1926), pp. 19–20.

xvii **'It had got filled ... become a place of darkness':** Joseph Conrad, *Heart of Darkness* (London: Penguin, 1989), p. 33.

xvii **That reputation sticks to the entire continent, as Wainaina reminds us:** 'Always use the word "Africa" or "Darkness" or "Safari" in your title. Subtitles may include the words "Zanzibar", "Masai", "Zulu", "Zambezi", "Congo", "Nile", "Big", "Sky", "Shadow", "Drum", "Sun" or "Bygone". Also useful are words such as "Guerrillas", "Timeless", "Primordial" and "Tribal".' Binyavanga Wainaina, 'How to Write About Africa', *Granta*, 2 May 2019.

xvii **Conrad was 'a thoroughgoing racist':** See Chinua Achebe, 'An Image of Africa: Racism in Conrad's *Heart of Darkness*', in *Hopes and Impediments* (London: Penguin, 2019), p. 11.

1. Prologue to an Adventure

1 **'I wouldn't be at home ... resting places themselves' [epigraph]:** Dylan Thomas, 'Letter to A. E. Trick, Summer 1935', in Paul Ferris (ed.), *The Collected Letters* (London: J. M. Dent & Sons Ltd, 1985), p. 191.

3 **'I find I can't see a landscape; scenery is just scenery to me':** Ibid., p. 192.

3 **'The dead Irish answer ... dead and damned forever':** Ibid., p. 191.

3 **'before the West died':** Dylan Thomas, 'Prologue to an Adventure', in Walford Davies (ed.), *Collected Stories* (London: Weidenfeld & Nicolson, 2014), p. 106.

3 **'a funny dimension':** Thomas, 'Letter to A. E. Trick, Summer 1935', p. 191.

4 **'I like maps, because they lie ... not of this world':** Wisława Szymborska, 'Map', trans. Clare Cavanagh, *New Yorker*, 7 April 2014.

6 **A semi-derelict training school for African elephants:** When I visited, the conservation agency African Parks was beginning to improve the surviving infrastructure as a base for new anti-poaching operations.

6 **Kony and his child soldiers ... the threat of kidnapping endured:** In 2008, a joint operation began between the Armed Forces of the Democratic Republic of Congo and the Ugandan army against Joseph Kony's Lord's Resistance Army (LRA) in and around Garamba. The LRA retaliated with a guerrilla campaign against the local population. In January 2009, LRA militants attacked the park's headquarters, killing fifteen staff and kidnapping two children. Poaching spun out of control, reaching a peak in 2014.

7 **'like a solid grey army on the march':** Armand Denis, *On Safari: The Story of My Life* (New York: E. P. Dutton & Co., 1963), p. 83.

8 **the Belgian conservationist ... details about the elephant school:** The biologist Jean Marc Froment. He collaborated on this book: Kes Hillman-Smith and José Kalpers (eds), with Luis Arranz and Nuria Ortega, *Garamba: Conservation in Peace and War* (published by the authors, 2015).

8   **The parade ground at Gangala-na-Bodio [picture caption]:** This rare
     picture, featuring the station commander on horseback in the parade
     ground at Gangala-na-Bodio in the late 1940s or early 1950s, was dug out
     of a private archive sourced by Froment.

9   **Gangala-na-Bodio was once run ... a hundred African mahouts:**
     Jean-Paul Harroy, *Biographie belge d'outre-mer*, t. VII-B (Brussels: Académie
     royale des sciences d'outre-mer, 1977), p. 275.

9   **a colonial-era film ... elephants were captured in the wild:** Travel Film
     Archive, 'Wild Elephant Round Up 1942', 3 June 2008, www.youtube.com/
     watch?v=m__JTQ7UqiM&t=503s

9   **'little fellows standing ... tied to the lines':** Edmund V. Leplae, 'Taming
     the African Elephant and Buffalo', *Illustrated London News*, 6 June 1925.

9   **To tame the elephants, the mahouts used the 'chicotte':** Johannes Du Plessis,
     *Thrice Through the Dark Continent: A Record of Journeyings Across Africa During
     the Years 1913–1916* (London: Longmans, Green and Co., 1917), p. 153.

9   **a man described as 'lean as a cudgel' ... 'angelic patience':** E. Leplae, 'La
     Domestication de l'éléphant d'Afrique au Congo belge', *Bulletin agricole du
     Congo belge* (London: L'Imprimerie nationale, 1918), p. 52.

9   **'one of the new industries on the Congo':** 'Congo Elephants', *The Globe*,
     10 December 1902.

10   **'elephantdozers':** David E. Reed, 'Letter to Walter S. Rogers, Institute of
     Current Affairs in New York', 3 March 1955, *Institute of Current World
     Affairs*, www.icwa.org/wp-content/uploads/2015/09/DER-36.pdf

10   **Buta:** 'Buta is, as nearly as possible, the centre of Central Africa. It's
     Piccadilly Circus, with its one-way traffic "Keep to the Right" in French
     and in Flemish.' Owen Tweedy, 'The Central African Highway',
     Geographical Journal, 75:1 (January 1930), p. 5.

10   **Hutsebaut ... to successfully raise an okapi in captivity:** In 1928, Brother
     Joseph Hutsebaut shipped an okapi to Antwerp Zoo – the first time an
     okapi translocation was successful – only for it to die of starvation during
     the Second World War. See Susan Lyndaker Lindsey, Mary Neel Green and
     Cynthia L. Bennett, *The Okapi: Mysterious Animal of Congo-Zaire* (Austin:
     University of Texas, 1999), p. 54, and James P. Chapin, 'The Birds of the
     Belgian Congo: Part I', *Bulletin of the American Museum of Natural History*,
     65 (1932).

12   **'looked as if they were carved out of lard':** Nadine Gordimer, 'The African
     Magician', *New Yorker*, 15 July 1961.

12   **'four great stubby feet waving in the air':** Nadine Gordimer, 'The Congo',
     Telling Times: Writing and Living, 1954–2008 (New York: W. W. Norton &
     Company, 2010), p. 93.

12   **Patrice Lumumba ... his body dissolved in sulphuric acid:** Georges
     Nzongola-Ntalaja, 'Patrice Lumumba: The Most Important Assassination

of the 20th Century', *Guardian*, 17 January 2011. For Britain's suspected involvement, see Gordon Corera, 'MI6 and the Death of Patrice Lumumba', *BBC News*, 2 April 2013.

12   **'all news from this remote corner ... have been among them':** Gordimer, 'The Congo', p. 92.

12   **the melodies evoked the soothing drone ... tame elephants in Asia:** Gordimer wasn't the only one to notice the connection. I found another description of Congolese mahouts in the 1920s singing Burmese and Indian lyrics to traditional Azande tunes. See Tracy Phillips, 'Farming with Elephants', *Living Age*, 334:4328 (April 1958), p. 736. See also Pushkar Sohoni, 'Translocated Colonial Subjects in Collaboration: Animals and Human Knowledge', *Transfers*, 8:1 (Spring 2018), p. 6.

12   **what distinguished the African and Asian species:** In 2021, the IUCN (International Union for Conservation of Nature) listed the African savannah elephant (*Loxodonta africana*) and African forest elephant (*Loxodonta cyclotis*) as separate species for the first time.

13   **forty-odd elephants were shipped ... tug of heavy loads:** After the Abyssinian campaign, some of the war elephants were decorated by Queen Victoria and redistributed to British circuses, others to America, including Jumbo II. For more on this story, including the botched attempt to execute Jumbo II using Thomas Edison's new electrocution technology, see the essay 'Jumbo II' in Elena Passarello's collection *Animals Strike Curious Poses* (London: Jonathan Cape, 2017).

13   **'the Africans have no notion ... but to kill and eat it':** 'News From Zanzibar', *East Anglian Daily Times*, 20 August 1879.

14   **In 1879 the number of African elephants ... figure it is now:** Elephant counts are notoriously unreliable. *National Geographic* estimated the elephant population in Africa in 1800 at twenty-six million. See www.education.nationalgeographic.org/resource/history-ivory-trade. The WWF has estimated there were around twelve million at the end of the nineteenth century. See www.worldwildlife.org/species/elephant. In 2016, IUCN research cited 415,000 African elephants, with unsurveyed areas accounting for maybe a further 117,000 to 135,000. See 'Poaching Behind Worst African Elephant Losses in 25 Years – IUCN Report', *IUCN*, 23 September 2016, www.iucn.org/news/species/201609/ poaching-behind-worst-african-elephant-losses-25-years-%E2%80%93- iucn-report

14   **'So Geographers in Afric-maps ... elephants for want of towns':** Jonathan Swift, 'On Poetry: A Rhapsody (1733)', in William Ernst Browning (ed.), *The Poems of Jonathan Swift, D.D.*, vol. 1 (Project Gutenberg, 2004), www.gutenberg.org/files/14353/14353-h/ 14353-h.htm#link2H_4_0077

14 **'Scramble for Africa':** Thomas Pakenham's *The Scramble for Africa* (London: Abacus, 1991) is a comprehensive history of European colonization across Africa between 1876 and 1912. Pakenham dates the phrase 'the scramble for Africa' to 1884.

15 **'A touching tale, if all were known' ... a 'strange prodigy':** Cited in Daniel Crawford, *Thinking Black: 22 Years Without a Break in the Long Grass of Central Africa* (New York: George H. Doran Company, 1912), p. 258.

15 **'Stuck high on the elephant's back ... struggle for supremacy':** Ibid.

15 **'invention of Africa':** See V. Y. Mudimbe, *The Invention of Africa: Gnosis, Philosophy, and the Order of Knowledge* (Bloomington: Indiana University Press, 1988).

16 **'A robin redbreast in a cage ... Puts all heaven in a rage':** William Blake, 'Auguries of Innocence' (*c.*1803), in R. H. Shepherd (ed.), *The Poems of William Blake* (London: Basil Montagu Pickering, 1874), p. 145.

16 **'Lord of Tuskers' ... hired to lead the expedition:** Crawford, *Thinking Black*, pp. 257–8.

17 **In 1863, he moved to Mesopotamia:** In 1879, Mesopotamia was also known as Ottoman, or Turkish Arabia.

17 **in the Age of Empire ... bonds of trade and communications:** E. J. Hobsbawm, *The Age of Empire: 1875–1914* (New York: Vintage Books, 1989), p. 9.

17 **The Indian Ocean before steam ... before the arrival of Islam:** Thomas Kerr Lynch, *The Navigation of the Euphrates and Tigris and the Political Rights of England Thereon* (London: Strangeways and Sons, 1884), cited in Camille Lyans Cole, 'Precarious Empires: A Social and Environmental History of Steam Navigation on the Tigris', *Journal of Social History*, 50:1 (19 April 2016), p. 23.

17–18 **the traditional ivory and East African slave trade ... coastal ports:** There is an interesting chapter on the complex feelings modern Africans have towards complicity in the trade of enslaved people through East Africa in Zeinab Badawi, *An African History of Africa: From the Dawn of Humanity to Independence* (London: W. H. Allen, 2024). 'As the Tanzanian archaeologist and historian Professor Felix Chami put it to me with some force, the fusion of African and Arab culture and the adoption of Islam created "a major problem in the history of coastal East Africa". He argued, and many African academics would agree, that Swahili empathy with Arabs made it easier for some Swahili to acquire non-Swahili African captives for human trafficking. The participation of some Africans in the trade of enslaved people is a topic most people across Africa find difficult to comprehend. It engenders feelings of shame and guilt among the descendants of enslavers and there are concerns that a franker conversation could foster divisions among communities and perhaps even hinder efforts at nation building' (pp. 214–15).

18 'slave nests': Colonel Gordon, September 1877, cited in George Birkbeck Hill (ed.), *Colonel Gordon in Central Africa, 1874–1879: From Original Letters and Documents* (London: Thos. De La Rue & Co., 1881), p. 274.

18 the shadowy trade ... worked for harems or diving for pearls: By the mid nineteenth century, it was estimated that up to thirty thousand of the Gulf's pearl divers were African. Abdul Sheriff, *Slaves, Spices and Ivory in Zanzibar: Integration of an East African Commercial Empire into the World Economy, 1770–1873* (Athens, OH: Ohio University Press, 1987), p. 37. Badawi's *An African History of Africa* describes how the Indian Ocean and eastern trade in enslaved Africans was different to the transatlantic: '[F]emale captives were more valued and are believed to have outnumbered males. Enslaved African women could be forced to work as sex slaves or enter the system of concubinage for nobles' (p. 225).

18 The numbers were staggering ... across the Red Sea: The 'Arab' slave trade in Africa has few reliable records, and estimates of the numbers involved vary widely. See Paul Lovejoy, *Transformations in Slavery: A History of Slavery in Africa* (Cambridge: Cambridge University Press, 2011), and Sheriff, *Slaves, Spices and Ivory in Zanzibar*.

19 boda-boda motorbikes: *Boda-boda* means 'shortcut to shortcut' in Swahili.

19 man-killing elephant, which he shot 'solely to avoid looking a fool': George Orwell, 'Shooting an Elephant', in *Shooting an Elephant and Other Essays* (Penguin Books, 2003), p. 40.

20 the elephant 'dying, very slowly and in great agony': Ibid., p. 39.

2. Shopping for an Elephant

21 '[N]o, I don't care ... about everything' [epigraph]: Ignacio Ruiz-Pérez, 'Blind Poet', in *Isles of Firm Ground*, trans. Mike Soto (Dallas: Phoneme Media, 2022), p. 29.

22 He called himself the country's 'proprietor': See Adam Hochschild, *King Leopold's Ghost: A Story of Greed, Terror and Heroism in Colonial Africa* (London: Pan Books, 2006), p. 87. This critically acclaimed book, first published in 1998 and updated in 2006, is essential to understanding the brutality of Leopold's Congo regime. Leopold's elephants are briefly mentioned on p. 66.

23–4 rounded up in the 'deepest forests of Kasai and the mountains in Urundi': *La Cité*, 10 June 1858, cited in 'Human Zoo: The Age of Colonial Exhibitions', *Exhibition Handbook* (AfricaMuseum, 9 November 2021–6 March 2022), p. 53.

24 His 1897 'human zoo' ... more than one in four Belgians as visitors: Belgium wasn't the only European nation to put on such colonial 'shows', though it was among the last – a topic the museum confronted in a temporary 2021 exhibition, entitled *Human Zoo: The Age of Colonial Exhibitions*.

24   **He was his parents' least favourite child:** See the detailed description of Leopold's childhood in Barbara Emerson, *Leopold II of the Belgians: King of Colonialism* (London: Weidenfeld & Nicolson, 1979), pp. 6–7.

24   **'Leopold is subtle and sly'...'he never takes a chance':** A. Vandenpeereboom, 'Mémoires', in J. Garsou, *Les Débuts d'un grand règne* (Brussels: 1931), vol. 1, pp. 30–1. Cited in Emerson, *Leopold II of the Belgians*, p. 23.

25   **'and then, with a thousand precautions...That is Leopold's way!':** Ibid.

25   **In this weird mix of exhibits...atrocities under the same roof:** Hochschild's initial description of the museum in *King Leopold's Ghost* did much to stir public discussion about its failings. In 2013, the museum shut its doors for a complete overhaul, reopening in 2018. However, as Hochschild's incisive 2020 essay in *The Atlantic* outlines, despite various efforts to decolonize the museum, there remain 'limitations'. See Adam Hochschild, 'The Fight to Decolonize the Museum', *The Atlantic* (January/February 2020).

25   **this is true of numerous collections all over the world:** The Belgians were by no means the only occupiers to steal artefacts from African countries. Perhaps the most famous hoard is the British collection of Nigeria's so-called 'Benin Bronzes', looted by British colonial troops from Benin City in 1897. In August 2022, London's Horniman Museum announced that it would transfer ownership of its seventy-two bronzes to Nigeria, where they would be displayed in Benin City's new Edo Museum of West African Art.

25   **much of what I was looking at...profoundly amoral terms:** At the time of my visit, a museum sign stated: 'In recent years, more and more voices have been raised in favour of transferring the illegally acquired part of Africa's heritage now in Western hands to the countries of origin. The AfricaMuseum is currently prioritising provenance research to ascertain how objects were acquired.'

25   **'There are only three of us':** This comment should be qualified by the fact I was travelling during a quiet period, towards the end of the Covid-19 pandemic.

25   **another statue of Leopold...warriors in loincloths and the king:** *The Congo, I Presume?* is a statue commissioned in 1997 to commemorate the Colonial Exhibition's centenary. See www.laphamsquarterly.org/roundtable/king-leopold-i-presume. During the Black Lives Matter protests in 2020, Leopold's face was covered in red paint.

25–6   **a man...responsible for the deaths of an estimated ten million Africans:** In *King Leopold's Ghost*, Hochschild grapples with the difficulty of proving statistics with a dearth of available evidence. However, in piecing together fragmented data and estimates – including the work of Belgian ethnographer Jan Vansina – Hochschild concludes that, during the 'Leopold' period, it's possible that Congo's population dropped by approximately ten million people. Hochschild, *King Leopold's Ghost*, pp. 225–34.

27   **the atrocities ... widely known, at home and abroad:** In 1908, Leopold II was forced to cede Congo to the Belgian state after reports of atrocities provoked international outrage. This was in no small part due to the efforts of the Congo Reform Association (CRA), founded in 1904 by Edmund Dene Morel, a British journalist and shipping clerk, and Roger Casement, a British consul in the Congo Free State, and future Irish nationalist. Horrified by first-hand testimony from Congolese people brutalized by Leopold's regime, the pair wrote blistering reports, successfully mobilizing public support and lobbying the British and US governments.

27   **'I am gathering proof ... desirability of overseas expansion':** Duke of Brabant, 'Letter to Pierre Chazal', 2 January 1861, cited in Emerson, *Leopold II of the Belgians*, p. 24.

27   **'Check out the history ... without possessions and without activity overseas':** Duke of Brabant, 'Letter to Henri-Alexis Brialmont', 26 July 1863, cited in Léon Le Febve de Vivy (ed.), *Documents d'histoire précoloniale belge (1861–1865): les idées coloniales de Léopold duc de Brabant* (Brussels: Académie royale des sciences coloniales, 1955), p. 19.

27   **'I will give them my Congo ... no right to know what I did there':** Hochschild, *King Leopold's Ghost*, p. 294.

27   **Among the documents spared ... travels before his accession in 1865:** The Goffinet family were close confidants of the king and, at his request, hid several thousand documents from his private family archives in a damp, walled-up cellar at a château south of Brussels. When the château was demolished in the late 1980s, Professor Jean Stengers, a pre-eminent Belgian historian, noticed a sudden influx of documents directly relating to Leopold I and Leopold II appearing in auction rooms. Together with a palace archivist, Stengers convinced the King Baudouin Foundation (a philanthropic foundation based in Belgium) to acquire the collection for the Royal Palace archives in 1993.

27   **port of Aden, the so-called 'Coal-hole of the East':** Richard Francis Burton, *Zanzibar: City, Island and Coast*, vol. 1 (London: Tinsley Brothers, 1872), p. 15.

27   **the Indian Ocean ... 'the English Lake':** Richard Seymour Hall, *Empires of the Monsoon: A History of the Indian Ocean and Its Invaders* (New York: Harper Collins, 1996), p. 354.

29   **whoever holds the tooth also holds the power to govern the country:** A genesis story derived from elephants confers power in parts of Asia. In the

tale of the Buddha's conception, his mother dreamed that a white elephant with six tusks entered her womb through her right side, heralding the birth of a world leader. In Hinduism, the elephant-headed Ganesha is worshipped as the god of beginnings.

29   **Wild herds would be driven ... in a centuries-old system of subjugation:** The system of wild elephant capture and taming in Ceylon was recorded by the Dutch traveller Jan Brandes in the late eighteenth century (see endpapers). Brandes drew the 'baptism' scene, showing a tamed elephant's head being blessed with water. The traditional 'kheddah' system in India also involved driving wild elephants into a stockade.

29   **When he visited Bharatpur in India ... royal collection of leopards:** It was near Bharatpur that the sixteenth-century Mughal emperor Akbar held court. He used mounted elephants as 'live' chess pieces in his palace courtyard and watched play from a specially constructed umpire stand. Akbar's son was said to have kept 113,000 elephants in captivity: 12,000 for active army service, a further 1,000 to carry their fodder, and another 100,000 for courtiers, officials, attendants and baggage. See S. S. Bist, J. V. Cheeran, S. Choudhury, P. Barua and M. K. Misra, 'The Domesticated Asian Elephant in India', in *Giants on Our Hands: Proceedings of the International Workshop on the Domesticated Asian Elephant* (Bangkok: Food and Agriculture Organization of the United Nations, Regional Office for Asia and the Pacific, 2002/3).

29   **Riding on them ... remarked Leopold in his diary:** Duke of Brabant, 'Voyage à Ceylon', 7 November 1864 to 6 May 1865, vol. 16 [APR].

29–30 **The animals made the forest 'crack open' ... challenging terrain:** Ibid.

30   **Leopold was covetous of everything ... stretching far behind:** Ibid.

30   **Congo's 'unspeakable richness':** *The Times*, 11 January 1876, cited in Tim Jeal, *Stanley: The Impossible Life of Africa's Greatest Explorer* (London: Faber & Faber, 2007), p. 230.

30   **'I intend to find out discreetly ... anything doing in Africa':** Leopold II, 'Letter to Baron Lambermont', 22 August 1875, in *Papiers Lambermont*, vol. 5, section 9, Service des Archives (of the Belgian Ministry of Foreign Affairs).

31   **countries behind the transatlantic trade ... Britain, France and the US:** British ships alone transported 3.4 million of the estimated twelve million West African victims of the Atlantic slave trade between 1640 and 1807. See 'Atlantic Worlds: Enslavement and Resistance', *Royal Museums Greenwich*, www.rmg.co.uk/stories/topics/history-transatlantic-slave-trade

31   **European explorers who had first gone ... libels and suspected suicides:** Was the source of the Nile Lake Tanganyika, imagined on the infamous 1856 'Slug Map' drawn by Jakob Erhardt in collaboration with two

German missionaries? The map hung on the walls of the Royal
Geographical Society in London and held the public spellbound. The
shape of the lake, drawn from hearsay, was described as looking like a slug
or salamander. It wasn't until 1858 that the first Europeans managed to
reach the lake's shores, but the two British explorers, Richard Burton and
John Hanning Speke, fell out. Speke claimed that Lake Victoria, not
Tanganyika, was the true source of the Nile. Their spat intensified in full
view of a public greedy for scandal. People were questioning if Burton was
even English, and if Speke – the day before a public debate with Burton –
didn't die in a shooting accident (as it was claimed) but had in fact
committed suicide.

31 **his famous call 'to heal this open sore of the world':** These were among
the last words Livingstone wrote, according to the inscription on his
tomb at Westminster Abbey.

32 **pseudo-scientific theory of 'race betterment' or eugenics:** The term
'eugenics', from the Greek *eugenes*, meaning 'well born', was coined by the
English scientist, mathematician and explorer Francis Galton in his 1883
book *Inquiries into Human Faculty and Its Development*. The theory, which
Galton used to describe 'the science which deals with all influences that
improve the inborn qualities of a race', was adopted and expanded to
justify increasingly murderous racism. This later included many of the
ideas adopted by Nazi Germany. Francis Galton, 'Eugenics: Its Definition,
Scope, and Aims', *American Journal of Sociology*, 10 (July 1904), p. 1.

32 **'White Heroes in Africa':** *Stanley and the White Heroes in Africa*, compiled by
D. M. Kelsey (St Louis and Philadelphia: Scammell & Company, 1890).

33 **'a high moral intervention':** Lieutenant-Colonel Liebrechts, *Léopold II,
fondateur d'empire* (Brussels: Office de Publicité, 1932), p. 12.

33 **'spirit of charity':** 'Invitation of King Leopold', cited in *The African
Repository*, vol. 53 (Washington City: American Colonization Society,
1877), p. 59.

33 **territory . . . 'as empty and bare as that of the Pole':** Émile Banning, *Africa
and the Brussels Geographical Conference*, trans. Richard Henry Major
(London: Sampson Low, Marston, Searle & Rivington, 1877), p. xi.

33 **'in a word, to pour upon it the treasures of civilization':** 'Invitation of
King Leopold', cited in *The African Repository*, vol. 53, pp. 58–9.

33 **dispatch back to Africa . . . recently released from plantation slavery:** A
year after Leopold's Brussels Geographical Conference, the American
Colonization Society published a letter arguing that there were 'millions
of colored civilized emigrants willing and anxious to go to the homes of
their ancestors in Africa'. Augustus Watson, 'African Continental Railroad,
25 September, 1877', in *The African Repository*, vol. 53, p. 120. John H. B.
Latrobe, president of the American Branch of the IAA, even suggested

Black Americans emigrate 'at their own cost'. See John H. B. Latrobe, 'Letter to Henry Shelton Sanford', 22 September 1877 [SM].

33–4   **New marble staircases … sumptuous gold and crimson damask:** These details are taken from the second chapter of Hochschild, *King Leopold's Ghost.*

34   **'instead of leaving … own needle in his own bundle of hay':** Banning, *Africa and the Brussels Geographical Conference*, p. 182.

34   **'military trading stations … both a moral and material support':** Samuel Baker, 'Letter to Leopold II', 20 September 1876 [APR].

34   **'worthy of this century of progress' … 'the current is with us':** Leopold II, cited in Liebrechts, *Léopold II, fondateur d'empire*, p. 13.

34   **'Need I say that … she is happy and satisfied with her fate':** Ibid.

34   **the British military hero Charles Gordon:** Also known as 'Chinese Gordon', 'Gordon Pasha' and 'Gordon of Khartoum', based on his British diplomatic and military career.

34   **'A horrid "end of the world" place this':** Charles Gordon, 'Letter to General Sir E. Stanton', 28 July 1876, in 'Unpublished Letters of George Charles Gordon', *Sudan Notes and Records*, vol. 10 (Sudan: University of Khartoum, 1927), p. 48.

35   **a complex British–Egyptian relationship:** The British were increasingly involved in Egypt's politics; while the region was ostensibly an autonomous province of the Ottoman Empire ruled by the Khedive, it was in reality on the cusp of becoming a British protectorate in all but name.

35   **'impolitic habit of telling political truths':** Richard Francis Burton, *Personal Narrative of a Pilgrimage to El-Medinah and Meccah*, fourth edition (London: Tylston and Edwards, 1893), cited in Edward Rice, *Captain Sir Richard Francis Burton* (Cambridge, MA: Da Capo Press, 2001), p. 233.

35   **'I say leave me alone … they have the poor':** Charles Gordon, 'Letter to Horace Waller', 4 October 1875 [BL].

35   **'You are bigots … you do not think of the other side':** Cited in George Birkbeck Hill (ed.), *Colonel Gordon in Central Africa, 1874–1879: From Original Letters and Documents* (London: Thos. De La Rue & Co., 1881), p. 257.

35   **'any of the men who worry about Africa':** Charles Gordon, 'Letter to Horace Waller', 12 October 1876 [BL].

35   **'Am I a tool to delude … some favour from our Government':** Charles Gordon, 'Letter to General Sir E. Stanton', 15 December 1874, in 'Unpublished Letters of George Charles Gordon', p. 11.

36   **'The [Congo] River is … the grand highway of commerce':** Henry Morton Stanley, 'To the Editors of "The Daily Telegraph" and "New York Herald." Loanda, West Coast of Africa, 5 September 1877', *Daily Telegraph*, 12 November 1877.

36 **'I do not wish to miss ... a share in this magnificent African cake':**
Leopold II, 'Letter to Baron Solvyns', 17 November 1877, cited in Jeal,
Stanley: The Impossible Life of Africa's Greatest Explorer, p. 231.

36–7 **the stain ... a massacre he'd allegedly ordered on Lake Victoria:** In
August 1876, the *Daily Telegraph* reported on a disturbing incident in
Central Africa that had happened a year earlier: in response to an
attempted robbery, Stanley ordered a revenge massacre at Bumbireh
Island (now Bumbire) on Lake Victoria. Forty-two people were killed, and
over one hundred more injured. The cold-blooded nature of Stanley's
brand of 'justice' raised eyebrows, even among the ordinarily sympathetic
press. Stanley delivered an impassioned defence of his actions to the Royal
Geographical Society, but the longer-term taint to his reputation was an
uncomfortable association with the 'moral dimensions of "exploration by
warfare"'. See Felix Driver, 'Henry Morton Stanley and His Critics:
Geography, Exploration and Empire', *Past and Present*, 133 (November
1991), p. 154.

37 **'In a word, we are going to attract as little attention as possible':** Jules
Greindl, 'Letter to Henry Shelton Sanford', 10 December 1878 [SM].

37 **'hospitable and scientific station[s]':** A. J. Wauters, 'Karéma: première station
de l'Association internationale africaine', in *Bulletin: Société belge de géographie*
(Brussels: Secrétariat de la Société belge de géographie, 1879), p. 724.

37 **'[There's] a feeling of ... something approaching to derision':** Henry
Morton Stanley, 'Letter to Henry Shelton Sanford', 19 October 1878, in
R. Stanley Thomson, *Congo: revue générale de la Colonie belge* (Brussels:
Goemaere, 1931), p. 11.

38 **French suggestion ... of creating an artificial sea by flooding the Sahara:**
The idea of creating a Sahara sea was first raised in 1874, and was
popularized by the endorsement of Ferdinand de Lesseps, the French
engineer behind the Suez Canal. The concept was simple, in so far as
creating an artificial sea could be: establishing a wetter, more fertile
climate in the Sahara's otherwise barren environment would provide
opportunities for trade and transport. The impracticability of the scheme
led to its abandonment in 1892.

38 **Gordon has just completed ... as well as a pet African one:** This
expedition is mentioned by Gordon in various pieces of correspondence,
including 'Letter to General Sir E. Stanton, 13 September 1878', in
'Unpublished Letters of George Charles Gordon', p. 41, and Charles
Gordon, 'Letter to Horace Waller', 17 May 1879 [BL].

38 **the deadly bite of the tsetse fly ... felled horses and cattle:** The fly carries
a parasite that can infect the bloodstream of both livestock and people,
causing nagana disease in cattle and horses, and sleeping sickness in
humans. Without effective treatment – only discovered in 1916 – the

disease can be fatal in both animals and humans. Various attempts at travelling the caravan route had been made with bullocks and carts – all of them failures because of the tsetse fly.

38 **stories like Jumbo's ... one of London's most well-known attractions:** In 1865, the London Zoological Society acquired Jumbo, a five-year-old African elephant, from the Jardin des Plantes in Paris. He had been captured in what is now Eritrea. During his time in Paris, he was so scabby that he was kept off-display. At the London Zoological Gardens, Jumbo grew to nearly eleven feet tall and became a sensation, giving rides to a young Winston Churchill. But in 1881, he became wildly aggressive, possibly because he went into musth, a hormonal surge in male elephants, or because of toothache caused by all the sticky buns he was fed. The Zoological Society decided to sell him, causing a public outcry. In 1882, Jumbo was shipped to America to join Barnum & Bailey circus, where he was the star performer. His aggression was held in check by a combination of brutal billhooks and the sedative effects of whisky. Tragedy struck one final time in 1885 when Jumbo was killed by a train. His carcass was stuffed and carried with the circus for another two years.

39 **'to watch for the favourable moment ... rare what they represent':** P. Crokaert Brialmont, *Éloges et mémoires* (Brussels: 1925), p. 416, cited in Léon Le Febve de Vivy, *Documents d'histoire précoloniale belge (1861–1865)*, p. 6.

39 **Basra:** At that time, also known as Bussorah.

40 **'Our genial host seemed equally at home ... and the comic':** William Perry Fogg, *Arabistan: or, the Land of 'The Arabian Nights'. Being Travels Through Egypt, Arabia, and Persia, to Bagdad* (Hartford, CT: Dustin, Gillman & Co., 1875), p. 342.

40 **'The hours of the short night ... great mulberry tree':** Ibid.

40 **Carter kept lions as pets ... two large English dogs:** According to one of Carter's foreign visitors, one of the dogs, Virginia, met an untimely end in a tussle with the lion-in-residence over possession of a bone. The lion was being kept on a chain and was due to be shipped off any day to a more permanent residence – London's Zoological Gardens. See Fogg, *Arabistan: or, the Land of 'The Arabian Nights'*, pp. 189–90.

40 **He'd shipped another ... to the Calcutta Zoological Gardens:** Eric Baratay and Elisabeth Hardouin-Fugier, *Zoo: A History of Zoological Gardens in the West* (London: Reaktion Books, 2002), p. 125.

40–1 **1840s Kilkenny ... where the streets had smelled of corpses:** Gustave de Beaumont, *Ireland: Social, Political, and Religious*, ed. W. C. Taylor, vol. 1 (London: Richard Bentley, 1839), pp. 268–70.

41 **'One might suppose [Kilkenny] to be dead':** Alexander Somerville, 'No. V. Kilkenny and Clonmel, Feb. 1 1847', in *Letters from Ireland During the Famine* (Manchester: J. Ainsworth, 1852).

41 **'Buímhís ("yellow month") ... and poor scraps of that sort':** Amhlaoibh Ó Súilleabháin (also known as Humphrey O'Sullivan) kept a diary of the famine. This entry dates from 26 July 1830, and is published in Tomás de Bhaldraithe's translation, *Diary of an Irish Country Gentleman, 1827–1835* (Cork: Mercier Press, 1979), p. 92.

42 **The coroner said it was a fit ... 'temporary insanity':** *Kilkenny Journal*, 5 December 1860.

42 **'His experience as a sailor ... in New York, Savannah and New Orleans':** Fogg, *Arabistan: or, the Land of 'The Arabian Nights'*, p. 342.

42–3 **'The Arabs round Bussorah grew to regard him ... the "White Shiek"** [sic]': *Times of India*, 13 September 1880.

43 **both fathered by drunkards who suffered from delirium tremens:** Stanley was illegitimate but it's thought his father may have been a Welshman called John Rowlands.

43 **Leopold and his proxies:** William Mackinnon tasked his London agent, Gerald Waller, with sourcing the king's elephants. Gerald was the younger brother of Horace Waller, who'd been pressing Charles Gordon to sign up to Leopold's schemes.

44 **There were signs of the coastal communities going 'rubber mad':** 'Memorandum: The Road from Dar-es-Salaam East Africa, Toward the Northern End of Lake Nyassa', 20 November 1878 [SOAS].

44 **There were none ... what they were a few years before:** George Sanderson, 'Letter to William Mackinnon', 2 April 1879 [SOAS].

44 **Leopold's associates turned to a menagerie in Hamburg:** This was Carl Hagenbeck's menagerie. Leopold's associates also tried Charles Jamrach's East London emporium. Young African elephants could easily be brought into line, said Jamrach; he later boasted how he walked eighteen of them like cattle through the streets of London from his ship. But Jamrach had a reputation for being expensive, selling rhinos for five hundred pounds apiece, which is the equivalent of around forty thousand pounds today. See 'A Jaunt to Jamrach's', *The Era*, 13 September 1884.

44 **Five had been recently trained ... the stock went to Berlin Zoo instead:** Gerald Waller, 'Letter to William Mackinnon', 18 March 1879 [SOAS].

44 **Leopold's men even started hustling England's travelling circus troupes:** Gerald Waller, 'Letter to William Mackinnon', 20 March 1879 [SOAS].

45 **'The one beating has lasted so far for the rest of his life'** [picture caption]: 'The Zoological Gardens', *London Evening Standard*, 3 June 1879.

45 **'ponderous performing elephants'** [picture caption]: 'Sanger's Grand National Amphitheatre', *Illustrated London News*, 28 December 1878.

46 **'nobody would ever know ... the name of the recipient':** Maximilien Strauch, 'Letter to Leopold II', 25 January 1879 [AEB].

3. The Paris of East Africa

48 'I was careful not to make . . . setting out upon a mere promenade'
[epigraph]: Richard Francis Burton, *Zanzibar: City, Island and Coast*, vol. 2
(London: Tinsley Brothers, 1872), p. 289.

51 it made sense to move the Omani court from Muscat to Zanzibar: This
news was apparently slow to reach Americans. In 1879, a visiting
American official wrote from Stone Town that 'Zanzibar is in Africa, and
not in Muscat as even the State Department seems to think'. Commodore
Robert Shufeldt, 'Journal No. 2', 10 October 1879, Shufeldt Papers, Library
of Congress, Washington, DC, cited in Norman R. Bennett, 'Americans in
Zanzibar: 1865–1915', *Essex Institute Historical Collections*, vol. 98 (Salem,
MA: Newcomb & Gauss Co., 1962), p. 53.

51–2 'When you play the flute . . . all Africa, as far as the Lakes, dances': Cited
in A. W. Smith, 'The Cloves of Zanzibar', *The Atlantic* (March 1948).

52 he described Africa's last public slave market . . . still doing a brisk trade:
The publication of Burton's account of Zanzibar was delayed for several
years after the manuscript was lost. According to Burton, he had originally
entrusted the manuscript to the apothecary at the island's British
consulate, with instructions to send it to the Royal Geographical Society
in London. According to the explorer's colourful account, the diary fell
into the hands of a skipper on the West African coast, was appropriated by
his widow, appeared at a London bookseller's stall, bought by an English
artillery officer, left in the hall of one of the British ministers of state, and
then spent eight years in the strong box of the Bombay branch of the
Royal Asiatic Society until someone eventually returned it to the author.
See Preface in Richard Francis Burton, *Zanzibar: City, Island and Coast*,
vol. 1 (London: Tinsley Brothers, 1872).

52 Men, women and children . . . sold for the price of a donkey, or less:
Alastair Hazell, *The Last Slave Market: Dr John Kirk and the Struggle to End
the East African Slave Trade* (London: Constable, 2012), p. 18.

52 Indian burghers resembling . . . clothes that were far too tight for them:
Burton, *Zanzibar: City, Island and Coast*, pp. 105–9.

52 Stone Town was being heralded as the 'Paris of East Africa': Daniel
O'Sullivan-Beare, 'Report on the Island of Pemba for the Year 1900',
Diplomatic and Consular Reports: Africa, no. 2653 (London: Harrison and
Sons, 1901), p. 15.

53 'The people of Zanzibar . . . the slaves they own': Ali bin Said al-Busaidi,
'Letter to John Kirk', 1 May 1891 [NLS].

56 A visiting missionary remarked . . . tracking the town from telescopes:
M. A. Pringle, *A Journey in East Africa: Towards the Mountains in the Moon*
(Edinburgh and London: William Blackwood and Sons, 1884), p. 28.

56 'and thus often becomes acquainted … not intended for his eye': Joseph Thomson, *To the Central African Lakes and Back: The Narrative of the Royal Geographical Society's East Central African Expedition, 1878–1880*, vol. 1 (London: Sampson Low, Marston, Searle & Rivington, 1878), p. 28.

56 'Kirkism': William Hathorne, 'Letter to Captain Emmerton, 12 December 1877', cited in Norman R. Bennet, 'William H. Hathorne: Merchant and Consul in Zanzibar', *Essex Institute Historical Collections*, vol. 99 (Salem, MA: Newcomb & Gauss Co., 1963), p. 126.

56 '[Kirk] has got to be a perfect snob … greatest gossip maker in the place': William Hathorne, 'Letter to Webb, 28 October 1879', cited in ibid., p. 144.

56 '[T]erribly vulgar, provincial and selfish … a gross eater': John Kirk, Diary, 17 May 1879 [NLS].

56 'to let you know the price I attach … to bring civilisation into Africa': Leopold II, 'Letter to John Kirk', 6 February 1879 [NLS]. The flattery – from not just this gift, but other direct correspondence from the king – played to Kirk's ego. 'You will have seen my report of the very kind notice taken by the King of the Belgians of my work', Kirk wrote to a colleague. 'Nothing was less expected.' John Kirk, 'Letter to H. W. Wylde', 16 April 1879 [NLS].

57 'free-and-easy suit of Tweeds and pith hat': Thomson, *To the Central African Lakes and Back*, vol. 2, p. 12.

57 French sunglasses were essential, and a … 'wide-awake' hat: John Hanning Speke, 'Captain Speke's Discovery of the Victoria Nyanza, the Supposed Source of the Nile, – Part II', p. 412, cited in Candice Millard, *River of the Gods: Genius, Courage, and Betrayal in the Search for the Source of the Nile* (London: Swift Press, 2023), p. 162.

57 popular how-to guide for … others 'who have to rough it': Francis Galton, *The Art of Travel: or, Shifts and Contrivances Available in Wild Countries*, fifth edition (London: John Murray, 1872), p. v. The first edition was published in 1854.

57 'I am told he has twice written … did not succeed in reaching the Lake': Stanley is referring to Lake Ngami in present-day Botswana. Henry Morton Stanley, 6 January 1872, 'Journal S.A. II, Full Transcript (10 November 1871 – Unyanyembe, 8 May 1872)', in Mathilde Leduc-Grimaldi and James L. Newman (eds), *Finding Dr. Livingstone: A History in Documents from the Henry Morton Stanley Archives* (Athens, OH: Ohio University Press, 2020), p. 236.

57–8 Galton's tips ranged from … rugs and dinner services: Galton, *The Art of Travel*, p. 169.

58 how to smuggle jewels by stitching them under your skin: 'The best place for burying them is in the left arm, at the spot chosen for vaccination. A traveller who was thus provided would always have a small

capital to fall back upon, though robbed of everything he wore.' Galton, *The Art of Travel*, p. 302.

58 **the peaked tropical hat … gauze veil to keep off mosquitoes:** 'That head-covering which London and Paris patronise must give place to the helmet and puggaree, or to a well-ventilated light cap.' Henry Morton Stanley, *The Congo and the Founding of Its Free State: A Story of Work and Exploration*, vol. 1 (New York: Harper & Brothers, 1885), p. 65.

58 **a good Stone Town opium dealer … visitors were caught short:** A Goanese shopkeeper called Andrew. See Arthur Dodgshun, 'Central African Expedition: List of Requirements', 29 March 1879 [SOAS].

58 **'A simple, commonsense cookery book':** Ibid.

58 **'a small gipsy tent, just sufficient to sleep in':** David Livingstone, *Missionary Travels and Researches in South Africa; Including a Sketch of Sixteen Years' Residence in the Interior of Africa, and a Journey from the Cape of Good Hope to Loanda on the West Coast; Thence Across the Continent, Down the River Zambesi, to the Eastern Ocean* (London: J. Murray, 1857), p. 230.

60 **'Armed with my experience' … an easy job of it:** Henry Morton Stanley, 'Letter to Ernest Cambier', 1879, in *The Congo and the Founding of Its Free State*, pp. 39–44.

60 **'rupture, ulcers, dysentery … or eaters of opium':** Ibid., p. 47.

60 **'Fashion was as dominant … and size among beads':** Thomson, *To the Central African Lakes and Back*, vol. 1, p. 35.

60 **gunbearers … double up as 'tent-boys, waiting or messenger-boys':** Henry Morton Stanley, 'Letter to Ernest Cambier', 1879, in *The Congo and the Founding of Its Free State*, p. 48.

60 **'without stinting yourself or men of any of the necessaries of life':** Ibid., pp. 41–2.

60 **'no caravan ever goes … without a number of slaves in the porters':** Thomson, *To the Central African Lakes and Back*, vol. 1, p. 17. Thomson also unpicks the European double standard, of employing enslaved people while nominally travelling to Africa to eradicate it, in the following note: 'The matter is very easily explained. Though we had slaves in our company, we did not engage them *as* slaves. They came to us offering to enter into engagements just like free men, and they were accepted and treated as though they were free men. What agreement they had previously entered into with their owners we knew not, and did not trouble ourselves to inquire' (p. 68).

61 **Livingstone's former caravan leader:** Thomson accused Abdullah Susi of being a drinker in ibid., p. 33. Outfitting his own caravan at the same time as Stanley, Thomson opted for Susi's former colleague on the Livingstone expedition, James Chuma.

61   **Kirk already loathed Stanley . . . souring his reputation with Livingstone:** Both Livingstone and Stanley had accused Kirk of failing to ensure the safe delivery of supplies to the interior, due to be dispatched from the coast in 1870. They were urgently needed to replenish Livingstone's struggling expedition. Kirk strongly denied these allegations, garnering the support of the British Foreign Office.

61   **'I gather from what [Stanley] does . . . the men he engages here':** John Kirk, 'Letter to H. W. Wylde', 16 April 1879 [NLS].

61   **'I am to coach [Dutalis] up in the "art" of exploration':** Henry Morton Stanley, 'Letter to Henry Shelton Sanford', 27 February 1879 [SM].

61   **'If Stanley is to be the guiding spirit . . . keep things well in hand':** John Kirk, 'Letter to Gerald Waller', 30 May 1879 [SOAS].

61   **He accused Stanley of trying to 'make mischief' for the British:** John Kirk, 'Letter to H. W. Wylde', 16 April 1879 [NLS].

61–2 **'[Dutalis] says he does not know . . . he may be somehow associated':** Ibid.

64   **I was letting 'Fantasy Zanzibar' dominate my impressions:** 'Fantasy Zanzibar' is a phrase belonging to the Zanzibar-born British author Abdulrazak Gurnah, whom I met in Stone Town on a return visit. He agreed to sit for a portrait for a newspaper article I was writing. I suggested a pretty, filigree-work balcony I'd found a few days before, framed by some palm fronds. 'Fantasy Zanzibar', said Gurnah. So I changed the venue to a local beach close to the High Court where Gurnah used to play as a child.

64   **'one of the fairest gems of Nature's creation':** Stanley, 6 January 1871, 'Journal S.A. 7, Full Transcript (1871)', p. 64.

64   **Burton was less flattering . . . a few months of Zanzibar air:** Burton, *Zanzibar: City, Island and Coast*, p. 183.

64   **I relied in part upon the novels . . . fled Stone Town as a refugee:** One of the characters in Gurnah's 1988 novel *Pilgrims Way* describes the tensions underlying Zanzibar's melting-pot history: 'One of these days, these people that we've been making slaves of for centuries will rise up and cut the throats of their oppressors. Then the Indians will go back to India and the Arabs will go back to Arabia, and what will you and I do? . . . We'll get slaughtered.' Abdulrazak Gurnah, *Pilgrims Way* (London: Bloomsbury Publishing, 2021), p. 198.

65   **'the burning blasts of an African sirocco':** Thomson, *To the Central African Lakes and Back*, vol. 1, p. 5.

65   **'Oh! The glare, the furnace heat . . . We were all upset':** Joseph Mullens, 'Letter to John Whitehouse', 30 May 1879 [CRL].

66   **'Maps and plans and books . . . were strewn about on all sides':** 'The King of the Belgians' Expedition: Landing the Elephants in Africa', *Times of India*, 22 July 1879.

67 **'Ship-tea, bad enough … "bouquet du Chinsurah [sic]" in general':**
Joseph Mullens, 'Letter to John Whitehouse', 30 May 1879 [CRL].

69 **'wandering like lost sheep in the wilderness':** Thomson, *To the Central African Lakes and Back*, vol. 1, p. 40.

69 **Kirk at least had a potential ally … to protect British interests:** John Kirk, 'Letter to Gerald Waller', 29 May 1879 [SOAS].

69 **For not only was Kirk familiar … briefly kept a juvenile himself:** The king of Buganda (now part of Uganda) had recently gifted Sultan Barghash a baby African elephant, which was palmed off on a local farmer who then gave it to Kirk. Kirk understood that keeping elephants was an expensive, specialist business, which was why he sent his unwanted gift to the governor of Bombay, who bestowed it on a grand vizier in Hyderabad. See 'African Exploration', *Pall Mall Gazette*, cited in *The Star*, 29 July 1879.

69 **a self-important sergeant … than was contained in a handbook:** Referred to in the sources as 'P. Gallagher', whose unfortunate legacy in Africa was to be described as nothing more than an annoyance. Gallagher worked for the Bombay Commissariat.

69 **'[the sergeant] has joined … but there will be trouble with the man':** John Kirk, 'Letter to Gerald Waller', 30 May 1879 [SOAS].

70 **'full of infinite graces … let forth his soul in passionate song':** Thomson, *To the Central African Lakes and Back*, vol. 1, p. 25.

70 **'rarely pausing to begin … never changing one':** Revd R. M. Heanley, *A Memoir of Edward Steere* (London: George Bell and Sons, 1888), p. 161.

71 **'They have all studied medicine … graduated in the art of war':** 'The King of the Belgians' Expedition: Landing the Elephants in Africa'. The 'extraordinary completeness' of the missionaries' outfit was also noted: 'it literally contained everything, from a needle to an anchor, from a cabin biscuit to the most tempting preserves and potted meats'.

71 **As soon as the *Chinsura* … to join Carter's royal parade:** Universities' Mission to Central Africa, Zanzibar Diary, 1864–1888 [ZNA].

71 **'The importance of this step can hardly be overrated':** Cited in Heanley, *A Memoir of Edward Steere*, p. 245.

75 **Within a few weeks … banished the teaching of history in schools:** 'History was banished from schools immediately after the revolution. It was not formally reintroduced until the late 1990s'. Omar Ramadhan Mapuri, 'Historia Kufundishwa Tena Zanzibar', *An-Nuur* (9–16 May 1997), cited in Jonathon Glassman, *War of Words, War of Stones: Racial Thought and Violence in Colonial Zanzibar* (Bloomington and Indianapolis: Indiana University Press, 2011), p. 306. Dr Ida Hadjivayanis, Senior Lecturer in Swahili Studies at SOAS University in London, suggested there was more nuance at play when I consulted her on this point; according to her sources, history was still taught in schools, but was heavily censored to fit with the new political agenda.

76   'race-baiting': The phrase is used in Glassman, *War of Words, War of Stones*,
     p. 7. See also Abdulrazak Gurnah, 'Writing', in *Map Reading: The Nobel
     Lecture and Other Writing* (London: Bloomsbury, 2022), p. 5. 'A new,
     simpler history was being constructed, transforming and even obliterating
     what had happened, restructuring it to suit the verities of the moment',
     declared Gurnah in his 2021 Nobel Prize acceptance speech.

76   'In the world of Herodotus ... of such circumstances it is born': Ryszard
     Kapuściński, *Travels with Herodotus* (London, New York and Toronto:
     Penguin, 2008), p. 76.

76   to build a convincing myth, nation builders need to get their history
     wrong: This point is derived from the statement made by Ernest Renan,
     which is cited in Glassman, *War of Words, War of Stones*, p. 6.

4. Sink or Swim

77   'A brief description of a road ... all those still to come' [epigraph]:
     George Saunders, *A Swim in a Pond in the Rain: In Which Four Russians
     Give a Masterclass on Writing, Reading and Life* (London and Dublin:
     Bloomsbury, 2022), p. 27.

78   'the history of humanity is the story of supply chains': Horatio Clare,
     'The Truckers who Keep Our World Moving', *Financial Times*, 20 May
     2022.

79   'the first in savage Africa': *Standard*, 23 August 1879.

80   'Indeed, [Kirk] could not have been ... lain on his own shoulders': The
     article's unnamed but accusatory source or author was possibly Sergeant
     P. Gallagher, who'd sailed with the elephants from Bombay.

80   'No one could exactly say ... like buffaloes in shallow rivers': Ibid.

80   'led them all to fussing': William Mackinnon, 'Letter to Henry Shelton
     Sanford', 26 June 1879 [SM].

81   'wonderful orange-blossomed gold-mohr tree[s]': Edward Lear, 7 June
     1874, in Ray Murphy (ed.), *Edward Lear's Indian Journal: Watercolours and
     Extracts from the Diary of Edward Lear (1873–1875)* (London: Jarrolds,
     1953), p. 147.

81   'monsoon sojourn': Edward Lear, 16 July 1874, in ibid., p. 162.

81   'all quite remarkable ... "there is nothing to be seen at Poona"': Edward
     Lear, 9 June 1874, in ibid., p. 148.

81   'elephants no end': Edward Lear, 1 July 1874, in ibid., p. 159.

81–2 'The crowd shouted and jostled ... helter-skelter on all sides': 'The King
     of the Belgians' Expedition: Landing the Elephants in Africa', *Times of
     India*, 22 July 1879.

84   the first elephant was winched ... a manoeuvre 'anxiously debated': Ibid.

84 **On her back was Luximor:** Also spelled 'Luximan', according to the
     expedition's official list of mahouts and elephant attendants held in the
     Papers of Sir William Mackinnon at SOAS in London.

84 **'She must sink or swim ... I was fast losing all hope':** 'The King of the
     Belgians' Expedition: Landing the Elephants in Africa.'

86 **carrying ... up the wide stone elephant stairs to Pune's Parvati Temple:**
     'There are some hundreds of these steps, which are some eight feet deep,
     and all are laid upon a slope. The elephant is the only animal that could
     be safely used for the ascent, on account of the slipperiness of these stones,
     worn smooth by the feet of pilgrims.' 'Visit to Parbuttee (from Our Special
     Correspondent.) Poona, Monday, Nov. 15', *Times of India*, 17 November 1875.

86 **Sundar Gaj ... an animal 'in the prime of elephant life':** Joseph Mullens,
     'Letter to John Whitehouse', 30 May 1879 [CRL].

86 **'Haven of Peace' ... its Persian-Arabic name was meant to evoke:** From
     the Persian-Arabic 'Bandar-ul-Salaam', cited in 'Dar es Salaam: City, Port
     and Region', *Tanzania Notes and Records*, 71 (1970), p. 1.

87 **'an infected spot' featuring little more than ... snakes and rats:** Joseph
     Thomson, *To the Central African Lakes and Back: The Narrative of the Royal
     Geographical Society's East Central African Expedition, 1878–1880*, vol. 1
     (London: Sampson Low, Marston, Searle & Rivington, 1878), p. 74.

87 **the second-fastest-growing city in Africa:** 'According to U.N. projections,
     the continent will have 18 cities with more than five million people by
     2030, up from eight in 2018. Today 21 of the world's 30 fastest growing
     cities, including the top ten, are African. Dar es Salaam – currently Africa's
     fifth most populous city – ranks second, behind Kampala in neighboring
     Uganda. It's projected to grow from six million people today to 13.4
     million by 2035, crossing the "megacity" threshold of 10 million people
     sometime before 2030.' See Jonathan W. Rosen, 'This Tanzanian City May
     Soon be One of the World's Most Populous. Is it Ready?', *National
     Geographic*, 5 April 2019.

88–9 **John Magufuli, then president ... made things a little easier for me:** John
     Magufuli, the fifth president of Tanzania, was voted in on a tide of
     goodwill in 2015 after promising to tackle corruption and wasteful
     government spending. He was nicknamed the 'Bulldozer'. But his policies
     inched the country close to authoritarianism. He was notoriously
     intolerant of criticism, working to repress civil society and political
     opposition. He died suddenly in March 2021 at the height of the global
     Covid-19 pandemic, which sparked intense speculation about the cause of
     his death. His government, however, was quick to deny he was a victim of
     the virus given his loud-spoken assurances that the infection could be
     countered by saunas and prayer.

89   **Nyerere ... widely loved as the 'father of the nation':** One village I passed in western Tanzania was called Asante Nyerere ('Thank you Nyerere').

92   **'Accompanied by the people of Dar es Salaam shouting':** A. J. Wauters, 'IX. La Caravane de M. Carter', in 'L'Éléphant d'Afrique et son rôle dans l'histoire de la civilisation africaine', *Bulletin: Société belge de géographie* (Brussels: Secrétariat de la Société belge de géographie, 1880), pp. 177–8.

92   **so thick ... a route would literally have 'to be felt for':** Edward Coode Hore, *Tanganyika: Eleven Years in Central Africa* (London: Edward Stanford, 1892), p. 29.

93   **'extraordinary growth of grass ... willing to resent this interference':** 'Memorandum: The Road from Dar-es-Salaam East Africa, Toward the Northern End of Lake Nyassa', 28 November 1878 [SOAS].

93   **The road 'seems better to travel ... for most of the way':** John Kirk, 'Letter to William Mackinnon', 3 May 1879 [SOAS].

93   **'The difficulty here is again to find men fit for Africa':** John Kirk, 'Letter to William Mackinnon, 18 September 1877 [SOAS].

93   **spending all their time 'bird, beetle and butterfly killing':** W. Mayes, 'Letter to William Mackinnon', 26 September 1877 [SOAS].

93   **'I cannot tell you the obligation ... to your East African Road':** Frederick Carter, 'Letter to William Mackinnon', 6 August 1879 [SOAS].

93   **'[I]t's like the king's highway ... could not drive a dog cart':** Frederick Carter, cited in William Beardall, 'Letter to Gerald Waller', 7 September 1879 [SOAS].

93–4 **'a triumphal progress ... see the strange procession pass':** L. K. Rankin, 'The Elephant Experiment in Africa: A Brief Account of the Belgian Elephant Expedition on the March from Dar-es-Salaam to Mpwapwa', *Proceedings of the Royal Geographical Society and Monthly Record of Geography*, 4:5 (May 1882), p. 274.

94   **street vendors slipped between the trucks ... spaces were too tight:** The street vendors are known as *machinga* – a Swahili colloquialism meaning 'the marching guys'.

94   **Bongo Flava:** Derived from *ubongo* (meaning 'brainland') and *flava* (meaning 'flavour'), combining melodic love ballads and American-style rap and hip-hop. 'In respect to its origins, the word *bongo* (the augmentative form of *ubongo*, "brain") means "Tanzania" in Swahili slang, with an allusion to the "big brain" necessary to survive in the country.' Maria Suriano, 'Hip-Hop and Bongo Flavour Music in Contemporary Tanzania: Youths' Experiences, Agency, Aspirations and Contradictions', *Africa Development*, 36:3–4 (2011), p. 113.

95   **'The scenery ... recalled Yorkshire to one's mind':** Rankin, 'The Elephant Experiment in Africa', p. 274.

95 **The polluted Msimbazi River ... between the hills and the port:** 'According to Shahidi wa Maji, a civil society group, nearly a quarter million people along the Msimbazi face serious health risks linked to the river's "toxic mixture of industrial effluent, chemicals, abattoir waste and human sewage."' Rosen, 'This Tanzanian City May Soon be One of the World's Most Populous'.

95 **Various conservation measures ... plant species are found nowhere else:** Pugu's relic forest, and the contiguous Kanzinagani reserve, covers some four thousand square hectares, which is about twelve times the size of Central Park in New York. At the time of writing, there were twenty-seven rangers employed to protect four areas in these hills: Pugu, Ruvu, Masanganya and Kanzinagani.

95–6 **charcoal in nylon bags on the back of bikes ... the seated drivers:** I later walked around the back of the local ranger HQ in the Pugu town of Kisarawe, where the poaching problem was clear. There were heaps of confiscated sacks of charcoal, about sixty motorbikes and six pedal bikes, all taken in less than five months.

96 **the landscape Rankin had described in detail:** See Rankin, 'The Elephant Experiment in Africa'.

97 **'thick as a man's thigh ... binding the tree-trunks as with bands of iron':** Thomson, *To the Central African Lakes and Back*, vol. 1, p. 144.

97 **poultices for sprains ... the local bad spirit, Mweneembago:** For more, see Lloyd Wantz, *The Medicine Man among the Zaramo of Dar es Salaam* (Uddevalla: Scandinavian Institute of African Studies and Dar es Salaam University Press, 1990), p. 33.

99 **Zaramo women love music and sex ... how to make men happy:** In other parts of Tanzania, there is plenty of evidence that female genital mutilation, though illegal, still exists. In 2019, I worked with the Kuria people on the western fringes of the Serengeti National Park. FGM was still being practised. A teacher, who was against FGM, said to me: 'The difference is the women now bring their own razor to stop the spread of HIV rather than share a blade.'

5. Miss Kisabengo

101 **'Everything flows ... So it is with memory' [epigraph]:** Ryszard Kapuściński, *Travels with Herodotus* (London, New York and Toronto: Penguin, 2008), p. 77.

102–3 **Britain's diminishing biodiversity passing me by ... Or a hawk moth:** Britain has lost almost half its biodiversity since I was born in the 1970s. See 'Biodiversity in the UK: Bloom or Bust?', *First Report of Session 2021–22*, UK Parliament, publications.parliament.uk/pa/cm5802/cmselect/cmenvaud/136/136-report.html. The country ranks in the bottom ten per cent of all countries globally. See Josh Davis, 'UK has "Led the World" in Destroying the Natural Environment', *Natural History Museum*, 26 September 2020. It's a similar story across Europe. In Germany, around a quarter of plant species and a third of animal species are considered endangered. See 'Biodiversity', *Federal Ministry of Education and Research*, www.bmbf.de/bmbf/en/research/environment-and-climate/biodiversity/biodiversity_node.html

103　**Tanzania has one of the fastest-growing populations in the world:** The population is expanding between two and three per cent each year. Caroline Kimeu, 'What Tanzania Tells Us About Africa's Population Explosion as the World hits 8bn People', *Guardian*, 15 November 2022.

103　**'pacing along as if they had an appointment at the end of the world':** Karen Blixen, *Out of Africa* (London: Penguin, 2001), Kindle Loc. 263.

103　**a third of the country falling under some kind of protection:** Maurus Msuha et al. (eds), 'National Human–Wildlife Conflict Management Strategy 2020–2024', United Republic of Tanzania Ministry of Natural Resources and Tourism (2020), p. 17.

104　**Carter nicknamed him 'Old Musty':** L. K. Rankin, 'The Elephant Experiment in Africa: A Brief Account of the Belgian Elephant Expedition on the March from Dar-es-Salaam to Mpwapwa', *Proceedings of the Royal Geographical Society and Monthly Record of Geography*, 4:5 (May 1882), p. 284.

104　**The mahouts called him 'Must Wallah':** Frederick Carter, 'Letter to William Mackinnon', 6 August 1879 [SOAS].

104　**He was proving 'very troublesome and unmanageable':** John Kirk, 'Letter to William Mackinnon', 17 September 1879 [SOAS].

104　**Sundar Gaj often had to be worked . . . the same in Africa:** Ibid.

104–5　**'The feline caresses . . . frolicking' . . . same tactic on another male:** Adolphe Burdo, *Les Belges dans l'Afrique centrale: voyages, aventures et découvertes d'après les documents et journaux des explorateurs: de Zanzibar au Lac Tanganika* (Brussels: P. Maes, 1886), p. 69.

105　**In the midst of the trickery . . . 'weep and moan like children':** Ibid.

105　**The slimy water was so bad . . . get through a cup of tea:** Drinking tea on an expedition was so important to the British, Galton gave more than two pages to his 'Theory of Tea-Making' in his explorer's handbook. See Francis Galton, *The Art of Travel: or, Shifts and Contrivances Available in Wild Countries*, fifth edition (London: John Murray, 1872), pp. 208–11. The missionary Edward Hore made a joke of it when a mug of water was delivered to the dinner table containing several tadpoles. '"Look here, what do you mean by bringing *little hippopotami* in my water?"' See Edward Coode Hore, *Tanganyika: Eleven Years in Central Africa* (London: Edward Stanford, 1892), p. 35.

105 'splendid, likely-looking game country': Rankin, 'The Elephant Experiment in Africa', p. 277.

108 At the peak of the poaching scourge ... three kilograms per tusk: Doran Ross, *Elephant: The Animal and Its Ivory in African Culture* (Berkeley: University of California Press, 1992), cited in Lina Jansson, 'How to Stop the African Elephant Population from Extermination: Causes, Achievements, Consequences', university thesis (Huddinge: Södertörns University College, 2006), p. 14. Further research suggests that the average weight of an African savannah bull elephant's tusk is now between fifty and seventy-nine kilograms. There has also been a rise in tuskless elephants, with researchers hypothesizing that the species is evolving in response to generations of ivory poaching.

108 Modern tests on nineteenth-century piano ... slaughter had penetrated: Research into the carbon isotopes in historical ivory has helped scientists identify which terrain the East African elephant originally inhabited: coastal, Rift Valley or inland lakes. This has informed a greater understanding of the 'moving frontier' of elephant extraction in the nineteenth century. For a nuanced interpretation of the data, see Ashley Coutu, Julia Lee-Thorp, Matthew J. Collins and Paul J. Lane, 'Mapping the Elephants of the 19th Century East African Ivory Trade with a Multi-Isotope Approach', *PLOS One* (October 2016).

109 People were using the ivory ... for their homesteads: See *Tippoo Tib: The Story of His Career in Central Africa, Narrated from His Own Accounts by Dr Heinrich Brode* (London: Edward Arnold, 1907), p. 128.

109 Tanzania's government chooses ... back into conservation [picture caption]: Over the years, Tanzania has built up a huge stockpile of tusks held in a top-secret government 'Ivory Room' – which, by the last count, amounted to a value of about fifty million dollars. See a 2013 National Geographic Television Special documentary, *Battle for the Elephants*, by investigative journalists Aidan Hartley and Bryan Christy.

111 From 1870 to 1890, the manufacture ... increased fourfold [picture caption]: Arthur Loesser, *Men, Women & Pianos: A Social History* (New York: Dover Publications, 1954), p. 549.

112 Today, the mountains' reputation ... outshines even Pugu: At the last official count, the Uluguru Mountains had at least a hundred and thirty-five plant species, three amphibians and two birds (Loveridge's sunbird, with its bottle-green head and reddish neckerchief, and the yellow-breasted Uluguru bushshrike) which aren't found anywhere else in the world. For more, see Colin Watkins, *A Walking and Wildlife Guide to the Uluguru Nature Reserve* (Cambridge: Banson, 2009), p. 15.

112 an Uluguru antelope so elusive ... photographed for the first time in 2003: The Abbott's duiker may or may not still be present in the

Ulugurus. Little is known about the antelope, and sources differ on its distribution patterns.

112 **breast-shaped peaks, 'each crowned with a nest of huts':** Rankin, 'The Elephant Experiment in Africa', p. 278.

112 **'the inhabitants could ... there was a world beyond them':** Ibid.

112 **the spear-carrying Zaramo people with their 'Van Dyke beards':** Ibid., p. 276.

112 **'The people crowded together ... least movement of the elephants':** Ibid., p. 278.

112 **splendid streams ... 'pebble-bottomed and clear as crystal':** Ibid., p. 279.

112 **The hills were 'abodes of peace and plenty':** Ibid., p. 278.

112 **the land glittering with flecks of 'gold-dust':** Ibid., p. 279.

112 **'I look back upon the scene ... and take possession of it':** Henry Morton
–13 Stanley, *How I Found Livingstone: Travels, Adventures and Discoveries in Central Africa: Including an Account of Four Months' Residence with Dr. Livingstone* (New York: Scribner, Armstrong & Co., 1872), p. 122.

113 **'Where a man feels at home ... where he's meant to go':** Ernest Hemingway, *Green Hills of Africa* (New York: Scribner, 2002), p. 200. This was Hemingway's account of a safari he took in East Africa with his wife in 1933. Along the way, he had the chance to exhibit his hunting skills, bagging black rhino and greater kudu. On publication, the book was hailed as 'the best-written story of big-game hunting anywhere' by the *New York Times*. C. G. Poore, 'Ernest Hemingway's Story of His African Safari: A Fine Book on Hunting and Writing and Life and Death in the African Afternoon', *New York Times*, 27 October 1935.

113 **'Up in this high air ... Here I am, where I ought to be':** Karen Blixen, *Out of Africa* (London: Penguin, 2001), Kindle Loc. 122–3.

113 **Simbamwene:** Stanley writes the same place name as 'Simbamwenni'. Travellers and explorers in Africa often misheard words and then spelled them phonetically.

113 **Kisabengo, a charismatic 'robber and kidnapper':** Stanley, *How I Found Livingstone*, p. 117.

113 **Stanley nicknamed her 'Amazon Simbamwenni' ... with disdain:** Ibid., p. 134.

114 **Cameron ... also haughtily dismissed 'Miss Kisabengo':** Verney Lovett Cameron, *Across Africa* (New York: Harper & Brothers, 1877), p. 55.

114 **'We marched past ... disregarding the demands of its present ruler':** Ibid., p. 53.

114 **'[Miss Kisabengo] possesses the will ... as was her robber sire':** Ibid. By 1879, Pangiro had given up her leadership to a male relative. If Carter met her, he made no mention of it in his surviving letters.

114 **an occasional 'squat and ill-favoured' woman:** Rankin, 'The Elephant Experiment in Africa', p. 276.

114   **Women were, as one missionary put it, 'supernumeraries':** Alexander
Mackay, 'Letter to Henry Wright', 18 September 1876 [CRL], cited in
Stephen J. Rockel, 'Enterprising Partners: Caravan Women in Nineteenth
Century Tanzania', *Canadian Journal of African Studies / Revue canadienne
des études africaines*, 34:3 (2000), p. 763.

114   **'Her figure ... offered in marriage to whosoever would have her':**
Joseph Thomson, *To the Central African Lakes and Back: The Narrative
of the Royal Geographical Society's East Central African Expedition,
1878–1880*, vol. 1 (London: Sampson Low, Marston, Searle & Rivington,
1878), pp. 264–5.

115   **'It gives great life to the party ... better than a horse or a bullock':**
Galton, *The Art of Travel*, p. 7.

115   **good for 'hearsay gossip ... fond of carrying weights':** Ibid., p. 8.

115   **'All the chiefs of the caravan carried ... "plenty of them"':** Richard
Francis Burton, *The Lake Regions of Central Africa*, vol. 1 (London:
Longman, Green, Longman and Roberts, 1860), p. 211.

115   **she 'disordered the caravan ... a few measures of rice':** Ibid., p. 211. This
passage is cited in Rockel, 'Enterprising Partners: Caravan Women in
Nineteenth Century Tanzania'. I am indebted to Rockel for this summary
on caravan women. His research details the rarely recorded, little-studied
subject of women's roles in the region's nineteenth-century caravan
industry.

115   **'I looked at the skies, and I looked at the ground':** Thomson, *To the
Central African Lakes and Back*, p. 245.

115   **ran away and hid his head ... their large 'mammæ':** Ibid., p. 262.

115   **'future historians would be wise to write only in Latin':** Burdo, *Les Belges
dans l'Afrique centrale*, p. 324.

116   **'There are no limits ... crimes of the imperialists and their agents':**
'Intensify the Revolution by O. R. Tambo: The "Morogoro Conference",
Morogoro, Tanzania, 25 April to 1 May 1969', *South African History Online*,
www.sahistory.org.za/archive/intensify-revolution-o-r-tambo-morogoro-
conference-morogoro-tanzania-25-april-1-may-1969

116   **'My roads had to be 12 feet x 10 feet to let the co[mpany] pass':** Frederick
Carter, 'Letter to Tom Cadenhead', 7 August 1879 [SM].

116   **'No loaded animal save an elephant could have accomplished them':**
Frederick Carter, 'Letter to William Mackinnon', 6 August 1879 [SOAS].

116   **'Picture to yourself ... as would bridge the Thames':** Frederick Carter,
'Letter to Tom Cadenhead', 7 August 1879 [SM].

117   **the Uluguru cave ... which women used to visit to improve their
fertility:** 'The hill tribes, however, still receive strangers hospitably into
their villages. They have a place visited even by distant Wazaramo
pilgrims. It is described as a cave where a P'hepo or the disembodied

spirit of a man, in fact a ghost, produces a terrible subterraneous sound, called by the people Kurero or Bokero; it arises probably from the flow of water underground. In a pool in the cave women bathe for the blessing of issue, and men sacrifice sheep and goats to obtain fruitful seasons and success in war? Burton, *The Lake Regions of Central Africa*, p. 88.

120 'In the Uluguru Mountains, our streams never run dry': See Sophy Roberts, 'Tanzania's Mountain Marvels', *Financial Times*, 20 August 2022.

121 the plain turned into 'one vast lake, a small Tanganyika': Henry Morton Stanley, 1 May 1871, 'Journal S.A. 7, Full Transcript (1871)', in Mathilde Leduc-Grimaldi and James L. Newman (eds), *Finding Dr. Livingstone: A History in Documents from the Henry Morton Stanley Archives* (Athens, OH: Ohio University Press, 2020), p. 85.

121 '[The] horrors ... until but five sickly worn-out beasts remained': Stanley, *How I Found Livingstone*, p. 141.

121 the caravan would camp, 'nested like Noah's dove': Stanley, 1 May 1871, 'Journal S.A. 7, Full Transcript (1871)', p. 85.

121 the land was 'as level as a billiard table': Ibid., p. 23.

121 giant elephant footprints, 'half as large again as those of our animals': Rankin, 'The Elephant Experiment in Africa', p. 280.

6. Big With Blessing

124 'The white man is very clever ... we have fallen apart' [epigraph]: Chinua Achebe, *Things Fall Apart* (London: Penguin, 2001), p. 166.

126 'Pass Terrible': Richard Francis Burton, *The Lake Regions of Central Africa*, vol. 1 (London: Longman, Green, Longman and Roberts, 1860), p. 213.

126 In the Mkata marshes, around a hundred men died each month: John Iliffe, *A Modern History of Tanganyika* (Cambridge: Cambridge University Press, 1979), p. 137.

127 African soldiers who fought and fell for a European war: The role of Africans during the First World War – as well as their names and identities – remains conspicuously overlooked. 'Official records put the death toll of the Africans who served Britain in the East Africa campaign at around 100,000, but many historians estimate it at up to three times that.' David Lammy, 'How Britain Dishonoured its African First World War Dead', *Guardian*, 3 November 2019.

130 To spare himself the discomfort ... 'long, rank grass': 'The Late Rev. Dr. Mullens', *Missionary Observer* (November 1879), in John Clifford (ed.), *General Baptist Magazine for 1879*, vol. 81 (London: E. Marlborough and Co., 1879), p. 461.

131 all ran 'smoothly and harmoniously': Ibid.

131 The experience was 'like a huge picnic': Ebenezer Southon, Journal, 7 July 1879 [SOAS].

131 'The men did their work . . . his wonted health and spirits': 'The Late Rev. Dr. Mullens', p. 461.

131 In 1858, Burton was conveyed . . . after suffering partial paralysis: Richard Francis Burton, 'The Lake Regions of Central Equatorial Africa with Notices of the Lunar Mountains and the Sources of the White Nile; Being the Results of an Expedition Undertaken Under the Patronage of Her Majesty's Government and the Royal Geographical Society of London, in the Years 1857–1859', *Journal of the Royal Geographical Society*, vol. 29 (1859), p. 17.

131 'annoyances . . . even when the sun is shining': Edward Baxter, 'Letter to Henry Wright', 9 August 1880 [CRL].

131 Annie Hore . . . join her missionary husband on Lake Tanganyika: She also wrote a book about it: Annie B. Hore, *To Lake Tanganyika in a Bath Chair* (London: Sampson Low, Marston, Searle & Rivington, 1886).

132 'a pleasant springiness': Ibid., p. 41.

132 'I could see nothing of the country . . . bushes and trees gliding by': Ibid., p. 11.

132 'Though always carried . . . longed for the relief of a walk': Ibid., p. 87.

132 'indeed we had no gilt tent-knobs . . . or canteens': Ibid., p. 50.

132 '[which] was . . . the quickest on record by any European': Ibid., p. 106.

134 Pulmalla had even carried the Prince of Wales through Pune: L. K. Rankin, 'The Elephant Experiment in Africa: A Brief Account of the Belgian Elephant Expedition on the March from Dar-es-Salaam to Mpwapwa', *Proceedings of the Royal Geographical Society and Monthly Record of Geography*, 4:5 (May 1882), p. 274. The future king of England is said to have toppled from his howdah on that hurried occasion.

135 Carter described walking . . . 'keeping the ball always rolling': Frederick Carter, 'Letter to Tom Cadenhead', 7 August 1879 [SM].

135 'I have got my men . . . has to be done with my own hands': Ibid.

135 'useless except to ride the elephants . . . boys without experience': Frederick Carter, 'Letter to William Mackinnon', 6 August 1879 [SOAS].

135 The mahouts had to be 'nursed and looked after like babies': Ibid.

135 accusations that the Africans were 'stupid brutes': Frederick Carter, 'Letter to Tom Cadenhead', 7 August 1879 [SM].

136 Kilkenny Union Workhouse . . . tours of the 'Famine Experience': Inside the mall there were brown exhibition plinths marking various places of historical interest, including the site of a mass grave between a clothes store and a shop selling trainers. The former workhouse infirmary was a Starbucks.

136 'I cannot tell you how often I have longed for you to help me': Frederick Carter, 'Letter to Tom Cadenhead', 7 August 1879 [SM]. 'These two gallant

men were like David and Jonathan in their love and devotion to each other', a London newspaper later observed, perhaps carrying a dose of insinuation: the Old Testament story was often used by the Victorians as a coded reference to homosexuality. See 'Captain Carter and Mr. Cadenhead', *The Graphic*, 9 October 1880.

136 **'From what I have written ... coming out just as I stand now':** Frederick Carter, 'Letter to Tom Cadenhead', 19 August 1879 [SM].

136 **'It's downright hard work ... without one pleasure of any kind':** Ibid.

136 **'There is a great future ... hills and mountains cover the country':** Ibid.

137 **turn Mpwapwa into ... a 'centre of light for the lakes around':** Henry Wright, 'Letter to Edward Baxter', 20 May 1879 [CRL].

137 **deal with the local chief ... convince about Christ's redemption:** A. T. Matson, 'The Instructions Issued in 1876 and 1878 to the Pioneer C.M.S. Parties to Karagwe and Uganda: Part I', *Journal of Religion in Africa*, 12:3 (1981), p. 197.

137 **the Mpwapwa chief said he 'hoped they would stay for a hundred years':** Ibid.

137 **Arab-Swahili caravans now marching 'out of sight ... dead of night':** Joseph Thomson, *To the Central African Lakes and Back: The Narrative of the Royal Geographical Society's East Central African Expedition, 1878–1880*, vol. 1 (London: Sampson Low, Marston, Searle & Rivington, 1878), p. 304.

137 **'So far as I can learn ... all trace of them is eventually lost':** John Kirk, 'Letter to the Marquis of Salisbury', 23 June 1879, in *Correspondence with British Representatives and Agents Abroad, and Reports from Naval Officers and the Treasury, Relative to the Slave Trade*, vol. 5, (London: Harrison & Sons, 1880), p. 245.

137–8 **Africa '[is] a cloud which is "big with blessing"':** Henry Wright, 'Instructions of the Committee to Mr George Sneath Returning and Mr Charles Stokes and Mr H. S. Penrose Proceeding to Join the Nyanza Mission', 26 March 1878 [CRL].

138 **Africans were desperate for salvation ... all argued for some time:** The 1870s saw a 'turn of the tide' for missionary societies. This gained momentum with Livingstone; as the CMS's nineteenth-century biographer wrote, he 'effected more by his death even than he did by his life' (Eugene Stock, *The History of the Church Missionary Society*, vol. 3 (London: Church Missionary Society, 1899), p. 73). Then along came Stanley: on 15 November 1875, the *Daily Telegraph* published one of his letters written from the shores of Lake Victoria, describing the spiritual potential of Buganda's ruler, Mutesa I. Because of Stanley's proselytizing, Mutesa was now observing both the Muslim Sabbath *and* the Christian – and that was achieved by a layman in just a few days! The balance could easily be tipped, wagered Stanley, and Islam would tumble 'to the ground.'

'But, oh that some pious, practical Missionary would come here! What a field and a harvest ripe for the sickle of civilization ... Here, gentlemen, is your opportunity – embrace it' (Henry Morton Stanley, 'Mtesa's Capital, Uganda', 14 April 1875, published in 'New African Expedition', *Daily Telegraph*, 15 November 1875). This was PR manna for the CMS, which had struggled to generate interest in Central Africa since the first Protestant mission to Africa three decades earlier. It was after reading Stanley's letter to the *Daily Telegraph* that an anonymous donor injected a game-changing five thousand pounds into the CMS coffers for a new wave of Africa missions to get started.

138 **fresh recruits found nothing left ... except a pile of rubbish:** The new recruits arrived in April 1878, in the thick of a scandal. A month before, another CMS employee, Alexander Mackay, had come through Mpwapwa on his way to Uganda. Against London's orders, Mackay had not only been openly hostile to Arab slavers, but also shot and wounded four porters, forcing Kirk to declare him an outlaw. See Alexina Mackay Harrison, *A. M. Mackay: Pioneer Missionary of the Church Missionary Society to Uganda* (London: Hodder & Stoughton, 1890).

138 **'I should not be surprised ... carried off by a gust of wind':** Edward Baxter, 'Letter to Henry Wright', 6 June 1880 [CRL].

138 **'With all I made one agreement ... permanent home at Mpwapwa':** Joseph Last, 'Letter to Henry Wright', 6 June 1879 [CRL].

138–9 **'a slave boy ... as well as the services and meetings':** Ibid.

139 **'I can often tell a story ... would not care to listen to me':** Joseph Last, 'Letter to Henry Wright', 20 January 1879 [CRL].

140 **Among the most committed members ... his plans to get to heaven:** '"*Kwa Imani Kabika Isa Masiya*" ("By Faith in Jesus Christ")'. Joseph Last, 'Letter to Henry Wright', 6 June 1879 [CRL].

140 **'[a] man of robust and virile personality':** R.N.L., 'Obituary: Joseph Thomas Last', *Geographical Journal*, 83:4 (April 1934), p. 352.

140 **A suspected cold ... twenty-nine miles shy of Mpwapwa:** 'The Late Rev. Dr. Mullens', *Missionary Observer* (November 1879), cited in Clifford (ed.), *General Baptist Magazine for 1879*, p. 462.

140 **the official medical report ... 'inflammation of the rectum':** Ebenezer Southon, 'London Missionary Society Third Central Africa Expedition Medical Report: Saadani to Mpwapwa from June 16th to July 12th 1879', 12 July 1879 [SOAS].

141 **Tito had worked as a 'houseboy':** 'Boy' or 'boi' was the term used for boys or men who worked as domestic servants for Europeans.

141 **pombe:** A home-brewed beer often made with millet.

142 **'We have no church papers. They're all in your country, in England':** Chamwela was referring specifically to documentation from the earliest

days of the Anglican mission, which are part of the Church Missionary Society Archive kept at the Cadbury Research Library in Birmingham, England.

143 **'Sunday is a happy day ... people coming and going to church':** Joseph Last, 'Letter to Henry Wright', 6 June 1879 [CRL].

143 **'The men and boys ... women, in their gay cotton clothes on the other':** Ibid.

145 **Baxter was 'more and more astonished' at Last's growing expenditure:** Edward Baxter, 'Letter to Henry Wright', 12 August 1879 [CRL].

145 **'I never was a drunkard ... many cases in which they are':** Joseph Last, 'Letter to Henry Wright', 1 September 1879 [CRL].

145 **'The Royal Elephant Expedition has ... things for presents':** Ibid.

145–6 Last had **'no idea whatever ... from what he would at home':** Edward Baxter, 'Letter to Henry Wright', 18 September 1879 [CRL].

146 **'two or three of these wise beasts ... on a missionary tour':** 'The Elephant in Africa', *American Missionary*, 34:7 (July 1880).

146 **'a delightful nook, 800 feet above the valley':** This is according to Annie Hore, who enjoyed the same 'oasis' three years later when she was carried in on her bath chair. Hore, *To Lake Tanganyika in a Bath Chair*, p. 19.

146 **Enslaved as a child, Majwara ... life in this emerging mission town:** The youngest son of a Bugandan chief, Majwara was kidnapped into slavery at a young age. He served as a gunbearer on Stanley's 1871 journey to find Livingstone. In 1872, Majwara set out from the coast again and entered Livingstone's service. In 1873, he marched at the head of the party that carried Livingstone's body back to the coast. The following year, Majwara entered Stanley's service again, accompanying him all the way to the mouth of the Congo River. After a stint serving as Joseph Last's cook in Mpwapwa in the late 1870s, Majwara moved on to another missionary station at Ujiji. After all he'd survived, Majwara drowned in 1886, when his boat capsized on Lake Tanganyika. For parts of this story, see Sir John Milner Gray, 'Livingstone's Muganda Servant', *Uganda Journal*, 13:2 (September 1949).

146 **'I often think of Maaghil ... than would be good for a dozen men':** Frederick Carter, 'Letter to Tom Cadenhead', 19 August 1879 [SM].

146 **Carter's old home ... foreign produce imported from England:** Tristram J. Elllis, *On a Raft, and Through the Desert*, vol. 1 (London: Field & Tuer, 1881), p. 2.

147 **'Well-arranged and comfortable' ... yellow-blossomed acacias:** These descriptions are largely taken from an account by John Henry Gray, *A Journey Round the World in the Years 1875–1876–1877* (London: Harrison, 1879), and William Perry Fogg, *Arabistan: or, the Land of 'The Arabian Nights'. Being Travels Through Egypt, Arabia, and Persia, to Bagdad* (Hartford:

Dustin, Gillman & Co., 1875). Both men stayed with Carter during the course of their travels.

147 **fig trees taken from the biblical . . . located a few miles upriver:** The trees were 'still revered as the lineal descendants of Adam and Eve's inanimate costumier,' wrote Carter's house guest. 'American Excursion to Eden,' *Stamford Mercury*, 6 October 1871.

147 **the elephant experiment already 'a complete success':** Frederick Carter, 'Letter to William Mackinnon,' 6 August 1879 [SOAS].

147 **'[We] have passed through . . . by a white man and unsurveyed':** Ibid.

147 **'mountains and incessant hills . . . steep banked streams and rivers':** Ibid.

147 **'carrying loads . . . the elements of doubt cleared up':** Ibid.

148 **The lake looked promising . . . eagles 'with wattles like a turkey':** Rankin, 'The Elephant Experiment in Africa,' p. 284.

148 **'There is an almost constant fusilade . . . rifles from the deck':** Fogg, *Arabistan: or, the Land of 'The Arabian Nights'*, p. 193.

148 **The species was rendered extinct in Mesopotamia just forty years later:** In what is now known as Iraq, the last-known Persian lion was said to have been killed on the lower Tigris in 1918 – the proverbial nail in the coffin to a staggering tale of slaughter, given the wildlife that used to roam these regions. Royal hunts in the ninth century BCE describe the bag of a single event: 450 lions, 390 wild bulls, 30 elephants, 200 ostriches. See Robert T. Hatt, *The Mammals of Iraq* (University of Michigan: Museum of Zoology, 1959), p. 21. While hunting may have devastated Iraq's wildlife at the start of the twentieth century, war has pretty much finished it off: the eight-year Iran–Iraq war laid waste to Iraq's mountain habitats. In addition, Iraq president Saddam Hussein ordered the destruction of nearly all Basra's twelve million date palms to prevent sneak assaults. Iraq's famous marshes – the region's largest wetlands – were drained to flush out rebels. Then in 2003 came the US-led invasion. Accumulatively, this has resulted in an ecosystem in collapse.

149 **'our porters could scarcely be compelled even to lend their knives':** Rankin, 'The Elephant Experiment in Africa,' p. 287.

149 **'a souvenir of the death . . . so many noble lives have been sacrificed':** 'The Royal Belgian Elephant Expedition in Africa,' *The Globe*, 11 November 1879.

149 **Leopold should blame the Indian government . . . 'behaved very meanly':** John Kirk, 'Letter to William Mackinnon,' 17 September 1879 [SOAS].

150 **'just <u>for fear</u> of any accident happening to the Indian ones':** Ibid.

150 **'a victim of too-herculean labours and an insufficiency of food':** Rankin, 'The Elephant Experiment in Africa,' p. 287.

150 **up and down hills . . . 'like the side of a house':** Frederick Carter, 'Letter to William Mackinnon,' 6 August 1879 [SOAS].

150   the elephant, 'fat and round at starting' ... from his flanks: Rankin, 'The Elephant Experiment in Africa', p. 287.

150   'It had been the most difficult to manage ... and succeeded': 'The Royal Belgian Elephant Expedition in Africa.'

150   'such an ass that I cannot trust him with the simplest thing': Frederick Carter, 'Letter to Tom Cadenhead', 7 August 1879 [SM].

151   'I dare not leave my camp ... if I do something is sure to happen': Frederick Carter, 'Letter to Tom Cadenhead, 19 August 1879 [SM].

151   'I fear Popelin's gang will spoil mine ... short marches will not suit me': Frederick Carter 'Letter to Tom Cadenhead, 7 August 1879 [SM].

151   a tall and robust 'son of the north', a 'warlike' professional soldier: Thomson, *To the Central African Lakes and Back*, vol. 2, p. 251.

151   muscles 'made of steel': Adolphe Burdo, *Les Belges dans l'Afrique centrale: voyages, aventures et découvertes d'après les documents et journaux des explorateurs: de Zanzibar au Lac Tanganika* (Brussels: P. Maes, 1886), pp. 62–3.

152   'These men should never have been sent ... not fit for African hardships': Frederick Carter, 'Letter to Tom Cadenhead', 19 August 1879 [SM].

152   Van den Heuvel was ... 'disgusted with the whole thing': Ibid.

152   'I have no instructions ... I would have been half way across by now': Ibid.

152   '[Carter] has given out ... throw up his contract if he likes it or not': W. H. Hathorne, 'Letter to Henry Morton Stanley', 28 June 1879, cited in Norman R. Bennett, 'Stanley and the American Consuls at Zanzibar', in *Essex Institute Historical Collections*, vol. C (Salem, MA: Newcomb & Gauss Co., 1964), p. 54.

152   'I think he is a "muff" and talks too much': Ibid.

153   'the mailmen [ran] the gauntlet every journey': Ebenezer Southon, Journal, 14 April 1880 [SOAS].

154   the skin was stripped ... body surrounded by ransacked books: Smith, Mackenzie & Co., 'Letter to Lay Secretary of the Church Missionary Society', 7 January 1879 [CRL]. Penrose's bones and the broken remains of his caravan lay scattered around the scene of his murder for many years, a grisly passing point for travellers on their way inland.

154   all were watching 'how far the example may spread': Edward Steere, 'Letter to Anonymous', 4 February 1879 [CRL].

154   '[F]or now having attacked ... not be so slow to attack Europeans again': Joseph Last, 'Letter to Henry Wright', 5 March 1879 [CRL].

154   'Our troubles will begin at Mpwapwa': Rankin, 'The Elephant Experiment in Africa', p. 286.

7. ACACIA HORRIDA

155 **'Mmoja anapokimbia asipigwe ... tone la maji' [epigraph]:** Euphrase
Kezilahabi, *Dunia Uwanja wa Fujo* (Nairobi: East African Literature
Bureau, 1975), p. 21, cited in Katriina Ranne, 'Drops that Open Worlds:
Image of Water in the Poetry of Euphrase Kezilahabi', master's thesis
(Helsinki: University of Helsinki, May 2006), p. 28.

156 **In the autumn of 1897, after gold ... glint in the South African veld:** A
version of this family history was first published in Sophy Roberts, 'Out in
the Open', *Condé Nast Traveler*, March 2024.

157 **a quarter of the globe's surface ... a half-dozen nation states:** This
calculation was made in Eric Hobsbawm, *The Age of Empire: 1875–1914*
(New York: Pantheon, 1987), p. 59.

157 **'I looked at this land and people ... worth some effort to reclaim':** Henry
Morton Stanley, *In Darkest Africa, or the Quest, Rescue and Retreat of Emin,
Governor of Equatoria*, vol. 2 (New York: Charles Scribner's Sons, 1891), p. 446.

157 **the dreaded Marenga-Mkali, or 'desert of bitter waters':** Joseph Thomson,
*To the Central African Lakes and Back: The Narrative of the Royal
Geographical Society's East Central African Expedition, 1878–1880*, vol. 2
(London: Sampson Low, Marston, Searle & Rivington, 1881), p. 262.

157 **The Chunyo water was ... 'extremely offensive to the palate':** Henry
Morton Stanley, *How I Found Livingstone: Travels, Adventures and Discoveries
in Central Africa: Including an Account of Four Months' Residence with
Dr. Livingstone* (New York: Scribner, Armstrong & Co., 1872), p. 172.

157 **The brush was as sharp ... thorns could pierce a human eyeball:**
Adolphe Burdo, 'Rapport succinct sur la route suivie par l'expédition
Burdo, depuis Mpwapwa jusqu'à Kouihara (Ounyanyembé)', in
'Association internationale africaine', *Bulletin: Société belge de géographie*
(Brussels: Secrétariat de la Société belge de géographie, 1880), p. 499.

157–8 **'If I were to speak for a month ... hard work without water':** Frederick
Carter, 'Letter to George Sutherland Mackenzie', 16 September 1879 [SM].

158 **In the Marenga-Mkali, Carter began to suffer a run of hallucinations:** Ibid.

159 **European travellers reach for quinine ... 'much like pepper and salt':**
Camille Coquilhat, cited in Johannes Fabian, *Out of Our Minds: Reason
and Madness in the Exploration of Central Africa* (Berkeley and Los Angeles:
University of California Press, 2000), p. 66.

159 **'Wine is generally helpful ... can and must resort to it':** Pierre Dutrieux,
'Étude sur les maladies et l'acclimatement des Européens dans l'Afrique
intertropicale', in *Association internationale africaine: rapports sur les marches
de la première expédition* (Brussels-Etterbeek: Verhavert Frères et Soeurs,
1879), p. 134.

159 **Van den Heuvel's abundant medicine chest ... dared not even touch:** The notion of 'Travel as Tripping' is explored widely in a fascinating book that reveals how early European explorers worked under the influence of opiates, alcohol, fever and fatigue. See Fabian, *Out of Our Minds*. For Dr Van den Heuvel's medicine chest, see p. 65: 'lead sulphate and quinine, tannin [an astringent], emetics, cantharidin [an alkaloid], *chloridine*, citric acid, Epsom salts, aloe, benzine, drops of senna [a purgative], rhubarb, kermesite [an expectorant], and so on ... five bottles of Warburg elixir, frequently used, Arabian elixir, also called Missionary's elixir, invented by the abbé Loyet, mustard plaster, *charpie* [shredded cotton dressing] plus a display of poisons I will take care not to touch.'

159 **They 'looked as if they would not live an hour':** Frederick Carter, 'Letter to George Sutherland Mackenzie', 16 September 1879 [SM].

159 **'A wonder of endurance':** Frederick Carter, 'Letter to Unknown', 12 September(?) 1879 [SOAS].

160 **tears in wild elephants ... common among those kept in captivity:** Sylvia K. Sikes, *The Natural History of the African Elephant* (London: Weidenfeld & Nicolson, 1971), cited in Heathcote Williams, *Sacred Elephant* (London: Jonathan Cape, 1989), p. 93.

160 **if they're starving, they'll eat anything:** In 1965, the stomach of a disembowelled elephant in Uganda was found to contain bottle tops, broken glass, a sardine-tin opener, stones and coins. See John Hanks, *A Struggle for Survival: The Elephant Problem* (London: Country Life Books, 1979), cited in Williams, *Sacred Elephant*, pp. 92–3.

161 **Famines came and went:** In the 1860s and 1870s, there was one serious famine each decade. In the early 1880s, they started to become much more frequent – a combination of climatic cycles and unreasonable demand on the region's diminishing resources. As the frequency of famine increased, social ties, weakened by wars and slavery, made communities even more vulnerable. See John Iliffe, *A Modern History of Tanganyika* (Cambridge: Cambridge University Press, 1979), p. 70.

162 **caravan numbers running up ... significant supplies of food and water:** Carl Christiansson, *Soil Erosion and Sedimentation in Semi-arid Tanzania: Studies of Environmental Change and Ecological Imbalance* (Stockholm: Scandinavian Institute of African Studies, 1981), p. 176.

162 **'The large plain ... filth and refuse and ashes of many caravans':** Edward Hore, Journal, 17 June 1878 [SOAS].

162 **The rainy season ... was called 'the hunger period':** Christiansson, *Soil Erosion and Sedimentation in Semi-arid Tanzania*, p. 176.

162 **'One would think there was a school ... masters in foxy-craft':** Stanley, *In Darkest Africa*, vol. 2, p. 446.

162 **He likened the Gogo . . . 'clannish and full of fight':** Henry Morton Stanley, 'Kwihara, District of Unyanyembe, July 4, 1871', in Norman R. Bennett (ed.), *Stanley's Despatches to the New York Herald, 1871–1872, 1874–1877* (Boston: Boston University Press, 1970), p. 19.

162 **'A tax on thirst':** Adolphe Burdo, *Les Belges dans l'Afrique centrale: voyages, aventures et découvertes d'après les documents et journaux des explorateurs: de Zanzibar au Lac Tanganika* (Brussels: P. Maes, 1886), p. 226.

162 **the last of the well-water was more like a 'foul porridge':** Ibid.

162 **'Nothing but wholesale robbery':** Charles Stokes, 'Letter to Henry Wright', 23 October 1878 [CRL].

162 **the Ugogo hongo was 'a kind of water tax':** Ebenezer Southon, 'Letter to John Whitehouse', 6 August 1879 [SOAS].

162–3 **'Hence they would value it highly . . . make them pay for it':** Ibid.

163 **'they would be glad to see us gone . . . drink all their water':** Ibid.

163 **By the 1960s . . . the Gogo were the beggars of Tanzania:** Gregory Maddox, 'Environment and Population Growth: In Ugogo and Central Tanzania', in Gregory Maddox, James Giblin and Isaria N. Kimambo (eds), *Custodians of the Land: Ecology and Culture in the History of Tanzania* (Martlesham and Rochester: Boydell & Brewer, 1996), p. 60.

164 **giant kopjes . . . 'like a burial site of the Titans':** Burdo, *Les Belges dans l'Afrique centrale*, p. 442.

164 **China has pumped more than . . . into African countries:** See Carla D. Jone, Hermann A. Ndofor and Mengge Li, 'Chinese Economic Engagement in Africa: Implications for U.S. Policy', *Foreign Policy Research Institute*, 24 January 2022, www.fpri.org/article/2022/01/chinese-economic-engagement-in-africa/

165 **At the time of my visit, business was quiet:** I was travelling during the global Covid-19 pandemic, which meant international visitors were fewer than normal.

165–6 **the Itigi Thicket . . . the next step in Carter's journey:** Ernest Cambier, 'Chapitre II: Rapport sur la marche de M. Cambier de Mpwapwa à Thierra-Magazy', in 'Association internationale africaine: rapports sur les marches de la première expédition', *Bulletin: Société belge de géographie* (Brussels: Secrétariat de la Société belge de géographie, 1879), p. 365.

170 **'the Croesus of the Ugogo':** Burdo, *Les Belges dans l'Afrique centrale*, p. 439. Croesus, the last king of Lydia (modern Anatolia), was said to have derived his fortune from King Midas and his river of gold deposits.

170 **'[S]tranded in the middle . . . manslaughter is a mild name for it':** Frederick Carter, 'Letter to George Sutherland Mackenzie', 16 September 1879 [SM].

170–1 **Leopold would pay a monthly rent . . . both deals settled in cloth:** Steven Press, *Rogue Empires: Contracts and Conmen in Europe's Scramble for Africa*

(Cambridge, MA, and London: Harvard University Press, 2017), p. 100. Tim Jeal offers a slightly different calculation in *Stanley: The Impossible Life of Africa's Greatest Explorer* (London: Faber & Faber, 2007), p. 241: 'As a one-off payment, he handed over fifty pieces of cloth, three boxes of gin, five military coats, five knives, five cloth waist belts and five ample loincloths of superior quality. He also threw in with the annual £15 rent, "a monthly royalty of £2 worth of cloth". Jeal defends Stanley's intentions in the deals he struck: 'From the beginning of his time on the Congo to the end, he tried to look after the interests of the indigenous inhabitants.'

171 **'the ground . . . amidst a frozen deathly stillness' [picture caption]:** Walter Busse, 'Deutsch-Ostafrika I, Zentrales Steppengbiet', *Vegetationsbilder*, 5:7 (Jena: Karsten & Schenk, 1907), Tafel 40. Caption translation from the original German is my own.

175 **'His legs are folded under him . . . noisily through his trunk':** 'Extraits d'une lettre de M. Carter – Usekhé-Ugogo, A C, 28 septembre 1879', in 'Chronique géographique: Afrique. Association internationale africaine', *Bulletin: Société belge de géographie* (Brussels: Secrétariat de la Société belge de géographie, 1879), pp. 754– 5.

175 **The elephant's stomach was 'rising and falling like bellows at a forge':** Ibid., p. 755.

175 **'an inert mass of cold flesh . . . hammer is working inside':** Ibid.

176 **'the poor lost beast . . . I rid him of his ills with a shot':** Ibid.

176 **'It is a serious matter to shoot . . . if it can possibly be avoided':** George Orwell, *Shooting an Elephant and Other Essays* (London: Penguin, 2009), p. 35.

176 **Today's hunters are recommended . . . can't run on three legs:** 'How to Shoot an Elephant', *Fieldsports Channel*, 3 May 2017, https://www.fieldsportschannel.tv/how-to-shoot-an-elephant/

177 **the Ugogo water, 'so saturated with lime . . . kill an elephant':** 'Extraits d'une lettre de M. Carter', p. 755.

177 **Carter was 'a bit feverish . . . mahouts and Indian servants':** Maximilien Strauch, 'Letter to William Mackinnon', 14 October 1879 [SOAS].

177 **give Carter some 'friendly advice on how he should deal with staff':** Ibid.

177 **'Croesus' sent his men to enquire 'how [the elephant] . . . his consent':** 'Eastern Tropical Africa', *The Globe*, 18 December 1879. A few months later, when yet another Belgian expedition passed through the same settlement, the locals saw one of the Europeans light his pipe with a pair of opera glasses (using the lenses like a magnifying glass to concentrate the sunlight into an intense heat to ignite the tobacco). He was quickly dragged in front of a furious 'Croesus', whose people were fearful of yet more witchcraft: 'My white brothers had killed a divine elephant in Kanyene [sic], and, by this curse, compromised the harvests and delayed the rains.' See Burdo, *Les Belges dans l'Afrique centrale*, p. 77.

178   **no law to protect the elephant, like in India:** In 1879, the Elephants'
Preservation Act was introduced in India. The key outcome was the
prohibition of the killing and capture of wild elephants unless '(a) in
defence of himself or some other person; (b) when such elephant is found
injuring houses or cultivation, or upon, or in the immediate vicinity of, any
main public road or any railway or canal; or (c) as permitted by a license
granted under this Act.' The Elephants' Preservation Act, 1879 Act no. 6 of
1879', www.indiacode.nic.in/bitstream/123456789/12635/1/elephants%27_
preservation_act%2C_1879_no._6_of_1879_dated_22.03.1879.pdf

178   **'in a country like this ... these animals will be destroyed before long':**
'Extraits d'une lettre de M. Carter', p. 755.

178   **'the top management of elephant-related businesses':** Maximilien
Strauch, 'Letter to William Mackinnon', 16 October 1879 [SOAS].

178   **'[Gordon] is different ... no amount of salary will tempt him to
undertake it':** William Mackinnon, 'Letter to Henry Shelton Sanford',
28 October 1879 [SM].

178   **'there is not a single mahout of Bombay' ... a wild African elephant:**
'Extraits d'une lettre de M. Carter', p. 755.

178   **Carter would fail in 'wild elephant capturing ... if left to himself':** William
Mackinnon, 'Letter to Henry Shelton Sanford', 28 October 1879 [SM].

178–9   **'[A] quiet sober minded ... tone down the other a little':** Ibid.

179   **'the truest little weapon I ever fired out of':** A letter from Frederick Carter
to an unknown correspondent, dated 2 October 1879, described his giraffe
hunt. It was published in 'Central Africa', *The Field*, 24 January 1880.

179   **He shot a giraffe ... the final numbers 'do not count':** Ibid.

179   **'a very drunken trot, then a walk' ... 'like good beef':** Ibid.

8. THE LAND OF THE MOON

181   **'[I]t is the drama of human endeavour ... success or failure' [epigraph]:**
Joseph Conrad, 'Geography and Some Explorers', in Richard E. Curle (ed.),
Last Essays by Joseph Conrad (London and Toronto: J. M. Dent & Sons,
1926), p. 2.

182   **up to twenty thousand Nyamwezi a year travelling ... as porters:** This is
an estimate made by the French missionary François Coulbois, *Dix années
au Tanganyika* (Limoges: Pierre Dumont, 1901), p. 41. Cited in Norman
Robert Bennett, *Mirambo of Tanzania* (New York: Oxford University Press,
1971), p. 12.

182   **'A young man ... takes back a new name in honour of his visit':** Edward
Steere, *Collections for the Nyamwezi Language* (London: Society for
Promoting Christian Knowledge, 1885), p. 4.

183   **Stanley thought Unyamwezi 'a romantic name':** Henry Morton Stanley,
'21 September 1871, published in the *New York Herald*, 9 August 1872', in

Norman R. Bennett (ed.), *Stanley's Despatches to the New York Herald: 1871–1872, 1874–1877* (Boston: Boston University Press, 1970), p. 35.

183   **'Why is it called … many rites observed on such an occasion':** Ebenezer Southon, 'I. The History, Country and People of Unyamwezi', in 'Letter to John Whitehouse', 28 March 1880 [SOAS].

183   **To outsiders, Tabora felt remote … their journey to Central Africa:** When Burton came here in 1857 (the first European visitor), he referred to the settlement as 'Kazeh'. In his 1863 novel *Five Weeks in a Balloon*, Jules Verne further pushed 'Kazeh' into the European popular imagination as the setting for one of the balloon's most memorable landings. See Jules Verne, *Five Weeks in a Balloon; or, Journeys and Discoveries in Africa by Three Englishmen*, trans. William Lackland (New York: Hurst & Co., 1869), p. 110.

184   **the 'cruel prickles' … 'a vault bristling with spikes':** Adolphe Burdo, *Les Belges dans l'Afrique centrale: voyages, aventures et découvertes d'après les documents et journaux des explorateurs: de Zanzibar au Lac Tanganika* (Brussels: P. Maes, 1886), p. 79.

184   **Hyenas prowled among the thorn bushes … while they slept:** Adolphe Burdo, 'Rapport succinct sur la route suivie par l'expédition Burdo, depuis Mpwapwa jusqu'à Kouihara (Ounyanyembé)', in 'Association internationale africaine', *Bulletin: Société belge de géographie* (Brussels: Secrétariat de la Société belge de géographie, 1880), p. 506.

184   **'a horrible state of war … Englishmen are not welcome':** Charles Stokes, 'Letter to Henry Wright', 23 December 1878 [CRL].

184   **The bandits would launch … 'the stragglers and the cripples':** Ernest Cambier, 'Chapitre II: Rapport sur la marche de M. Cambier de Mpwapwa à Thierra-Magazy', in 'Association internationale africaine: rapport sur les marches de la première expédition', *Bulletin: Société belge de géographie* (Brussels: Secrétariat de la Société belge de géographie, 1879), p. 366.

184   **the elephants were in better condition than when they'd left the coast:** Frederick Carter, 'Letter to Maximilien Strauch', 30 October 1879 [SOAS].

184   **'in proper style', to borrow Stanley's phrase:** Henry Morton Stanley, 5 November 1871, 'Journal S.A. 73, Excerpts: (January 1871–May 1872)', in Mathilde Leduc-Grimaldi and James L. Newman (eds), *Finding Dr. Livingstone: A History in Documents from the Henry Morton Stanley Archives* (Athens, OH: Ohio University Press, 2020), p. 35.

185   **'His energetic face … take him for one of their co-religionists':** 'Letter from Doctor Dutrieux, published by La Flandre Libérale', *L'Indépendance belge*, 13 November 1879.

185   **Princess Margaret came on an official visit … dainty cornflower hat:** 'Princess Given Wild Welcome by Tribesmen', *Edinburgh Evening News*, 13 October 1956.

186 'A second Zanzibar': Arthur Dodgshun, 20 January 1879, 'Journals. From London to Ujiji, 1877–1879' [SOAS].

187 The enslaved would 'waddle about . . . four or five fathoms of chain': Edward Hore, 'Letter to Joseph Mullens', 10 January 1879 [SOAS].

187 'a mass of dirty back slums . . . scarce hidden from the eye': Ibid.

188 Tabora's Nyamwezi chief Isike: Isike was an arch diplomat, who preferred negotiation and alliances over armed conflict. He later returned to power and became a thorn in the sides of the colonizing Germans until he was defeated in 1893. He tried to blow himself up rather than surrender. 'His mangled but still living remains were hanged from a tree by the victors.' See Norman R. Bennett, 'Isike, *Ntemi* of Unyanyembe', in Mark Karp (ed.), *African Dimensions: Essays in Honor of William O. Brown* (Boston and New York: African Studies Center, Boston University and Africana Publishing Company, 1975), p. 66.

188 Mirambo's kingdom 'of ill defined limits': Southon, 'I. The History, Country and People of Unyamwezi.'

189 when Stanley met Mirambo, he'd expected . . . a 'terrible bandit': Henry Morton Stanley, *Through the Dark Continent*, vol. 1 (London: Sampson Low, Marston, Searle & Rivington, 1878), p. 492.

189 a wisp of blue cloth tied . . . like 'a vulgar cattle keeper': Jerome Becker, *La Vie en Afrique, ou Trois ans dans l'Afrique centrale*, vol. 1 (Paris and Brussels: J. Lebègue & Cie., 1887), p. 158.

189 'There is a large mixture of "don't care" . . . ever-changing fortune': Ebenezer Southon, Journal, 30 August 1879 [SOAS].

189 a brilliant military tactician . . . 'the black Bonaparte': Stanley, 28 August 1871, 'Journal S.A. 7, Full Transcript (1871)', p. 124.

189 Like Napoleon, Mirambo expanded . . . at an extraordinary pace: Mirambo first waged war against the Arabs of Tabora in 1871. Fighting was so fierce that Stanley was stranded in Tabora for three months that same year during his search for Livingstone.

189 'No one could tell . . . yesterday he was forty miles south of it': Southon, 'I. The History, Country and People of Unyamwezi.'

189 '[Boys] have sharper eyes . . . move with the ease of serpents': Stanley, *Through the Dark Continent*, vol. 1, pp. 492–3.

190 'Mirambo is the only man I fear very much': Charles Stokes, 'Letter to Henry Wright', 1 June 1880 [SOAS].

190 '[he] professes to be the friend . . . make himself stronger': Charles Stokes, 'Letter to Henry Wright', 17 February 1879 [SOAS].

190 'Every passing year . . . shall be in one language, customs and religion': Ebenezer Southon, 'IV. The History, Country and People of Unyamwezi continued', in 'Letter to John Whitehouse', 16 September 1880 [SOAS].

190 'Mirambo is for the time being ... head of a settled Kingdom': Bishop
    Steere, 'Letter to Unknown', 4 February 1879 [SOAS].
190 Chief Nyungu-ya-Mawe ... details that have passed down to us are
    fewer: What we do know is largely due to the painstaking research in
    Aylward Shorter's 1968 essay 'Nyungu-Ya-Mawe and the "Empire of
    Ruga-Rugas"'. *Journal of African History*, 9:2 (1968).
190 Nyungy-ya-Mawe: His name translates as 'the pot which cannot break'. See
    Shorter, 'Nyungu-Ya-Mawe and the "Empire of Ruga-Rugas"', p. 240.
190 'Pile on more logs!': Ibid., p. 242.
190 his men wore 'ghastly finery' ... necklaces of his victims' teeth: Adolphe
    Burdo, cited in ibid., p. 240.
190–1 Like Mirambo ... 'Kania Vanhu' ('Defecator of Men'): Ibid., p. 241.
191 he'd learned that a European ... skinned like a rabbit: Frederick Carter,
    'Letter to Maximilien Strauch', 30 October 1879 [SOAS].
191 Carter mocked the African chief ... water pumps were heavy artillery:
    Ibid.
191 He claimed the announcement ... all the ruga-ruga who 'infested' it:
    Ibid.
191 Mirambo and Nyungu-ya-Mawe ... African figures of authority: My
    ignorance irked me even more when I fell into conversation with a taxi
    driver in Dar es Salaam at the start of my journey. He wanted to talk
    about the indigenous leaders I needed to include in my book. 'We had
    brave chiefs, and crazy chiefs. Mirambo was really brave. And Mkwawa,
    who fought against the Germans,' said the driver. 'They cut off his head
    and put it into a museum in Tanzania. You should go and see it. The
    crazy one was called Kinjikitile Ngwale, who said to his people: "When
    the white people fire their guns, spray water and the bullets will turn
    to rain."'
        Kinjikitile Ngwale was a spirit medium who led the indigenous
    resistance against German rule in the 1905–7 Maji Maji War – an uprising
    named after a sacred 'bulletproof' water concoction (*maji*) which Ngwale
    persuaded his followers would keep them safe. The German suppression
    of the rebellion was brutal. Whole villages and crops were wiped out
    under a scorched-earth policy. The resulting famine killed up to three
    hundred thousand people.
        Chief Mkwawa, whose territory lay further south than the
    expedition route I was following, committed suicide in 1898 after a
    seven-year revolt against the country's German colonizers. His severed
    head was defleshed and first displayed as a trophy, then sent to Germany.
    His skull spent decades 'lost' in Germany, and was only returned to
    Mkwawa's grandson in the 1950s. It's now on display in a museum at
    Kalenga, in central Tanzania. Curiously, Mkwawa's skull's return to Africa

was a condition of the Treaty of Versailles which ended the First World War (a British official included the 'craniological curiosity' as a footnote to some of the war reparations Germany had to pay after their defeat in 1918). See Note 1 on paper scrap, FO 608/215/380, TNA, cited in Jeremiah J. Garsha, 'The Head of Chief Mkwawa and the Transnational History of Colonial Violence, 1898–2019', PhD dissertation (Cambridge: Cambridge University, 2019), p. 133.

In Dar es Salaam, I met with Edson Mhenga in October 2023. He was directly related to Mkwawa's youngest brother, Mhenga. 'Mkwawa was a warrior and leader with the courage to fight intruders and stand for his community,' said Edson. 'He was an exceptional leader. I admire him. I wish to have his courage. For me, his name means something. History can give you an idea of who you are. That's my authenticity. My blood. They brought the skull back from Europe, but according to the story, a German family kept Mkwawa's teeth. They experienced bad things, spiritual issues.' I asked Edson if he was angry. 'At this point, we don't get angry. We know bad things happened, but we can't change that. We know for sure our elders did something to stand up for us. But it's also sad to tell you this history, because I have to gather the sources to give it to you. I have to go online to find it.'

191–2 **'Perhaps in the future … darkness is not a subject for history':** Hugh Trevor-Roper, *The Rise of Christian Europe* (London: Thames & Hudson, 1965), p. 9.

192 **'Mature a plan of elephant stud,' instructed the king:** Leopold II, 'Letter to Maximilien Strauch,' 14 September 1879 [AEB].

192 **There were no memorials to the African experience of slavery:** '[T]he absence of memorials to the African experience to slavery and to the millions who died in the production of wealth for Europe and in the New World, have become a kind of global norm.' Howard W. French, *Born in Blackness: Africa, Africans and the Making of the Modern World, 1471 to the Second World War* (New York: Liveright, 2022), p. 120.

193 **The guard said *shikamoo* now carried a bad connotation:** Numerous people I consulted agreed with this interpretation, while other sources stood by the idea that *shikamoo* remains a common polite form of address to use with one's elders.

193 **'On my honor … [o]ne could almost wax poetic':** Henry Morton Stanley, *How I Found Livingstone: Travels, Adventures and Discoveries in Central Africa: Including an Account of Four Months' Residence with Dr. Livingstone* (New York: Scribner, Armstrong & Co., 1872), p. 262.

194 **'This was real, practical, noble courtesy … gratitude by storm':** Ibid., p. 264.

194 **'dishes of well-cooked curry … our own *cordon bleu':*** Verney Lovett Cameron, *Across Africa* (New York, Harper & Brothers, 1877), p. 122.

194 'bad food and in small quantities ... black dough': Frederick Carter, 'Letter to Tom Cadenhead', 19 August 1879 [SM].

194 an elephant's foot – 'a whiteish mass ... like marrow': 'A long march, to prevent biliousness, is a wise precaution after a meal of elephant's foot. Elephant's trunk and tongue are also good, and, after long simmering, much resemble the hump of a buffalo, and the tongue of an ox; but all the other meat is tough, and, from its peculiar flavour, only to be eaten by a hungry man.' David Livingstone and Charles Livingstone, *Narrative of an Expedition to the Zambesi and Its Tributaries; and of the Discovery of the Lakes Shirwa and Nyassa, 1858–1864* (London: John Murray, 1865), pp. 168–9.

194 In Carter's company, 'the fun never flagged for a moment': William Perry Fogg, *Arabistan: or, the Land of 'The Arabian Nights'. Being Travels Through Egypt, Arabia, and Persia, to Bagdad* (Hartford: Dustin, Gillman & Co., 1875), p. 342.

194 With Stokes, Carter struck up ... entertaining with 'unusual brilliancy': Ibid., p. 341.

195 'In Ireland long ago ... nor my time but somebody else's': A traditional beginning to an Irish folktale, cited in Susan Campbell Bartoletti, *Black Potatoes: The Story of the Great Irish Famine, 1845–1850* (Boston: Houghton Mifflin Company, 2001), p. 1.

195 '[T]his historical *tembè* ... so many travellers in Central Africa': Joseph Thomson, *To the Central African Lakes and Back: The Narrative of the Royal Geographical Society's East Central African Expedition, 1878–1880*, vol. 2 (London: Sampson Low, Marston, Searle & Rivington, 1881), p. 249.

196 White Fathers ... founded in 1868 by the French Archbishop of Algiers: The White Fathers became one of the region's most prominent Christianizing forces.

198 autograph hunters in pursuit of memorabilia: Stanley memorabilia auctions for large sums. A sale at Christie's in 2002 saw his travelling desk (complete with signature stamp) go for over ten thousand pounds.

198 The local names ... 'the one who makes a path on the road with her feet': 'Slave Trade in East Africa: Introduction', issued 30 November 1974, 526.502 [ATA].

198 There was a 1913 note ... a letter to Tabora's magistrate: P. Grünn, 'Letter to Mr Bauer', 2 December 1913, 526.503 [ATA].

198 '[They] have all been told ... remain with their late master, or otherwise': Unknown, 'Letter to Father Anton van Aken', 14 August 1922, 526.502 [ATA].

199 'Can you tell me anything of their history?': Unknown, 'Letter to Father Anton van Aken', 13 October 1924, 526.502 [ATA].

199   The burden of four men . . . 'much too heavy a load for the poor old
       lady': Frederick Carter, 'Letter to Maximilien Strauch', 30 October 1879
       [SOAS].
199   they were presented with 'more than was good for us': Ibid.
200   'hundreds and hundreds of men, women . . . screaming and laughing':
       Ibid.
200   'It was a day never to be forgotten by the people of Tabora': Ibid.
200   a quote widely repeated in Belgian newspapers: *L'Echo du Parlement*,
       7 March 1880; *Journal de Bruxelles*, 7 March 1880; *Courrier de l'Escaut*,
       10 March 1880.
200   'Good news for elephants!': Leopold II, 'Letter to Maximilien Strauch', 11
       October 1879 [AEB].
200   'The place looked so devoid of grace and completeness without': Henry
       Morton Stanley, *The Congo and the Founding of Its Free State: A Story of Work
       and Exploration*, vol. 1 (New York: Harper and Brothers, 1885), p. 147.
200   'News of the elephants have gone right through Africa': Frederick Carter,
       'Letter to Maximilien Strauch', 30 October 1879 [SOAS].
200   'the big master . . . power of the white man over the elephants': Ibid.
201   'already given more of a footing to Europeans . . . they can do anything':
       Ibid.
201   'Capt. C. asked me to write . . . I hope you will make the matter public':
       Charles Stokes, 'Letter to Henry Wright', 17 November 1879 [CRL].
201   '"the year of the Elephants"': L. K. Rankin, 'The Elephant Experiment in
       Africa: A Brief Account of the Belgian Elephant Expedition on the March
       from Dar-es-Salaam to Mpwapwa', *Proceedings of the Royal Geographical
       Society and Monthly Record of Geography*, 4:5 (May, 1882), p. 281.
201   'The spectacle of the elephants . . . the guns of the Spaniards': Maximilien
       Strauch, 'Letter to William Mackinnon', 6 February 1880 [SOAS].
201   ordered local authorities 'to place themselves . . . at my disposal':
       Frederick Carter, 'Letter to Maximilien Strauch', 30 October 1879 [SOAS].
201   He boasted . . . new base at Tabora that Van den Heuvel could oversee:
       Ibid.
202   'All the Arabs . . . I am come as English consul to Central Africa': Ibid.
202   'Sleepy fever' was also prevalent . . . affecting Carter's men: Stanley,
       29 August 1871, 'Journal S.A. 7, Full Transcript (1871)', p. 124. Tabora
       remains one of Tanzania's higher risk areas for sleeping sickness, spread
       by the tsetse fly.
203   During the First World War . . . annexed Tabora: It was only in November
       2023 that Belgium officially commemorated the contribution made by
       African soldiers in the 1914–18 world war. See Ugo Realfonzo, 'Belgium
       to Pay Tribute to Congolese Soldiers of 1914–1918 for the First Time',
       Brussels Times, 11 November 2023.

206 'You already know enough ... what we know and to draw conclusions':
Sven Lindqvist, *Exterminate All the Brutes*, in *The Dead Do Not Die* (New York: New Press, 2014), p. 13.

9. CHIEF OF CHIEFS

208 'Let me tell you more ... after all the chores of the day' [epigraph]:
Ngũgĩ wa Thiong'o and Charles Cantalupo, 'African Literature ... Says Who?', *Transition: You Are Next*, 120 (2016), p. 6.

209 a journey which took Cambier 'about a year and a half ... finished':
John Kirk, 'Letter to William Mackinnon', 26 July 1879 [SOAS].

209 Karema's 'miniscule potentate ... with the authorization to settle': A. J. Wauters, 'Karéma: première station de l'Association internationale africaine', *Bulletin: Société belge de géographie* (Brussels: Secrétariat de la Société belge de géographie, 1879), p. 726. The 'miniscule potentate' who signed the deal was called Kangoa, a puppet of the notorious elephant hunter Matumula, whose overlord was in turn Simba.

210 Simba: Also called Usawila in nineteenth-century sources. Near modern-day Uruwira, located around one hundred and forty miles southwest of Tabora.

211 'It's a triumph', reported Brussels' newspapers: *Journal de Bruxelles*, 16 November 1879.

211 He was 'practically kept ... as a prisoner' ... goods held hostage: Arthur Dodgshun, 'Letter to Joseph Mullens', 23 January 1879 [SOAS].

211 'There is Cambier ... but he must be met by a man': John Kirk, 'Letter to William Mackinnon', 25 May 1879 [SOAS].

211 one of Cambier's party ... accusations of witchcraft began to circulate:
'To mitigate the strangeness of my request in the eyes of the Sultan of Kouikourou, I simply expressed to him the desire to see the bones of wild beasts killed by his hunters and which are usually gathered like a trophy near the dwelling of the chiefs of the Unyamwezi. I examined and measured with apparent interest bones of hyenas, leopards, buffaloes, lions, on a second visit humans, and it was not until the third visit that I began to measure them with the most indifferent air in the world.' Pierre Dutrieux, 'Notes d'anthropologie', in 'Association internationale africaine', *Bulletin: Société belge de géographie* (Brussels: Secrétariat de la Société belge de géographie, 1880), pp. 102–3.

211 earth tremors 'preceded by a noise ... cart rolling rapidly': 'Lettre de M. Cambier, datée de Karema, 24 septembre 1879', in 'Association internationale africaine: rapport sur la marche de M. Cambier de Tabora à Karema', *Bulletin: Société belge de géographie* (Brussels: Secrétariat de la Société belge de géographie, 1880), p. 101, and 'The Belgian African Expedition', *The Graphic*, 20 March 1880.

211 'They told me that it was the soul ... death of an important
-12 personage': Ibid.

212 Broyon was regarded as one of the best-travelled ... East African
interior: Norman Bennett provides an excellent biography of Broyon's
East African activities in Norman R. Bennett, 'Philippe Broyon: Pioneer
Trader in East Africa', *African Affairs*, 62:247 (April 1963), pp. 157–63.

212 He married an African woman ... one of Mirambo's daughters:
Bennett's meticulous research suggests that, in fact, Broyon married a
formerly enslaved woman, and that she was unlikely to have been one of
Mirambo's daughters. See ibid.

212 He even signed his letters 'Philippe Broyon-Mirambo': *Bulletin de la
Société de géographie de Marseille*, 1 (1877), cited in Bennett, 'Philippe
Broyon: Pioneer Trader in East Africa', p. 156.

212 'There never seems to be any ... but Dodgshun was <u>ready</u>': Edward Hore,
'Letter to Anonymous', 16 April 1879 [SOAS].

213 'grossly ill used if not cheated by Broyon' ... dealing with the
consequences: John Kirk, 'Letter to William Mackinnon', 11 November
1879 [SOAS].

213 'an intelligent desire to know and understand things': Ebenezer Southon,
Journal, 30 August 1879 [SOAS].

213 '[Mirambo] handles a new thing as thoughtfully as a skilled mechanic':
Ibid.

213 'He appeared to weigh well every word': Ebenezer Southon, Journal,
1 September 1879 [SOAS].

214 Southon wrote ... Mirambo copied 'fairly well' underneath [picture
caption]: Ebenezer Southon, Journal, 7 September 1879 [SOAS].

215 a national park for tourists – the kind who carry cameras, not guns:
When Ugalla was designated a national park, the hunters argued that this
change in land use would turn into a conservation disaster, that no tourist
would spend either the time or the money to travel all the way out here.
They lobbied that it would be better if the government relied on the
hunting industry's premium trophy fees, and their model for 'sustainable
take-off' (shooting old male animals, for instance). See Sophy Roberts,
'Alone with the Animals in Tanzania's Newest National Park', *Financial
Times*, 2 April 2022.

216 Southon's rare nineteenth-century account of the wider region: Southon
spent three years living in Urambo, from 1879 to 1882. His unpublished
letters and diaries are held in the Council for World Mission Archive at
SOAS in London.

216 country 'royally prolific in vegetation': Ebenezer Southon, 'II. The History,
Country and People of Unyamwezi continued', in 'Letter to John
Whitehouse', 24 July 1880 [SOAS].

218 **big-game hunting is allowed in almost a third of the country:** See Nyangabo V. Musika, James V. Wakibara, Patrick A. Ndakidemi and Anna C. Treydte, 'Using Trophy Hunting to Save Wildlife Foraging Resources: A Case Study from Moyowosi-Kigosi Game Reserves, Tanzania', *Sustainability*, 14:1288 (2022), p. 2.

218 **a violent criminal gang, the Sanjo:** The 'Sanjo' are believed to be a violent splinter sect of migrant pastoralists known as the Nyantuzu. The word 'Sanjo' is used by local communities around western Tanzania's Ugalla River National Park.

219 **There simply wasn't the same abundance of mahogany:** When Ismail took on the job as head of anti-poaching, he said his ranger teams found some four hundred felled mahogany trees with a market value close to half a million dollars.

219 **flowering plants ... 'exceedingly beautiful' with 'exquisite perfumes':** Ebenezer Southon, 'II. The History, Country and People of Unyamwezi continued', in 'Letter to John Whitehouse', 24 July 1880 [SOAS].

219 **'something like maniacal laughter ... slurred, in a peculiar manner':** Ibid.

219 **the lion's heart was 'the sole property ... by him alone it is eaten':** Ebenezer Southon, 'III. The History, Country and People of Unyamwezi continued', in 'Letter to John Whitehouse', 23 August 1880 [SOAS].

219 **'King Mirambo told me ... rare to meet with one unless far north':** Ibid.

221–2 **'It was the first time ... deserves the title of "king of beasts":** The 1880 *Bulletin* of the Belgian Geographical Society cited this report, published in Stanley's *How I Found Livingstone: Travels, Adventures and Discoveries in Central Africa: Including an Account of Four Months' Residence with Dr. Livingstone* (New York: Scribner, Armstrong & Co., 1872), pp. 358–9. See A. J. Wauters, 'II. Quelques particularités sur l'éléphant', in 'L'Éléphant d'Afrique et son rôle dans l'histoire de la civilisation africaine', *Bulletin: Société belge de géographie* (Brussels: Secrétariat de la Société belge de géographie, 1880), p. 154.

222 **'forage in abundance' ... weaving along 'like she [was] drunk':** Frederick Carter, 'Letter to Maximilien Strauch', 17 December 1879 [SOAS].

224 **they wanted ... their people's long-term access assured:** I was told by the park authorities that the Nyamwezi have access to the national park for their rituals. However, they have to formally seek permission from the chief warden before entering the area.

224 **In the north, the Maasai ... made from foreign safari tourists:** For more context, see Jess Craig, '"It's Becoming a War Zone": Tanzania's Maasai Speak Out on "Forced" Removals', *Guardian*, 16 January 2023, and Stephanie McCrummen, 'The Great Serengeti Land Grab', *The Atlantic*, 8 April 2024.

224–5 more than thirteen thousand muskets ... trading house in Zanzibar:
Richard Francis Burton, *The Lake Regions of Central Africa*, vol. 1 (London: Longman, Green, Longman and Roberts, 1860), p. 364.

225   'Unless some steps are taken ... first-class breech-loading rifles':
Euan-Smith, 'Letter to the Earl of Rosebery', 28 June 1888, cited in R. W. Beachey, 'The Arms Trade in East Africa in the Late Nineteenth Century', *Journal of African History*, 3:3 (1962), p. 453. Beachey calculates that, between 1885 and 1902, a million firearms and well over four hundred thousand pounds in weight of gunpowder entered the German and British territories in East Africa.

225   'a troop of about three hundred ... old large calibre flintlock rifles':
Ernest Cambier, 'Rapport sur la marche de M. Cambier de Tabora à Karéma', in 'Association internationale africaine', *Bulletin: Société belge de géographie* (Brussels: Secrétariat de la Société belge de géographie, 1880), p. 91.

226   'Thank God! ... A sense of completion': Frederick Carter, 'Letter to Maximilien Strauch', 17 December 1879 [SOAS].

227   'A strange thing': Ibid.

227   How could this have happened ... in this last stage to let her rest:
Frederick Carter, Journal, 21 November 1879, cited in Frederick Carter, 'Letter to Maximilien Strauch', 17 December 1879 [SOAS].

227   The mahouts attributed it to ... 'aghin baho': A. J. Wauters, 'IX. La Caravane de M. Carter', in 'L'Éléphant d'Afrique et son rôle dans l'histoire de la civilisation africaine', *Bulletin: Société belge de géographie* (Brussels: Secrétariat de la Société belge de géographie, 1880), p. 181.

228   'I am very sore about her loss ... She is dead': Frederick Carter, Journal, 21 November 1879, cited in Frederick Carter, 'Letter to Maximilien Strauch', 17 December 1879 [SOAS].

10. Fish Without Number

229   'Certainly it's good to question ... out there on the edge' [epigraph]:
Barry Lopez, 'On the Border', in *Embrace Fearlessly the Burning World: Essays* (New York: Random House, 2022), p. 91.

230   amapiano: A musical style, originally from South Africa, which combines lounge, deep house and jazz, and often features a piano melody.

232   'An atrocious blunder ... favourite haunt of clouds of mosquitoes':
Joseph Thomson, *To the Central African Lakes and Back: The Narrative of the Royal Geographical Society's East Central African Expedition, 1878–1880*, vol. 2 (London: Sampson Low, Marston, Searle & Rivington, 1881), pp. 184–5.

232   'the cloud masses joined together ... vast, glass-like cylinder': Edward Coode Hore, *Tanganyika: Eleven Years in Central Africa* (London: Edward Stanford, 1892), p. 143.

232 **a black substance 'like bitumen' ... hidden underwater fissure:** Edward
Coode Hore, 'Lake Tanganyika: (Read at the Evening Meeting, November
28th, 1881)', *Proceedings of the Royal Geographical Society and Monthly
Record of Geography*, 4:1 (January 1882), p. 3.

234 **dead trees, 'killed by the recent rise ... sudden lowering':** Thomson, *To the
Central African Lakes and Back*, vol. 2, pp. 2, 6 and 23.

234 **'waste-pipe of the lake':** Hore, *Tanganyika: Eleven Years in Central Africa*,
p. 113.

235 **'Tanganyika, in the Swahili language ... slopes of its containing basin':**
Ibid., p. 161.

235 **'The Great Lake, the supreme goal, the Promised Land':** Adolphe Burdo,
*Les Belges dans l'Afrique centrale: voyages, aventures et découvertes d'après les
documents et journaux des explorateurs: de Zanzibar au Lac Tanganika*
(Brussels: P. Maes, 1886), p. 56.

235 **the kind of place where you 'dreamed of fairy things':** Thomson, *To the
Central African Lakes and Back*, vol. 2, p. 193.

235 **'the spoiled child of the station':** Burdo, *Les Belges dans l'Afrique centrale*,
p. 372.

237 **'This is a most fearful spot ... he would never have recommended it':**
Frederick Carter, 'Letter to Henry Shelton Sanford', 9 January 1880 [SM].

237 **a lake full of 'fish without number':** Local people had a legend about the
origins of Lake Tanganyika, wrote Burdo. The Lake was once a prosperous
town on a wide plain where there was also a deep spring. The spring was
owned by a young couple whose ownership depended on keeping its
existence secret. For this was not just any spring; it was a magic spring,
filled with 'fish without number', which provided the couple with endless
food. But the wife was having an affair. One day, she showed her lover the
magic spring. A terrible earthquake split the ground open, the plain
collapsed, the town was swallowed and the spring burst out, filling the
'frightful fissure' left behind with the waters of Lake Tanganyika. Burdo,
Les Belges dans l'Afrique centrale, pp. 88–91.

238 **'You may fancy how hard up we all are ... we shall get rather thin':**
Frederick Carter, 'Letter to Henry Shelton Sanford', 9 January 1880 [SM].

238 **Popelin described a 'sad season':** Émile Popelin, 'Letter to Maximilien
Strauch', 9 January 1880, in 'Extraits des rapports des voyageurs de
l'Association internationale africaine', *Association internationale africaine:
rapports sur les marches de la première expédition* (Brussels-Etterbeek:
Verhavert Frères et Soeurs, 1879), p. 116.

238 **'You can't go through the jungle ... immediately wet to the bone':** Ernest
Cambier, 'Letter to Maximilien Strauch', 6 January 1880, in 'Extraits des
rapports des voyageurs de l'Association Internationale Africaine', p. 114.

238 a country with 'abundant elephant': Maximilien Strauch, 'Letter to William Mackinnon', 16 December 1879 [SOAS].

238 'wild brutes with fangs ... claws dripping with blood': Frederick Carter, 'Letter to Henry Shelton Sanford', 9 January 1880 [SM].

238 'I have faced death ... never had a narrower escape than this': Ibid.

238–9 'I felt very like putting a bullet ... shaking all over': Ibid.

239 to make a trophy ... promised Carter a Christmas pudding: Ibid.

239 'if he had a fault at all ... exigencies of African travelling': Thomson, *To the Central African Lakes and Back*, vol. 2, p. 187.

239 'the only topic of conversation for people all around the lake': Burdo, *Les Belges dans l'Afrique centrale*, p. 372.

241 infamous for his 'noisy harangues': Edward Hore, 'Letter to Joseph Mullens', 27 May 1879 [SOAS].

241 'softening influence of music': Thomson, *To the Central African Lakes and Back*, vol. 2, p. 96.

241 the peculiar detritus ... including twelve boxes of fireworks: Ibid.

241 Mwinyi Heri ... a 'pushing, avaricious, and unscrupulous' man: Edward Hore, 'Letter to John Whitehouse', 9 February 1880 [SOAS].

241–2 'listened to open mouthed ... customs well nigh forgotten': Ibid.

242 Leopold's 'excellent' vision ... 'a very considerable supporter': Ibid.

242 'He lingers too long in the first station' ... 'He is sometimes like a child': Maximilien Strauch, 'Letter to Leopold II, Annotated by the King', 18 February 1880 [AEB].

242 '[W]ith his business ... floating and fighting down the swift flowing Congo': The word 'floating' is my best interpretation of the handwriting. Henry Shelton Sanford, 'Letter to Leopold II', 12 November 1879 [APR].

242 six men bound to a single chain ... stapled directly to the store shelves: A detailed description of the enslaved Africans in Ujiji is given in Edward Hore, 'Letter to Joseph Mullens', 10 January 1879 [SOAS].

242–3 four White Fathers ... hats tied on with silk cord chin-straps: Edward Hore, 'Letter to Joseph Mullens', 16 April 1879 [SOAS].

243 they kept themselves to themselves ... arrive from the coast: Edward Hore, 'Letter John Whitehouse', 2 March 1880 [SOAS].

243 'the right man in the right place ... he can turn his hand to anything': Frederick Carter, 'Letter to John Whitehouse', 7 February 1880 [SOAS].

243 Tanganyika's so-called 'sons of the waves': Burdo, *Les Belges dans l'Afrique centrale*, p. 480.

243 'strut about with a little cane ... and boast of their sailoring': Edward Hore, 'Letter to Joseph Mullens', 16 April 1879 [SOAS].

243 'grotesque-looking craft of the Arab merchants': Hore, *Tanganyika: Eleven Years in Central Africa*, p. 72.

243   'small catamarans, made up of ... the pith-tree strung together': Hore, 'Lake Tanganyika: (Read at the Evening Meeting, November 28th, 1881)', p. 7.

243   canoes ... good for baths: Hore, *Tanganyika: Eleven Years in Central Africa*, pp. 83–4.

243   a 'piratical' ship he called the *Calabash*: Ibid., p. 106.

243   with a jib, mizzen and rigging in 'English fashion': Ibid., p. 107.

243–4 'It is no secret that the rivers ... than at first appears': 'The White Sheikh, from a Correspondent in Bussorah: May 12', *Times of India*, 13 June 1879.

244   A modern steamer ... was 'absolutely necessary': Frederick Carter, 'Letter to Edward Hore', 29 March 1880 [SOAS].

245   make money by charging caravans a 'fair rate' for transport: Ibid.

245   The 'civilising effect' would be 'immense': Ibid.

245   'The constant visits of the steamer ... exposed from the natives': Ibid.

245   An English officer ... with a 'respectable able seaman as his chief mate': Perhaps Carter saw himself filling the role of the 'intelligent, sober, cool and clearheaded man' he recommended to take command, 'whose heart should be in the work and not simply in the pay he receives.' Frederick Carter, 'Letter to Edward Hore', 29 March 1880 [SOAS].

245   'I could of course fill pages ... before I leave Africa': Ibid.

246   the Ujiji tree where Stanley famously 'met' Livingstone: When Stanley met Livingstone under a mango tree at Ujiji, he delivered that famous line: 'Dr Livingstone, I presume?' His personal journal, however, only made mention of a 'pale-looking white man in a faded blue cap'; the following two pages were ripped out, perhaps to hide a later fabrication. See Tim Jeal, *Stanley: The Impossible Life of Africa's Greatest Explorer* (London: Faber & Faber, 2007), p. 25.

247   one of the most far-flung battles ... the Germans scuttled her: During the Battle for Lake Tanganyika, the Germans who were ordered to scuttle the ship also greased the engines before gently capsizing her in relatively shallow water. This meant that when she was lifted, her boilers and engines were still functional.

247   the British raised her again, this time turning her into a passenger ferry: The *Liemba* is thought to be the inspiration for the gunship sunk by the *African Queen* in the eponymous 1951 John Huston film.

248   the ship was retired to her berth in Kigoma for critical repairs: When I went back to Kigoma in October 2023 to fact-check my sources, I met up with Captain Titus again. He told me the *Liemba* was about to be repaired to the tune of sixteen million US dollars.

249   two armed motorboats ... surprise attacks on the Germans [picture caption]: For more, see Giles Foden, *Mimi and Toutou Go Forth: The Bizarre Battle of Lake Tanganyika* (London: Penguin, 2005).

250   **Carter was thrilled to be greeted with the moniker 'Lord of the Elephants':** Walter Hutley, 'Letter to Reverend J. O. Whitehouse', 20 February 1880 [SOAS].

250   **Carter whipped out his rifle and 'shot one or two of the savages':** Thomson, *To the Central African Lakes and Back*, vol. 2, p. 177.

250   **the administration of 'Bush Law' . . . 'a nation in himself':** Francis Galton, *The Art of Travel: or, Shifts and Contrivances Available in Wild Countries*, fifth edition (London: John Murray, 1872), p. 308.

250   **An 'intense feeling of hostility' in the community:** Thomson, *To the Central African Lakes and Back*, vol. 2, p. 184.

250   **Popelin displayed 'haughty disregard' for indigenous customs:** Ibid., p. 185.

251   **'move his little finger to assist them for either love or money':** Ibid., p. 184.

251   **'poor-looking elderly [chief] . . . eyes that never looked straight':** Log of the *Calabash*, 3 July 1879, in Hore, *Tanganyika: Eleven Years in Central Africa*, p. 114.

251   **'foreigner and outsider' . . . 'no personal friends in the bureau at Brussels':** Frederick Carter, 'Letter to Henry Shelton Sanford', 9 January 1880 [SM].

251   **'I keep myself and opinions . . . thoroughly in the background':** Ibid.

251   **he hollered a 'jolly "Halloo!"':** Thomson, *To the Central African Lakes and Back*, vol. 2, p. 180.

251   **The three men 'drew to each other like brothers':** Ibid.

251   **'a thousand miles from the faintest trace of civilization':** Ibid.

251   **Carter 'bursting with stories':** Joseph Thomson, 'Letter to John Kirk', 27 March 1880, in 'Geographical Notes', *Proceedings of the Royal Geographical Society and Monthly Record of Geography* (September 1880), p. 558.

251   **Carter often leaning . . . 'involuntarily or by mistake':** Thomson, *To the Central African Lakes and Back*, vol. 2, p. 180.

252   **By now 'fat, strong and well':** Frederick Carter, 'Letter to Henry Shelton Sanford', 9 January 1880 [SM].

252   **'utter want of . . . knowledge of the geography of Africa':** Thomson, *To the Central African Lakes and Back*, vol. 2, p. 188.

252   **Karema was clearly no place . . . single Roman Catholic missionary:** Ibid., p. 189.

252   **But at least they were alive . . . had saved them:** Ibid.

252   **Karema seemed to Thomson . . . eat together at the station that evening:** Ibid.

252   **'an Englishman, an Irishman . . . and a German':** Joseph Thomson, 'Letter to John Kirk', 27 March 1880, in 'Geographical Notes', p. 558. It's unclear which of the Belgians Thomson thought was German; by the time he published his book in 1881, he'd reassessed the nationalities as two

Belgians (Popelin and Cambier), an Irishman (Carter), an Englishman (Hore), a Frenchman (the missionary) and a Scotsman (himself).

252 'a sad tale of trial and utmost hardship': Thomson, *To the Central African Lakes and Back*, vol. 2, p. 190.

252 'The three captains ... without his favourite weapon': Ibid., p. 191.

252–3 'They put implicit faith in their guns ... do some bloody deed': Ibid.

253 'a few vigorous strokes of the cane': Émile Popelin, 'Letter to Maximilien Strauch', 9 December 1879, in 'Extraits des rapports des voyageurs de l'Association internationale africaine', *Association internationale africaine: rapports sur les marches de la première expédition* (Brussels-Etterbeek: Verhavert Frères et Soeurs, 1879), p. 107.

253 'all he had to do was to come out to Karema ... then return to Belgium': Thomson, *To the Central African Lakes and Back*, vol. 2, p. 188.

253 As for the elephants ... the 'utter unsuitability' of these animals: Ibid., p. 187.

253 elephants would do well in Africa as draft animals hitched to wagons: Edward Hore, 'Letter to John Whitehouse', 30 March 1880 [SOAS].

253 'We could find no question ... setting everybody right about Africa': Thomson, *To the Central African Lakes and Back*, vol. 2, p. 192.

253 Debaize's hurdy-gurdy ... to play feeble 'operatic selections': Thomson, 'Letter to John Kirk', 27 March 1880, in 'Geographical Notes', p. 558.

253 'old familiar airs': Thomson, *To the Central African Lakes and Back*, vol. 2, pp. 190–1.

253 'to assist members ... stationed there to assist, not to be assisted': Ibid., p. 174. Burdo issued a furious rebuttal in his book *Les Belges dans l'Afrique centrale*: '[A]re the British too proud to acknowledge the great deeds of others or accept any moral obligation towards them?' (p. 465).

254 earthquakes rumbling like 'distant tumbrils': This is Carter's description, cited in Edward Hore, Journal, 10 August 1880 [SOAS].

254 'afraid to leave Karema for any time' ... orders to arrive from Brussels: Frederick Carter, 'Letter to Henry Shelton Sanford', 15 April 1880 [SM].

254 'Do not I pray send a ship as happened before without a day's notice': John Kirk, 'Letter to William Mackinnon', 8 February 1880 [SOAS].

254 'I feel more savage at the poor elephants ... They haven't a chance!!!': Helen Kirk, cited in Gerald Waller, 'Letter to William Mackinnon', 12 January 1880 [SOAS].

255 'I hope you won't think it snobbish ... respect for The King': Quotations in this and the following paragraph in this chapter are all taken from Frederick Carter, 'Letter to Henry Shelton Sanford', 15 April 1880 [SM].

256 'The results of the year 1879 ... that of 1880 even richer in hopes': Henri Wauwermans, 'Les Explorateurs Belges en Afrique', *Bulletin de la Société de géographie d'Anvers*, vol. 4 (Anvers: Veuve de Backer, 1879), p. 417.

256   **"Failure" is a word I don't believe in ... success will be mine':** Frederick Carter, 'Letter to Henry Shelton Sanford', 15 April 1880 [SM].

256   **'[W]hen the white man turns tyrant ... freedom he destroys':** George Orwell, *Shooting an Elephant and Other Essays* (London: Penguin, 2003), p. 36.

257   **'I feel it night and day ... my skin is always like fire':** Frederick Carter, 'Letter to Henry Shelton Sanford', 15 April 1880 [SM].

11. Paradise Plains

258   **'[W]hen an elephant's mind ... impossible to change it' [epigraph]:** Frederick Carter, 'Letter to William Mackinnon', 6 August 1879 [SOAS].

259   **rising water levels had been 'stealing the land':** In 1879, Hore commented that the rains were so significant they rose a full two feet before Tanganyika 'finished stealing the land'. See Edward Hore, 'Letter to Joseph Mullens', 27 May 1879 [SOAS].

260   **Adolphe Burdo, hired to lead the third IAA expedition:** Burdo's account is a window on the extreme racism that was an integral part of European discourse at the time. As he made clear, the Belgian perception of African society was that 'polygamy is an honour, violence is a right and slavery is a law'. Adolphe Burdo, *Les Belges dans l'Afrique centrale: voyages, aventures et découvertes d'après les documents et journaux des explorateurs: de Zanzibar au Lac Tanganika* (Brussels: P. Maes, 1886), p. 292.

260   **'off to breathe the air' ... with 'one of his compatriots':** Ibid., p. 165.

261   **sending messages ... 'so that he is always aware of my movements':** Tom Cadenhead, 'Letter to Maximilien Strauch', 20 February 1880, 'Extraits des rapports des voyageurs de l'Association Internationale Africaine', in *Association internationale africaine: rapports sur les marches de la première expédition* (Brussels-Etterbeek: Verhavert Frères et Soeurs, 1879), p. 121.

261   **'My pride as an Englishman ... at this stage without a struggle':** *The Times*, 30 July 1880, cited in 'The Royal Belgian Expedition to Central Africa', *Sydney Morning Herald*, 29 September 1880.

261   **Arguments escalated ... best if the expedition divided:** Burdo, *Les Belges dans l'Afrique centrale*, p. 315.

262   **the two men lingered ... a brief and 'pleasant chat', and that was it:** Joseph Thomson, *To the Central African Lakes and Back: The Narrative of the Royal Geographical Society's East Central African Expedition, 1878–1880*, vol. 2 (London: Sampson Low, Marston, Searle & Rivington, 1881), p. 239.

262   **'terribly pulled down with fever' ... had trouble even speaking:** Ibid., p. 238.

262   **'dressed in white clothes ... glasses to protect the eyes':** Ibid., p. 240.

262   **'tiptoe of expectation':** Frederick Carter, 'Letter to Henry Shelton Sanford', 15 April 1880 [SM].

262 **a point of 'such turmoil'... 'to the point of worrying us':** Ernest Cambier, 'Letter to Maximilien Strauch', 11 July 1880 [SM].

262–3 **'This is the first time that I have not obeyed an order':** Ibid.

263 **he was in a terrible state, 'beaten down by fever':** Ibid.

263 **There was Wrori ... '[t]his you will understand is all on hearsay':** He gives the coordinates: 'about Lat 7"40S and Long about 35"40E'. Frederick Carter, 'Letter to Henry Shelton Sanford', 9 January 1880 [SM].

263 **the Ruaha region's dense elephant population ... far-sighted local chief:** 'We had heard strange stories about the extraordinary abundance of elephants in that country. They were said to be looked upon with such reverence that they were never molested, and had become so tame in consequence that the sight of a human being did not disturb them in the least. It appears that formerly there had been some grounds for such a story. A certain chief of Mahenge had had such a regard of these noble animals, that no one was permitted to disturb them.' This story is told by Joseph Thomson, who regretted that the Ruaha elephant populations had been depleted by the time he passed through. See Thomson, *To the Central African Lakes and Back*, vol. 1, p. 177.

263 **'new and more direct' to avoid the 'scoundrels in Ugogo':** Quotations in this and the following paragraph in this chapter are all taken from Frederick Carter, 'Letter to Henry Shelton Sanford', 15 April 1880 [SM].

264–5 **To mark the procession's departure ... travel 'like a prince':** Adolphe Burdo, 'Tablettes africaines: le drame de Pimboué', *La Meuse*, 20 and 21 August 1881.

267 **There was difficult marsh ... like 'an English park':** 'Captain Carter's Last March in Central Africa', *Proceedings of the Royal Geographical Society and Monthly Record of Geography*, 2:12 (December 1880), p. 762.

267 **'some splendid African ash trees':** Ibid.

267 **the morning broke 'clear, but bitterly cold':** Ibid.

267 **Swarms of tsetse thickened the air, 'nearly driving us mad':** Ibid.

267 **'like a flight of huts perched like emigrating birds':** Burdo, 'Tablettes africaines: le drame de Pimboué'.

267 **'lots of food for elephants ... at all times of year':** 'Captain Carter's Last March in Central Africa', p. 762.

268 **The females clustered ... centuries of killing by Sudanese ivory hunters:** See Sophy Roberts, 'Up Close with Elephants in Chad', *Financial Times*, 30 January 2015.

268 **But this old bull ... the infants following at a trot:** In the complicated matrix of modern conservation, this is where Tanzania's extensive national park system succeeds: nearly forty thousand square miles (almost equal to the size of Croatia) where hunting isn't allowed. Between 2014 and 2021, the country's elephant population increased by

17,000 elephants. See '2022 Elephant Conservation Report', *African Wildlife Foundation*, p. 3, www.awf.org/sites/default/files/2022-08/2022%20Elephant%20Conservation%20Progress%20Report.pdf

269   'pointing to one in Orion ... Let us go towards Sala, meaning home':
       Walter Hutley, Journal, 13 April 1880 [SOAS]. 'Waguha' refers to the people belonging to the Ha ethnic group living in the region of Lake Tanganyika.

269   'more accentuated, more precise ... like distant blowing of a tempest':
–70   Burdo, 'Tablettes africaines: le drame de Pimboué.'

270   Carter ordered his caravan ... Kasogera's 'great town' of Mpimbwe:
       'Captain Carter's last March in Central Africa', *Proceedings of the Royal Geographical Society and Monthly Record of Geography*, 2:12 (December, 1880), p. 763.

270   'fine-looking fellows ... heads shaved in several fantastic ways':
       Quotations in this and the following five paragraphs in this chapter are all taken from Carter's diary published in ibid., pp. 763–4.

273   His flag ... 'resembled that of the English' to an uncanny degree: Was it a flag that Mirambo took in 1871 from Stanley? 'Chronique géographique: Afrique', in *Bulletin: Société belge de géographie* (Brussels: Secrétariat de la Société belge de géographie, 1880), p. 610.

273–4 'impassive spectators ... will not allow you to be harmed': Burdo, 'Tablettes africaines: le drame de Pimboué.' Adolphe Burdo's version of the events at Mpimbwe appeared in the Belgian press, as well as in his 1886 book, *Les Belges dans l'Afrique centrale*.

274   Carter held his white handkerchief ... 'Rafiki! Rafiki!': Burdo, *Les Belges dans l'Afrique centrale*, p. 379.

275   Carter pulled out his watch and 'threw down his gun': Ernest Cambier, 'Letter to Maximilien Strauch', 30 June 1880 [SM].

12. Two Tin Boxes

278   'And whether ... That was a thought I had' [epigraph]: Johannes Fabian and Tshibumba Kanda Matulu, *Remembering the Present: Painting and Popular History in Zaire* (Berkeley and Los Angeles: University of California Press, 1996), p. 181.

279   'Do you see him? ... any given epoch of one's existence': Joseph Conrad, *Heart of Darkness* (London: Penguin, 1989), p. 57.

280   'the lisping accents of the lady traveller ... hospitable station to another': Alfred J. Swann, *Fighting the Slave-Hunters in Central Africa: A Record of Twenty-Six Years of Travel & Adventure Round the Great Lakes and of the Overthrow of Tip-Pu-Tib, Rumaliza and Other Great Slave-Traders, with an Introduction by Sir H. H. Johnston* (Philadelphia: J. B. Lippincott Company, 1910), p. vii.

280 **The trope that the past is another country where they do things differently:** Derived from L. P. Hartley's famous opening line to his 1953 novel, *The Go-Between*: 'The past is a foreign country: they do things differently there.'

280 **brother of the current Belgian king ... he'd never been there:** 'Belgium's Prince Laurent: "Leopold II never went to Congo", *Brussels Times*, 12 June 2020. Leopold wasn't the only European monarch who never visited their overseas territory. Queen Victoria, who was made empress of India in 1876, never set foot in India.

280 **'Captain Carter and Mr Cadenhead ... robber chief Mercambo':** 'The Belgian Central African Expedition', *The Times*, 11 August 1880. The announcement was taken from the previous day's scoop in *The Globe*: 'Latest Foreign News. The Belgian Central African Expedition. Murder of English Leaders.'

281 **'Contradictory talk and many different versions of the same story':** Ebenezer Southon, Journal, 9 August 1880 [SOAS].

281 **'tell his tale in his own way and time':** Ebenezer Southon, Journal, 11 August 1880 [SOAS].

281 **they should be saved 'at all costs':** Quotations in this and the following two paragraphs in this chapter are all taken from ibid.

282 **Snippets ... released 'by the family of the late Captain Carter':** 'Captain Carter's last March in Central Africa', *Proceedings of the Royal Geographical Society and Monthly Record of Geography*, 2:12 (December 1880), p. 761.

283 **In Belgium, for instance, extracts ... belonging to 'B. C. Carter':** 'ii) Copie d'extraits du journal de feu le capitaine B. C. Carter (22–24/06/1880) et d'une note sur l'assassinat de Carter et Cadenhead', in Fonds Storms, Émile, HA.01.0017 [RMCA].

283 **Leopold ... sent her a personally signed letter of condolence:** Maximilien Strauch, 'Letter to William Mackinnon', 12 August 1880 [SOAS].

283 **Leopold 'treats men as we use lemons ... throws away the peel':** August Beernaert in Jean Stengers, *Belgique et Congo: l'élaboration de la charte coloniale* (Brussels: La Renaissance du Livre, 1963), p. 98, cited in Adam Hochschild, *King Leopold's Ghost: A Story of Greed, Terror and Heroism in Colonial Africa* (London: Pan Books, 2006), p. 95.

283 **'The poor lady is very old and her wants are not many':** George Sutherland Mackenzie, 'Letter to Henry Shelton Sanford', 31 May 1881 [SM].

283 **she was left 'quite destitute':** George Sutherland Mackenzie, 'Letter to Henry Shelton Sanford', 1 October 1880 [SM].

284 **'Cruel events' ... Carter 'a true friend':** Ernest Cambier, 'Letter to Maximilien Strauch', 30 June 1880 [SM].

284 **Carter had 'paid dearly for the disobedience ... ordered to do so':** Ernest Cambier, 'Letter to Maximilien Strauch', 11 July 1880 [SM].

284 Cambier lamented the loss ... 'without having saved a thing': Ibid.

284 the news cast 'a gloom' ... 'with whom Carter was a great favourite': 'East Africa. From a Correspondent', *The Times*, 17 September 1880.

284 Mirambo was 'a deep dyed villain': Charles Stokes, 'Letter to John Kirk', 5 September 1880 [ZNA].

284 Stokes would eventually set up ... three thousand porters strong: Dismissed from the CMS mission for marrying an unbaptized African woman, Stokes was later found guilty by mock trial for trading weapons in Belgian territory. In 1895, he was hanged in a Congo forest by one of Leopold's henchmen.

284 his 'single chance of salvation' ... Cambier needed to head for Ujiji: Émile Popelin, 'Letter to Maximilien Strauch', 10 July 1880 [SM].

285 She'd started 'staggering and shaking with convulsive chills': Ernest Cambier, 'Letter to Maximilien Strauch', 15 September 1880 [SM].

285 'the joy of the small colony' of Karema: Adolphe Burdo, *Les Belges dans l'Afrique centrale: voyages, aventures et découvertes d'après les documents et journaux des explorateurs: de Zanzibar au Lac Tanganika* (Brussels: P. Maes, 1886), p. 372.

285 'Any news ... the silence which is accorded to our expeditions': 'Chronique locale', *La Meuse*, 21 October 1880.

285 '[T]his now opens a new phase in Africa history': John Kirk, 'Letter to Gerald Waller', 25 August 1880 [SOAS].

285 '[I]t has caused me an emotion ... thirst for retaliation': Maximilien Strauch, 'Letter to William Mackinnon', 12 August 1880 [SOAS].

285 'no doubt gave the order ... for the purpose of the murder': John Kirk, cited in Gerald Waller, 'Letter to William Mackinnon', 15 October 1880 [SOAS].

286 '"Boss" of the whole country': Gerald Waller, 'Letter to William Mackinnon', 15 October 1880 [SOAS].

286 'Hitherto, disease ... so many of the explorers of the Dark Continent': *Standard* quoted in 'African Explorers Killed', *New York Times*, 23 August 1880.

286 the gangs of Mirambo's ruga-ruga were 'ravaging' all Ugalla: Émile Popelin, 'Letter to Maximilien Strauch', 10 July 1880 [SM].

286 'there was nothing I could do ... as quickly as possible': Ibid.

286 'as long as these men exist there will be nothing to do': Ibid.

286 'to make a point of reducing Mirambo ... to helplessness forever': Émile Popelin, 'Letter to Maximilien Strauch', 15 July 1880 [SM].

287 Across the region, panic was spreading 'like a gunpowder flame': Burdo, *Les Belges dans l'Afrique centrale*, p. 366.

287 'They frolicked joyfully ... forehead of a black marble colossus': Ibid., p. 411.

287 **the unflattering portrait Thomson had written of the Belgian doctor:**
One of the most 'startling' points in Thomson's book, wrote a reviewer
for *The Field* in 1881, was 'his revelation of the incompetency for their
purpose of various official and other agents now in East Africa. That
part of the Dark Continent, indeed, would seem at the time of his visit
to have been quite thick with white men, emissaries of foreign
governments, missionaries, &c., most of whom were actively engaged in
showing "how not to do it".' 'The Central African Lakes', *The Field*, 21
May 1881.

287 **'in a district where cows could be counted ... could not get a drop of
milk':** Joseph Thomson, *To the Central African Lakes and Back: The
Narrative of the Royal Geographical Society's East Central African Expedition,
1878–1880*, vol. 2 (London: Sampson Low, Marston, Searle & Rivington,
1881), p. 253.

288 **Mirambo 'is not given to assassinating white men':** Ebenezer Southon,
'The Murder of Messrs. Carter and Cadenhead: To the Editor of The
Times, 16 August 1880', *The Times*, 18 August 1880.

288 **'placed his faith thoroughly in the English':** Quotations in this paragraph
in this chapter are all taken from Edward Hore, 'Letter to John
Whitehouse', 30 November 1880 [SOAS].

289 **kidnapping attempt by Mirambo ... not knowing she was already dead:**
'East Africa. From a Correspondent'.

289 **Mirambo's actual intention ... as some of the rumours went:** Burdo, *Les
Belges dans l'Afrique centrale*, p. 391.

289 **what future for Christians and commerce could there be?:** 'East Africa.
From a Correspondent'.

289 **'the sympathy and support ... will be against Mirambo and his allies':**
John Kirk, 'Letter to Ebenezer Southon', 12 August 1880 [SOAS].

290 **'make safe for travellers those countries ... now subject to outrage':** 'East
Africa. From a Correspondent'.

290 **'a motley crew' ... instructed in the 'intricacies of the goose-step':** 'The
King of the Belgians' Expedition: Landing the Elephants in Africa', *Times
of India*, 22 July 1879.

290 **'in odds and ends of different uniforms' ... 'as tall as himself':** Ibid.

290 **'filibustering expeditions':** 'The Annual Address on the Progress of
Geography', in *Proceedings of the Royal Geographical Society and Monthly
Record of Geography*, vol. 2 (London: Edward Stanford, 1880), p. 415.

291 **Southon issued a warning ... about the rapidly deteriorating security:**
Ebenezer Southon, 'Letter to Ralph Thompson: Annual Report of the
Urambo Mission', 31 December 1881 [SOAS].

292 **'The Belgian colours float ... the living incarnation of the Fatherland':**
Guillaume Ramaeckers, 'Letter to the Brussels Committee', 15 November

1881, in Jerome Becker, *La Vie en Afrique, ou Trois ans dans l'Afrique centrale*, vol. 2 (Paris and Brussels: J. Lebègue & Cie., 1887), pp. 93–4.

Epilogue

293 **'The off forefoot of my donkey ... go and measure for yourself'** [epigraph]: Cited in Wilfrid Scawen Blunt, 'Preface by the Editor', in Lady Anne Blunt, *Bedouin Tribes of the Euphrates*, vol. 1 (New York: Harper & Brothers, 1879), p. 10.

294 **a paper about the translocation of animals by colonial powers:** Pushkar Sohoni, 'Translocated Colonial Subjects in Collaboration: Animals and Human Knowledge', *Transfers*, 8:1 (Spring 2018).

295–6 **'He scans the skies ... and live in peace':** This verse, written by Don W. Thomson, is from a poem called 'The Surveyor' published on the flyleaf of Don W. Thomson, *Men and Meridians: The History of Surveying and Mapping in Canada*, vol. 3: *1917–1947* (Ottawa: Canadian Government Publishing Centre, 1969).

298 **looking 'no more dangerous than a cow':** George Orwell, *Shooting an Elephant and Other Essays* (London: Penguin, 2003), p. 35.

298 **'aghin baho':** So spelled in the expedition notes.

298 **Tajuddin's diagnosis ... elephants died as a result of maltreatment:** Not knowing traditional Urdu words for elephant ailments, the various vets I contacted in Europe, Africa, India and North America suggested that Sosankalli's illness could equally have been elephant pox, laminitis, septicaemia, foot rot or even sleeping sickness from a tsetse bite. The consensus was she would have died anyway, with or without the infection. Asian elephants might be powerhouses, but they're not machines.

299 **one of the very few animals to also recognize their own reflection in a mirror:** For more, see Ed Yong, 'Elephants Recognize Themselves in Mirror', *National Geographic*, 28 September 2008.

299 **animals should be free ... the time for training elephants is finished:** There are estimated to be around 2,675 captive elephants in India, according to a 2019 statistic (see K. M. Pavithra, 'Data: More than 60% of Captive Elephants in India are in Private Custody', *Factly*, 1 April 2024). India's 1972 Wildlife Protection Act prohibits the poaching, trafficking, sale and transfer of elephants. It is largely illegal to buy and sell elephants in India. But the reality is that the laws are often ignored, and human–wildlife conflict is worsening with India's expanding population.

299 **'Without memory one cannot live ... determines the contours of the human soul':** Ryszard Kapuściński, *Travels with Herodotus* (London, New York and Toronto: Penguin, 2008), p. 75. This is an extension of Aristotle's ancient, polarizing notion that animals are brute beasts morally available for human exploitation because we have souls and they do not. The books I relied on to explore a different philosophical approach to animal rights include: J. M. Coetzee, *The Lives of Animals* (Princeton: Princeton University Press, 2016); John Berger, 'Why Look at Animals', *About Looking* (New York: Pantheon Books, 1980); and Martha C. Nussbaum, *Justice for Animals: Our Collective Responsibility* (New York: Simon & Schuster, 2024).

300 **'If animals deserved ... we might have to do something about it':** '[C]ourts, when considering the confinement of elephants and chimpanzees, have conceded that such animals evince many of the qualities that give humans legal standing, but have declined to follow through on the implications of this fact.' Elizabeth Barber, 'What Would It Mean to Treat Animals Fairly?', *New Yorker*, 16 December 2023, referencing Lawrence Wright, 'The Elephant in the Courtroom', *New Yorker*, 28 February 2022.

300–1 **The mahouts' names ... Luximan Zenkuttee:** The accuracy of the transcribed names listed is hard to verify because of difficult handwriting and nineteenth-century spellings. This list is according to a letter of 7 May 1879 sent from Sd. W. Willoughby, Lt. Colonel for Commissary General, to the British India Steam Navigation Co. Limited, now held in the Papers of Sir William Mackinnon at SOAS in London.

301 **the ivory was used to adorn Colonel Strauch's African office:** Maximilien Strauch, 'Letter to Leopold II', 13 November 1879 [AEB].

302 **around 2.1 million Africans were enslaved ... last to close:** For more context on these numbers, see Paul Lovejoy, *Transformations in Slavery: A History of Slavery in Africa* (Cambridge: Cambridge University Press, 2011). In email correspondence from May 2024, Professor Lovejoy added that many of those enslaved were also sent to the Mascarenes and lesser numbers to other Indian Ocean islands, especially from the last third of the eighteenth century through the nineteenth century.

302 **'To the British ... their lively imaginations conjured up':** See Abdul Sheriff, *Slaves, Spices and Ivory in Zanzibar Integration of an East African Commercial Empire into the World Economy, 1770–1873* (Athens, OH: Ohio University Press, 1987), p. 35.

303 **sixty-three per cent of Tanzania's population identifies as Christian:** Office of International Religious Freedom, '2022 Report on International Religious Freedom: Tanzania', US Department of State (June 2022).

303–4 **'Lying invitingly ... a beautiful lady waiting for a proposal':** 'Road a Final Piece of Karema Port Jigsaw Puzzle', [Tanzania] *Daily News*, 11 May 2023.

304 **In February 2023, I travelled to Iraq ... for a British newspaper:** Sophy Roberts, 'Iraq, 20 Years On', *Financial Times*, 6 March 2023.

305 **'My officers ... with assegais, and that was the end of it':** 'Extract from Sinbad the Tourist (by the author of Zit and Xoe), XI. The Horse Trade', *Times of India*, 24 September 1887. An assegai is a slender spear.

306 'see the Scorpion in it, star by star': Gertrude Bell, 'Letter to Unknown', 11 September 1921, cited in Georgina Howell, *Queen of the Desert: The Extraordinary Life of Gertrude Bell* (Dublin: Pan Books, 2015), p. 413.

306 'African business is a long-term business': Leopold II, 'Letter to Maximilien Strauch', 23 May 1879 [AEB].

306 'The Belgian flag lies at the door of the new world': A. J. Wauters, *Voyages en Afrique: de Bruxelles à Karema: le royaume des éléphants* (Brussels: J. Lebègue & Cie, n.d.), p. 87.

307 The 'iron horse' was built: A. M. Mackay, January 1889, cited in Alexina Mackay Harrison, *The Story of the Life of Mackay of Uganda Told for Boys* (London: Hodder & Stoughton, 1891), p. 319.

307 'burglars breaking into a safe': Joseph Conrad, *Heart of Darkness* (London: Penguin, 1989), p. 61.

307 'no heroism ... disfigured the history of human conscience': Joseph Conrad, 'Geography and Some Explorers', *National Geographic* (March 1924), in R. Curle (ed.), *Last Essays* (London: Dent, 1926), p. 25.

307 Then in 1984, a final attempt ... elephant-back wildlife safaris: For more on this, see Alan Root, *Ivory, Apes and Peacocks: Animals, Adventure and Discovery in the Wild Places of Africa* (London: Vintage Books, 2013), pp. 257–9, and Kes Hillman-Smith and José Kalpers (eds), with Luis Arranz and Nuria Ortega, *Garamba: Conservation in Peace and War* (published by the authors, 2015). Alan Root also made a film, *Garamba: The Impossible Elephants*, which is available to view on www.alanroot.org. In the early 1990s, another attempt to commercialize African elephant-back safaris was made in Botswana's Okavango Delta. Then in 2016, Botswana introduced new legislation which banned the riding of elephants altogether. In Asia, on the other hand, the use of working elephants remains widespread. In places like Assam in India, you will still encounter scrawny, overworked elephants in chains. Elephant-back tourism is on the wane, but it's not over yet.

308 'The elephant is the most ... as matter can approach spirit': Georges-Louis Leclerc, *The Natural History of Quadrupeds*, vol. 2 (Edinburgh: Thomas Nelson and Peter Brown, 1830), p. 185.

Select Bibliography

This bibliography focuses on the texts I relied on most for wider context, along with a selected list of journals, newspapers and periodicals, and the archives I consulted. The Notes (pp. 317–79) give more detailed citations, as well as fiction, essays, short films and websites that may be of further interest.

BOOKS

Chinua Achebe, *Hopes and Impediments* (London: Penguin, 2019)

J. F. Ade Ajayi, *General History of Africa*, vol. 4: *Africa in the Nineteenth Century Until the 1880s* (Nairobi: UNESCO and East African Educational Publishers, 2014)

Association internationale africaine: rapports sur les marches de la première expédition (Brussels-Etterbeek: Verhavert Frères et Soeurs, 1879)

Zeinab Badawi, *An African History of Africa: From the Dawn of Humanity to Independence* (London: W. H. Allen, 2024)

Émile Banning, *Africa and the Brussels Geographical Conference*, trans. Richard Henry Major (London: Sampson Low, Marston, Searle & Rivington, 1877)

Jerome Becker, *La Vie en Afrique, ou Trois ans dans l'Afrique centrale*, vols 1 and 2 (Paris and Brussels: J. Lebègue & Cie., 1887)

Norman R. Bennett (ed.), *Stanley's Despatches to the New York Herald, 1871–1872, 1874–1877* (Boston: Boston University Press, 1970)

——*Mirambo of Tanzania* (New York: Oxford University Press, 1971)

Adolphe Burdo, *Les Belges dans l'Afrique centrale: voyages, aventures et découvertes d'après les documents et journaux des explorateurs: de Zanzibar au Lac Tanganika* (Brussels: P. Maes, 1886)

Richard Francis Burton, *The Lake Regions of Central Africa: A Picture of Exploration*, vols 1 and 2 (London: Longman, Green, Longman and Roberts, 1860)

——*Zanzibar: City, Island and Coast*, vols 1 and 2 (London: Tinsley Brothers, 1872)

Verney Lovett Cameron, *Across Africa* (New York: Harper & Brothers, 1877)

Felix Driver, *Geography Militant: Cultures of Exploration and Empire* (Hoboken, NJ: Wiley-Blackwell, 2000)

Barbara Emerson, *Leopold II of the Belgians: King of Colonialism* (London: Weidenfeld & Nicolson, 1979)

Johannes Fabian, *Out of Our Minds: Reason and Madness in the Exploration of Central Africa* (Berkeley and Los Angeles: University of California Press, 2000)

Howard. W. French, *Born in Blackness: Africa, Africans and the Making of the Modern World, 1471 to the Second World War* (New York: Liveright, 2022)

Francis Galton, *The Art of Travel: or, Shifts and Contrivances Available in Wild Countries*, fifth edition (London: John Murray, 1872)

Kes Hillman-Smith and José Kalpers (eds), with Luis Arranz and Nuria Ortega, *Garamba: Conservation in Peace and War* (published by the authors, 2015)

E. J. Hobsbawm, *The Age of Empire: 1875–1914* (New York: Vintage Books, 1989)

Adam Hochschild, *King Leopold's Ghost: A Story of Greed, Terror and Heroism in Colonial Africa* (London: Pan Books, 2006)

Edward Coode Hore, *Tanganyika: Eleven Years in Central Africa* (London: Edward Stanford, 1892)

John Iliffe, *A Modern History of Tanganyika* (Cambridge: Cambridge University Press, 1979)

Tim Jeal, *Stanley: The Impossible Life of Africa's Greatest Explorer* (London: Faber & Faber, 2007)

Mathilde Leduc-Grimaldi and James L. Newman (eds), *Finding Dr. Livingstone: A History in Documents from the Henry Morton Stanley Archives* (Athens, OH: Ohio University Press, 2020)

David Livingstone, *Missionary Travels and Researches in South Africa; Including a Sketch of Sixteen Years' Residence in the Interior of Africa, and a Journey from the Cape of Good Hope to Loanda on the West*

Coast; Thence Across the Continent, Down the River Zambesi, to the Eastern Ocean (London: J. Murray, 1857)

Paul Lovejoy, *Transformations in Slavery: A History of Slavery in Africa* (Cambridge: Cambridge University Press, 2011)

Anne Luck, *Charles Stokes in Africa* (Nairobi: East African Publishing House, 1972)

V. Y. Mudimbe, *The Invention of Africa: Gnosis, Philosophy, and the Order of Knowledge* (Bloomington: Indiana University Press, 1988)

Thomas Pakenham, *The Scramble for Africa* (London: Abacus, 1991)

Alan Root, *Ivory, Apes and Peacocks: Animals, Adventure and Discovery in the Wild Places of Africa* (London: Vintage Books, 2013)

Edward Said, *Culture and Imperialism* (London: Vintage, 1994)

——*Orientalism* (London: Penguin Classics, 2019)

Eric Scigliano, *Seeing the Elephant: The Ties that Bind Elephants and Humans* (London: Bloomsbury, 2006)

Abdul Sheriff, *Slaves, Spices and Ivory in Zanzibar: Integration of an East African Commercial Empire into the World Economy, 1770–1873* (Athens, OH: Ohio University Press, 1987)

Henry Morton Stanley, *How I Found Livingstone: Travels, Adventures and Discoveries in Central Africa: Including an Account of Four Months' Residence with Dr. Livingstone* (New York: Scribner, Armstrong & Co., 1872)

——*Through the Dark Continent, or, The Sources of the Nile, Around the Great Lakes of Equatorial Africa, and Down the Livingstone River to the Atlantic Ocean*, vols 1 and 2 (London: Sampson Low, Marston, Searle & Rivington, 1878)

——*The Congo and the Founding of Its Free State: A Story of Work and Exploration*, vols 1 and 2 (New York: Harper & Brothers, 1885)

Joseph Thomson, *To the Central African Lakes and Back: The Narrative of the Royal Geographical Society's East Central African Expedition, 1878–1880*, vols 1 and 2 (Sampson, Low, Marston, Searle & Rivington, 1881)

Ngũgĩ wa Thiong'o, *Globalectics: Theory and the Politics of Knowing* (Nairobi, Kampala, Dar es Salaam and Kigali: East African Educational Publishers, 2013)

Tippoo Tib: The Story of His Career in Central Africa, Narrated from His Own Accounts by Dr Heinrich Brode (London: Edward Arnold, 1907)

A. J. Wauters, *Voyages en Afrique: de Bruxelles a Karéma: le royaume des éléphants* (Brussels: J. Lebègue & Cie, n.d.)

Journals

African Affairs

Bulletin de la Société de géographie d'Anvers

Bulletin de la Société de géographie de Marseille

Bulletin: Société belge de géographie

Canadian Journal of African Studies / Revue canadienne des études africaines

Essex Institute Historical Collections

Geographical Journal

Journal of African History

Proceedings of the Royal Geographical Society and Monthly Record of Geography

Proceedings of the Royal Geographical Society of London

Sudan Notes and Records

Tanzania Notes and Records

Transition

Uganda Journal

Newspapers and Periodicals

The Atlantic

Brussels Times

Daily Telegraph

The Field

Financial Times

Gazetteer of the Bombay Presidency

Gazetteer of the Persian Gulf, Oman and Central Arabia

The Globe

Granta

The Graphic

Guardian

Illustrated London News

L'Indépendance belge

Journal de Bruxelles
Kilkenny Journal
London Evening Standard
La Meuse
Missionary Observer
National Geographic
New York Herald
New York Times
New Yorker
Standard
The Times
Times of India

ARCHIVES

Below are the archives I consulted while researching this book, preceded by their abbreviated forms as cited in the Notes.

AEB   Archives de l'État en Belgique, Brussels
AMAE Archives du Ministère belge des Affaires étrangères, Brussels
       —Archives africaines
       —Archives diplomatiques
APR   Archives du Palais Royal, Brussels
       —Goffinet Archives
ATA   Archives of Tabora Archdiocese, Tabora
BL   Bodleian Libraries, Oxford
       —Archive of Horace Waller
       —Papers of Sir Thomas Fowell Buxton, 3rd Baronet
       —Papers of the United Society for the Propagation of the
        Gospel
CRL   Cadbury Research Library, Birmingham
       —Church Missionary Society Archive
LMA   London Metropolitan Archives, London
       —Inchcape Group
LPL   Lambeth Palace Library, London
       —Tait Papers
NA   The National Archives, London

NAI   National Archives of India, Delhi
NLS   National Library of Scotland, Edinburgh
       —The Kirk Papers
PEM   Peabody Essex Museum, Salem
       —Edward D. Ropes Papers (1882–1888)
RGS   Royal Geographical Society, London
RMCA Royal Museum for Central Africa, Tervuren
       —Fonds Cambier, Ernest
       —Fonds Cornet, Frantz
       —Fonds Hanolet, Léon
       —Fonds Harroy, Jean-Paul
       —Fonds Laplume, Jules
       —Fonds Lemaire, Charles
       —Fonds Offermann, Pierre
       —Fonds Ramaeckers, Jules
       —Fonds Reichard, Paul
       —Fonds Stanley, Henry Morton
       —Fonds Storms, Émile
       —Fonds Tennant, Dorothy
       —Fonds von Wissmann, Hermann
SM   Sanford Museum, Florida
       —Henry Shelton Sanford Papers
SOAS   SOAS (School of Oriental and African Studies), London
       —Correspondence of William Beardall
       —Council for World Mission / London Missionary Society
         Archive
       —Papers of Sir William Mackinnon
ZNA   Zanzibar National Archives, Zanzibar City

Acknowledgements

Seven years ago, I was travelling by train from London to Dorset when I overheard a heated three-hour conversation a young woman was having with her brother. She was a recent history graduate. He was talking to her about a job in law. She said she wanted to travel and write. Just before I got off the train, I interrupted and asked her to google my work, and if she was interested by any of it, to give me a call. She did, and the next day I hired her. It was one of the most rewarding meetings of my life. In the end, book writing is an act of stamina, which Serena Strang understands better than anyone. She helps me juggle other writing jobs to make the balance sheet work. For *A Training School for Elephants*, her work in the archives has been indefatigable. Serena's uncompromising pursuit of clarity, as a writer, editor and researcher, is all over this book. Without her, I quite simply would never have got to the end of it.

For the numerous people who helped me on the road, please refer to the book itself. Especially important to me were my two companions in Tanzania, Remtula ('Rem') Nasary and Wolfe Purcell. These introductions were both made by Wolfe's father, Roland Purcell, whose original thinking is a constant inspiration. His generosity in time and knowledge also made my journey possible.

I owe a special debt to the Arusha-based conservation tourism company Nomad Tanzania, who assisted with some of the logistics in the Mahale, Katavi and Ruaha national parks. My most sincere thanks to Natalia Dabo, Alex Edwards, Lizzie Farren, Mark Houldsworth, Petra Meyr, Jacky Mosha, Butati Nyundo, Samantha Simpson and David Stone.

Thank you also to Charlie Mason not only for his hospitality in Arusha, but for the attention he gave the manuscript in all its painful stages.

Behind the scenes in Tanzania and Zanzibar, thank you to Kim Axmann, Ally Abdallah Baharoon, Luke Bailes, Fabia Bausch, Alex Chetkovic, Tobias Fidelis, Lorenz Herrmann, Tony Hughes, Derek Hurt, Emma Impink, Jamila Mahmoud Juma, Fadhili Samahani Kejeri, Lucious Killo, Dr Allan Herbert Kijazi, Jules Knocker, Rian and Lorna Labuschagne, Mouse McConnell, Annie and Mike McEnery, Edson Mhenga, Dr Asha-Rose Migiro, Ryan Mitchell, Isaac Mziga, Dr Damas D. Ndumbaro, Luke Naylor-Perrott, Anthea Rowan, Baraka Samwel Sadiki, Ben Simpson, Grace Soso, Idd Suburi, Lillian Shirima and Catherine Sinclair-Jones.

I owe a significant debt to wildlife biologist Jean Marc Froment, whom I met once (and only briefly) on an airstrip on the Uganda–DRC border. Jean Marc gave this book nuances it would have otherwise been without. In the Democratic Republic of Congo, thanks to photographer Tom Parker; conservationist Jean Labuschagne; Fran Read, who made my original visit possible with African Parks; and wildlife biologist and safari guide Michael Lorentz, who read and reread this manuscript, providing me with constant insight and support.

In other places I visited for this book, my thanks to the following:

In Belgium: Patrick Maselis, Thomas Rasson, and Dirk H. M. De Waele, author of *A Missionary in Congo: Broeder Jozef Hutsebaut 1886–1954* (Sinaai: 1996). Dirk and his wife Helena kindly shared their ancestor's fascinating story in Buta.

In India: Toby Sinclair for enabling my visit to India, and catching a significant mistake in a late draft of this book. In Pune: Zeba Mahat for translation work, and Dr Uday S. Kulkarni and Saili K. Palande Datar for their assistance on the city's history.

In Iraq: Sara Barbieri, Brady Binstadt and Shayan Kamal for tracking down some of Carter's history on the Tigris River.

In Myanmar: Nicholas Chan and Melissa Ong for taking me to the region which inspired George Orwell's 'Shooting an Elephant' – it was a game changer for me – and to Aung Myo Chit and Jon Miceler for their knowledge of captive elephants and conservation.

Thank you to Richard Mitchelson at Rocam–AKE International Group for their ongoing security support, including in Iraq; to

Jason Gibbs at Nomad Travel in London for always having my back; and to Laura O'Sullivan.

For help accessing various archives, I'm grateful to Patricia Bergin, Honorary Librarian at the Kilkenny Archaeological Society; Katie Fallon, Customer Support Assistant at Adam Matthew; Baudouin D'hoore, Archives of the Royal Palace, Brussels; Joanne Ichimura, Special Collections Archivist (CWM) at SOAS; Fuad Mohd, Zanzibar National Archives; Tom Morren and Anne Welschen, archivists for Cultural Anthropology and History, and Mathilde Leduc-Grimaldi at the Royal Museum for Central Africa; Darren Ray, at Brigham Young University; Brigitte Stephenson, Curator of the Sanford Museum.

For their assistance navigating some of my questions around elephant-related veterinary science and animal welfare: Lisa Choegyal; Dr R. J. Harvey; Professor Michele Miller, Faculty of Medicine and Health Sciences, Stellenbosch University; Susan Mikota, Director of Veterinary Programs and Research at Elephant Care International; Dr Jenny Pastorini and Dr Christian Schiffmann, members of the IUCN Asian Elephant Specialist Group; John Roberts; Belinda Stewart-Cox, Conservation Advisor at the British Asian Trust; Sreedhar Vijayakrishnan, Centre for Conservation and Research, Sri Lanka. Most of all, I want to thank Dr Pete Morkel, one of Africa's most pioneering wildlife veterinarians and conservationists.

Other people who have helped me along the way: Will Bolsover, David Chancellor, Richard Hamilton, Will Knocker, Will Jones, Rosanna Menza, Nicolas Monti, Jessica Mousley, Martha North, Mehdi Rheljari, Susan Ridder, Alastair Vere-Nicoll, Dave Waddell and Justin Wateridge. Thank you to Imogen Chan-Lee for her close reading of an early manuscript; Connie Doxat for her help researching historical photographs; my son Danny Fisher for the website that accompanies the book, as well as his thoughtful text edits; my nephew Max Baldock who read and reread working drafts; Dr Ida Hadjivayanis, Senior Lecturer in Swahili Studies at SOAS University, who agreed to take on the sensitivity read; Alex Hotchin for her beautiful maps; Jamie Barnes for his video editing; and my editor

Tom Robbins at the *Financial Times*, who not only enables unusual stories, but always makes my writing better. Tom's support also includes commissioning articles which cross over with some of the places in this book, all of which are fully referenced in the Notes.

At Transworld, special thanks to my editors Sharika Teelwah and Susanna Wadeson for their absolute clarity when I couldn't see my way through the story; Phil Lord and Marianne Issa El-Khoury for making the design come together; Hannah Winter and Sally Wray for all the attention they've given to the marketing and publicity; Vivien Thompson for holding the moving parts in such a steady place with infinite patience; and Kate Parker for being the best, most rigorous of copy-editors any writer could hope for. At Grove Atlantic, thanks to Morgan Entrekin and Zoe Harris; to Justina Batchelor, Natalie Church, JT Green, Judy Hottensen, Rachael Richardson and Deb Seager; the US cover was designed by Dan Rembert, using type design by Becca Fox, and the sensitivity read by Lynn Brown. As always, particular thanks to my agent Sophie Lambert and her colleagues Alice Hoskyns and Kate Burton at C&W Agency for working so hard to support me.

In the 2003 prologue to *Orientalism*, his seminal book on postcolonialism, the Palestinian-American literary critic Edward Said refused to believe the clash of civilizations was 'unending, implacable, irremediable'.* Sometimes, that optimism has been elusive. My closest friends and family have tolerated endless anxieties as I've tried to engage with some of the difficulties, and I am grateful to them all for encouraging me to keep at it when I wanted to give up. Special thanks to Alice Daunt, Catherine Fairweather, my father Johnny Roberts and my long-term colleague, photographer Michael Turek, who came with me on a return trip to Tanzania in 2023. Michael's pictures are now a part of everything I do. And so is his friendship, not just to me, but to my husband, John, and our two sons, Jack and Danny. Those three people live most closely with my absences. They're always funny, loving, incisive, and for those reasons, I owe them my biggest thanks of all.

* Edward Said, *Orientalism* (London: Penguin, 2019), p. xi.

Picture Acknowledgements

Maps
Alex Hotchin.

1. Prologue to an Adventure
Page 7: Elephants in Garamba, 2015. © Tom Parker. **Page 8:** Elephants standing to attention at Gangala-na-Bodio. © Jean Marc Froment, sourced from a private archive. Originally published in Kes Hillman-Smith and José Kalpers (eds), with Luis Arranz and Nuria Ortega, *Garamba: Conservation in Peace and War* (published by the authors, 2015). **Page 10:** Elephants ploughing in Congo. © Jean Marc Froment, sourced from a private archive. Kes Hillman-Smith and José Kalpers (eds), with Luis Arranz and Nuria Ortega, *Garamba: Conservation in Peace and War* (published by the authors, 2015). **Page 11 (top):** The main boulevard in Buta in the 1930s with a young elephant out on a promenade. Courtesy of Yale Divinity School Library. Missionary Postcard Collection (RG 101), Special Collections. **Page 11 (bottom):** Buta's wildlife expert, Broeder Jozef Hutsebaut, riding his elephant, Ndjoku. Courtesy of the family archive of Dirk and Helena De Waele-Verschelden. **Page 19:** Logging elephants in Myanmar, 2018. © Ken Kochey.

2. Shopping for an Elephant
Page 26 (top): The Congolese brought to Belgium in 1897 to go 'on display' in Leopold's ancestral royal hunting grounds at Tervuren. Courtesy of the Royal Museum of Central Africa, Tervuren. Anonymous photo, 1897. All rights reserved. **Page 26 (bottom):** The graves of the seven Congolese who died in the run-up to the 1897 'human zoo' exhibit. Courtesy of the Royal Museum of Central Africa, Tervuren. 1930. © RMCA Tervuren. **Page 28:** Caricature of Leopold

riding an elephant. Courtesy of The Royal Archives, Brussels. Anonymous artist, *circa* 1900. **Page 32:** Jacob Wainwright with Livingstone's coffin. © Michael Graham-Stewart / Bridgeman Images. **Page 45 (top):** A menagerie sale of an elephant in London. Penta Springs Limited / Alamy Stock Photo. **Page 45 (bottom):** Acrobat swinging from elephant's trunk. Courtesy of the National Fairground & Circus Archive, University of Sheffield.

3. The Paris of East Africa
Page 54 (top): Ivory on display alongside merchants in Stone Town. Courtesy of Zanzibar National Archives. **Page 54 (bottom):** Four porters carrying a piece of ivory in Zanzibar. CPA Media Pte Ltd / Alamy Stock Photo. **Page 55 (top):** Ivory shipment at Royal Albert Dock, London. The Print Collector / Hulton Archive / Getty Images. **Page 55 (bottom):** Billiard ball dealer. © Look and Learn / Bridgeman Images. **Page 59 (top):** Diagram of the various activities possible within a tent. Francis Galton, *The Art of Travel* (London: John Murray, 1872). **Page 59 (bottom left):** Illustration of an anti-mosquito 'globe'. Copyright unknown. **Page 59 (bottom right):** Stanley in a cap of his own design. Royal Geographical Society / Getty Images. **Page 66:** Frederick Carter, published in *The Graphic*, 9 October 1880. © Illustrated London News Group / Mary Evans Picture Library. **Page 74:** Peter Sudi standing inside the Church of St John. © Sophy Roberts.

4. Sink or Swim
Page 82: Edward Lear on an elephant. Reproduced with kind permission of the South West Heritage Trust [ref: SHC DD/SH/62/337]. **Page 83:** Elephant being hoisted from ship. Hulton Deutsch / Corbis Historical / Getty Images. **Page 85 (top):** Cranes used to lift elephants. From the Bulletin of the Society of Geography of Antwerp, 1879. © Bibliotèque nationale de France. **Page 85 (bottom):** Map showing the disembarkation route of elephants. From the Bulletin of the Society of Geography of Antwerp, 1879. © Bibliotèque nationale de France. **Page 90:** Nyerere holding independence sign. Keystone / Hulton Archive / Getty Images. **Page 99:** Nassoro Saidi Jaswa, photographed in Kisarawe, 2023 © Michael Turek.

5. Miss Kisabengo

Page 106: A bestiary elephant. Courtesy of The Master and Fellows of Trinity College, Cambridge. **Page 107:** *The Siege of the Elephant*, etching and engraving, attr. Joannes van Doetecum I and Lucas van Doetecum after Alart du Hameel. © The Trustees of the British Museum. **Page 109:** A 1989 ivory burn in Kenya. © Tom Stoddart / Getty Images. **Page 110:** Men in Zanzibar holding elephant ivory. Chronicle / Alamy Stock Photo. **Page 111:** A wagonload of ivory tusks worth $9,000 on its way to the Pratt, Read & Company factory in Deep River, Connecticut. Courtesy of Deep River Historical Society.

6. Big With Blessing

Page 126: Station master at Kilosa. © Sophy Roberts. **Page 127:** The construction of the Central Railway. Ullstein Bild / Getty Images. **Page 128:** Members of German Parliament in train carriage. Ullstein Bild / Getty Images. **Page 130 (left):** Fellow passengers in the sleeper cabin on the Dar–Kigoma train. © Sophy Roberts. **Page 130 (right):** A local train stop on the Central Railway. © Sophy Roberts. **Page 132:** European being carried by Africans. National Museum of Tanzania. **Page 133 (top):** European being carried over a river. Courtesy of Zanzibar National Archives. **Page 133 (Bottom):** Female missionaries being carried in hammocks, in a forest, Nyasa, Tanzania, *circa* 1893–4. Call no. 05950. Courtesy of Unity Archives / Moravian Archives, Herrnhut, Germany. **Page 134:** Sister Hauffe sitting on a one-wheeled cart. Call no. 10973. © Werner Hauffe. Courtesy of Unity Archives / Moravian Archives, Herrnhut, Germany. **Page 139:** Children holding an image of the crucifixion. Courtesy of Nicolas Monti Collection. **Page 144 (left):** Portrait of Tito Habeli. © Sophy Roberts. **Page 144 (right):** Portrait of Sylivester Chamwela. © Sophy Roberts. **Page 145 (left):** Portrait of Robert Chiteme, St Paul's Church. © Sophy Roberts. **Page 145 (right):** Choir outside St Paul's Church. © Sophy Roberts.

7. Acacia horrida

Page 161: Ugogo baobab trees © Sophy Roberts. **Page 167 (top):** Theodore Roosevelt with a dead elephant. This image, taken by his son Kermit Roosevelt in 1909, is presented by the Theodore Roosevelt Birthplace National Historic Site courtesy of the

Theodore Roosevelt Center at Dickinson State University. **Page 167 (bottom)**: An elephant shot down, Rutenganio, Tanzania, *circa* 1898–1914. Call no. 03217. Courtesy of Moravian Archives, Herrnhut, Germany. **Page 168 (top)**: Sir Hesketh Bell, surrounded by hunting trophies. Photographer unknown. No known copyright. **Page 168 (bottom)**: Untitled hunter, trophy room #VII, Dallas, Texas, 2011, from the series 'Safari Club' © David Chancellor. **Page 171**: A path cut through a thorn thicket in Ugogo. Image from Walter Busse, 'Deutsch-Ostafrika I, Zentrales Steppengbiet', *Vegetationsbilder*, 5:7 (Jena: Karsten & Schenk, 1907). **Page 173 (top left)**: Henry Mtemi Mazengo II. © Sophy Roberts. **Page 173 (top right)**: Sukuma herdsmen. © Sophy Roberts. **Page 173 (bottom left)**: Eda Mpwepwe. © Sophy Roberts. **Page 173 (bottom right)**: Kanunga Namayan Marau. © Sophy Roberts.

8. The Land of the Moon
Page 187: Tippu Tip. CPA Media Pte Ltd/ Alamy Stock Photo. **Page 188:** Tippu Tip's ivory collection at Stanley Falls. Chronicle / Alamy Stock Photo. **Page 196:** The museum at Kwiharah. © Michael Turek. **Page 197:** Plan of the House at Kwiharah. Verney Lovett Cameron, *Across Africa* (New York: Harper & Brothers, 1877). No known copyright. **Page 205:** A domesticated zebra leaping over a jump. Paul Thompson / FPG / Stringer / Getty Images.

9. Chief of Chiefs
Page 214 (top left): Mirambo in regalia. Unknown photographer. No known copyright. **Page 214 (top right)**: Sample of Chief Mirambo's handwriting, sent to the Reverend J. O. Whitehouse by Dr Ebenezer Southon. CWM/LMS. Central Africa. Incoming correspondence. Box 2, Folder 2 (1879), Council for World Mission Archive, SOAS Library. **Page 214 (bottom)**: Wanyamwezi porters. Call no. 02683. Courtesy of Unity Archives / Moravian Archives, Herrnhut, Germany. **Page 220 (left)**: Balthazary Gitamwa Boa. © Sophy Roberts. **Page 220 (right)**: Ismail Omari. © Sophy Roberts. **Page 223:** Chief Lindyati Finulla. © Sophy Roberts.

10. Fish Without Number

Page 236 (top left): A flooded village edge on the eastern shore of Lake Tanganyika. © Sophy Roberts. **Page 236 (top right):** Local girls playing, Karema. © Sophy Roberts. **Page 236 (bottom left):** Sister Lydia, Karema. © Sophy Roberts. **Page 236 (bottom right):** Flooded river. © Sophy Roberts. **Page 244:** Drawing of the *Calabash* on Lake Tanganyika during a storm. From Edward Hore, *Eleven Years in Central Africa* (London: Edward Stanford, 1892). **Page 249 (top left):** MV *Liemba* on Lake Tanganyika. © Sophy Roberts. **Page 249 (top right):** Malilo Omani. © Sophy Roberts. **Page 249 (bottom):** HMS *Mimi* being pulled off a plateau. Courtesy of The National Archives.

11. Paradise Plains

Page 266 (left): Rem. © Sophy Roberts. **Page 266 (right):** Wolfe. © Sophy Roberts. **Page 269:** Paradise Plains. © Sophy Roberts. **Page 274:** The baobab where Carter fell. © Michael Turek. **Page 275:** Chief Alex Savery Kalulu, with his two sisters. © Michael Turek.

Epilogue

Page 296: Nineteenth-century view of Parvati Hill, Pune. FLHC DBA4 / Alamy Stock Photo. **Page 297 (left):** Shrine at Parvati Temple, Pune. © Sophy Roberts. **Page 297 (right):** Parvati Temple, Pune. © Sophy Roberts.

Printed endpapers (hardback only)

Front: Elephants in their pen. NG-1985-7-2-80. *The World of Jan Brandes, 1743–1808: Drawings of a Dutch Traveller in Batavia, Ceylon and Southern Africa*, Max de Bruijn, An Duits, Remco Raben (ed.), pp. 262–71, 278–80 met afb., cat.nr. 76, Rijksmuseum. **Back, left:** Wild elephants being driven into a stockade. NG-1985-7-2-101. *The World of Jan Brandes, 1743–1808: Drawings of a Dutch Traveller in Batavia, Ceylon and Southern Africa*, Max de Bruijn, An Duits, Remco Raben (ed.), pp. 262–71 (afb.), 274, cat.nr. 73, Rijksmuseum. **Back, right:** Elephant being baptized. NG-1985-7-2-87. *The World of Jan Brandes, 1743–1808: Drawings of a Dutch Traveller in Batavia, Ceylon and Southern Africa*, Max de Bruijn, An Duits, Remco Raben (ed.), pp. 262–71, 287 (afb.), 290–91, cat.nr. 81, Rijksmuseum.

www.atrainingschoolforelephants.com

The book's website includes links to archival film, and behind-the-scenes footage of the author's journey.

Index

About the Author

Sophy Roberts is a British journalist and author based in West Dorset. She is a regular contributor to *FT Weekend* and other international titles. Her critically acclaimed first book, *The Lost Pianos of Siberia*, was a *Sunday Times* Book of the Year in 2020, and went on to be published in eight more languages.

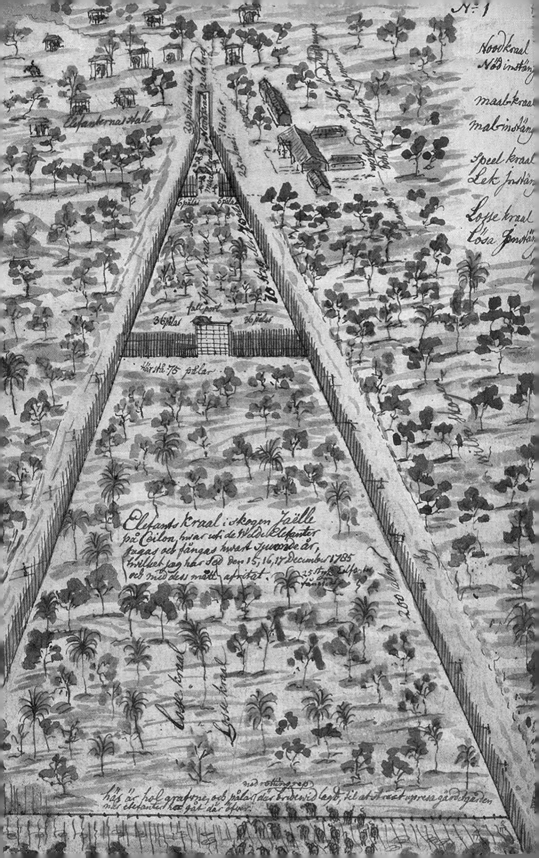

N:1

Hoodkraal
Nöd instäng.

maalkraal
mad instäng

Speel kraal
Lek Instäng

Losse kraal
Lösa Instäng

Elefanternas Stall

29 pålar

19 pålar

25 pålar

16 Hög Lång Port

6 pålar   6 pålar

fall port

36 pålar   36 pålar

Här stå 75 pålar

Elefants kraal i skogen Jaëlle
på Ceilon, hwar uti de Wilde Elefanter
tagas och fängas hwart 3:nonde år,
hwilket jag här sed den 15, 16, 17 December 1785
och med dess mått afritat.   15 Styk Elefanter
fängslades.

200 lång

Höde kraal

Loke kraal

med rotting rep

här är hål grafne, och pålar där bredewid lagd, til at ej wästt upresa gärdsgården
med elefanter hoo gåt där öfwer.